ALOFT

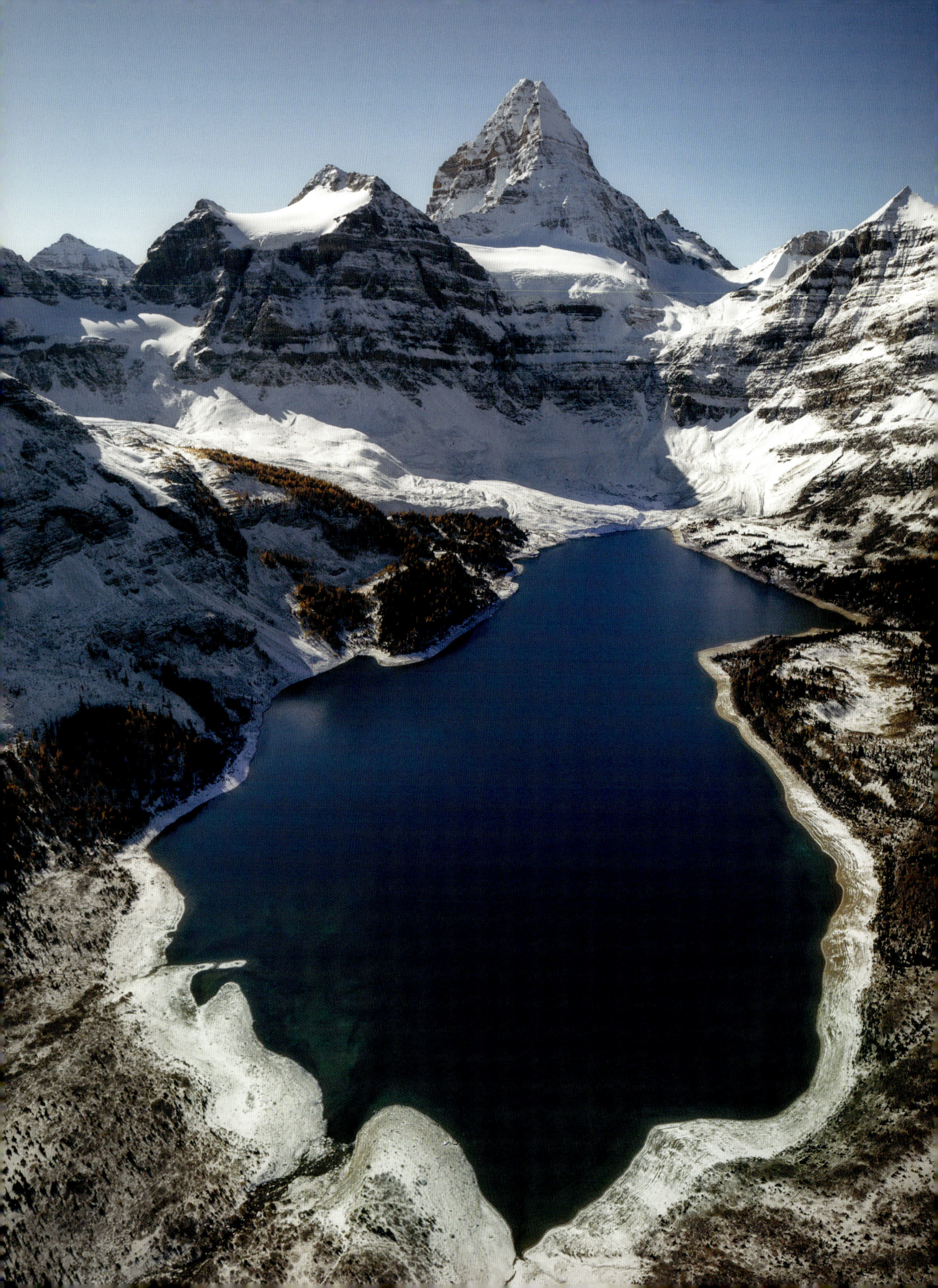

aloft

CANADIAN ROCKIES AERIAL PHOTOGRAPHY

Paul Zizka

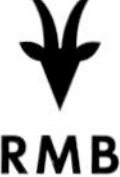

INTRODUCTION

Ever since I can remember, I've been drawn to high places. It explains why I left the flatter lands of eastern Canada 20 years ago and found another home in the mountains. There's something about having the world spread out at your feet that is utterly intoxicating. It's not only about the aesthetics, although for a photographer that's definitely part of the equation. Another part of the appeal is less tangible, beyond the realm of the visible. The perspective and freedom that those loftier views offer are unparalleled – and addictive. From up high you feel acutely aware of your own insignificance, yet also like the whole world is at your fingertips.

I'm also drawn upwards because of a deep-rooted desire to see my beloved Canadian Rockies from a different angle. I experience so much joy in rediscovering familiar valleys and peaks from a completely different perspective. As I gaze out at all those landmarks from a high perch, I reflect on the various stories I've attached to them over the years.

For my first decade of wandering around the Rockies and career as a landscape and adventure photographer, I "earned" my altitude. Hiking, scrambling and mountaineering were my gateways to moments spent up above the treeline, looking down at the winding rivers, turquoise lakes, sweeping forests and shimmering glaciers. I'd be curious to know how many metres I gained in order to collect the images that appear in my previous books. While I still primarily rely on my feet as I seek photographs that fulfill me, in more recent years I've had the opportunity to leave firm ground altogether and fly by helicopter over the Canadian Rockies on multiple occasions.

The first time I ever flew was during a rescue off of Castle Mountain in 2009 after an unfortunate climbing incident in which my partner broke his foot on Eisenhower Tower. Though we were only in the air for mere minutes, and I had the safety of my friend front-of-mind, I could not help but be blown away by how quickly Castle Mountain, an icon, became almost unrecognizable. I was immediately struck by the boundless potential for photography that flying could open up.

Since then, through my commercial assignments, as well as some personal work over the last few years, I've boarded helicopters several times, hovering over much of the Canadian Rocky Mountains UNESCO World Heritage Site, which comprises the contiguous national parks of Banff, Jasper, Kootenay and Yoho, as well as Mount Robson, Mount Assiniboine and Hamber provincial parks.

Shooting from a ridge, face or summit, with one's boots firmly on the ground, is for me more exciting, creatively speaking. The availability of foregrounds allows for a lot more compositions. There is also the possibility of using the human element or long exposures on a tripod in order to make images more compelling. There's the luxury of time and immersion with one's surroundings. And of course there's the fact that a journey and effort are required to afford the heights as opposed to finding yourself up high in an instant, and that journey can offer countless photo opportunities along the way.

Yet, photographing from a doorless helicopter offers unique opportunities and can be extremely productive. In fact, all of the images found in this book were photographed over a total of perhaps eight to ten hours! The ability to reposition the camera at a moment's notice and improve an angle without the limitations of spatial barriers makes for very fruitful sessions. What's more, seeing the summits from above them provides a perspective that even a mountaineer can't obtain.

Even though aerial photography does not require much in terms of physical effort, it still presents specific challenges. Even with the doors off, the angles are often limited. With the wind, proper communication, which is paramount for a productive shoot, can be extremely difficult. With all the motion involved, image sharpness can be hard to achieve. Weather can wreak havoc on the best-laid plans. Along with the ever-changing conditions, the possibilities for images are so plentiful that aerial photography can be mentally taxing as one has to constantly adapt and assess conditions and camera settings. Removing the doors of the aircraft means becoming very exposed to the elements, such as bone-chilling temperatures and powerful winds. Finally, there's the fact that you find yourself hundreds of metres above the ground in a tiny metal box that is at the mercy of the weather. Unlike in mountaineering, where safety largely comes down to one's own skills and decision making, flying means trusting a pilot's skills in order to get up and down safely. When I find our position slightly unnerving, I focus on my purpose out there and keep shooting – it keeps my mind from wandering!

Interestingly, creating the images was not the most difficult part in making this book. The sorting and selecting that ensued were much more arduous. Though I'd created a handful of books before this one, the process never gets easier. Photographers are close to their work and the image selection process is always painful. Out of thousands of images I started out with, 135 remain.

I am proud of every single image in this book. They all meet my personal standards as a photographer. But aesthetics were only part of the equation in the elaborate selection process. I also had to consider variety: geographically, seasonally and compositionally. For that reason, herein you will find images from various seasons and areas, with some images featuring well-known, iconic locations and others that highlight more obscure backcountry locations. Some images were processed in black-and-white to emphasize drama and structure, while others showcase the fantastic array of colour the Rockies can offer. Some were shot wide, top-down, while others were shot with a telephoto lens, towards the horizon.

Ultimately, what I've aimed to provide is a different perspective on the Canadian Rockies and one that highlights their unparalleled beauty. I hope it gives you a new sense of scale of this magnificent place and that you enjoy the chance to gain a birds-eye view of Canada's celebrated mountain range. May your own explorations bring you sweeping views and a fresh outlook, no matter how high your adventures take you.

ACKNOWLEDGEMENTS

Aerial photography is so much about teamwork, and I'm very much indebted to the great helicopter companies and pilots who were team players and instrumental in making this book happen. Thanks to Alpine Helicopters, Yellowhead Helicopters and Rockies Heli Canada for their assistance. I started out the photo selection with thousands of images in front of me and could not have completed the selection process without the help of Meghan Ward and Kahli Hindmarsh, who provided honest, unbiased input on the images. I'm also thankful to Parks Canada for being flexible when the weather fooled us, over and over. Thanks also to Rocky Mountain Books, specifically Don Gorman and Chyla Cardinal, for once again allowing me to see my work in print and share it with the world. Lastly, thanks so much to my family: my wife, Meghan, and our daughters Léa and Maya. Your support means the world to me.

DEDICATION

I would like to dedicate this book to my parents,
Claire and Jacques, as well as my brother Étienne.
They have always supported my adventures
even if those took me a few provinces away.

Opposite: The Rundle range rises above the Trans-Canada Highway near Canmore.

Overleaf: Mount Lougheed and Canmore's iconic Three Sisters on a summer evening.

Following spread: A bluebird day over the Bow Valley and the Three Sisters, Canmore.

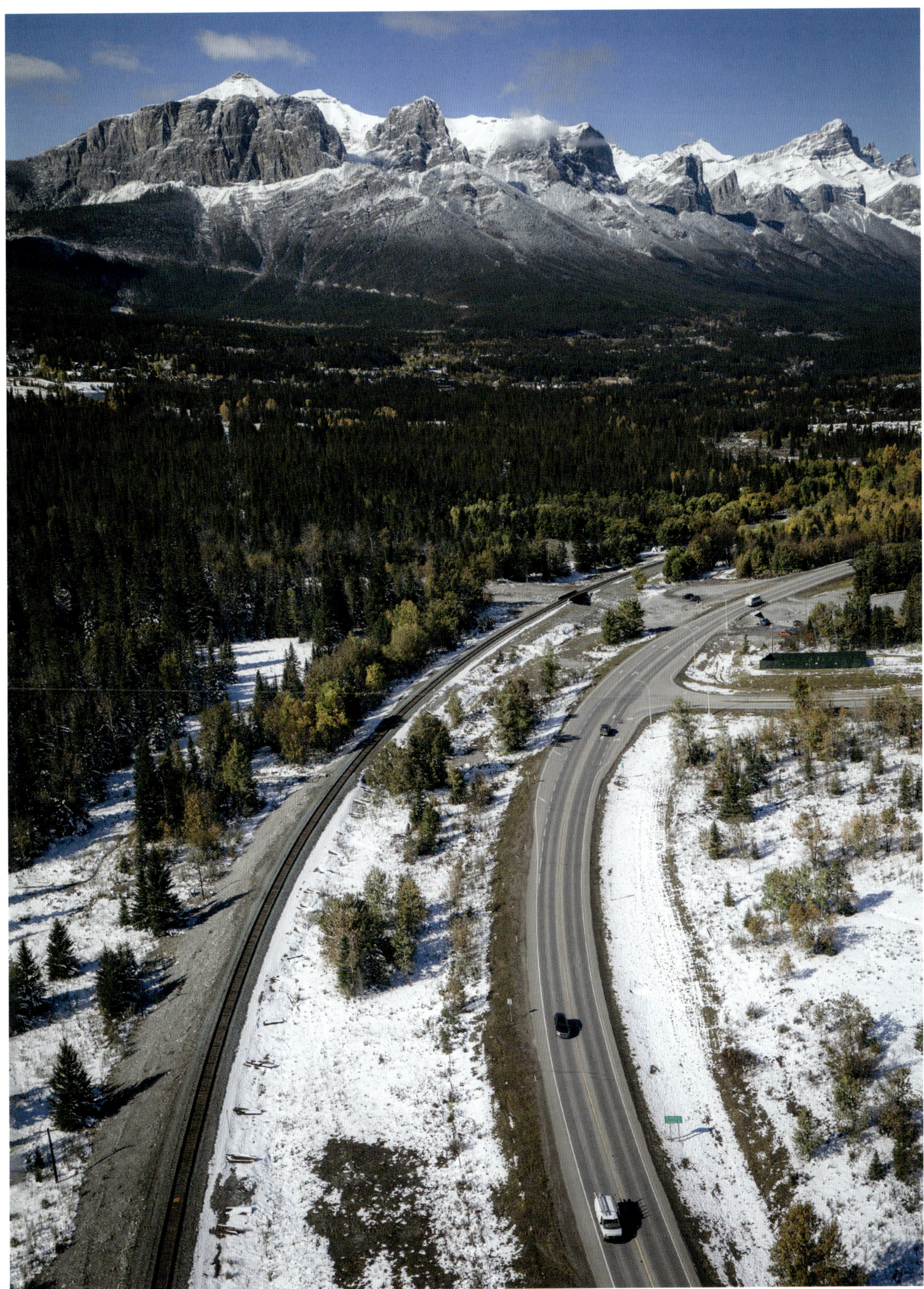

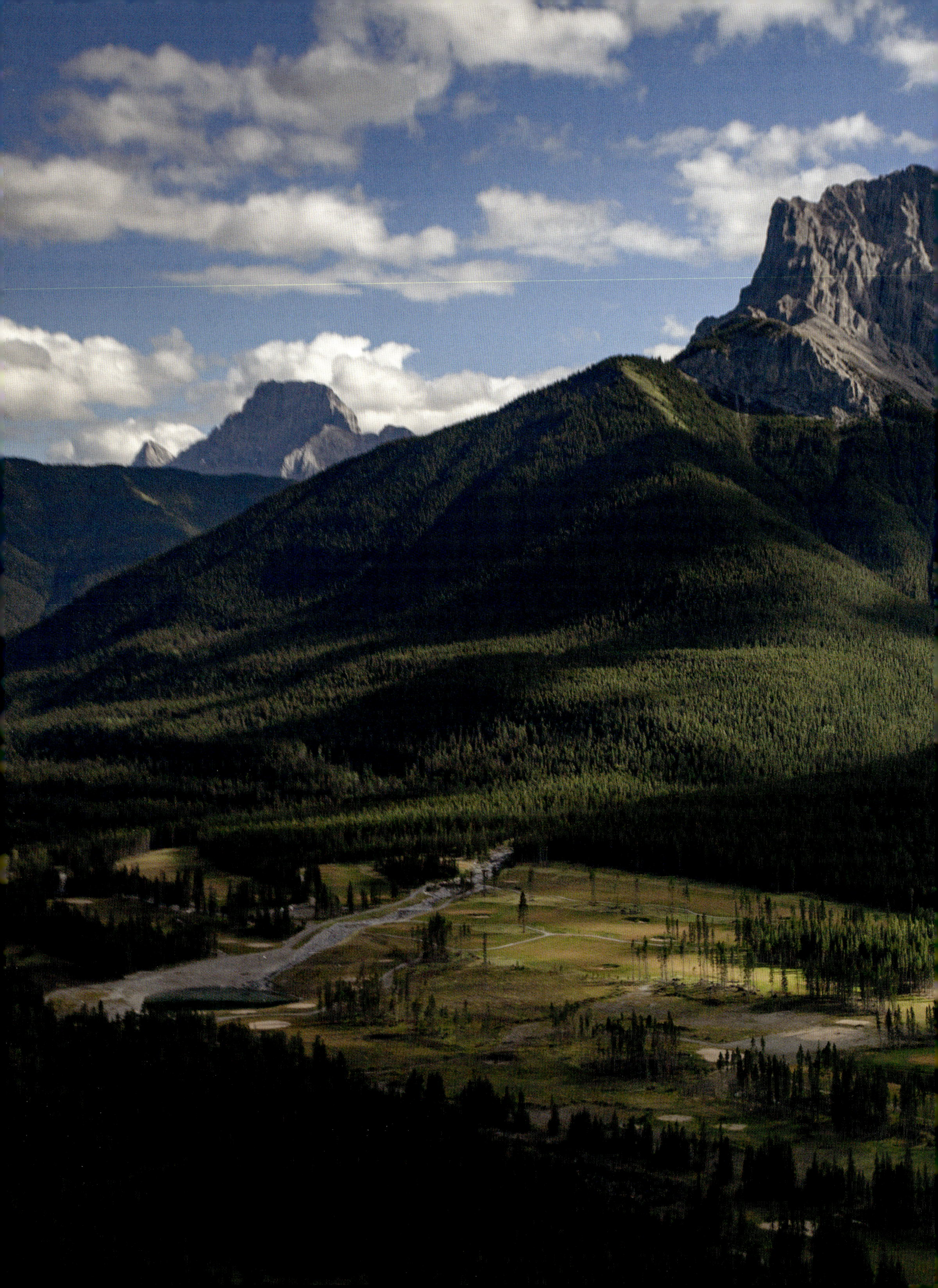

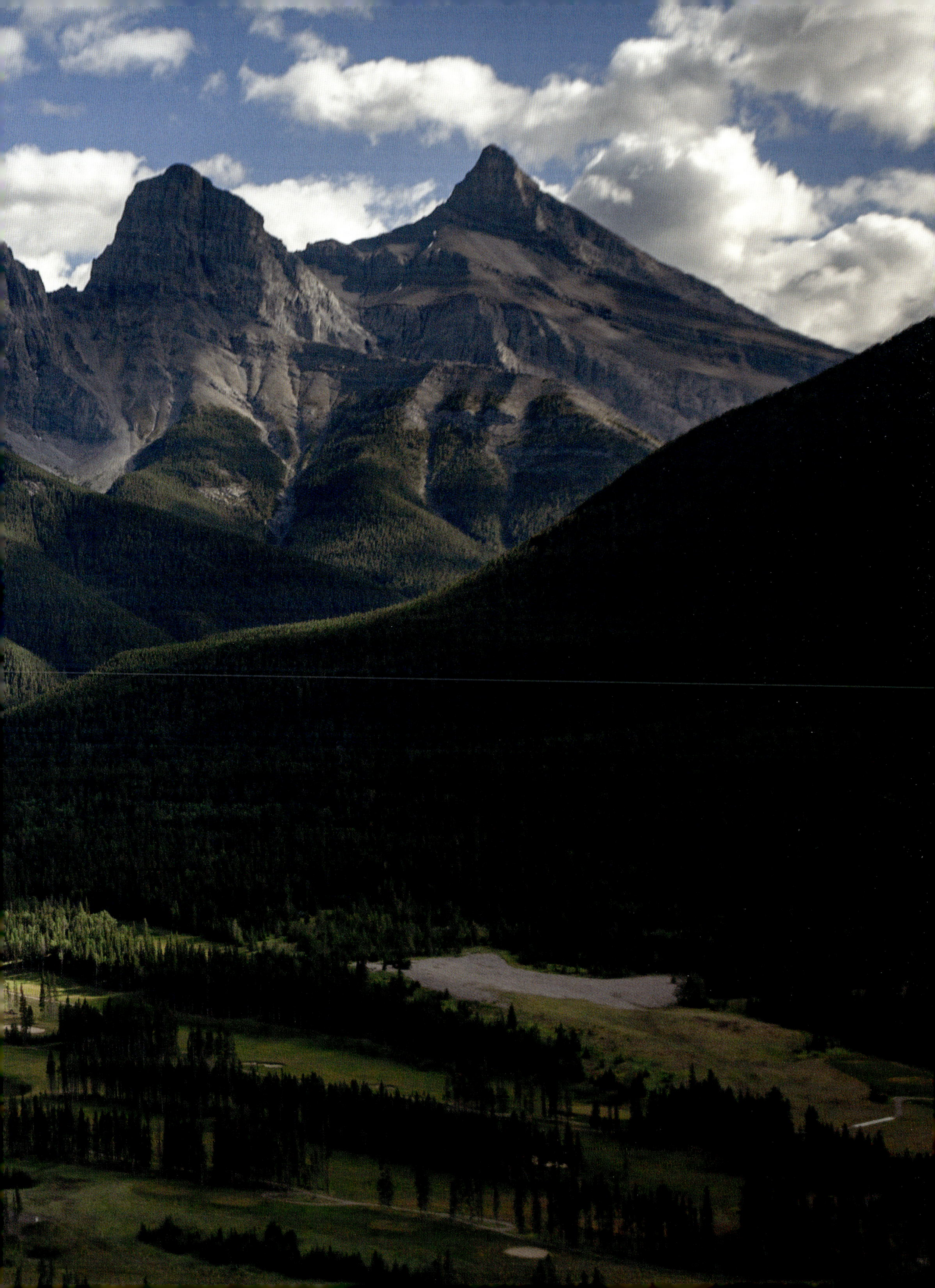

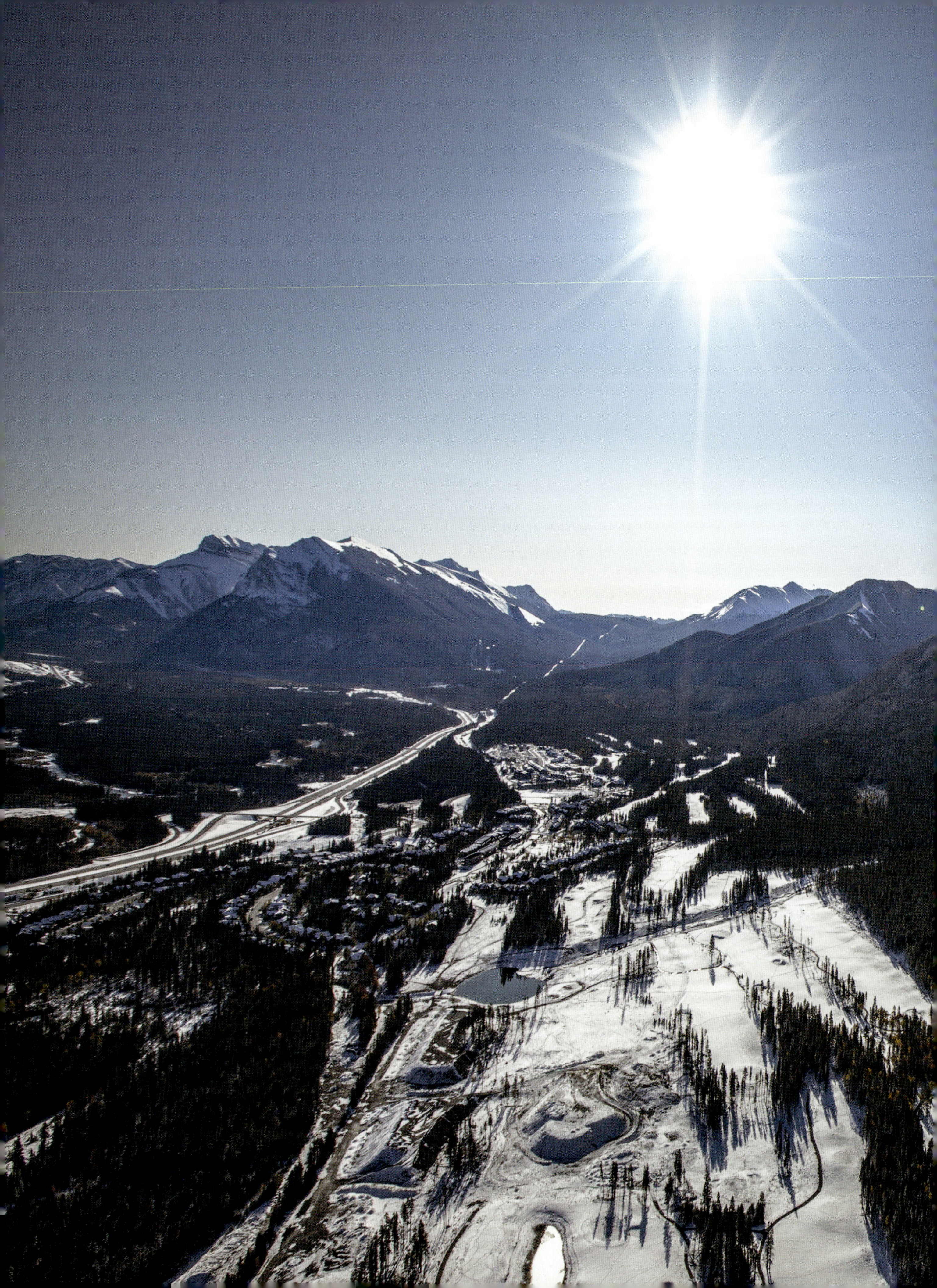

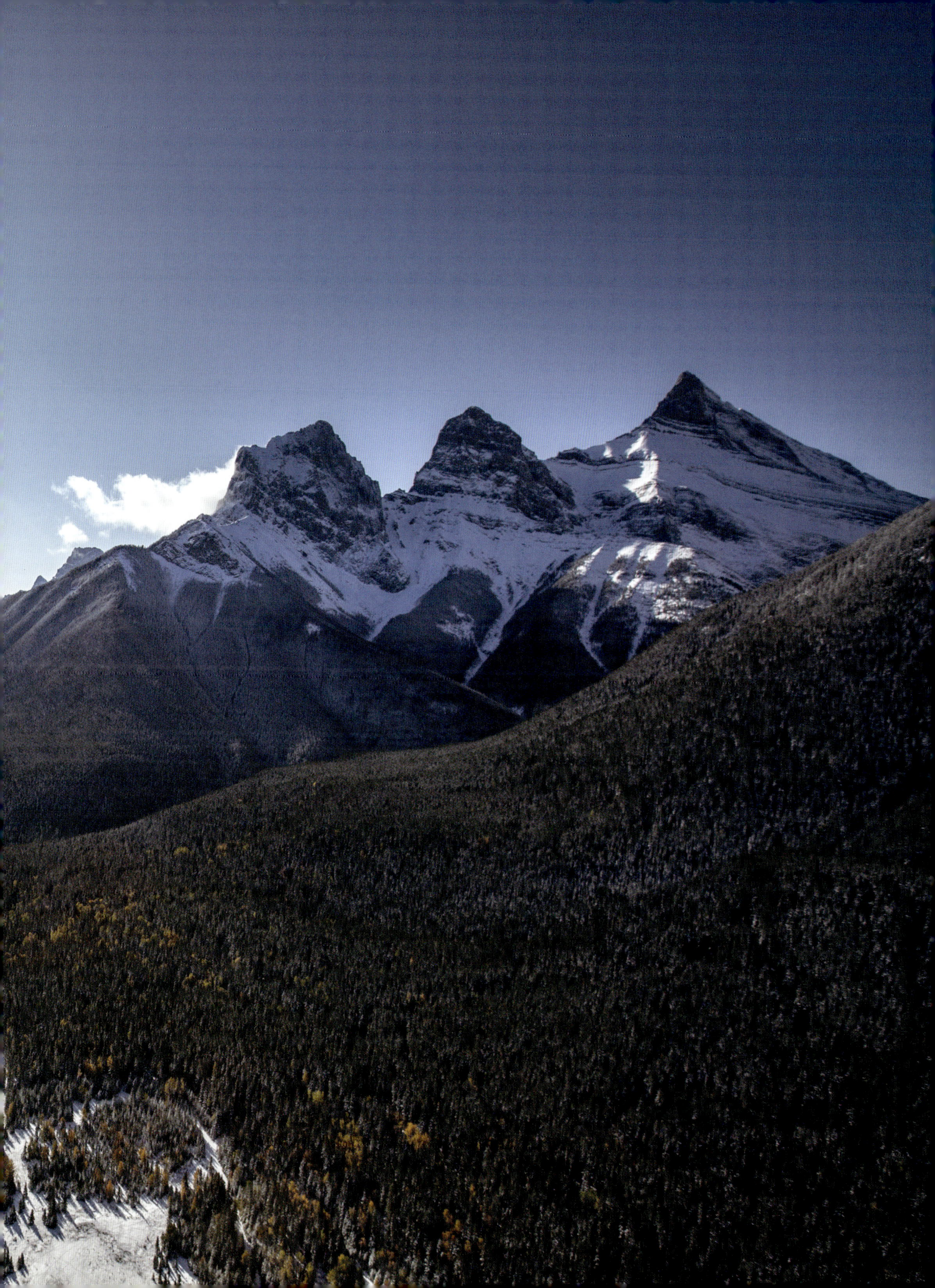

Opposite: The flatirons and couloirs of the Front Ranges on a brilliant winter's day.

Overleaf: Mount Assiniboine rises above a trio of lakes, (l–r) Magog,
Sunburst and Cerulean, after the first snowfall of the season.

Following spread: Lake Magog and the cabins
of Assiniboine Lodge at the height of larch season.

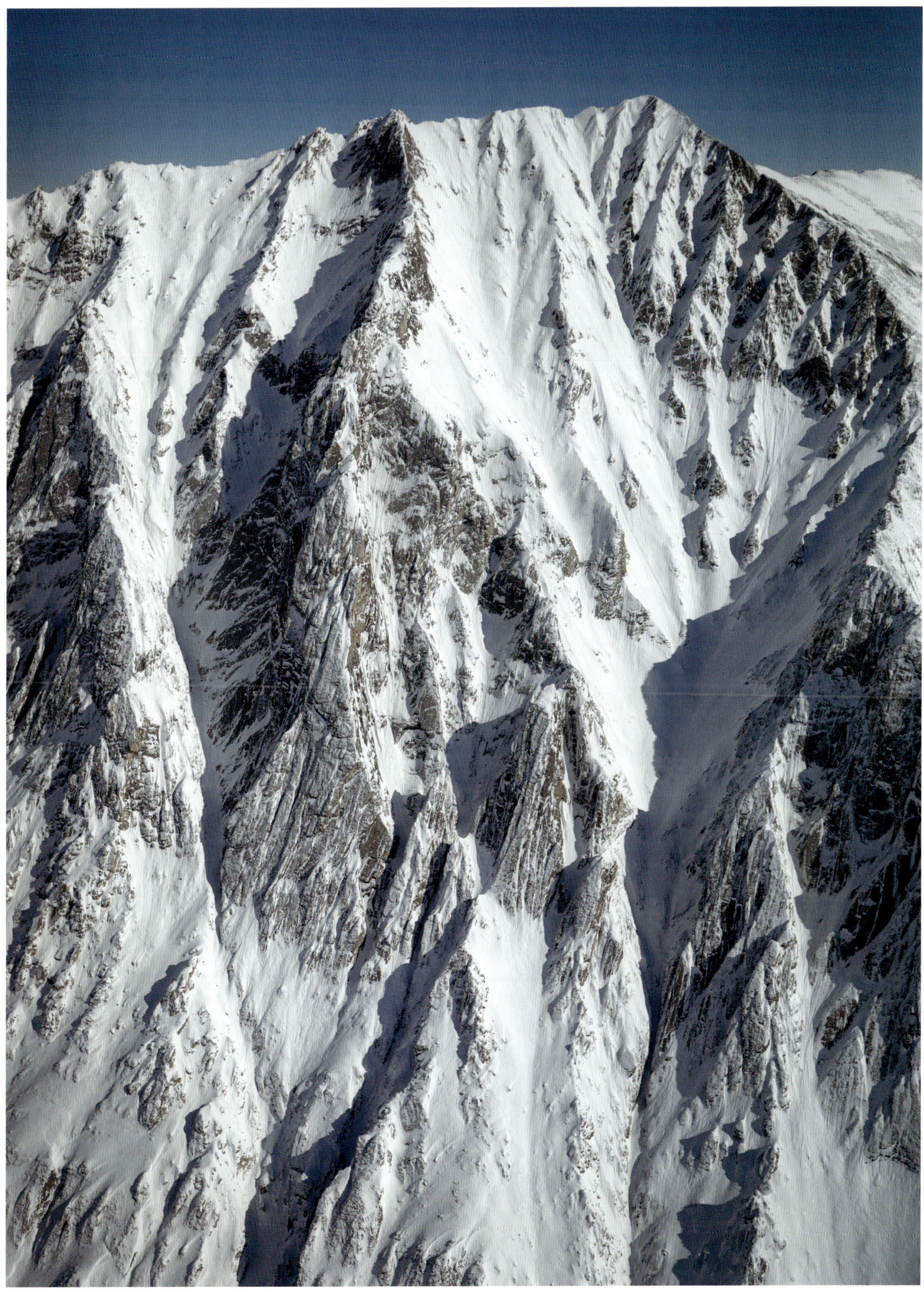

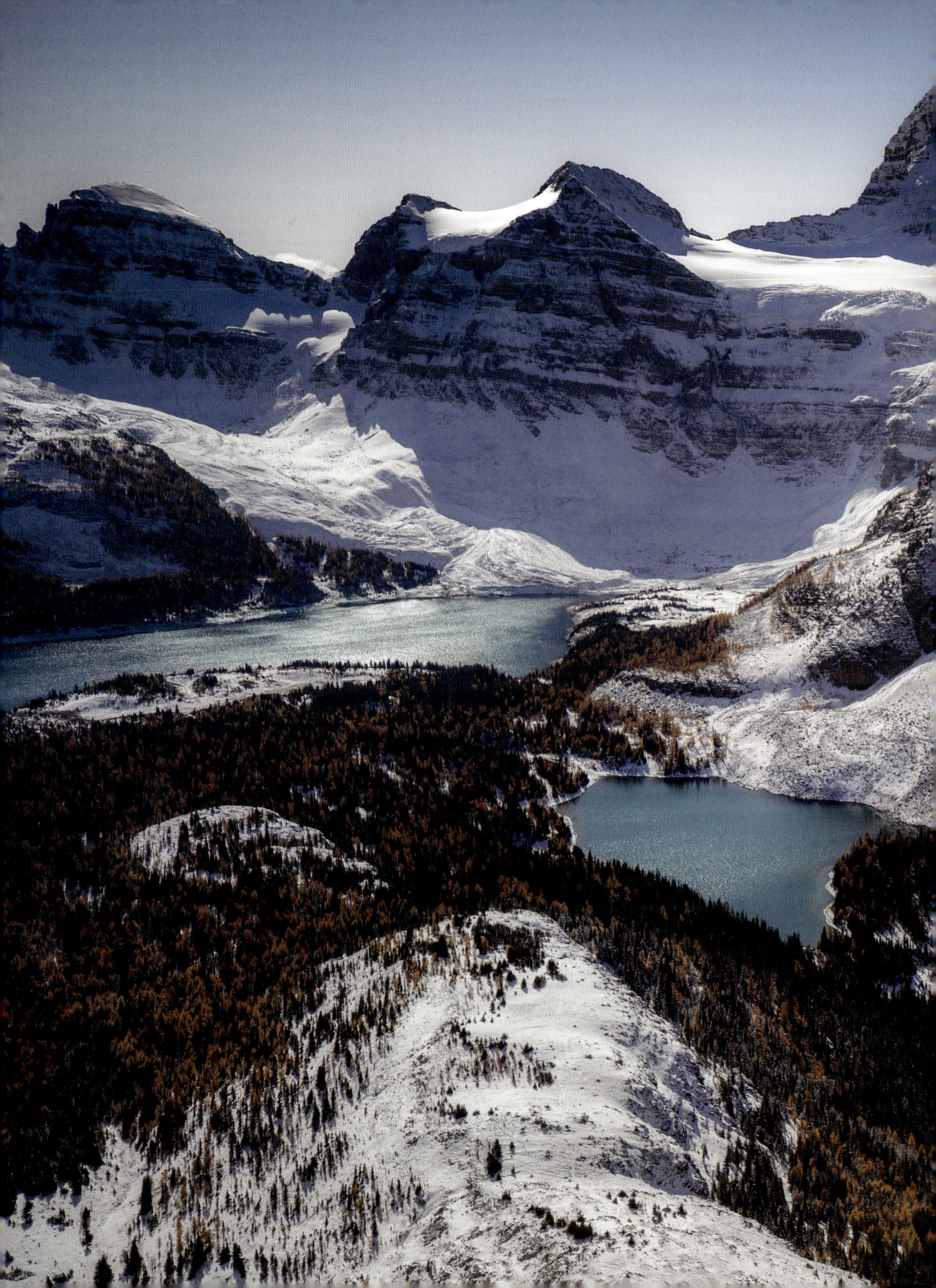

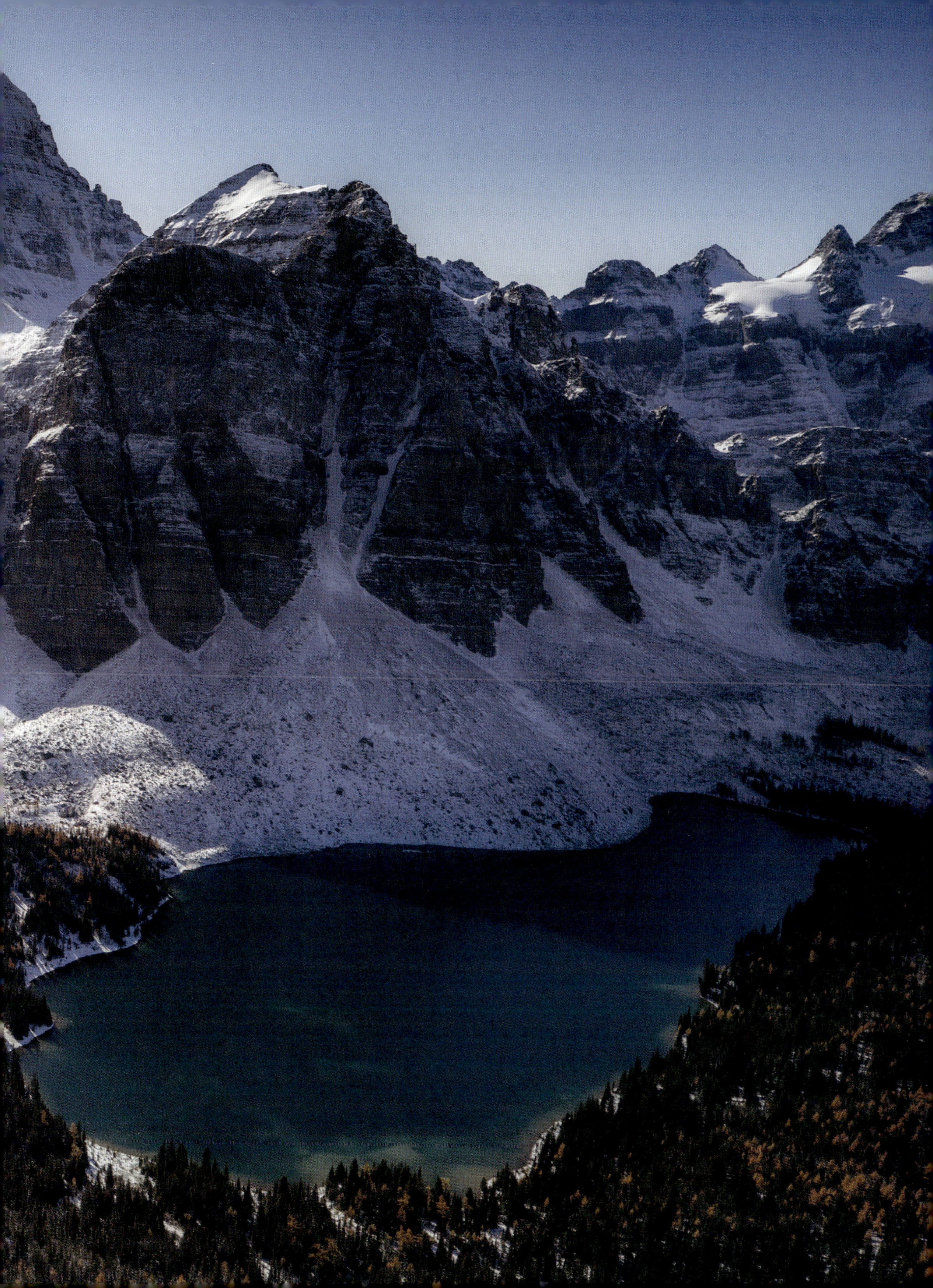

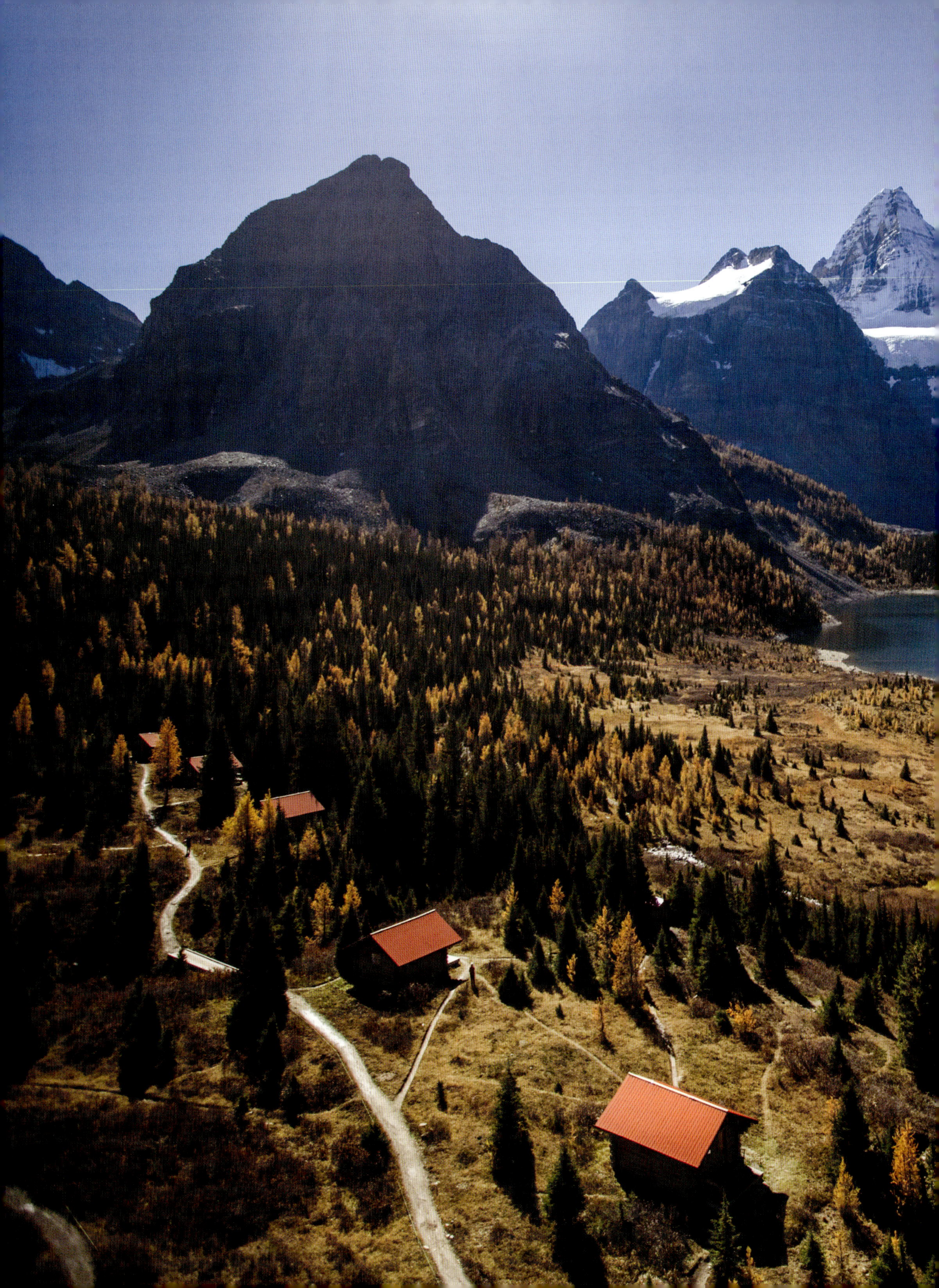

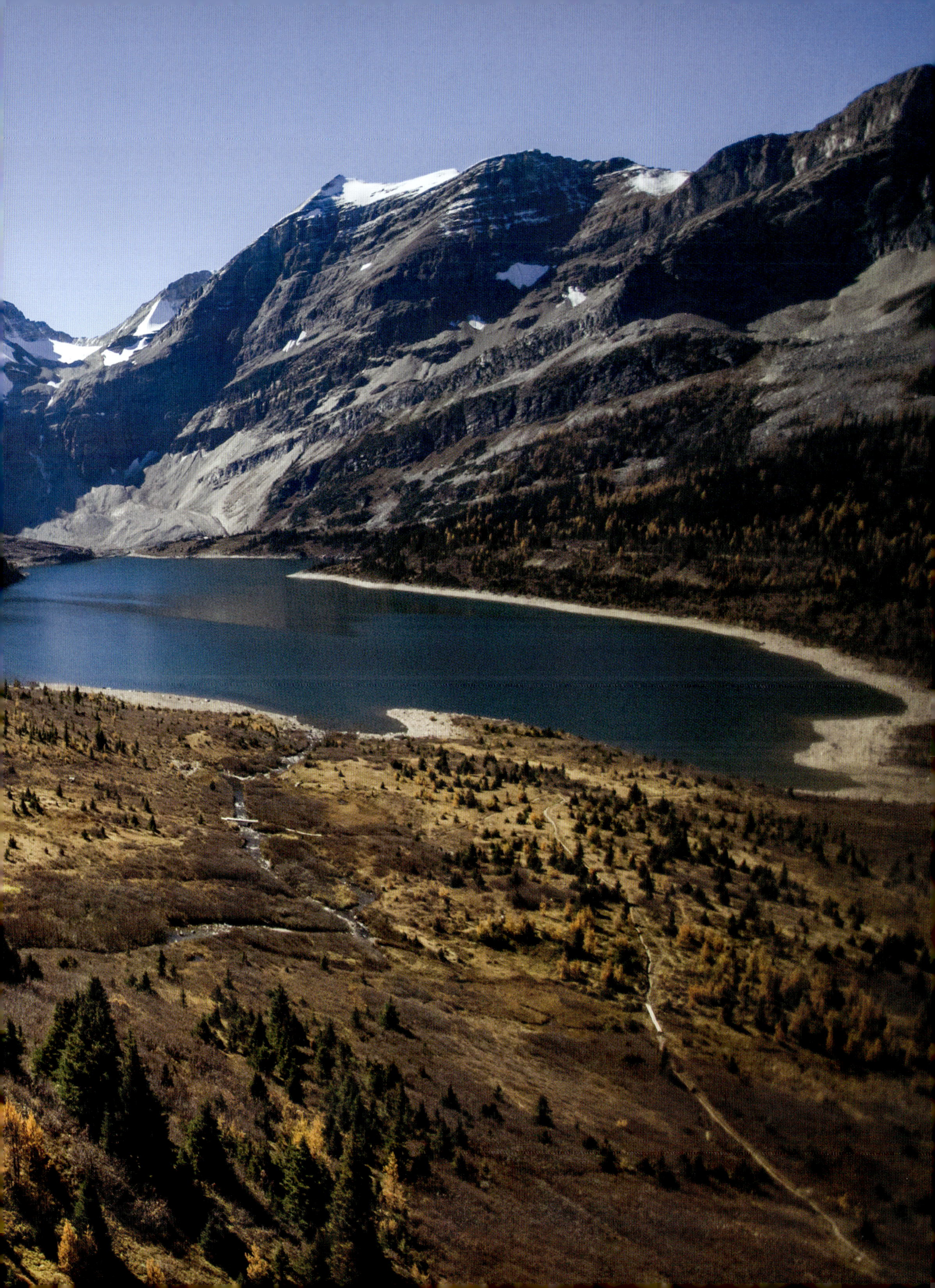

Opposite: The impressive east face of Mount Assiniboine rises nearly
two kilometres above Gloria (top) and Terrapin (bottom) lakes.

Overleaf: Clouds are reflected in Two Jack Lake, with Mount Rundle in the distance.

Following spread: Mount Inglismaldie rises over the turquoise waters
of Lake Minnewanka, the largest lake in Banff National Park.

Final spread: A boat cruises up the 21-kilometre-long Lake Minnewanka.

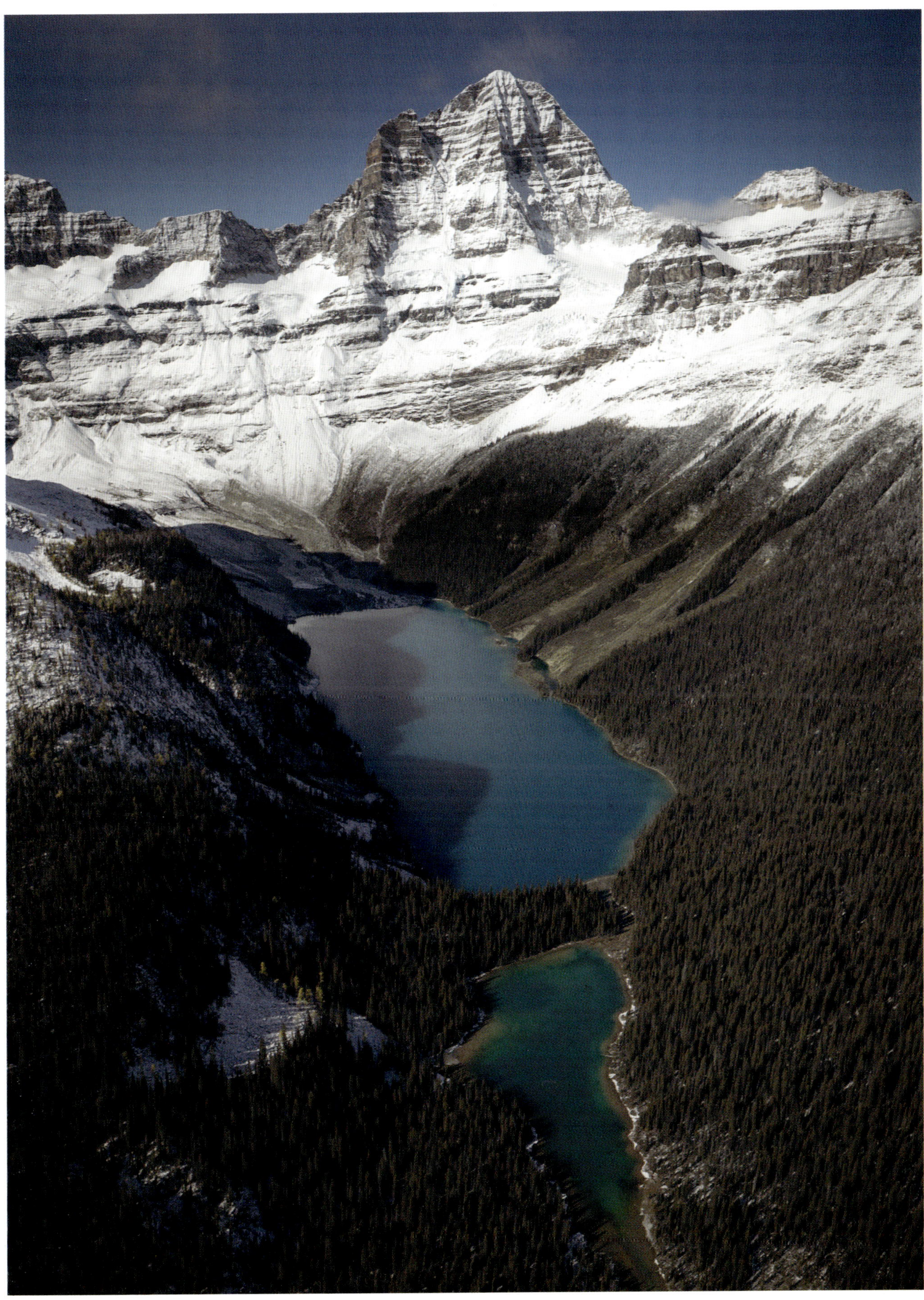

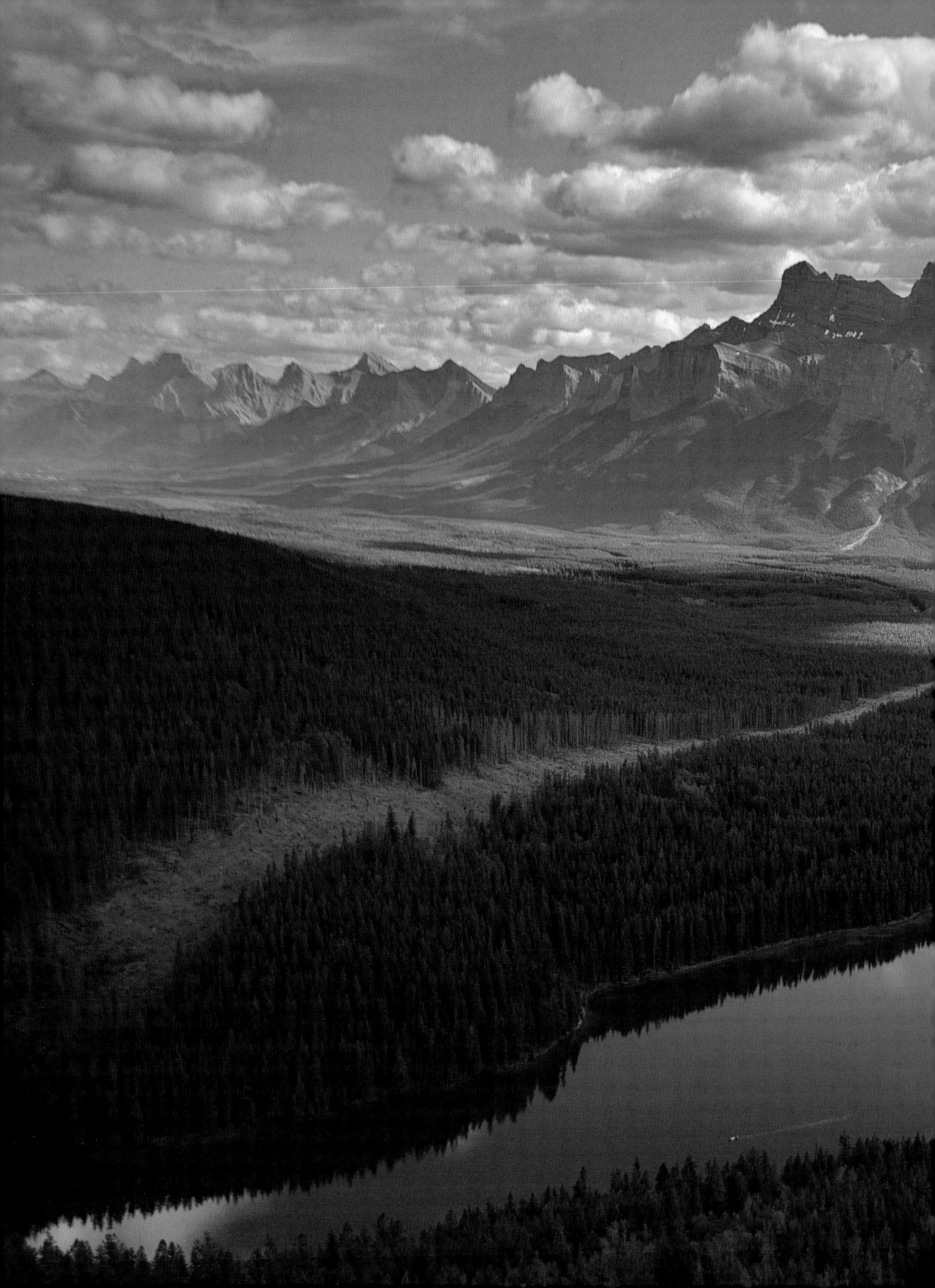

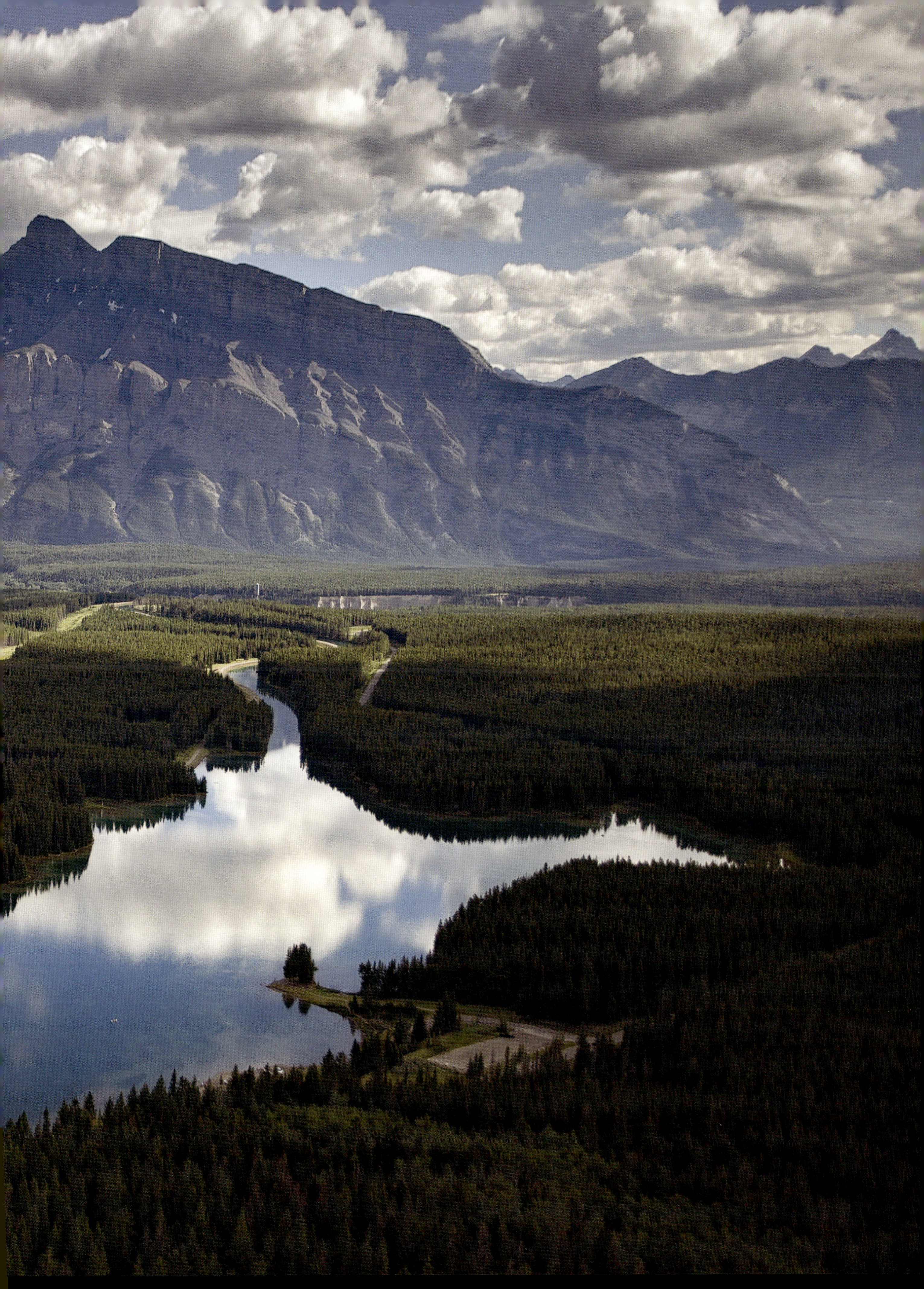

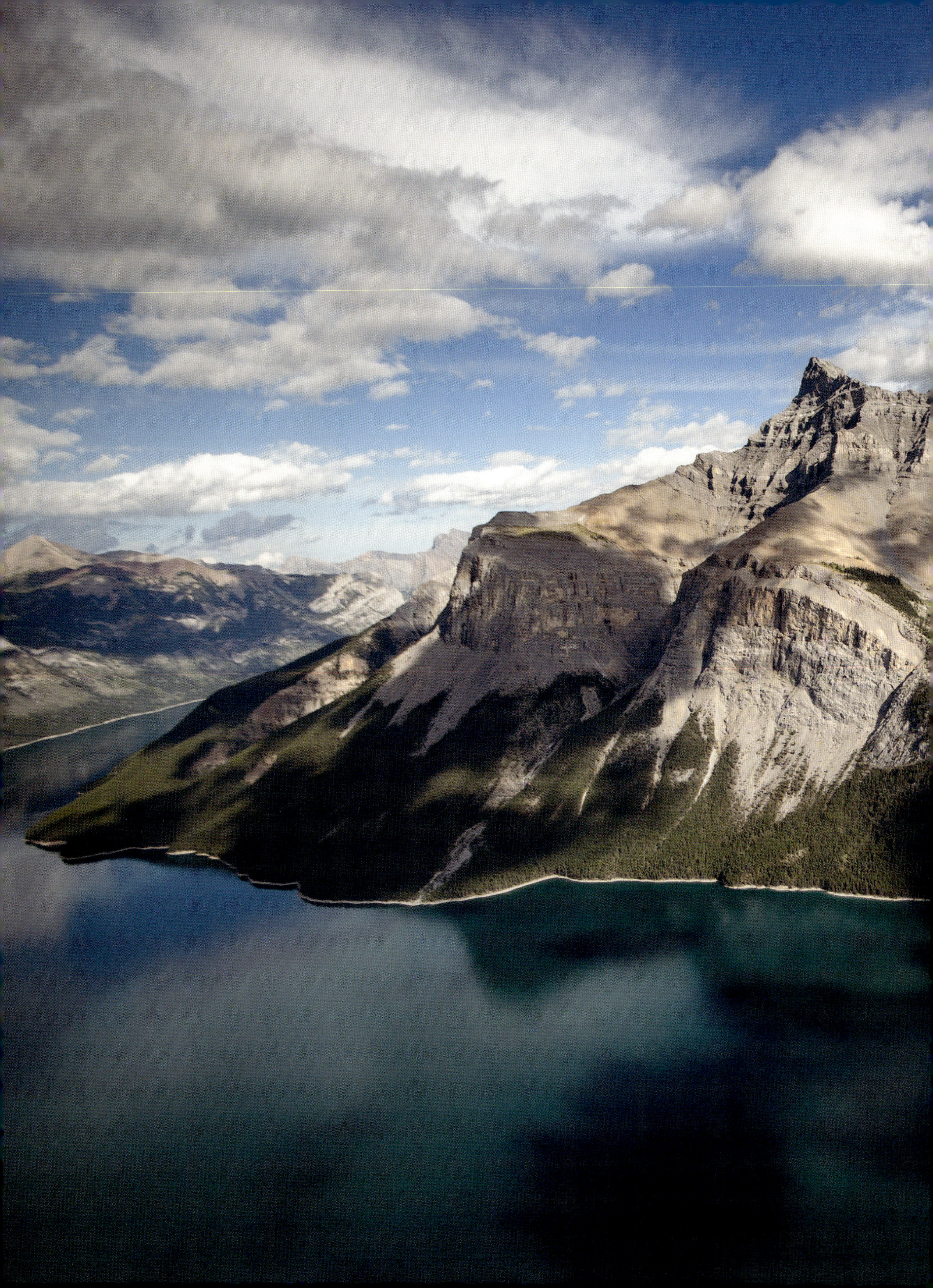

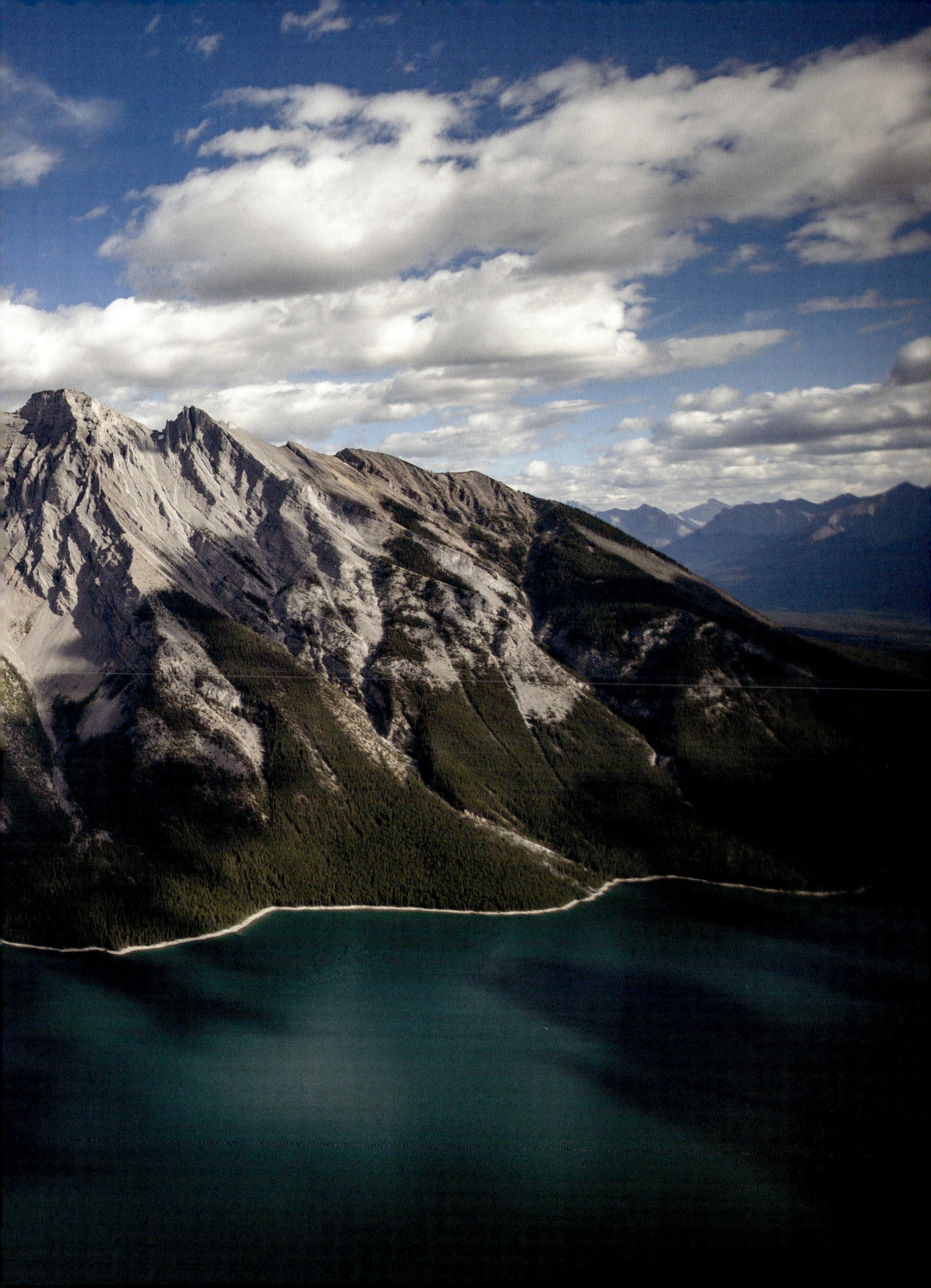

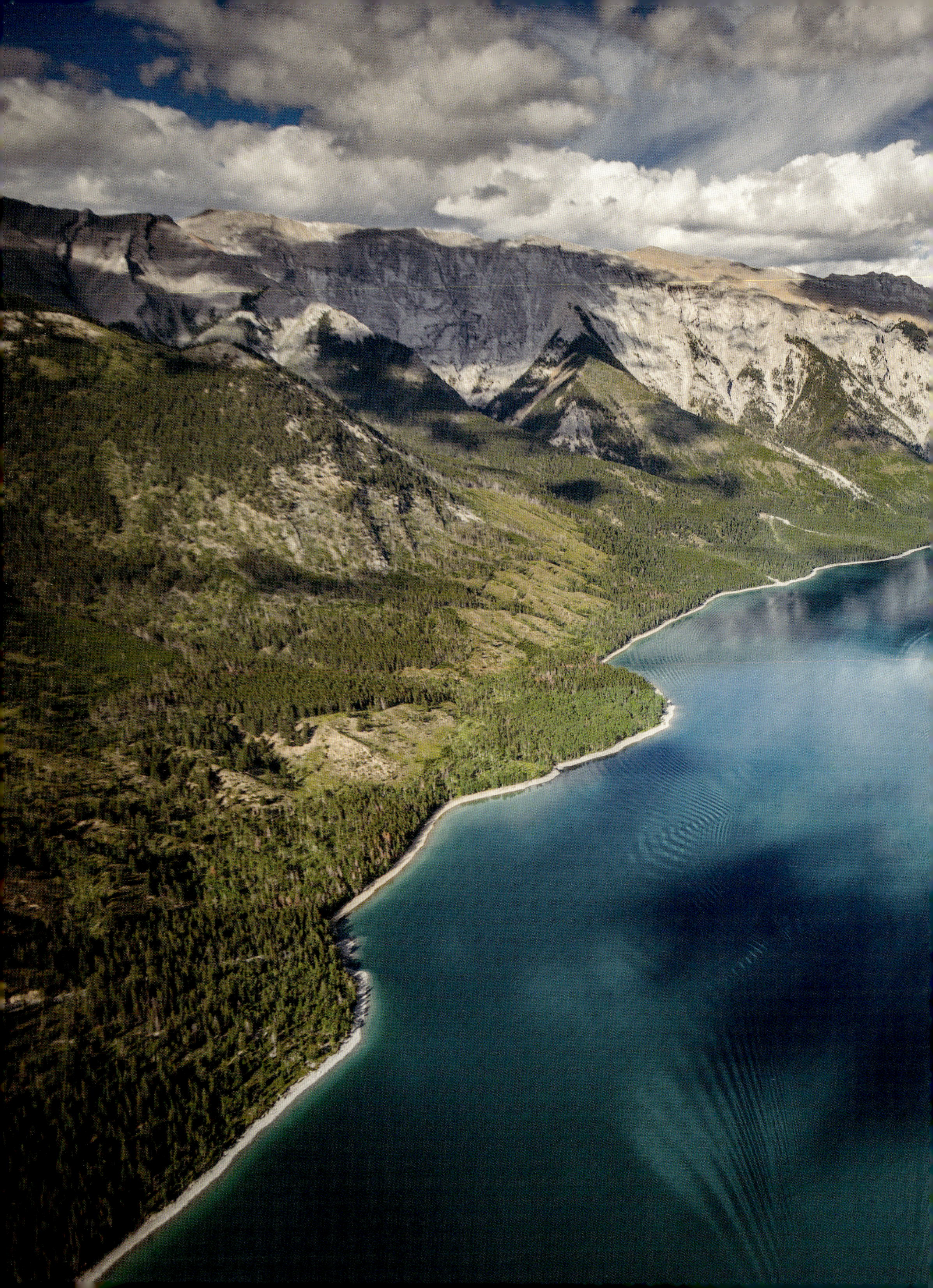

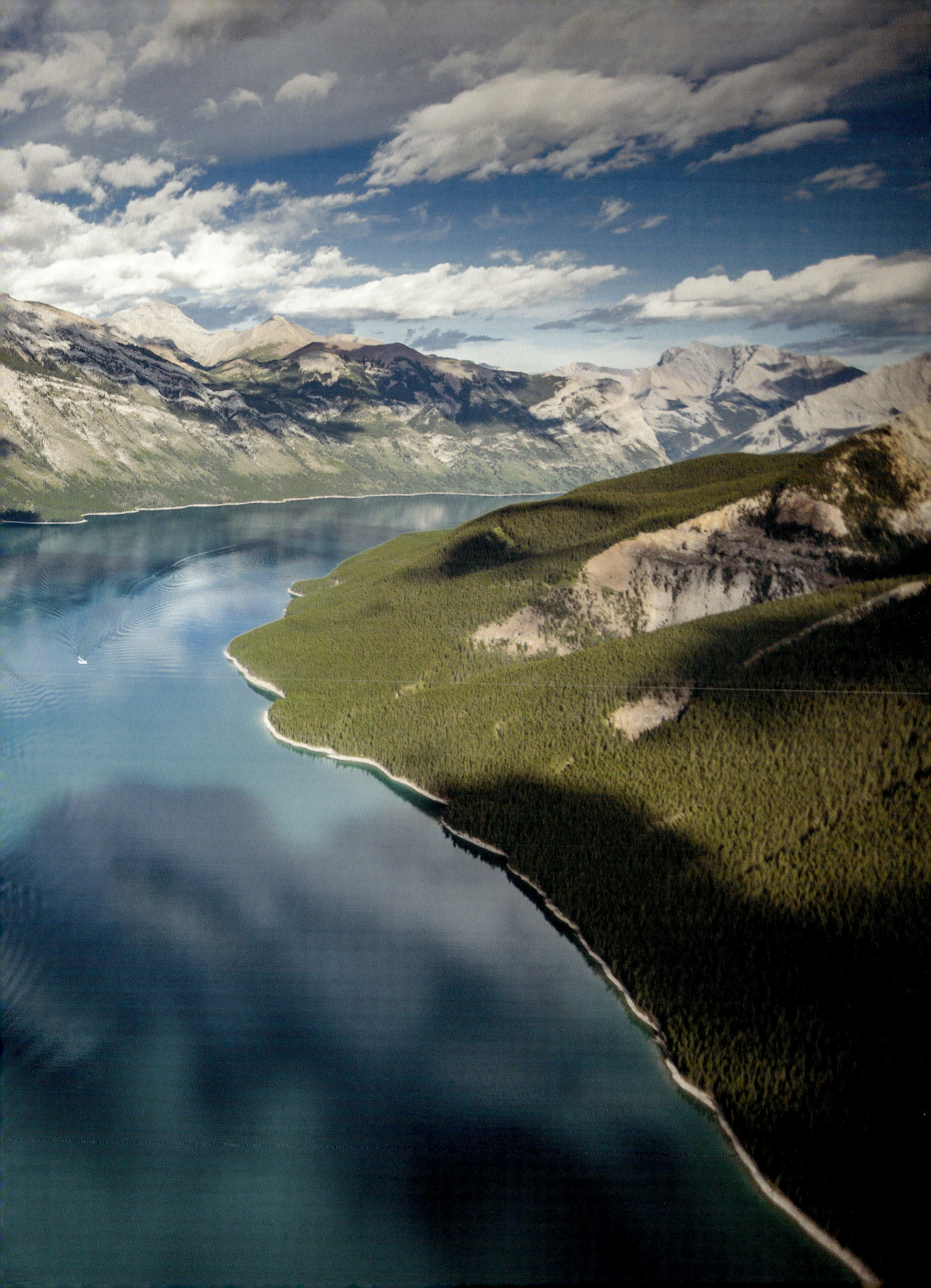

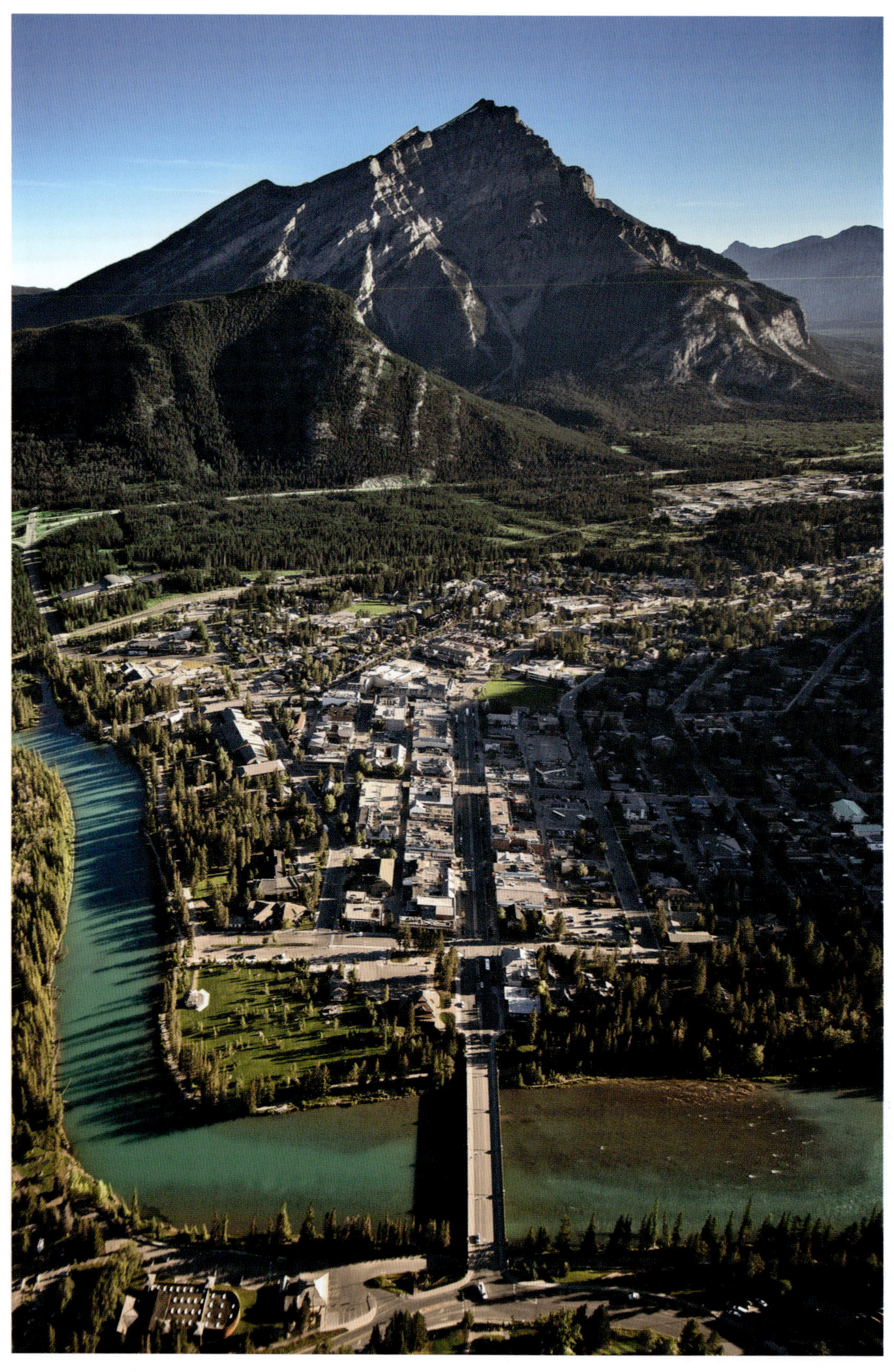

Above: The Town of Banff was designed with Banff Avenue (pictured here) oriented for optimal views of Cascade Mountain.

Opposite: The Bow River snakes towards the Town of Banff with the Massive Range looming beyond.

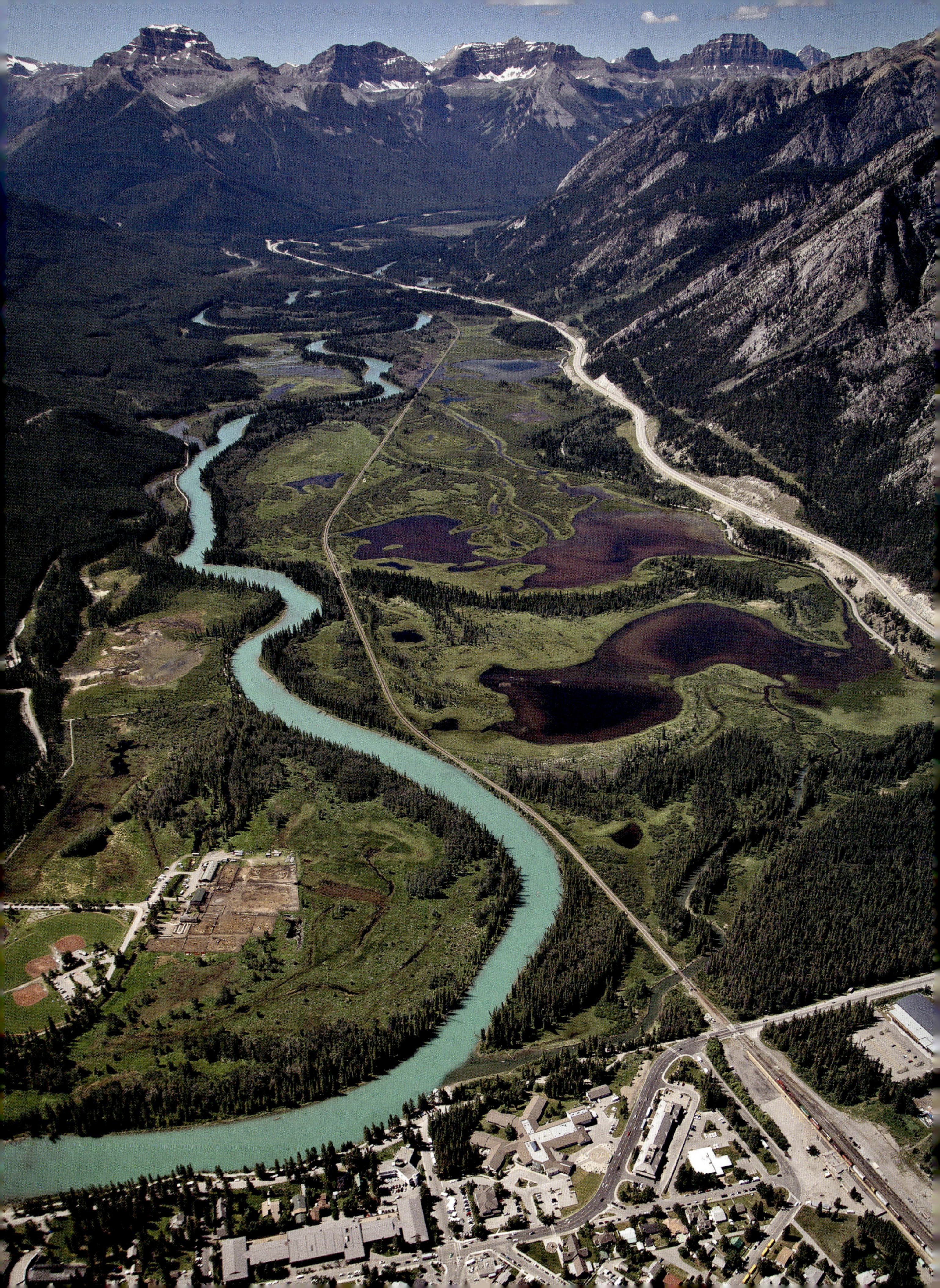

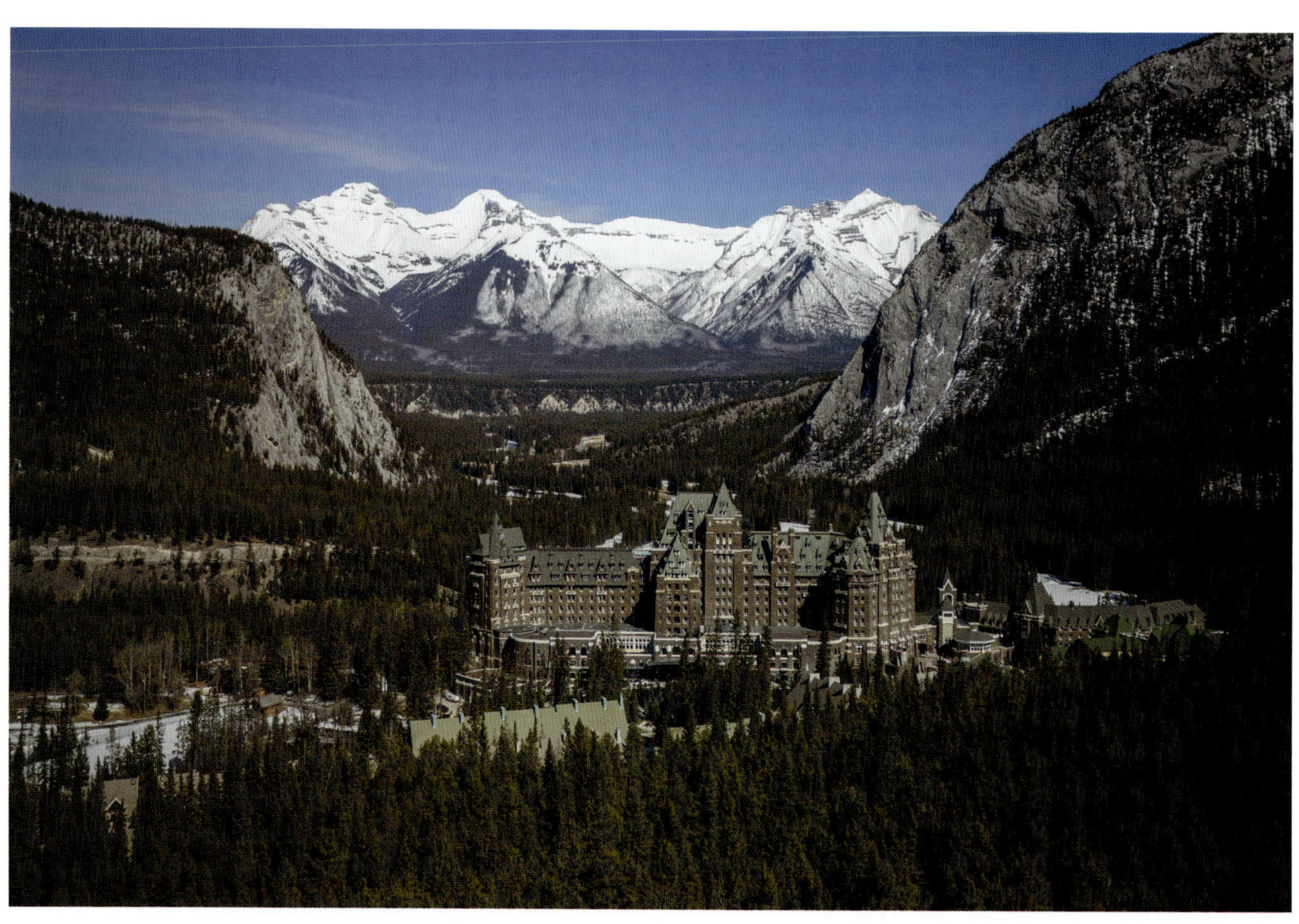

Above: First opened in 1888, the Fairmont Banff Springs Hotel overlooks
the gap where the Bow River carves its way towards the Prairies.

Opposite: In the centre, from bottom to top: Fairmont Banff Springs Hotel,
Bow Falls, Banff Centre for Arts and Creativity, and Cascade Mountain.

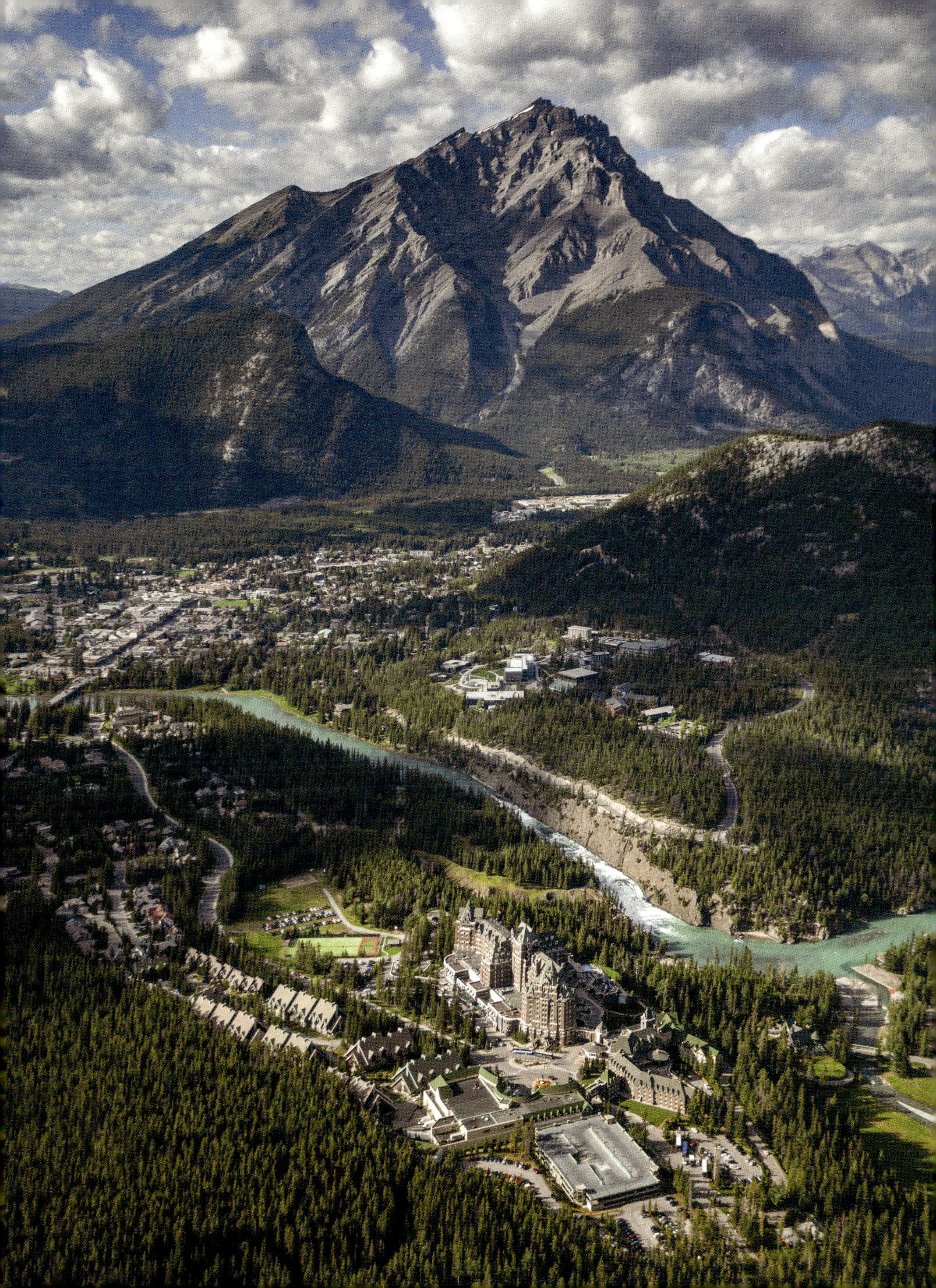

Opposite: First light on a north-facing aspect of Mount Rundle.

Overleaf: The Bow River and Bow Falls split the Town of Banff into two parts,
joined only by a driving bridge and pedestrian bridge (both not pictured in the image).

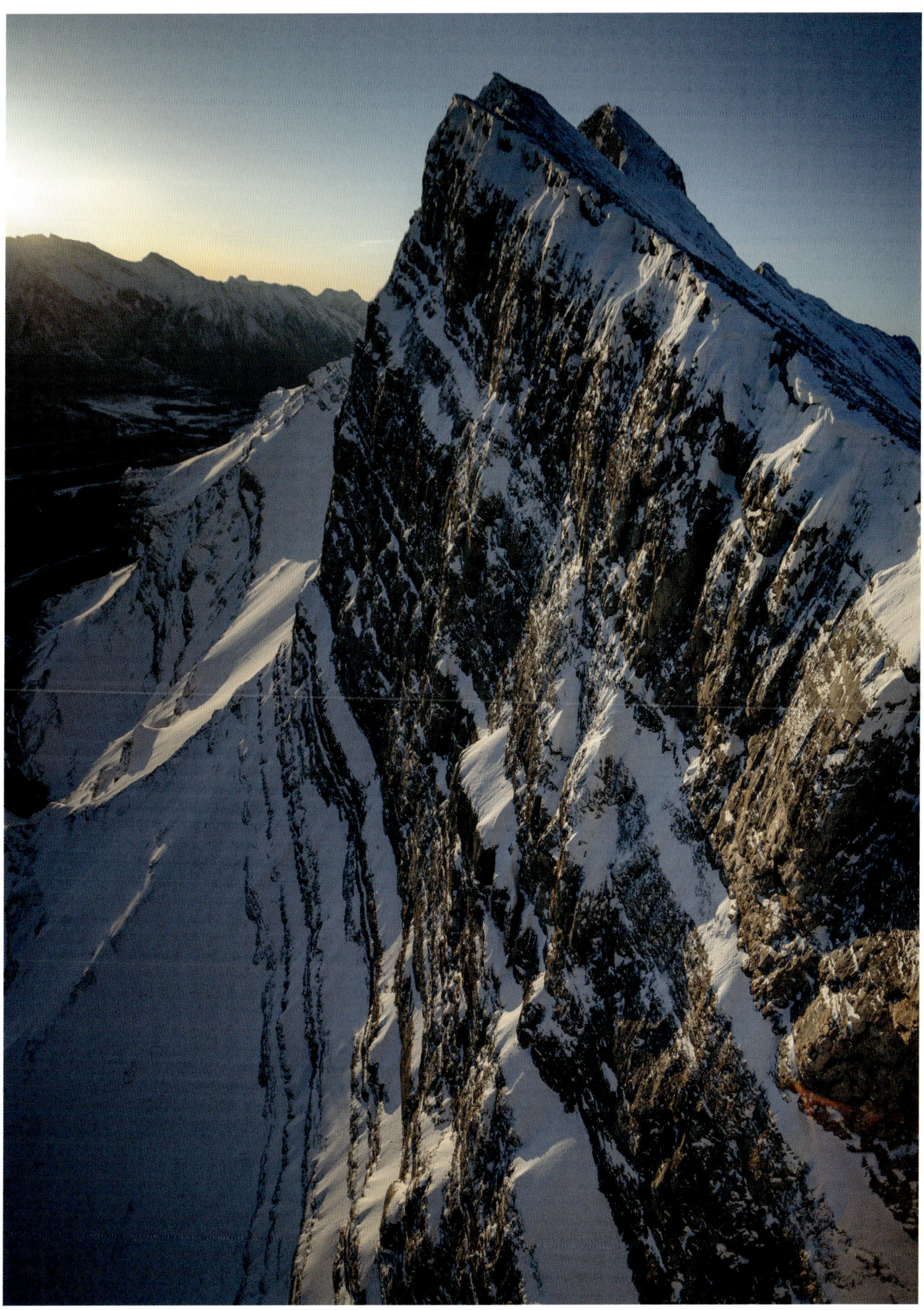

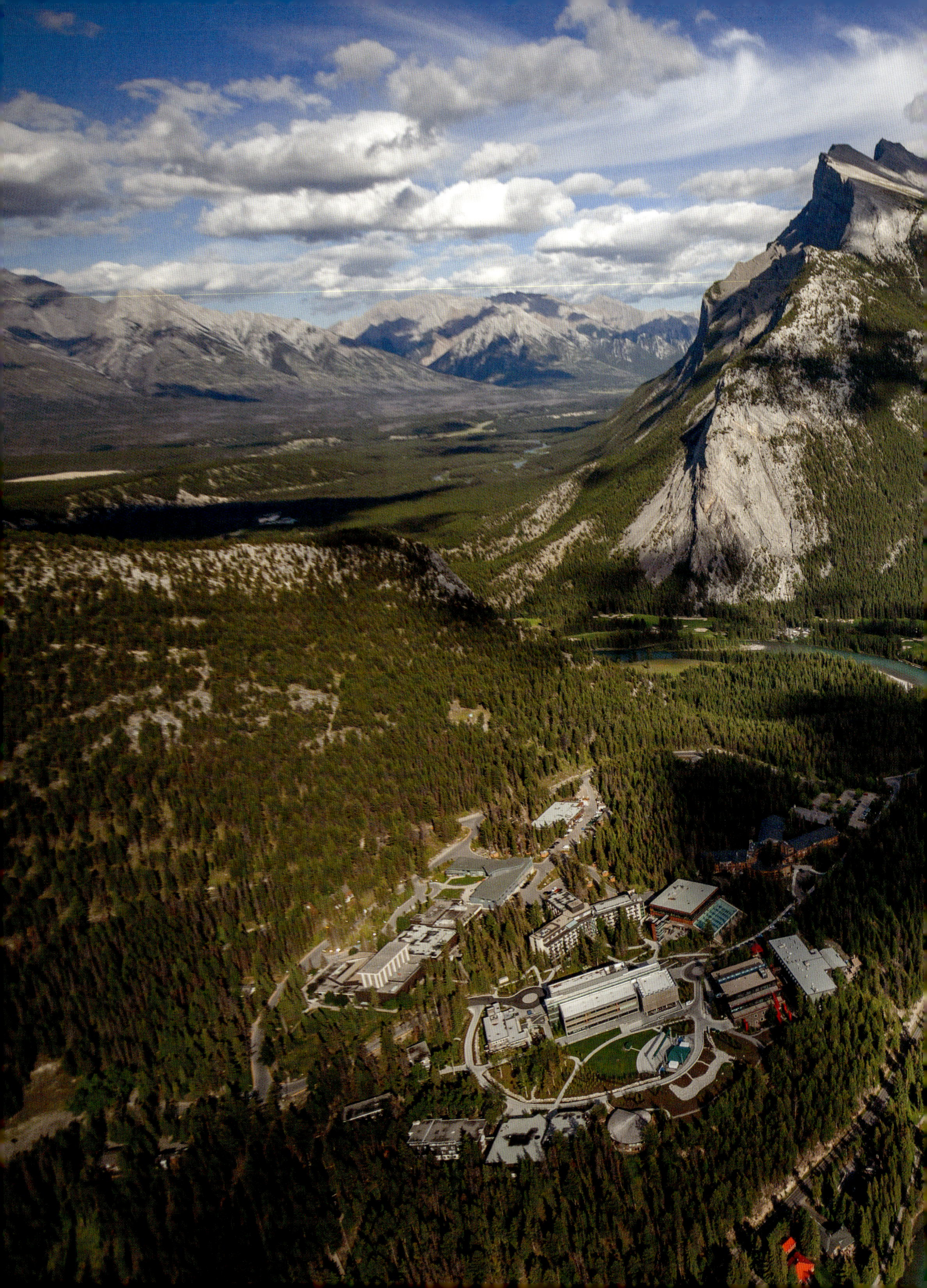

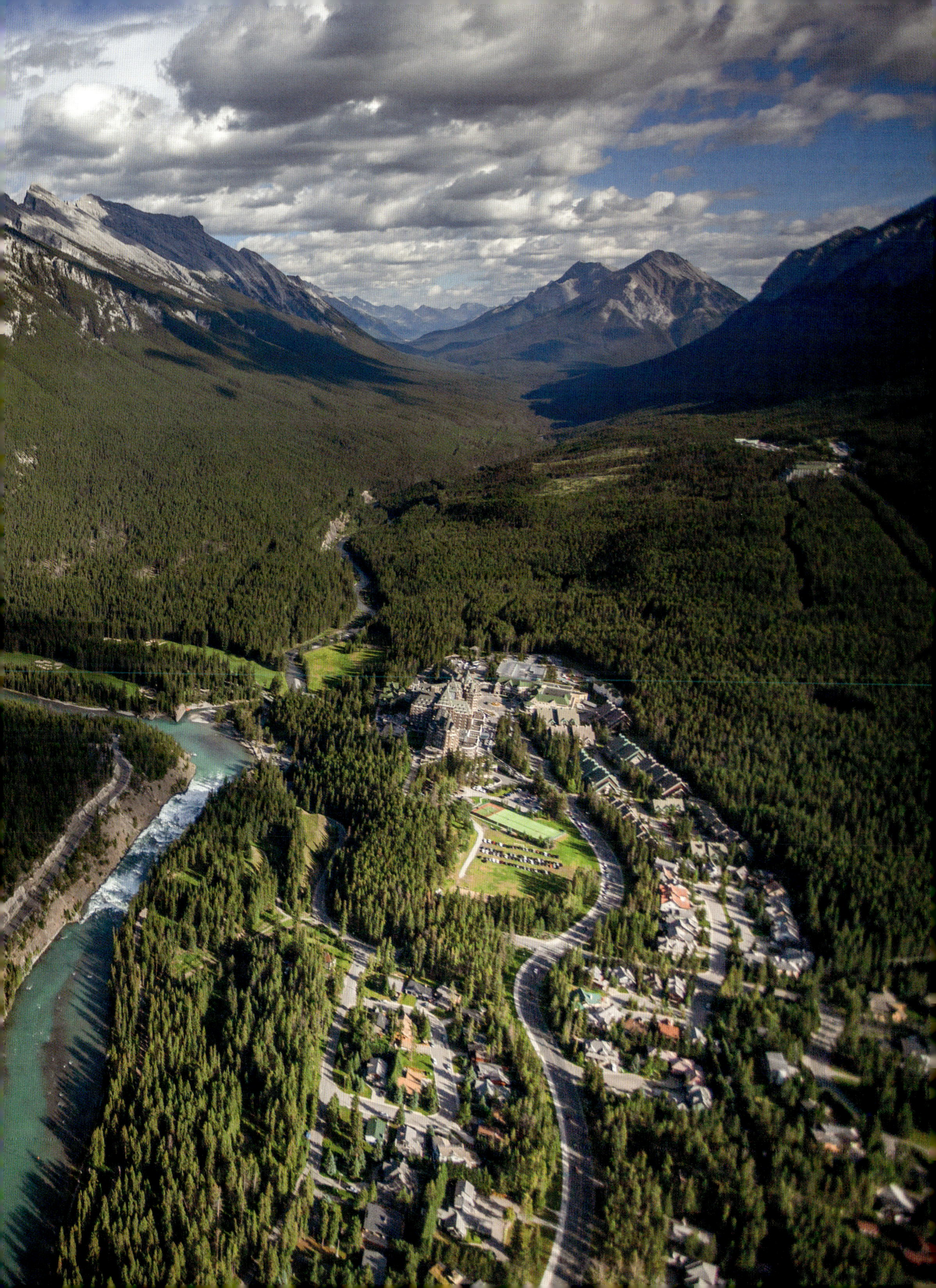

Opposite: The upper terminal of the Banff Gondola
is situated on a high ridge on Sulphur Mountain.

Overleaf: Amazing light on the limestone slabs of the west face of Mount Louis.

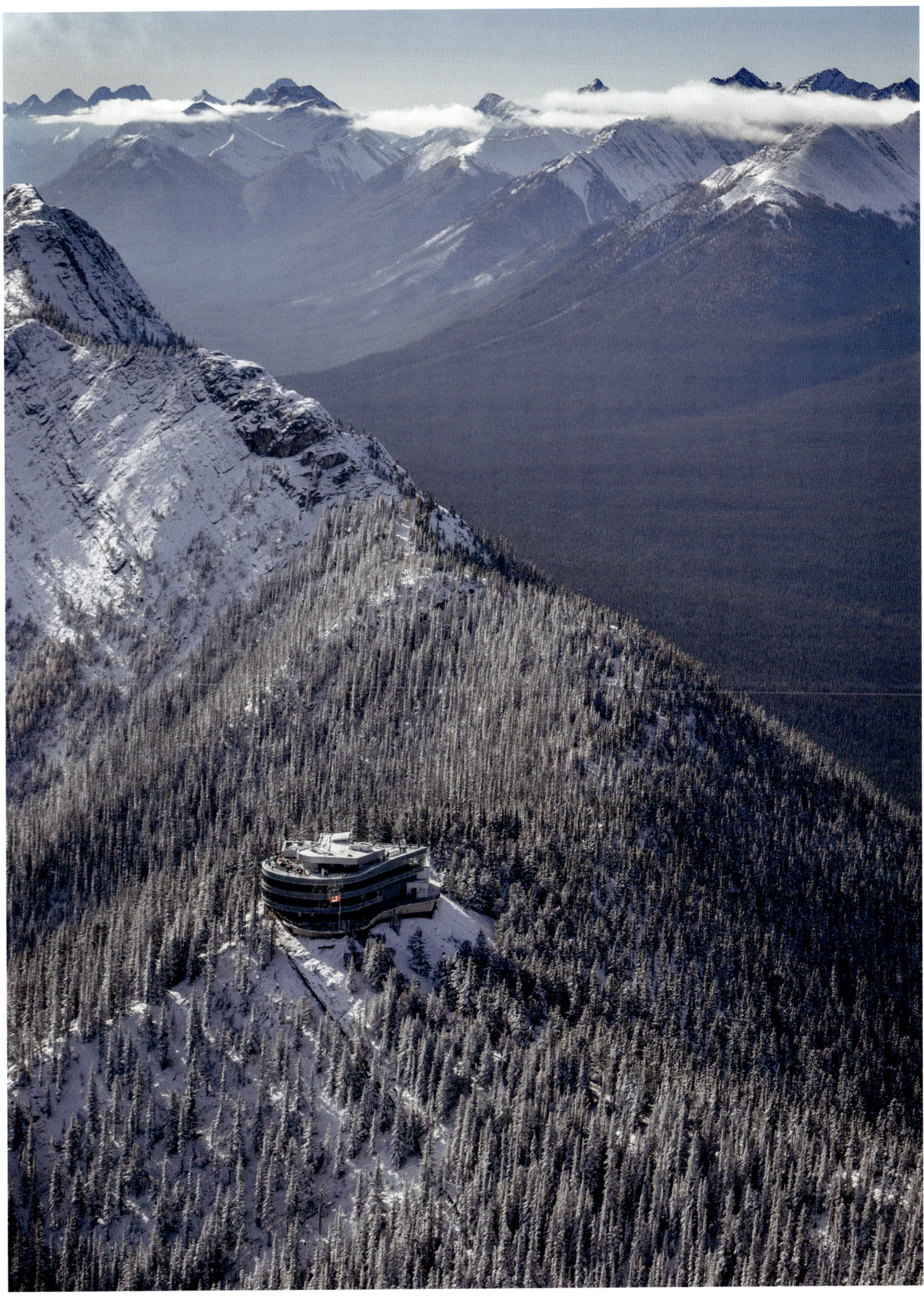

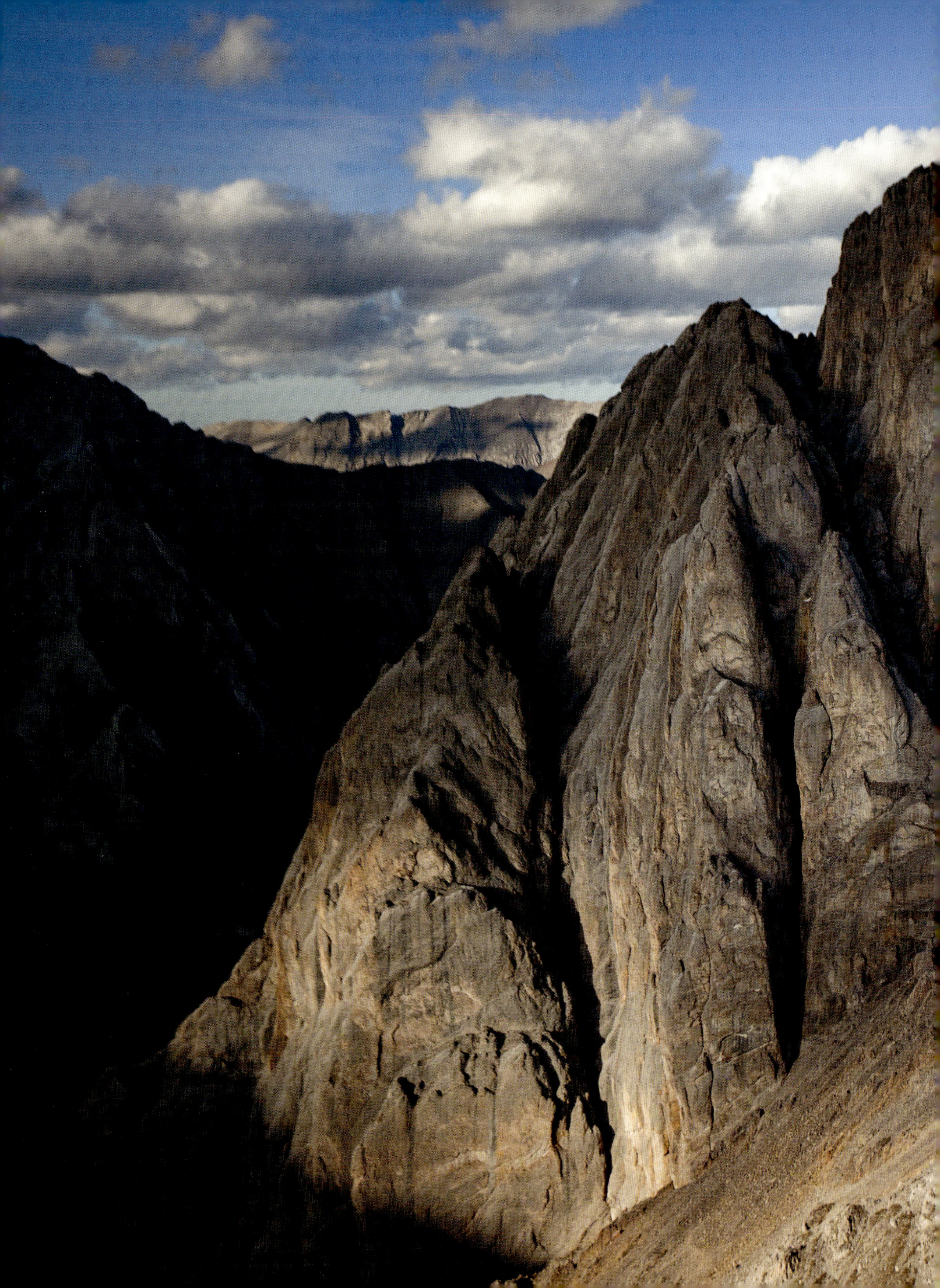

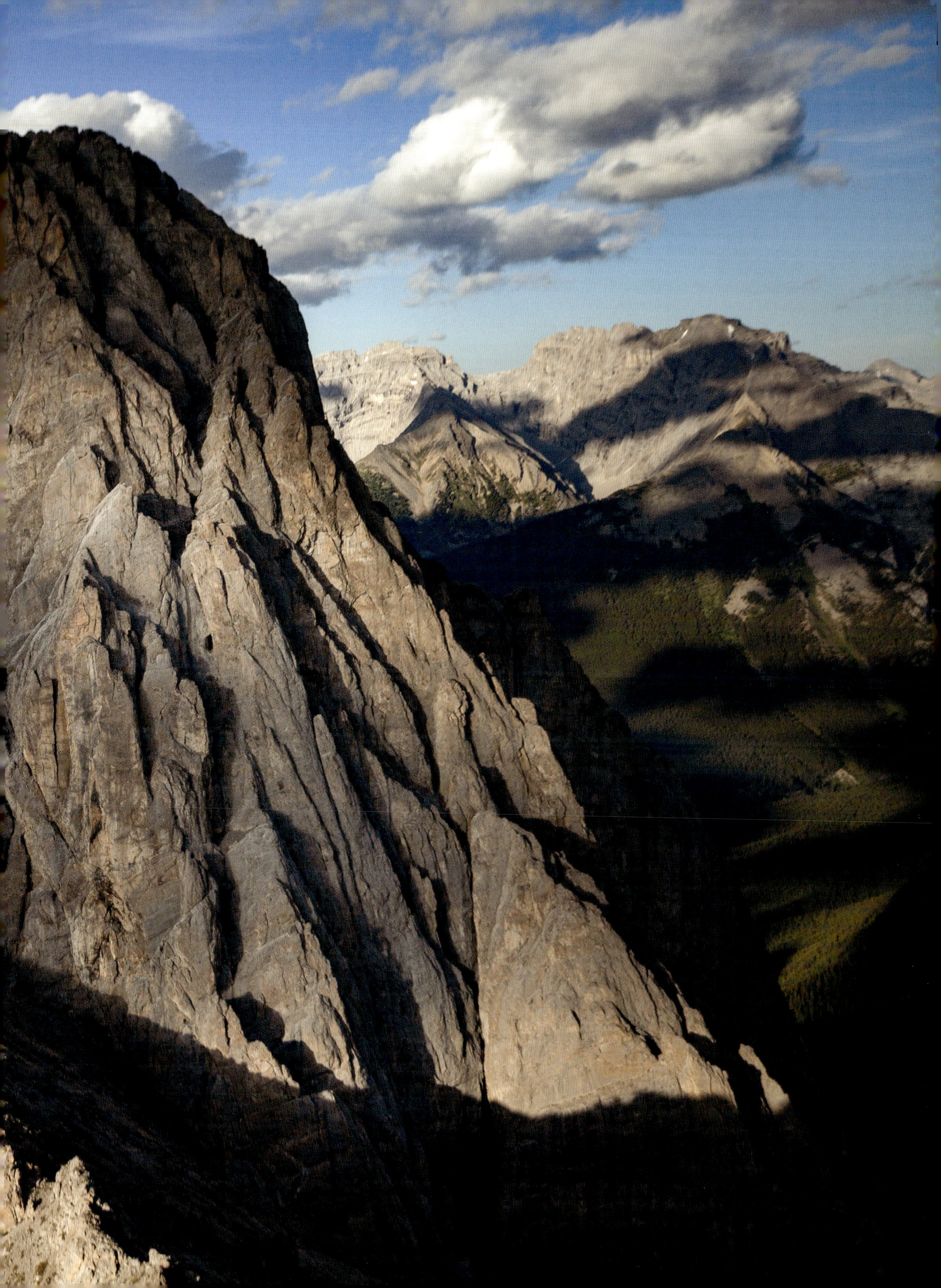

Opposite: The sheer faces of Mount Louis have beckoned climbers since the peak's first ascent, by A.H. MacCarthy and Conrad Kain in 1916.

Overleaf: A family favourite for local skiers, Mount Norquay has a tradition of skiing that dates back to 1926.

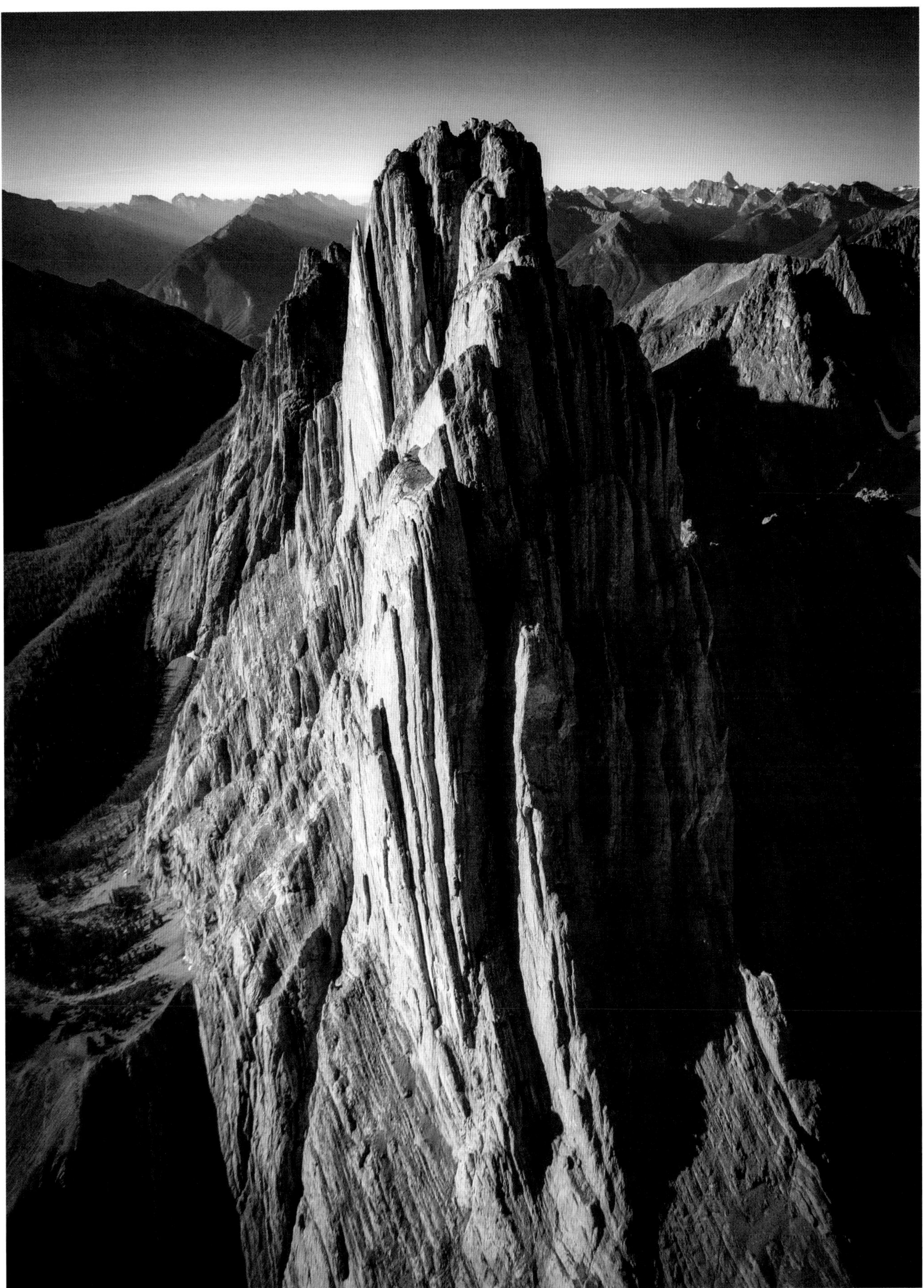

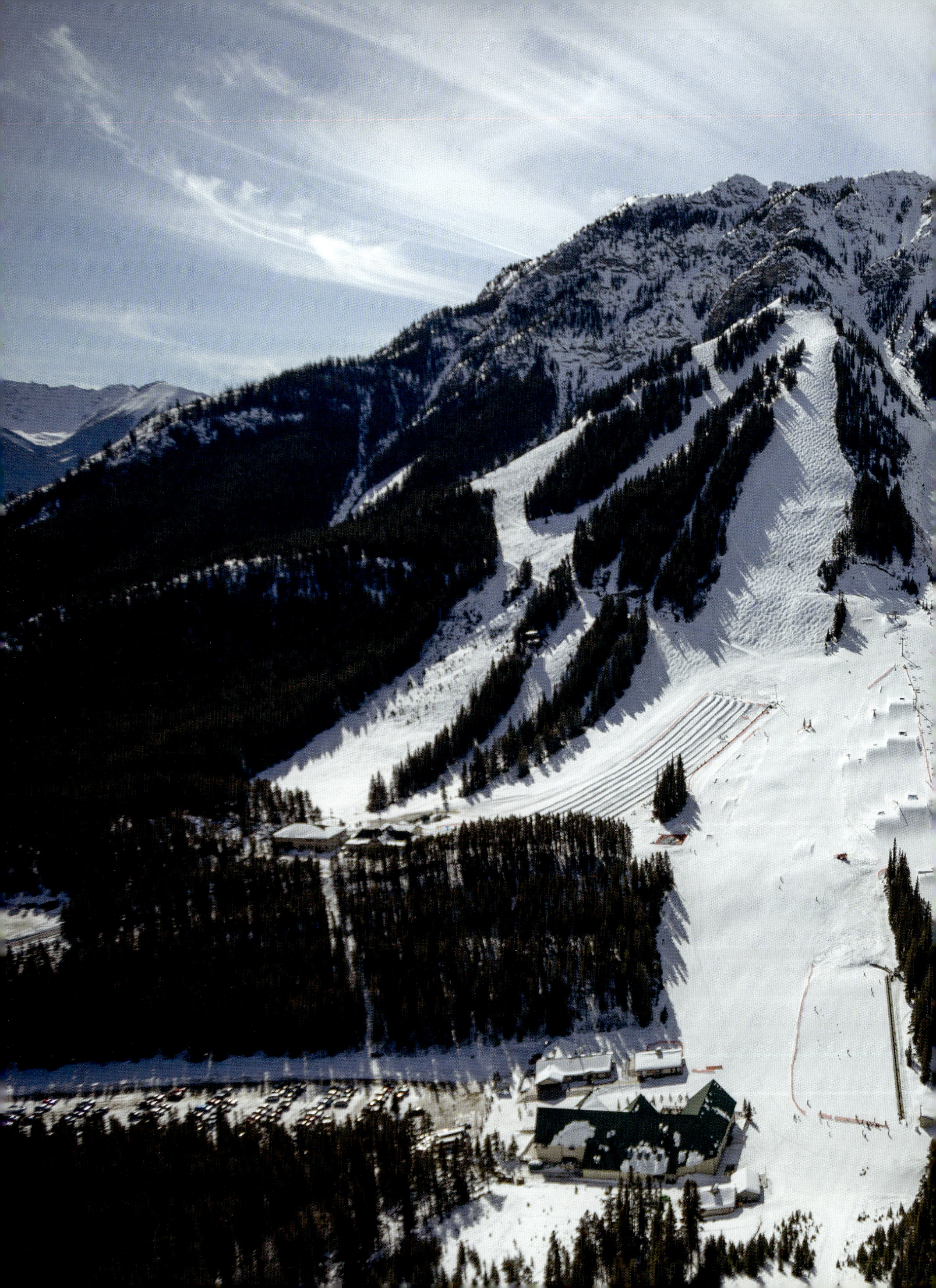

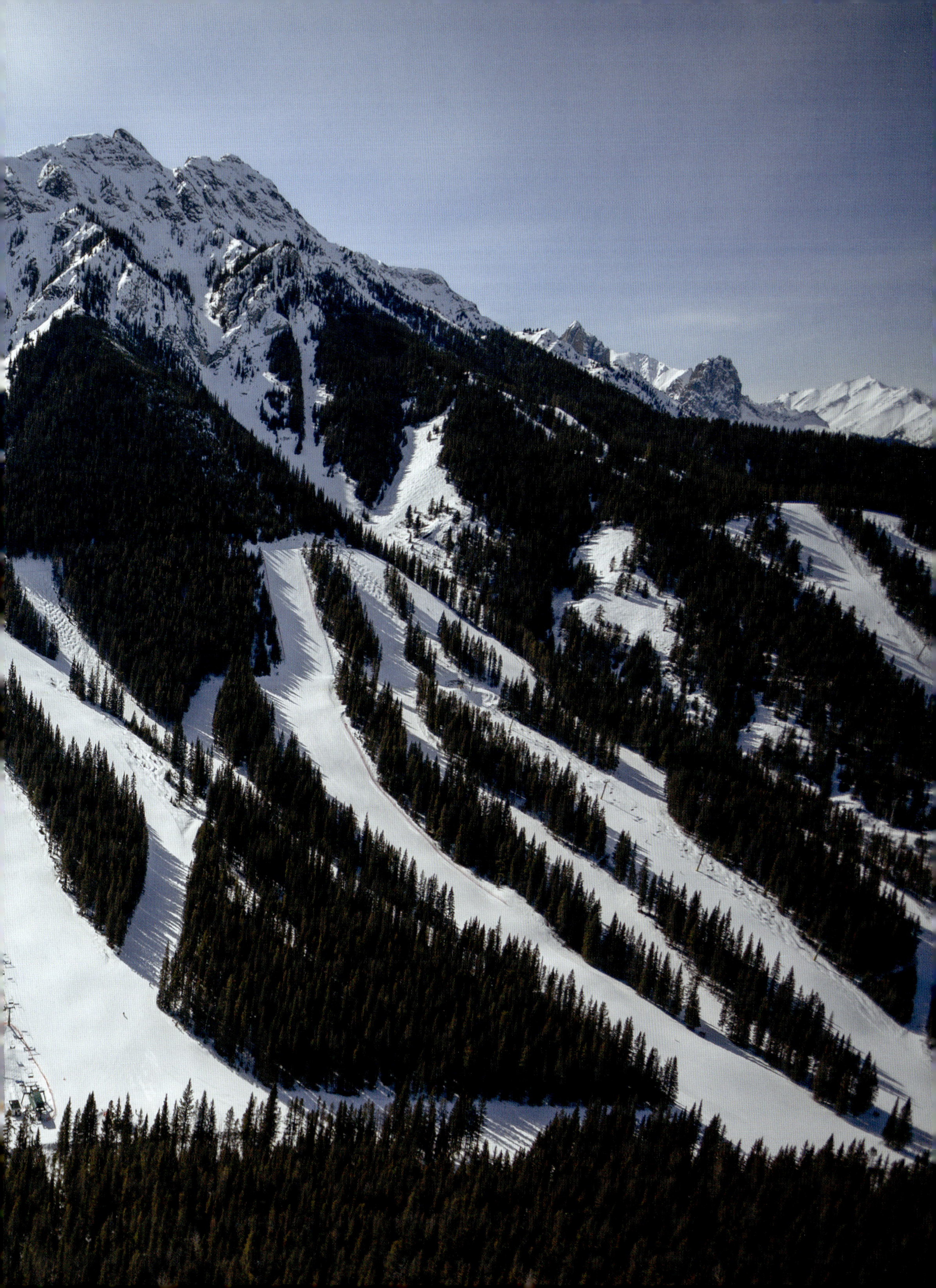

A unique perspective on the marshlands surrounding
Vermilion Lakes outside the Town of Banff.

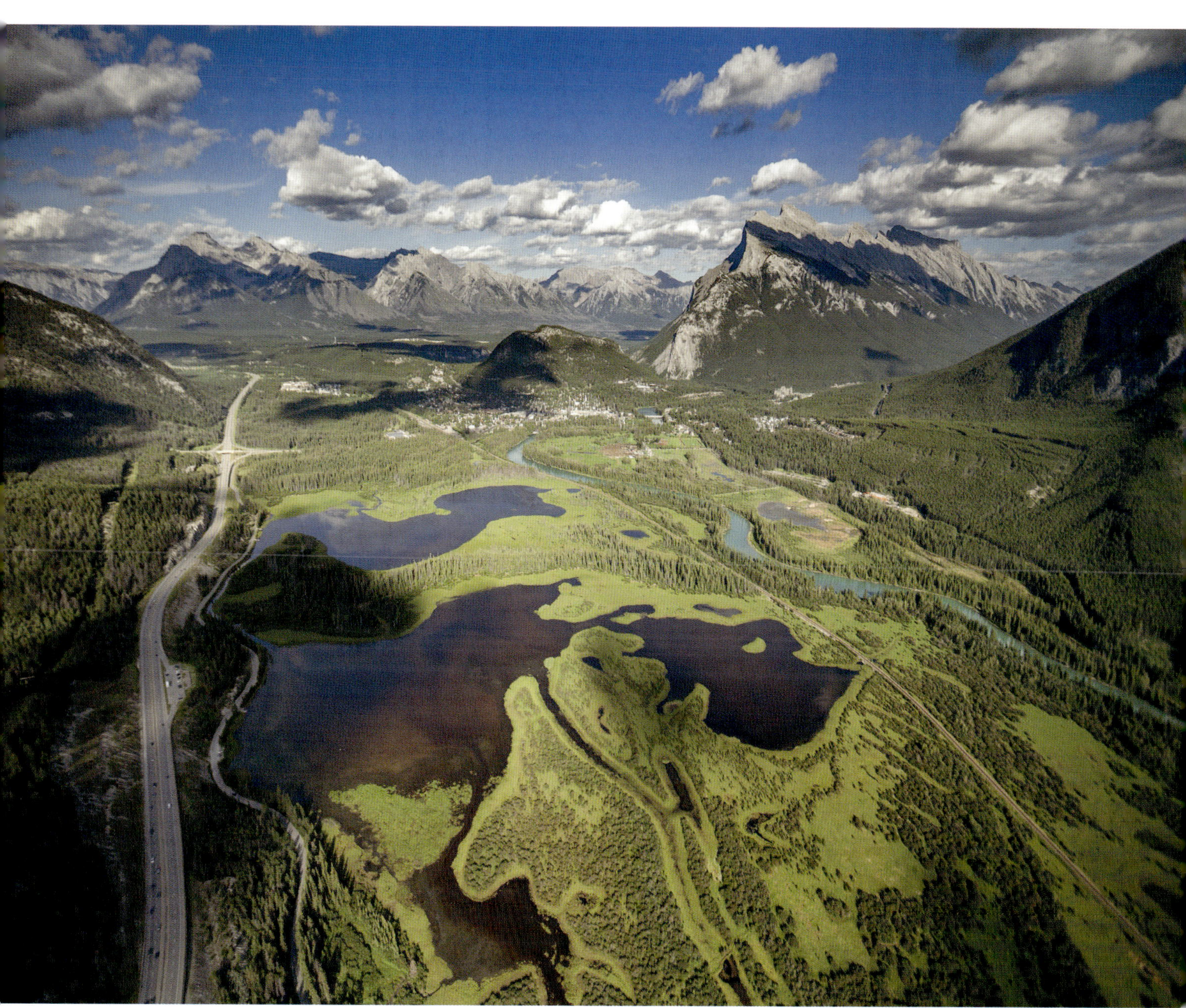

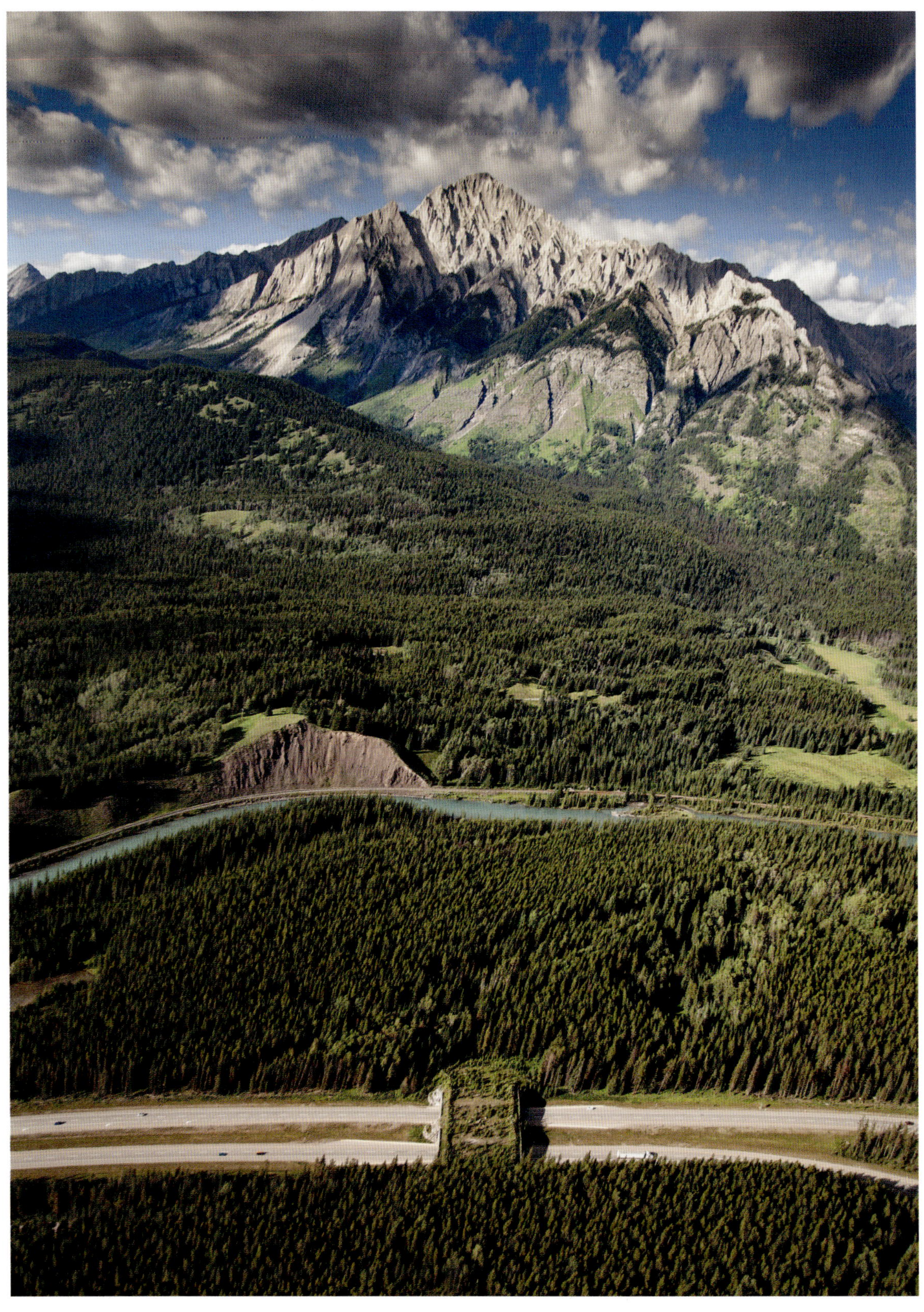

To protect wildlife from vehicle collisions, Banff National Park has 6 overpasses and 38 underpasses that assist animals in safely crossing to the other side, secured with a 2.4-metre high fence that lines both sides of the Trans-Canada Highway. This network of overpasses and underpasses is one of the most respected around the world and has greatly reduced wildlife–vehicle crashes.

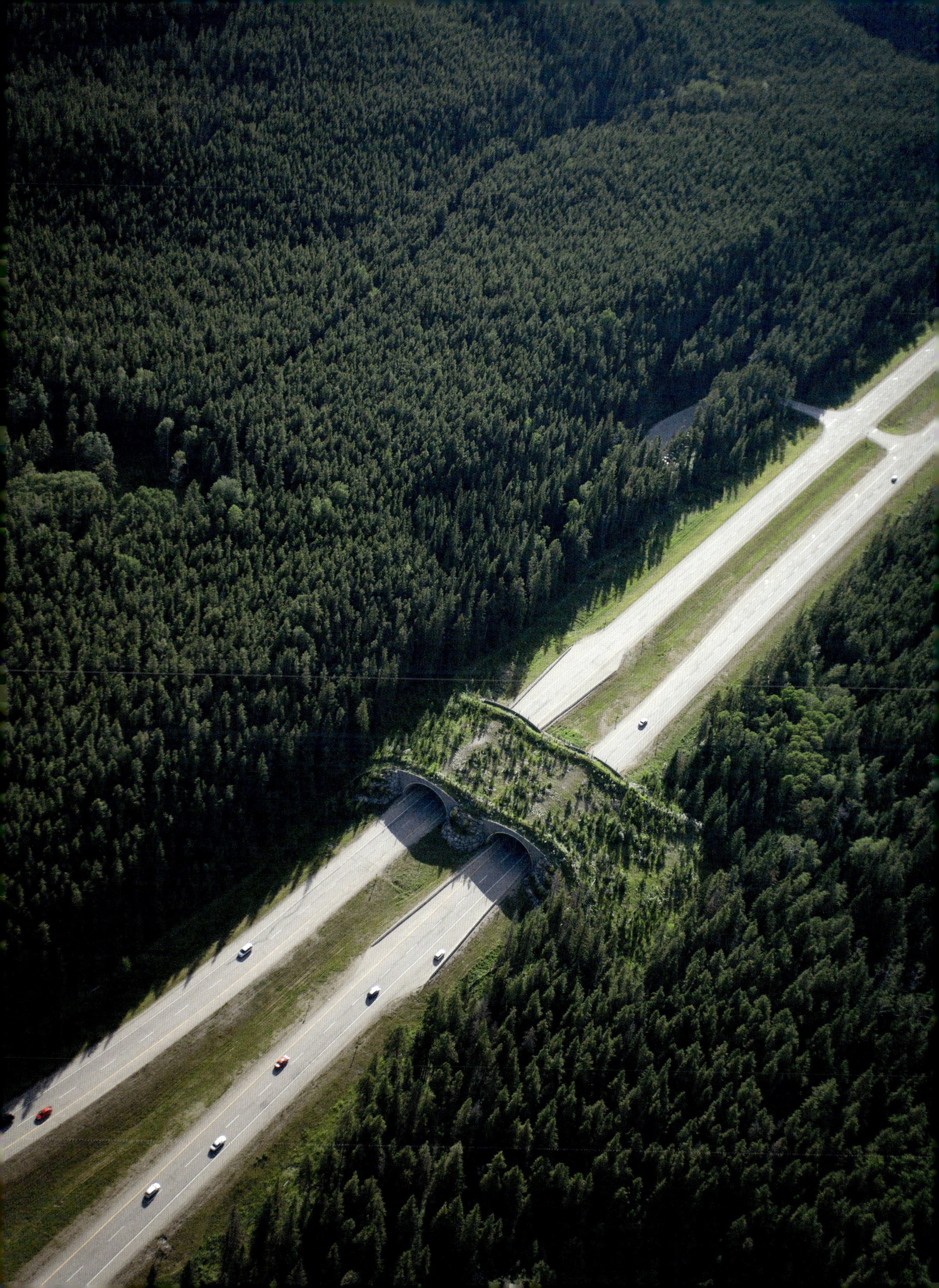

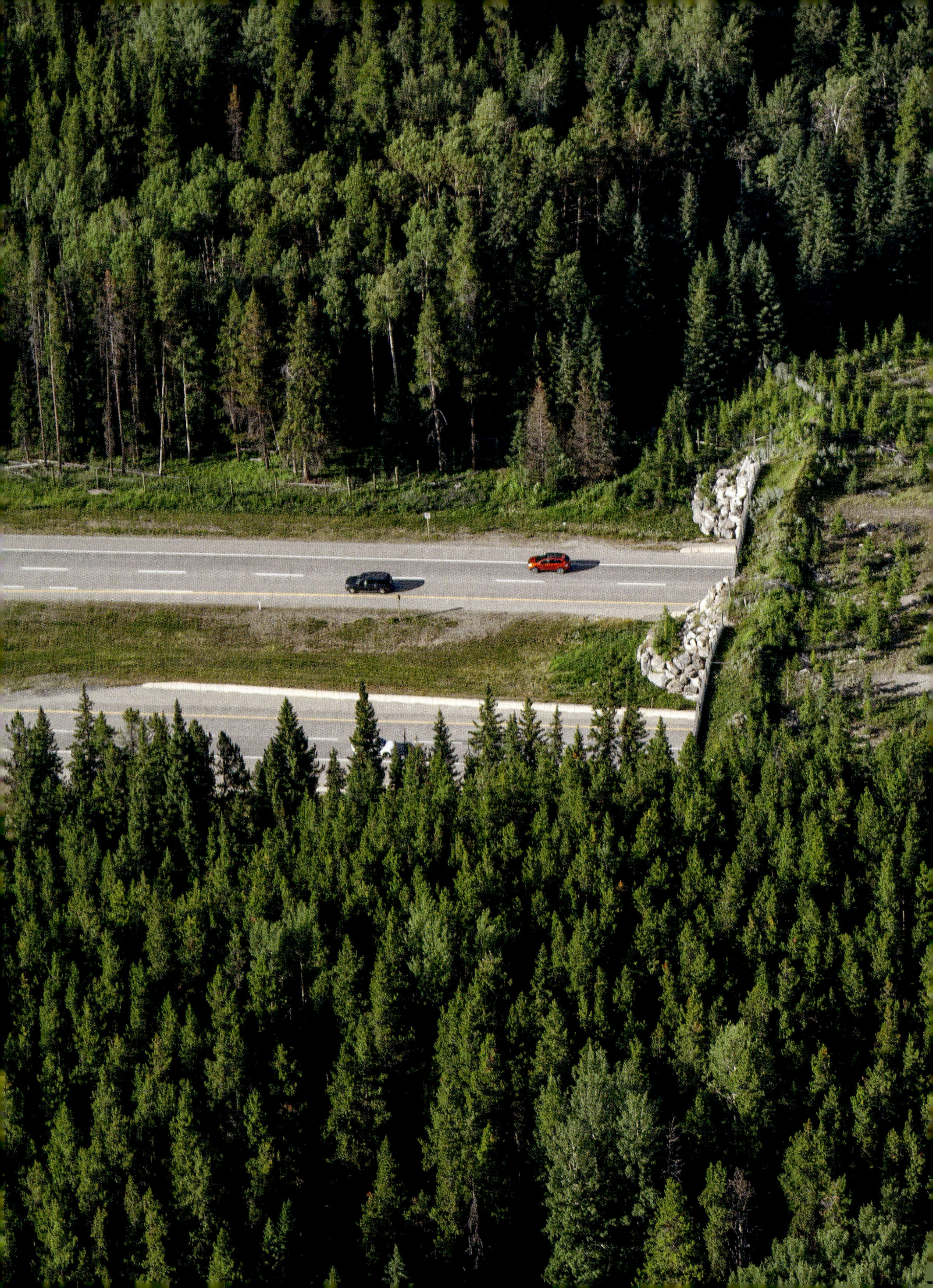

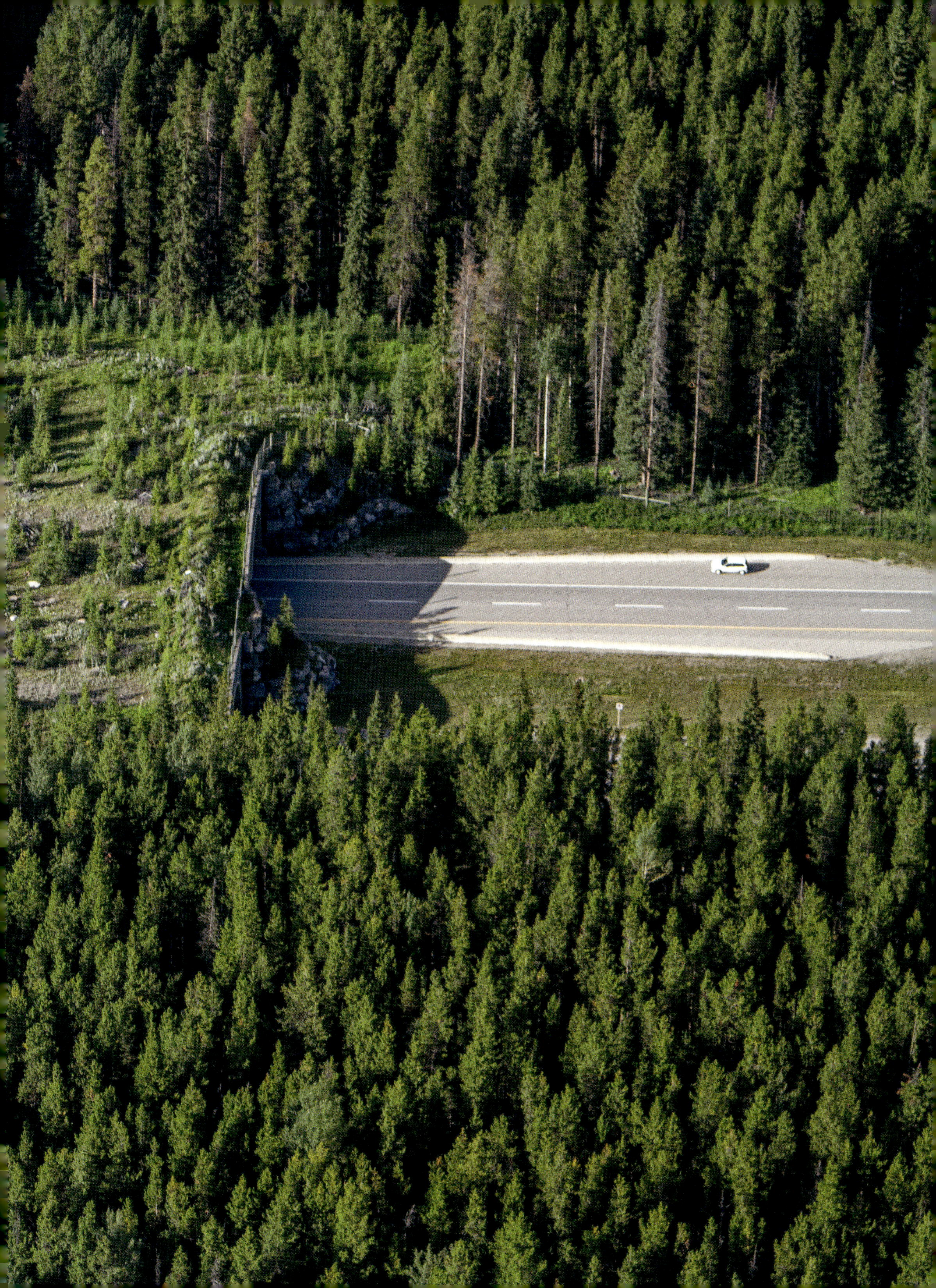

Opposite: James Hector originally named Castle Mountain after its shape. It was called Mount Eisenhower from 1946 to 1979 until "Castle Mountain" was reinstated due to public pressure.

Overleaf: Beautiful Rockbound Lake occupies a glacial cirque behind Castle Mountain.

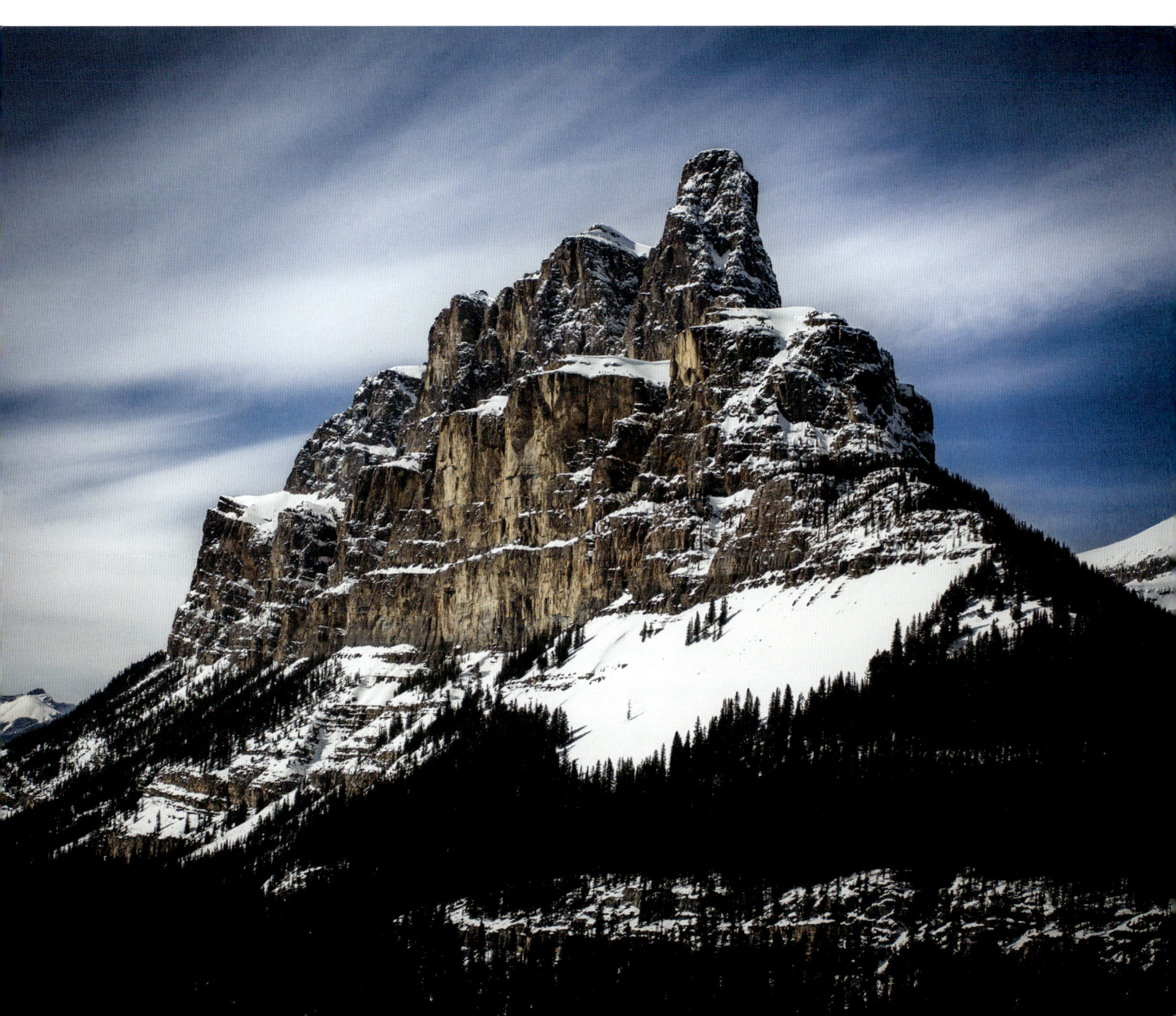

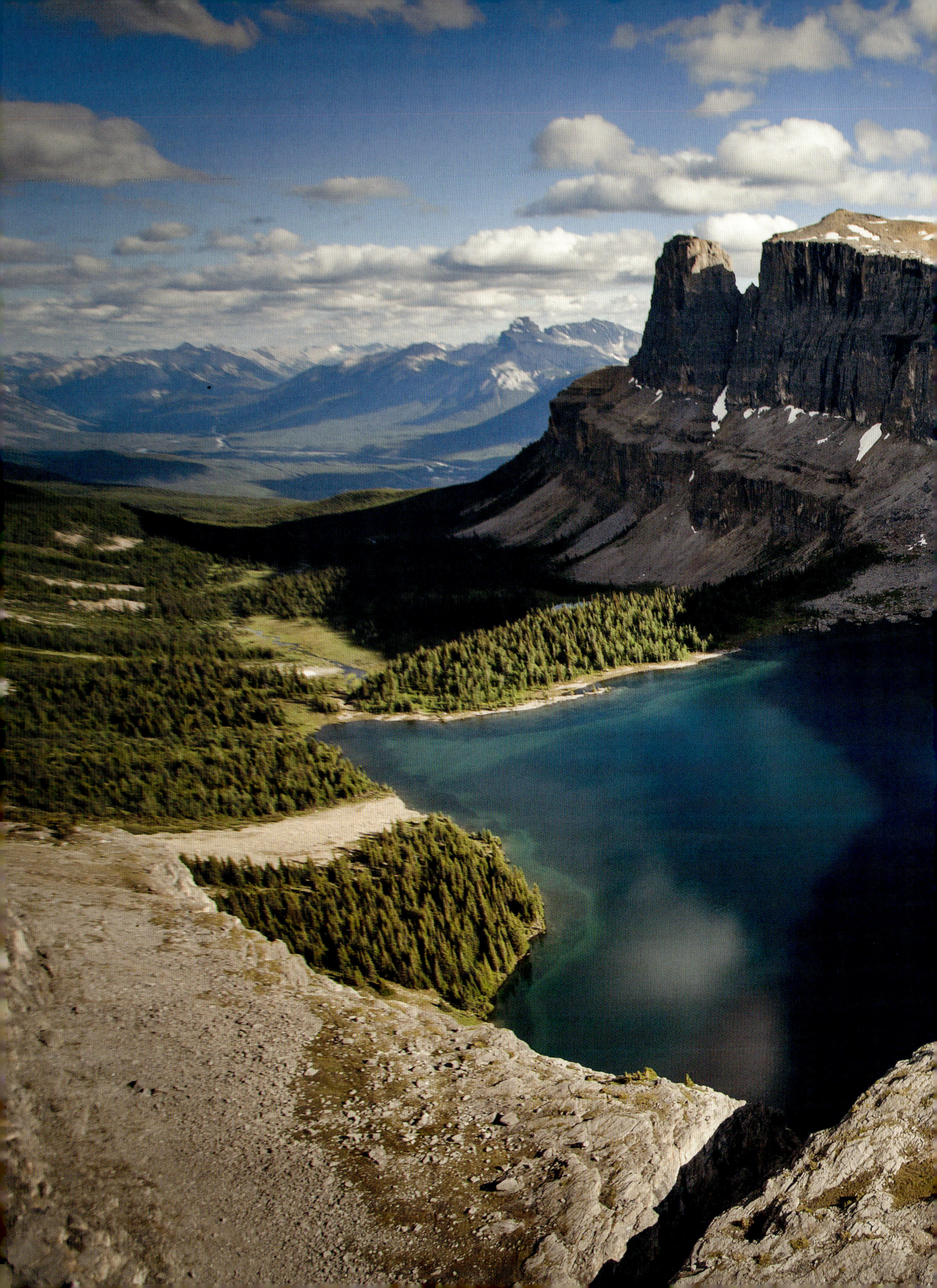

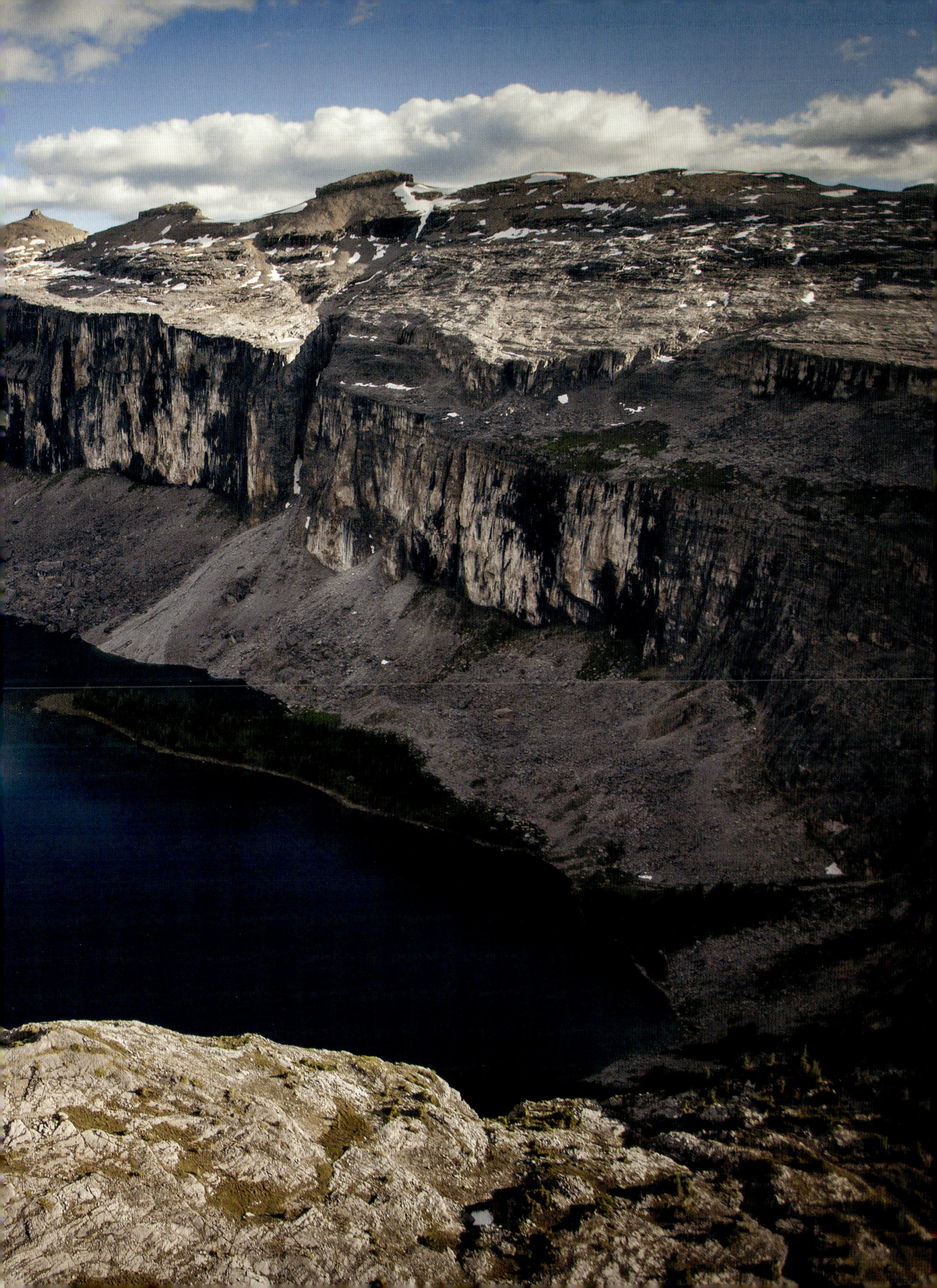

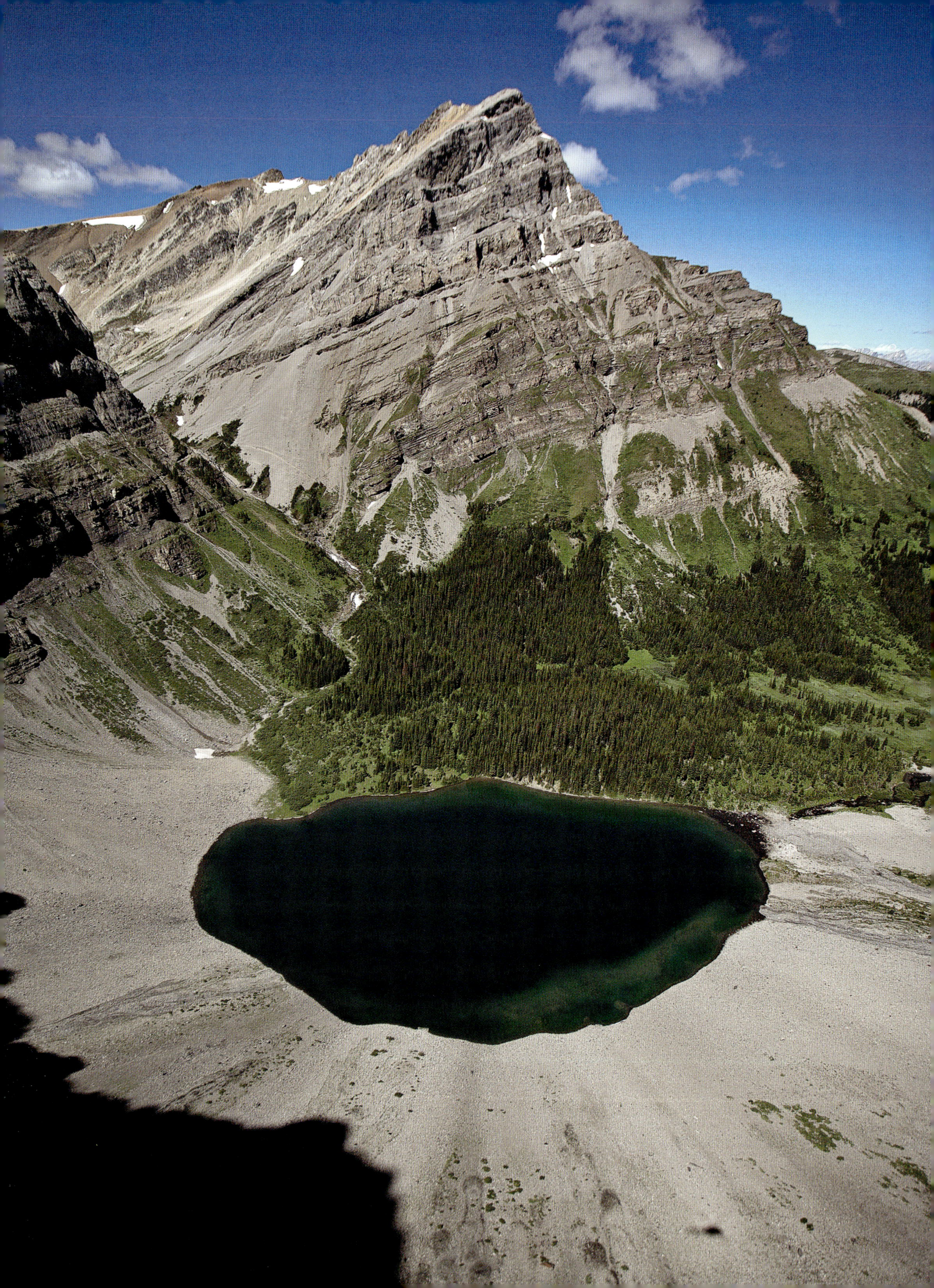

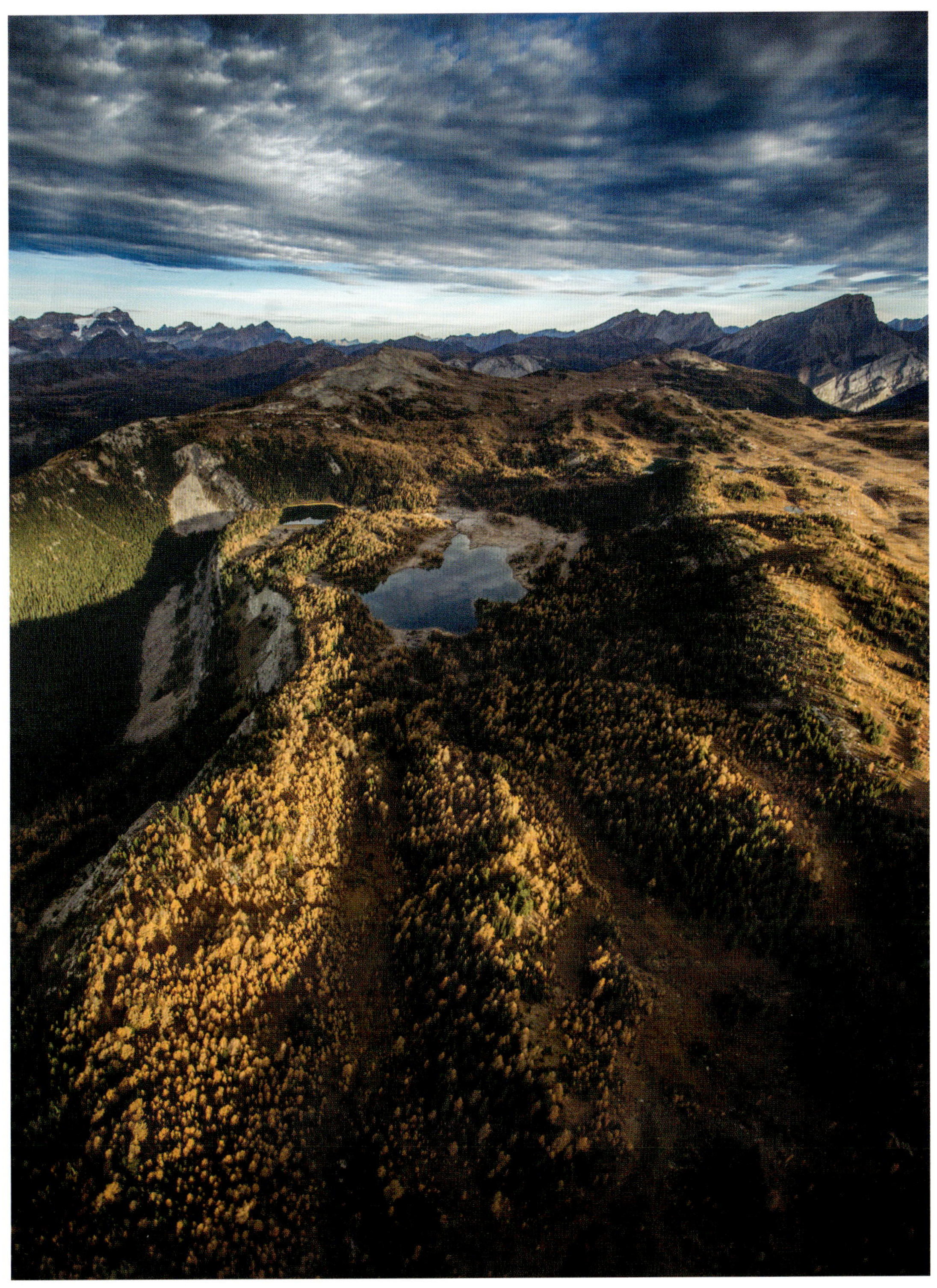

Opposite: Bourgeau Lake is a popular hiking destination near Banff.

Above: A moody autumn day over Sunshine Meadows,
one of the best places to see the larch trees at their brightest.

Overleaf: A stunning winter day at Banff's Sunshine Village, one of the park's three ski resorts.

Following spread: The three lakes of Sunshine Meadows (Laryx, Grizzly and Rock Isle)
glisten as the familiar pyramid of Mount Assiniboine dominates the skyline.

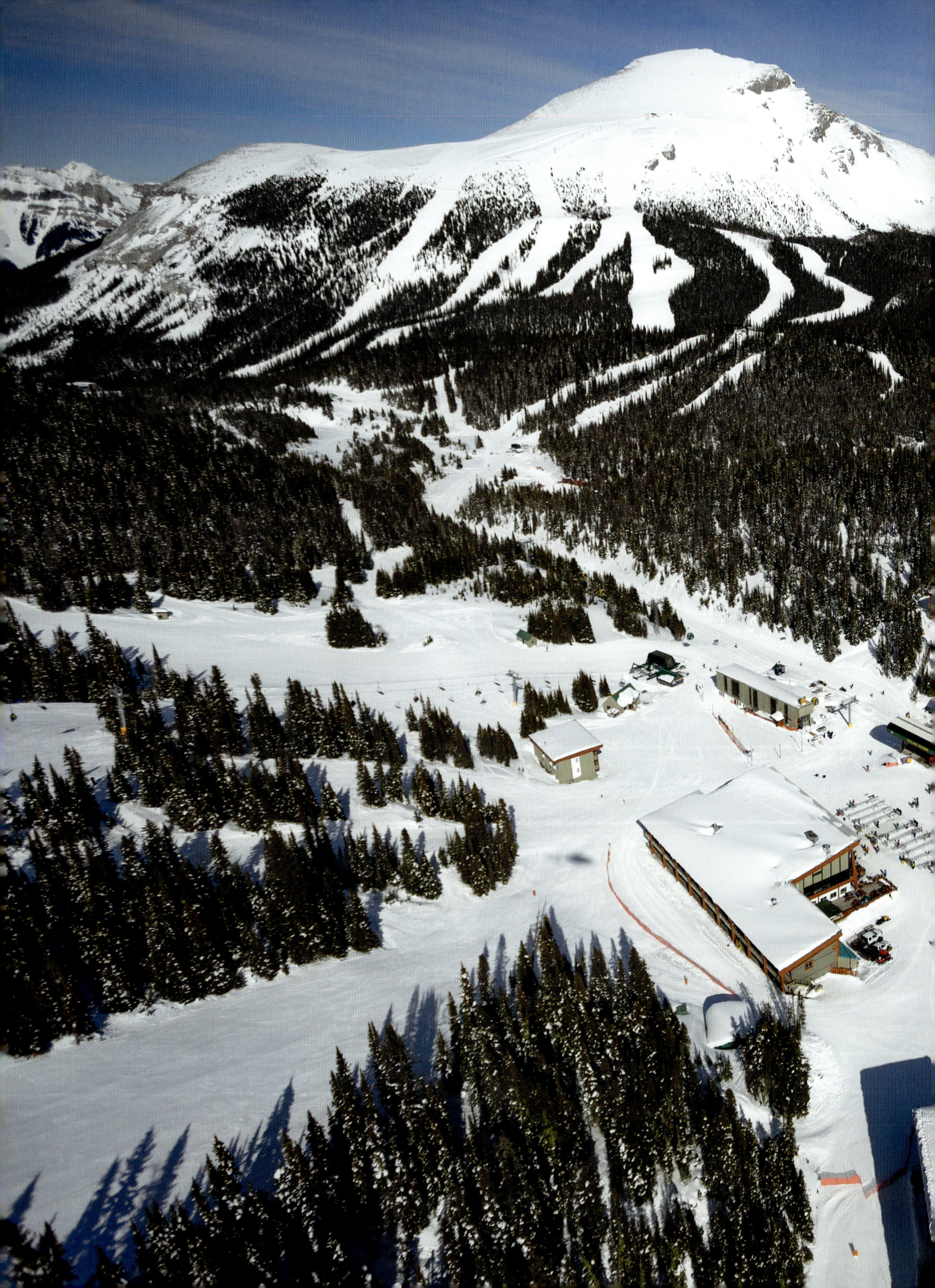

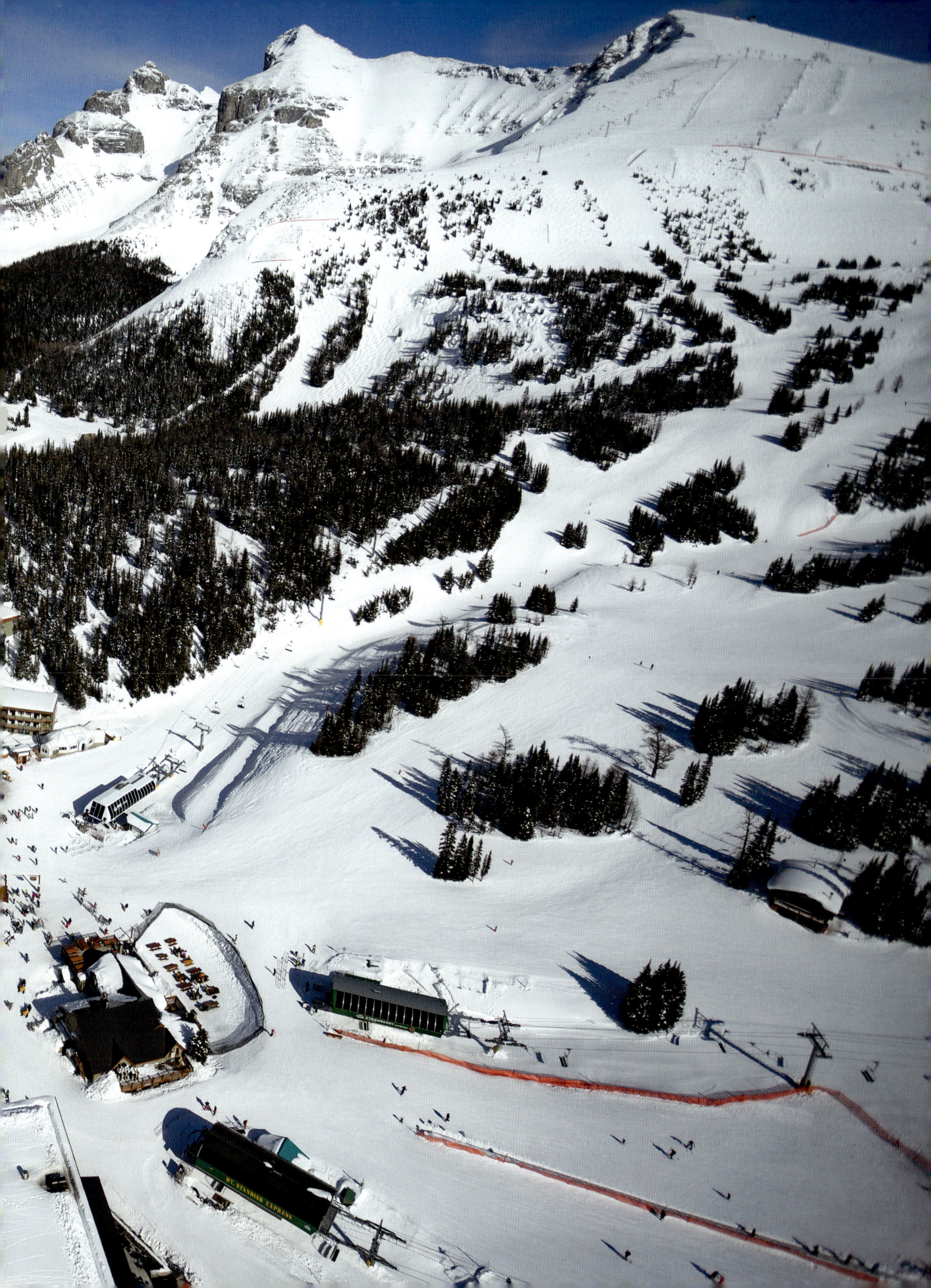

MT. STANDISH EXPRESS

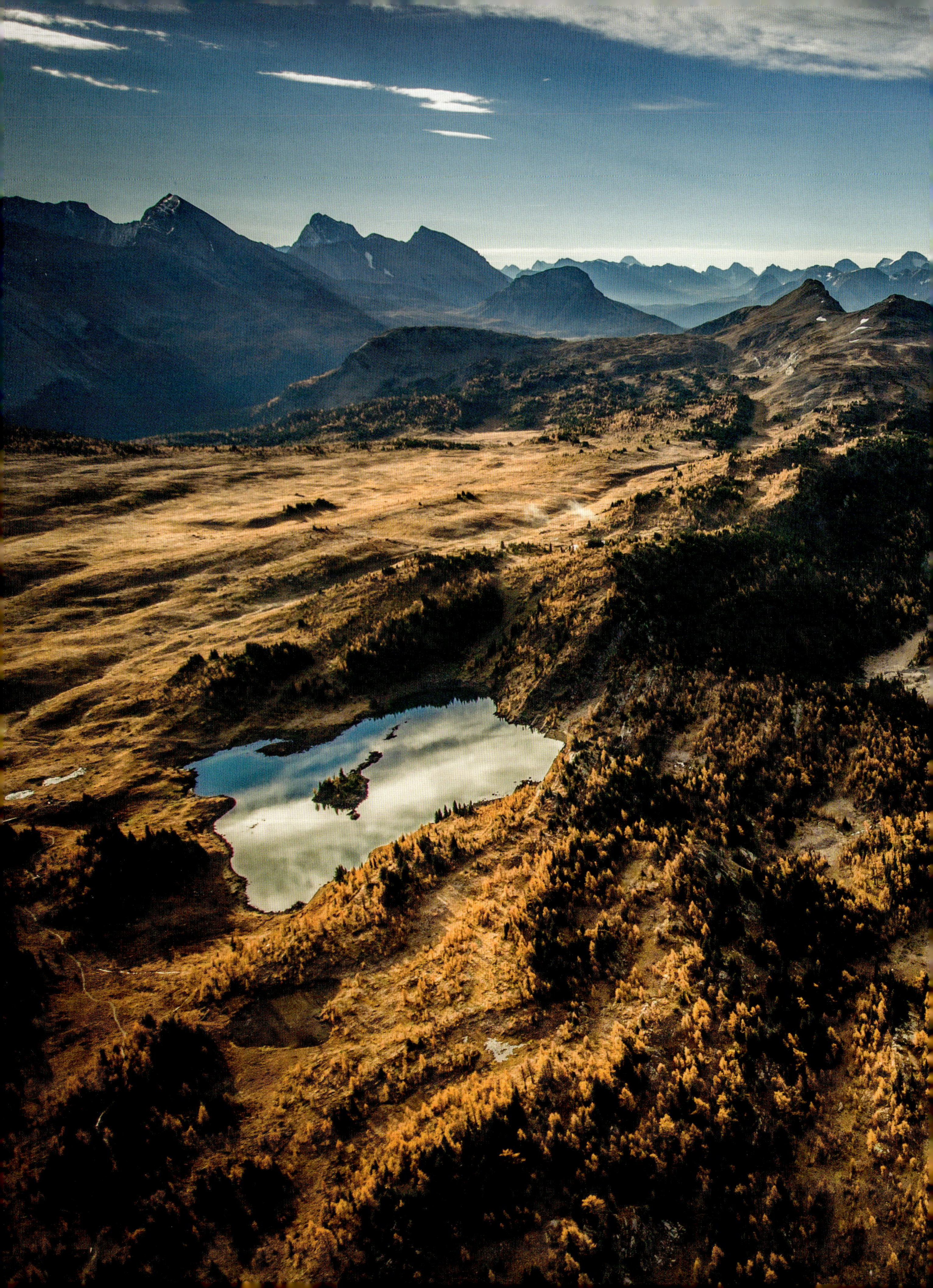

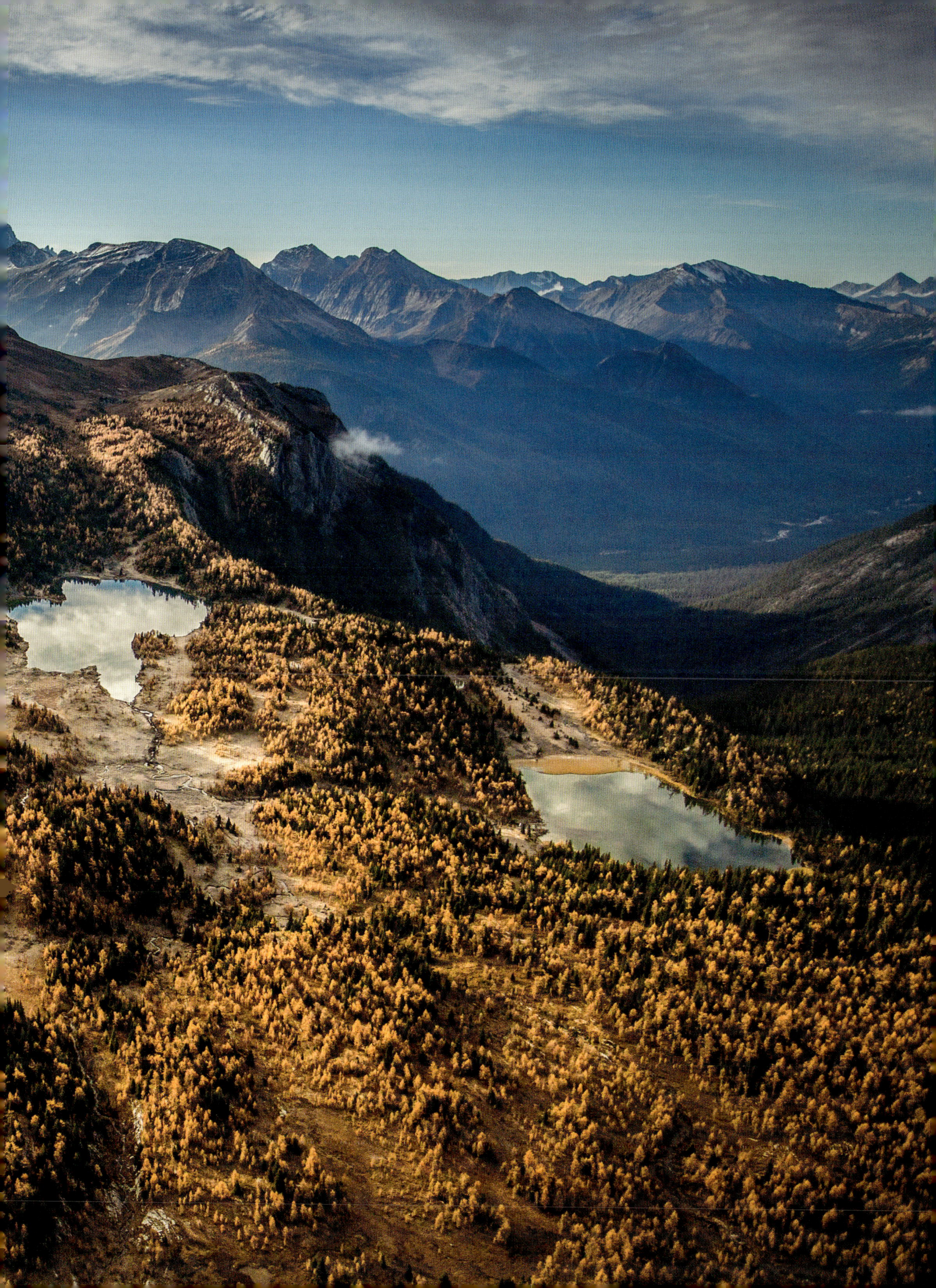

Redearth Creek snakes its way past Shadow Lake Lodge.
A few kilometres farther along, the creek merges with the Bow River.

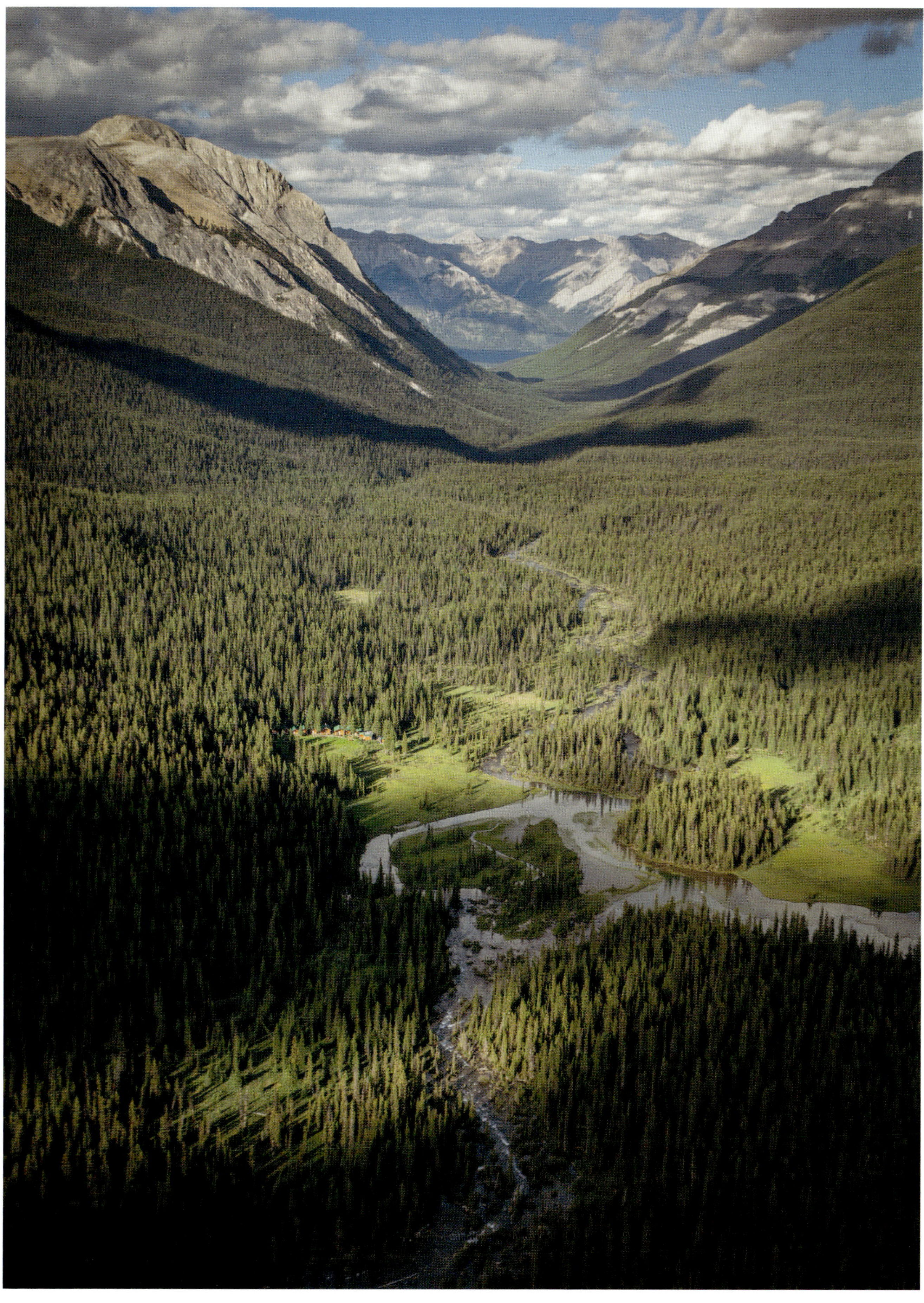

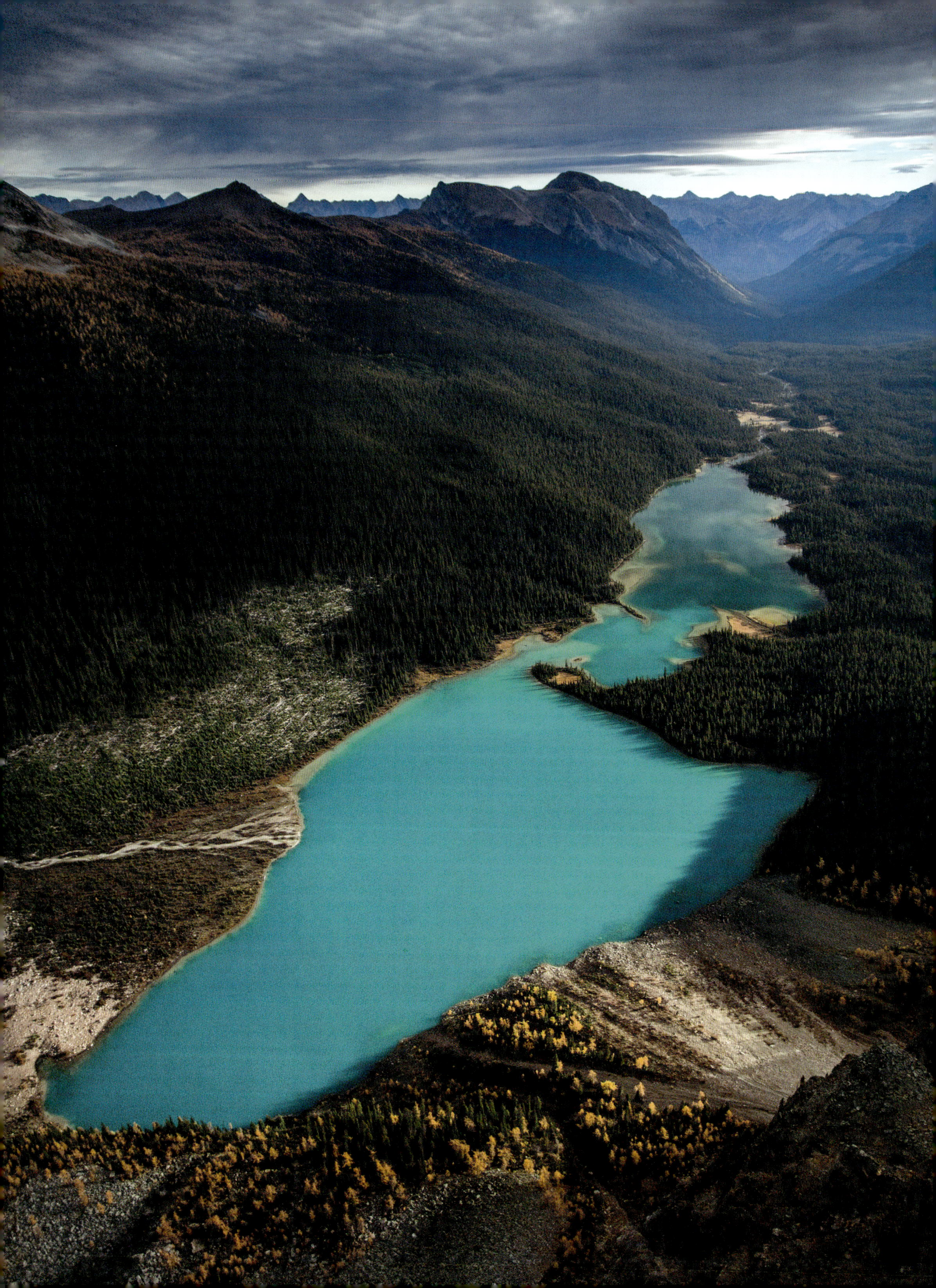

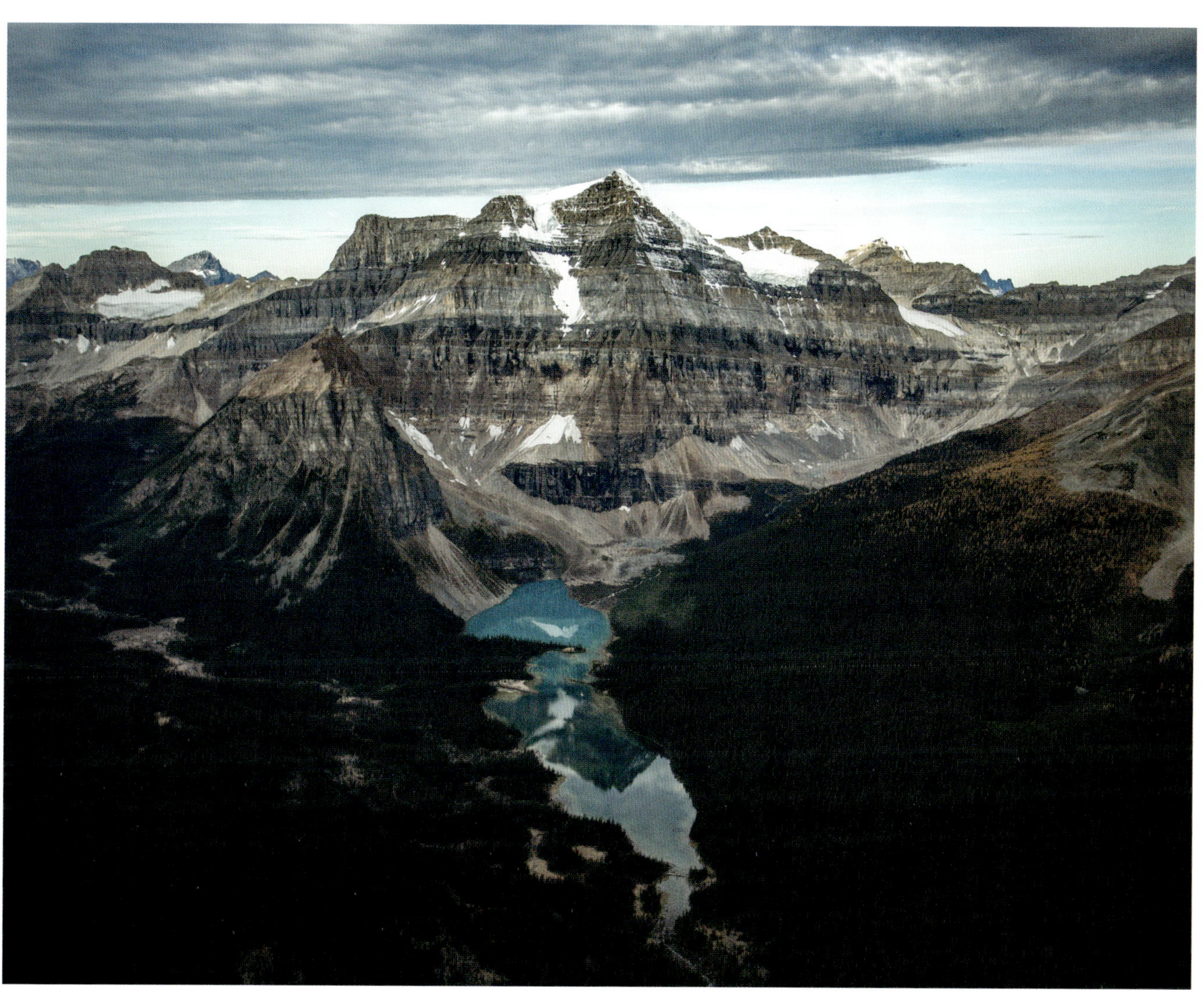

Opposite: Shadow Lake is one of the most stunning lakes of the Banff backcountry.

Above: Hulking, glacier-capped Mount Ball stands tall above the placid waters of Shadow Lake.

Opposite: A small waterfall empties into Lower Twin Lake on a fall day
near the Great Divide. The sedimentary layers of Storm Mountain loom above.

Overleaf: The two jewels of Skoki – Zigadenus Lake (l) and Myosotis Lake (r) –
lie below the Wall of Jericho in one of Banff's prime backcountry areas.

Following spread: The Twin Lakes display vastly different colours
at the base of Storm Mountain, where a small glacier clings on.

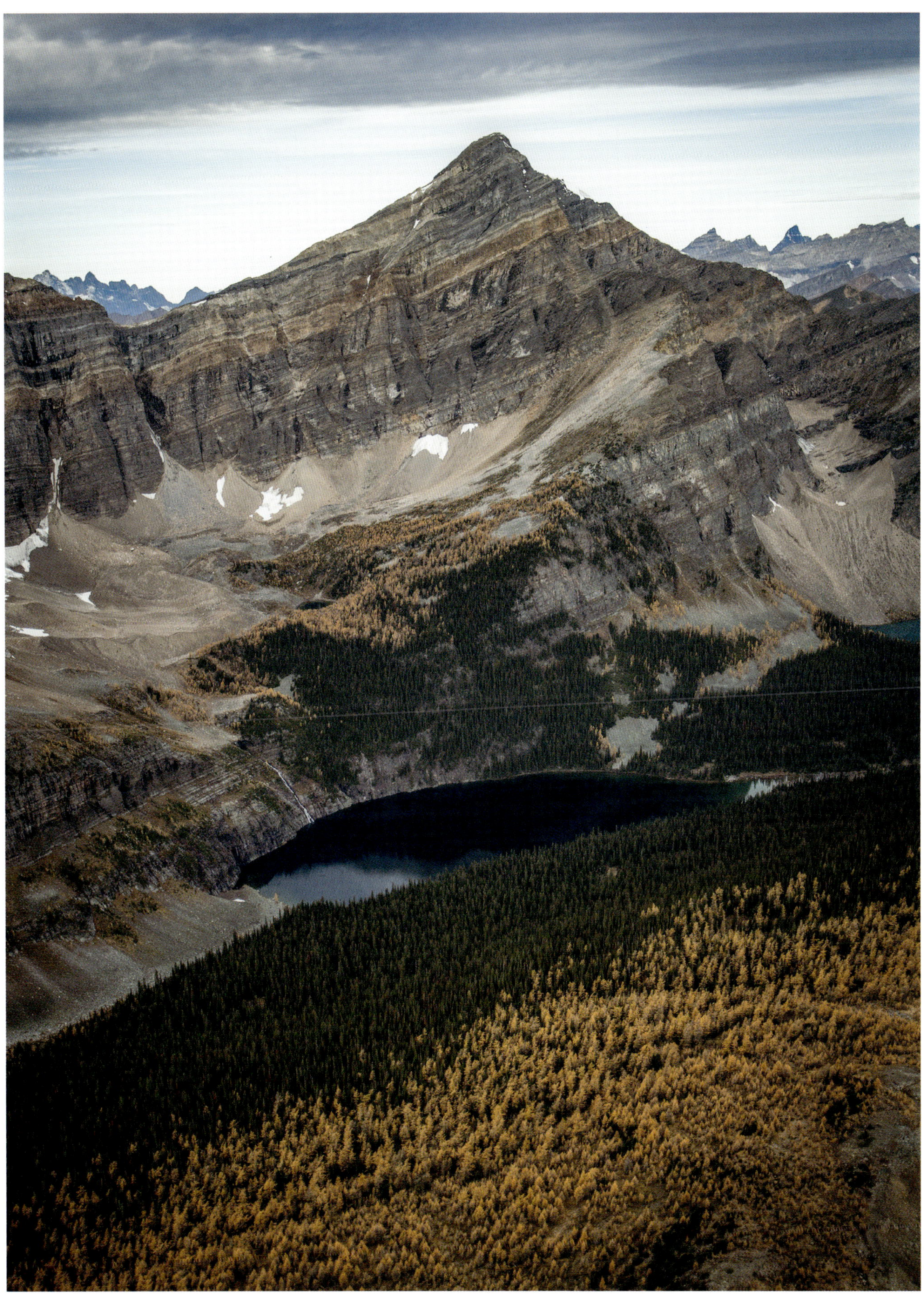

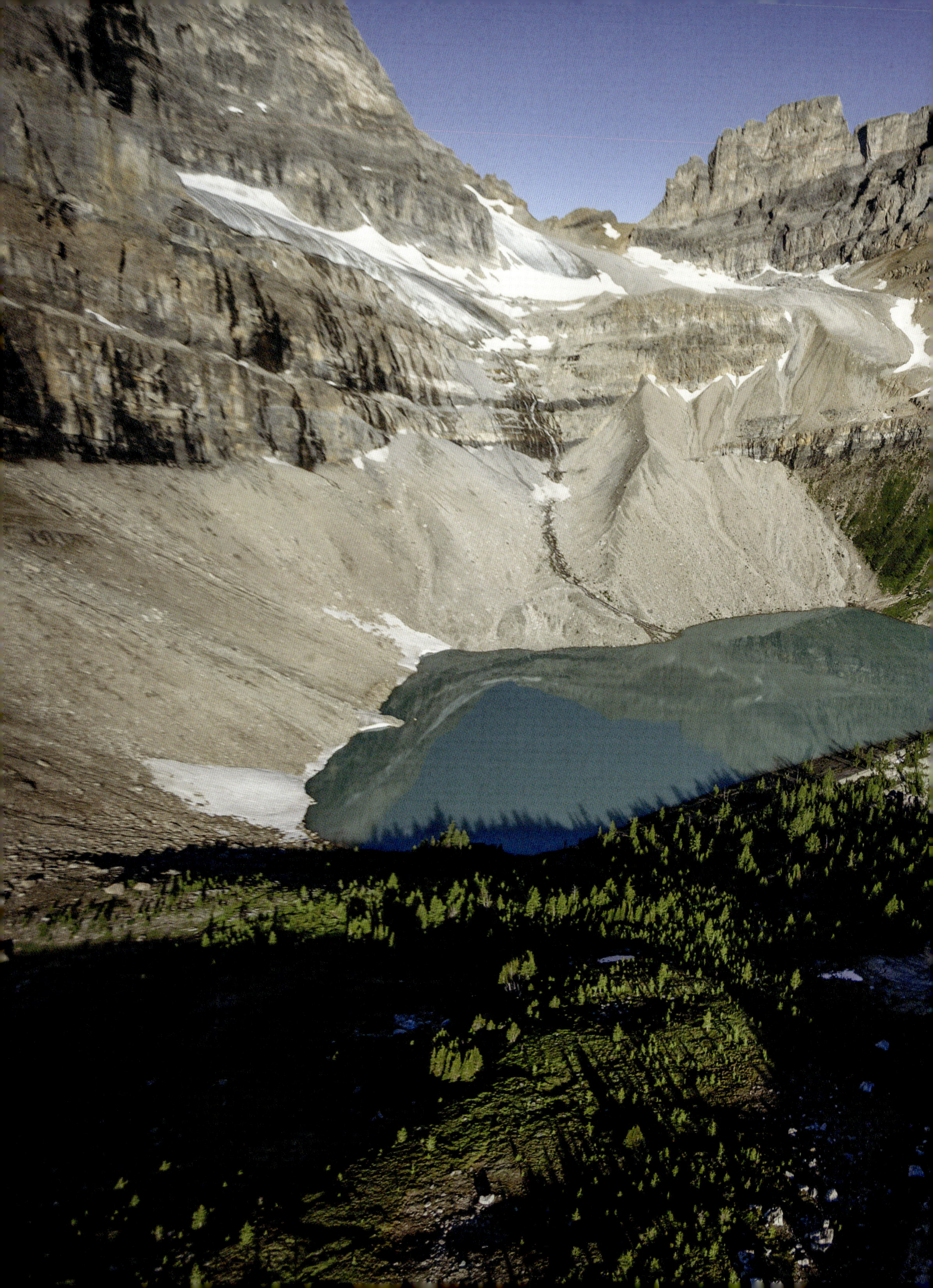

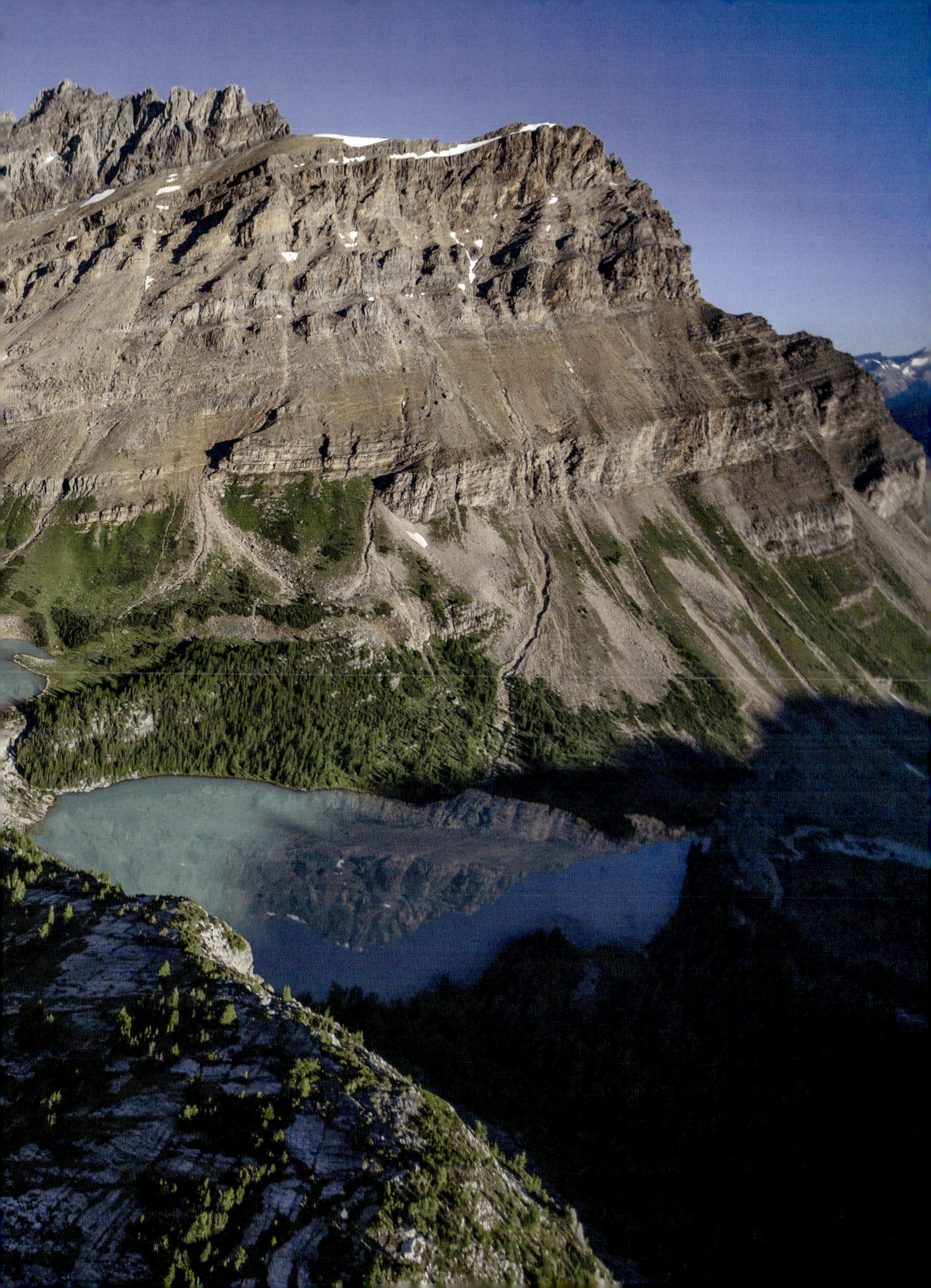

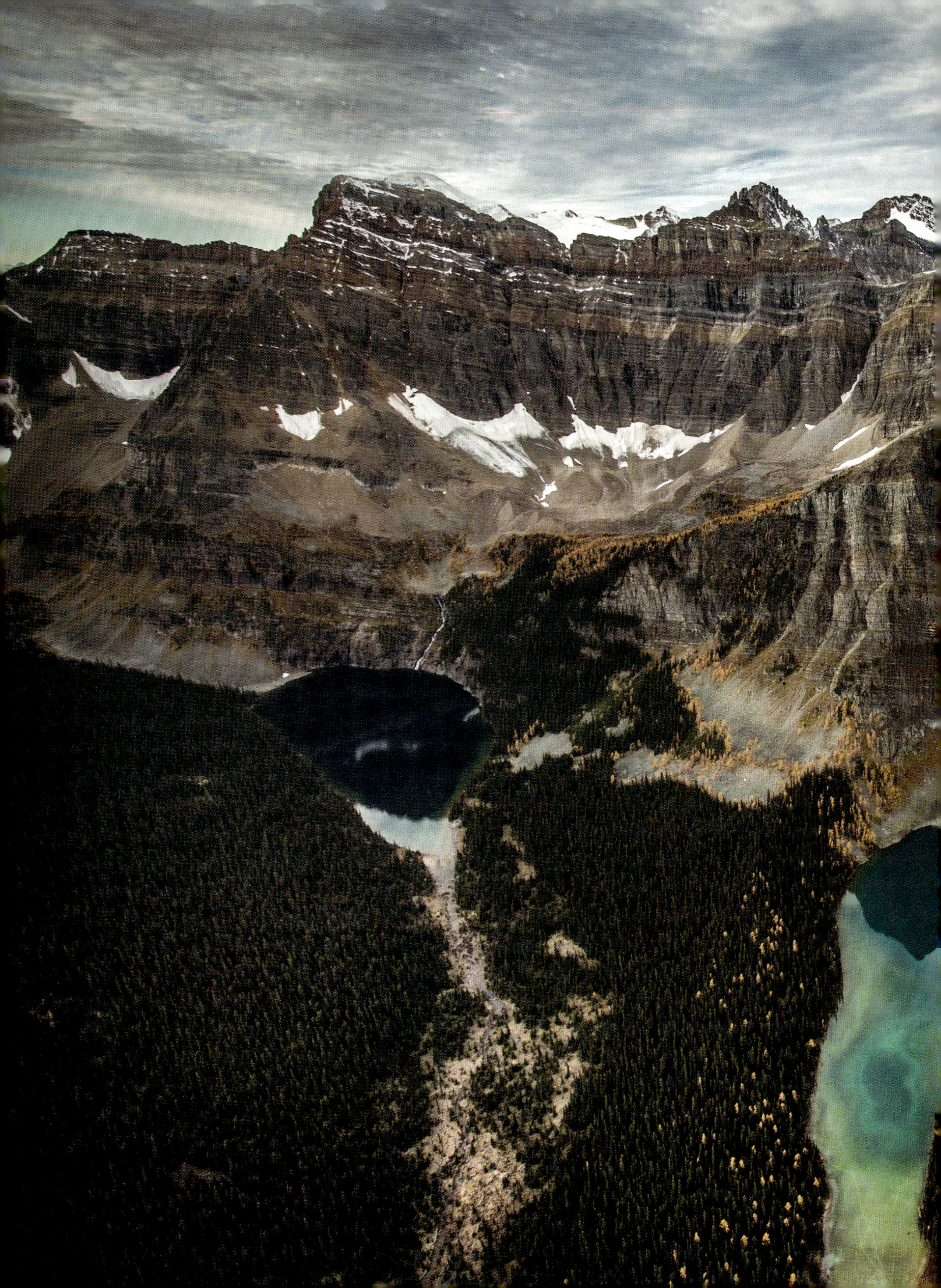

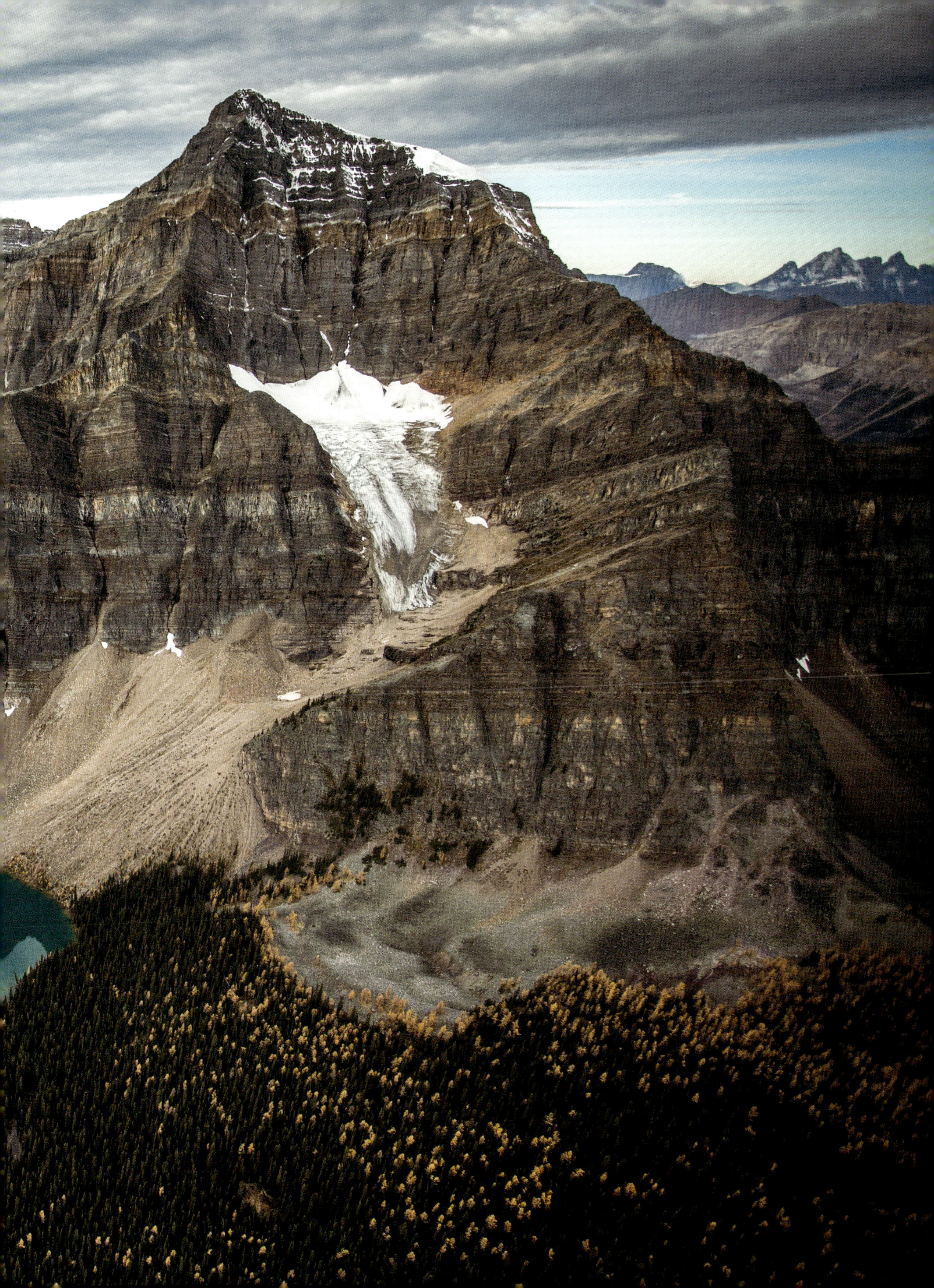

Taylor Lake occupies an enchanting site among larch trees and quartzite slopes.
In the background are mounts Bident and Quadra.

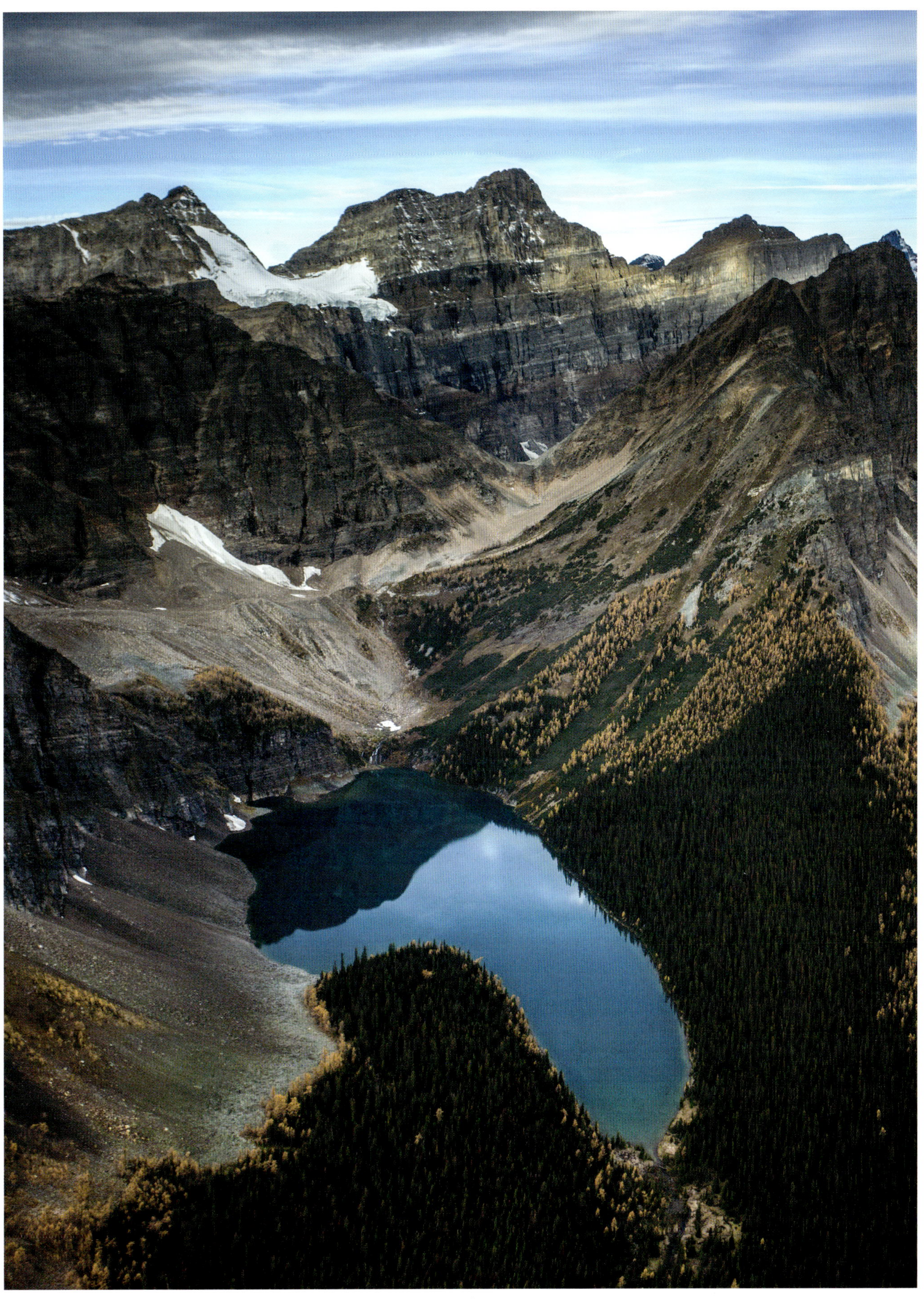

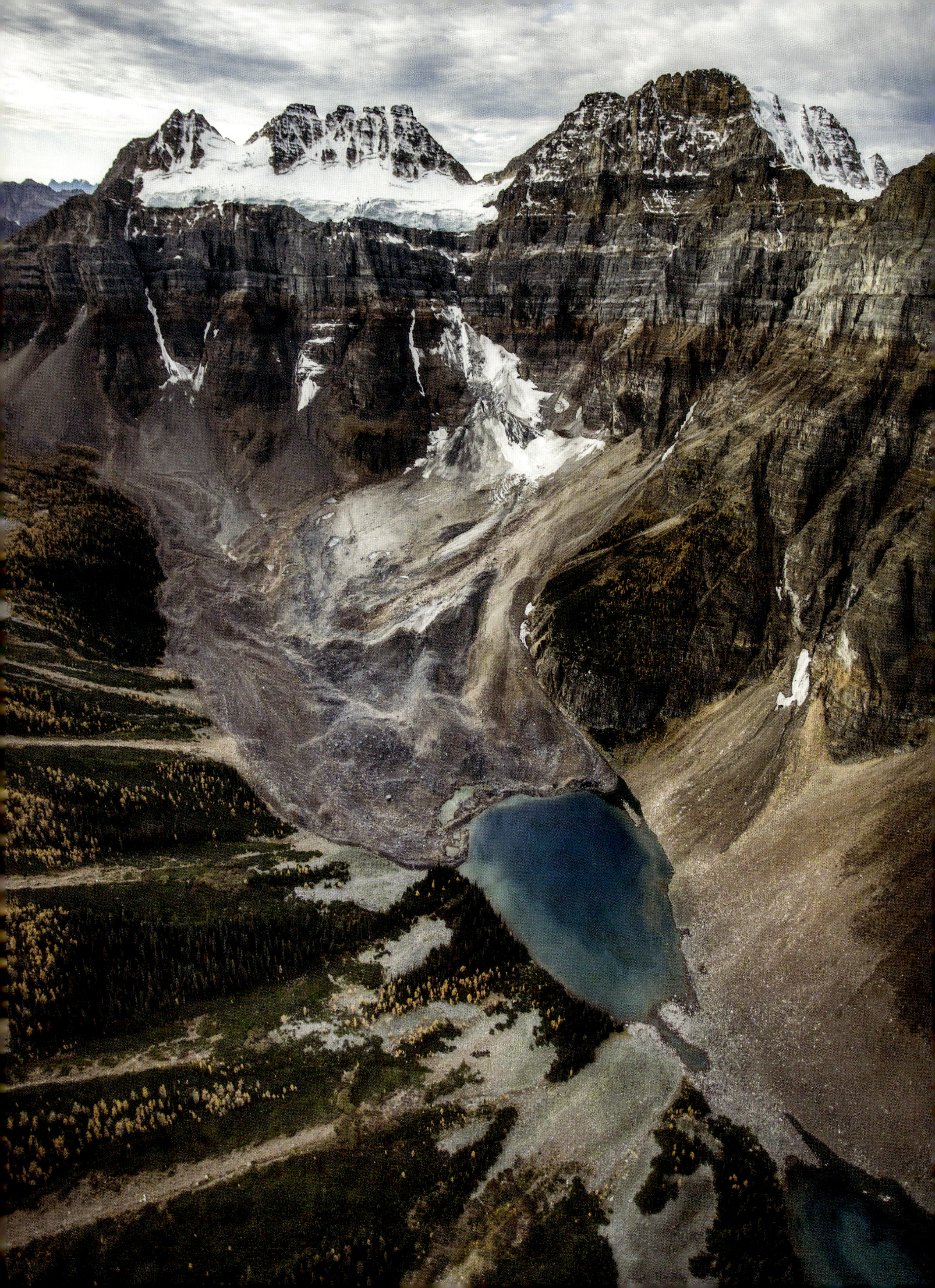

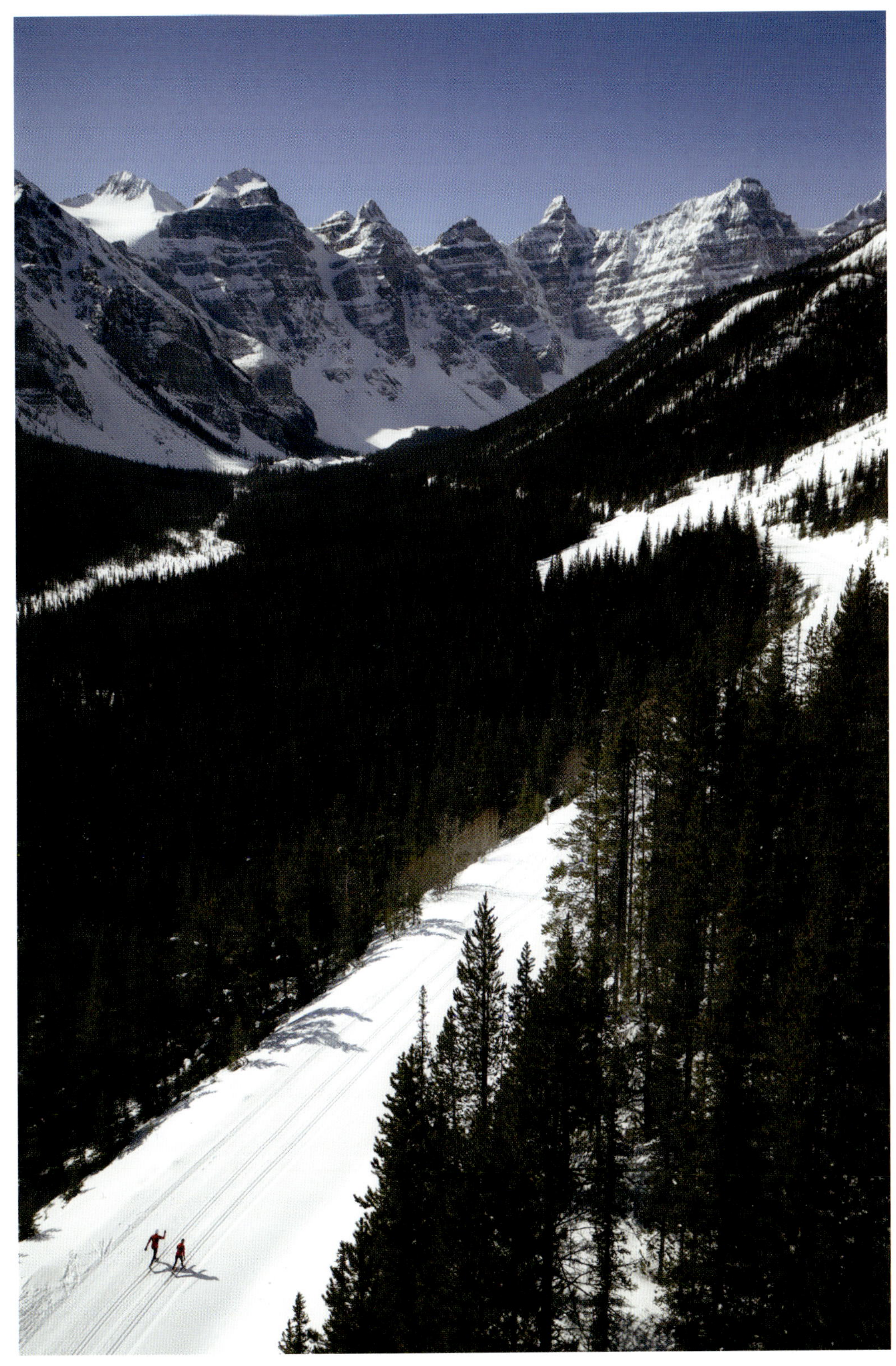

Opposite: The incredible blue of Consolation Lakes and the yellow of nearby larch trees contrast with the stark world of rock and ice above. At the head of this stunning valley lies the impressive trio of mounts Bident, Quadra and Babel.

Above: In the winter, the road to Moraine Lake turns into an epic cross-country ski track.

Overleaf: A top-down view of world-famous Moraine Lake. The colour is something one never forgets.

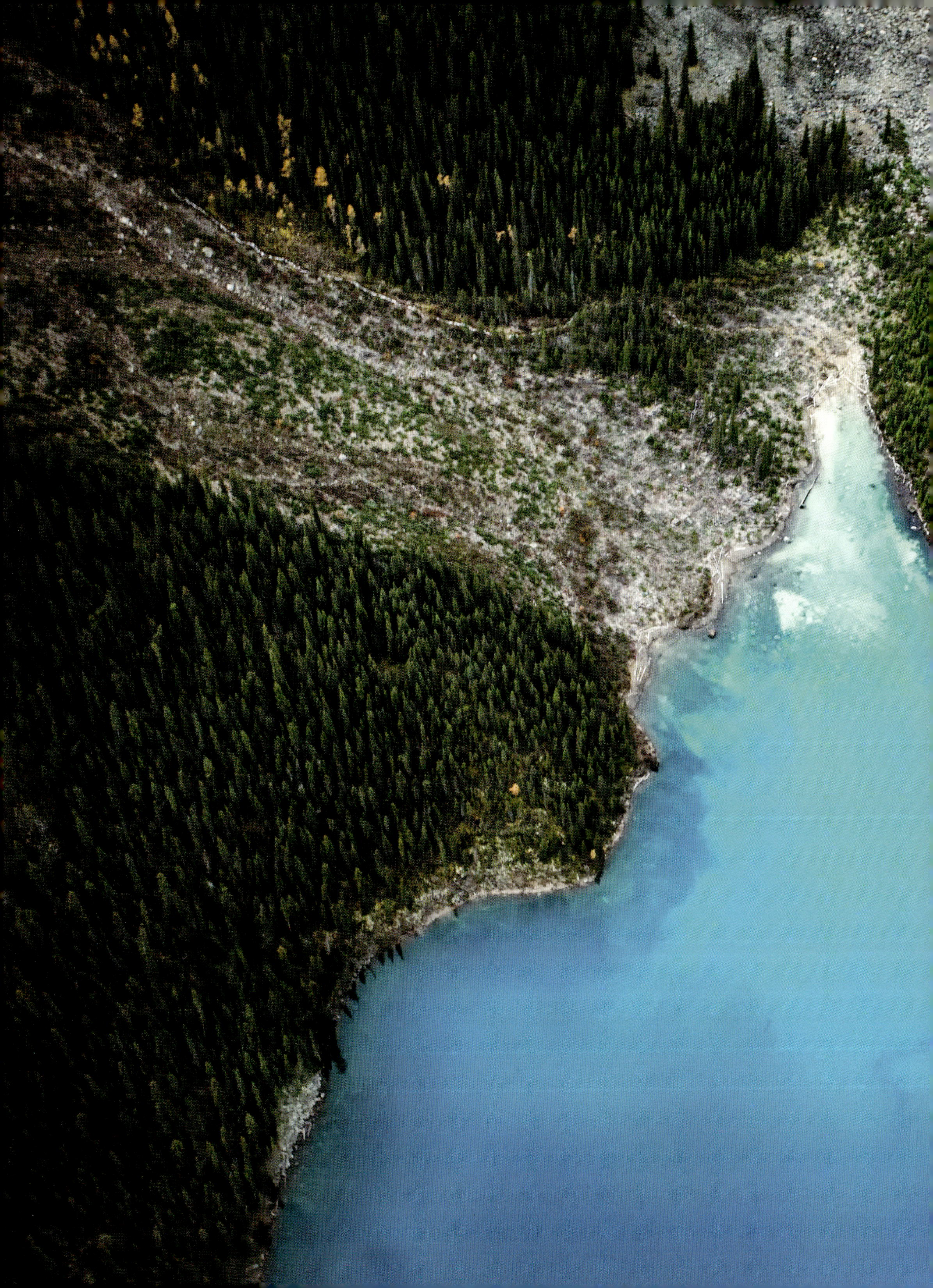

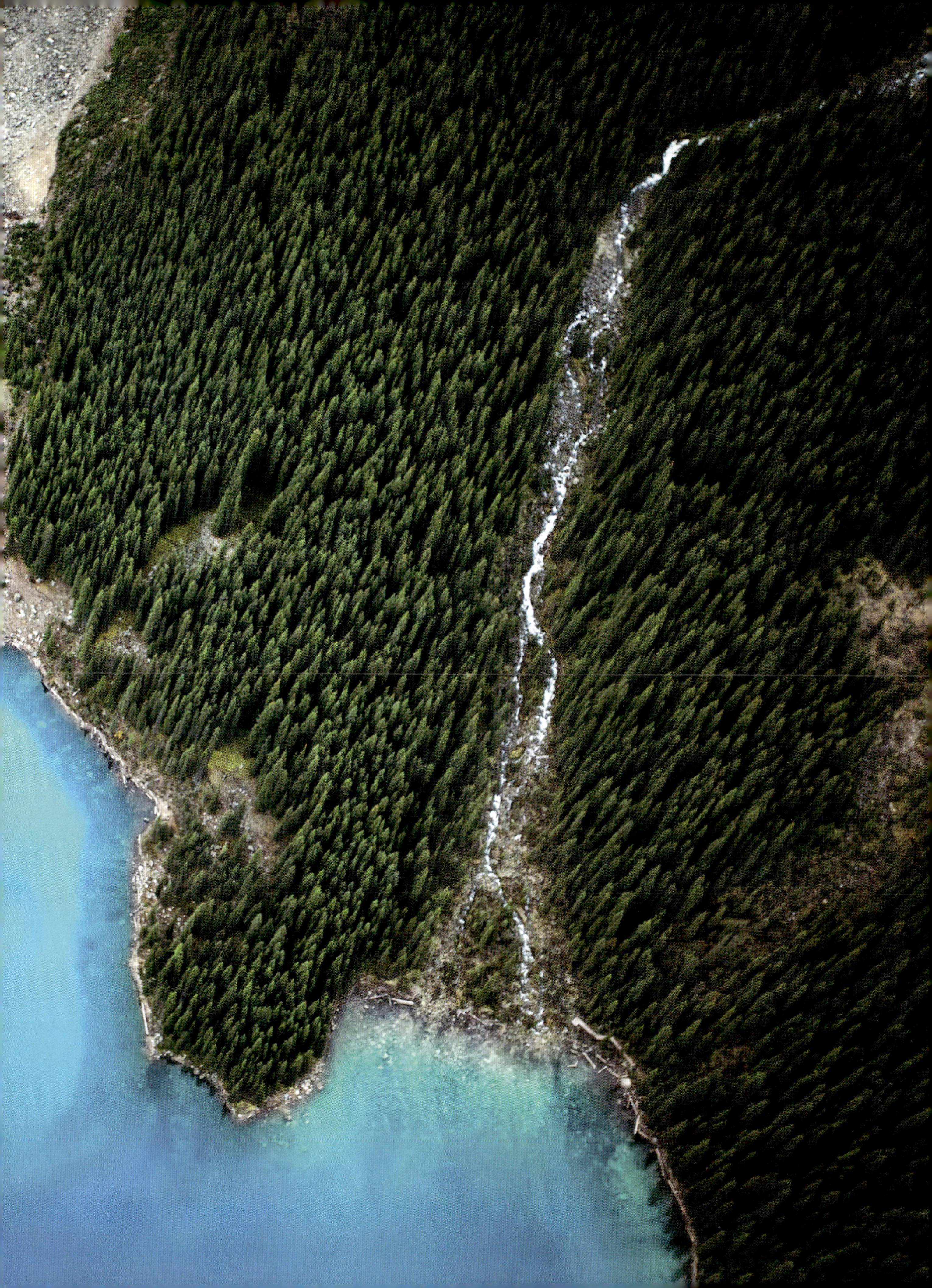

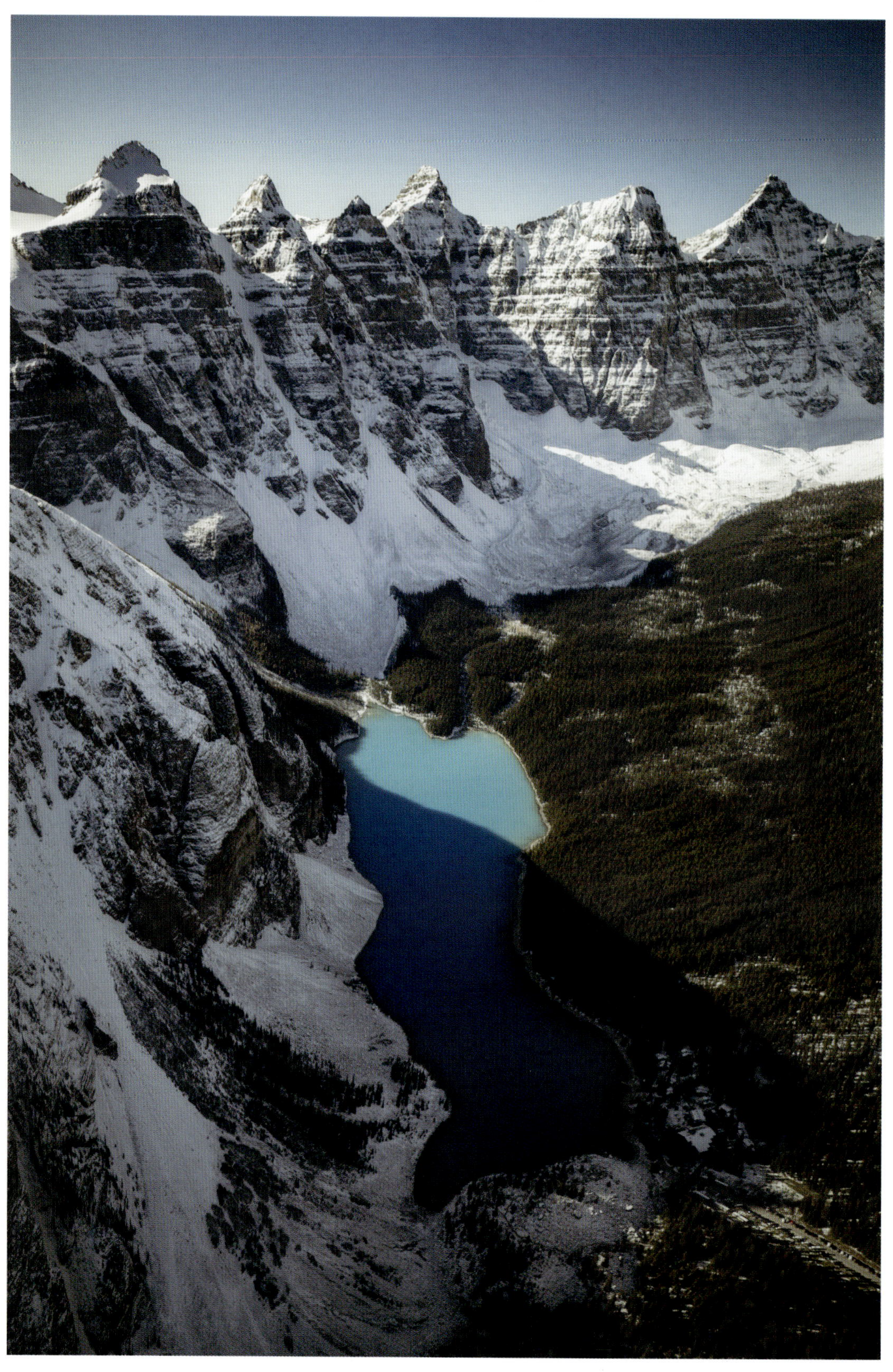

Above: Six of Moraine Lake's famous "Ten Peaks" are visible in this image taken just before the lake froze. The backdrop of Moraine Lake is one of the world's longest uninterrupted rock walls.

Opposite: The unbelievably blue ink stain of Moraine Lake is nestled below the Great Divide in this autumn view.

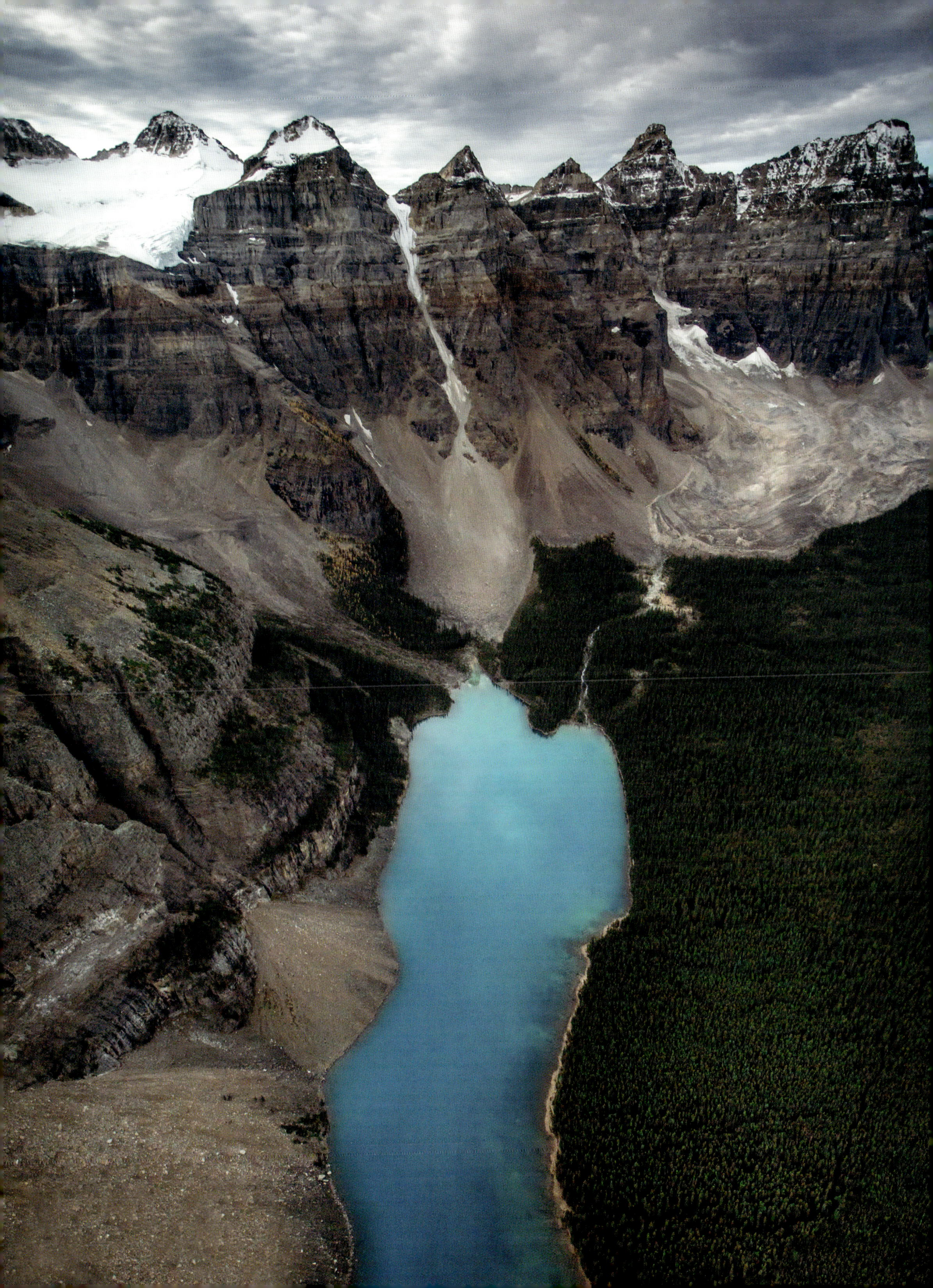

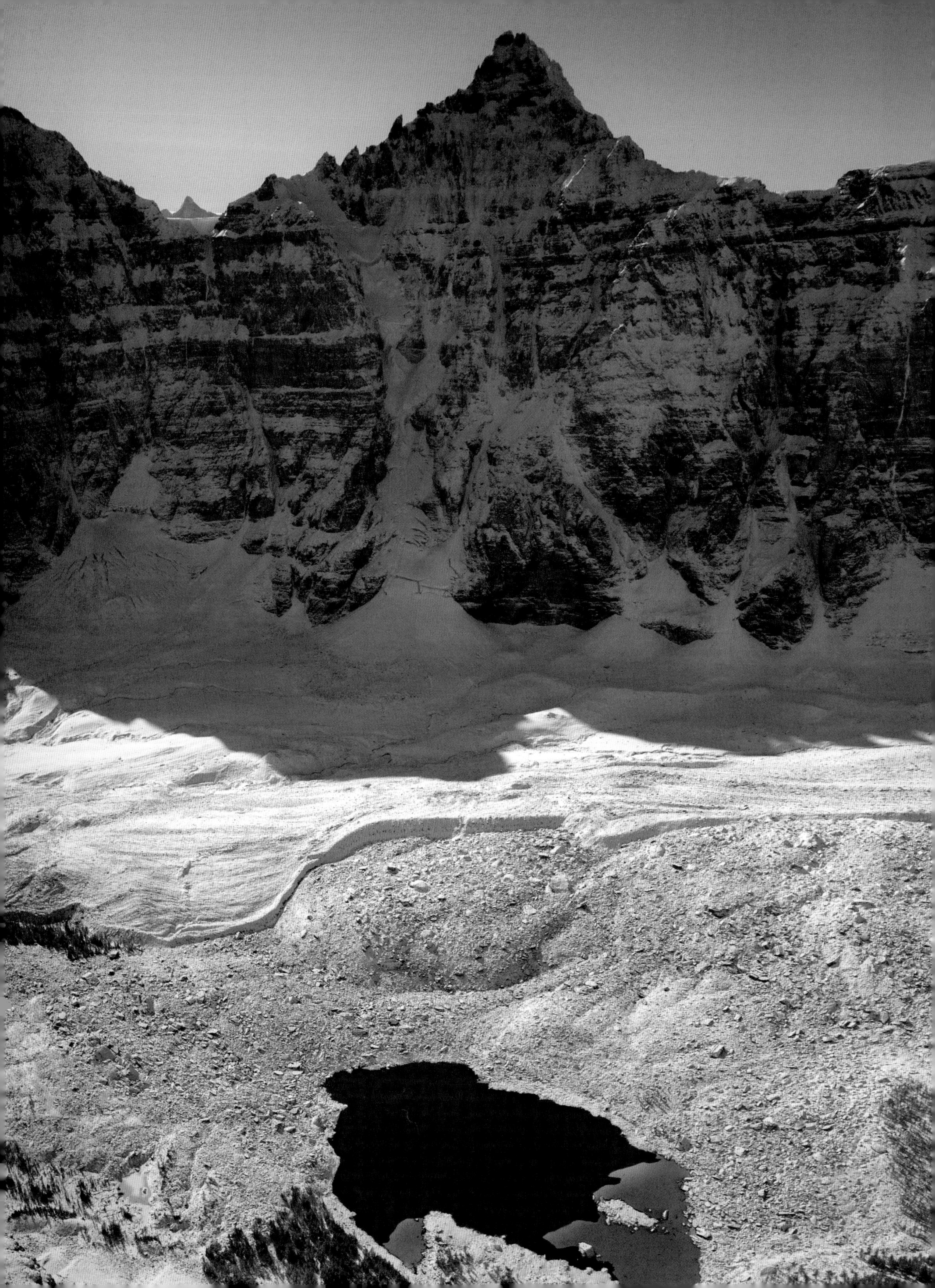

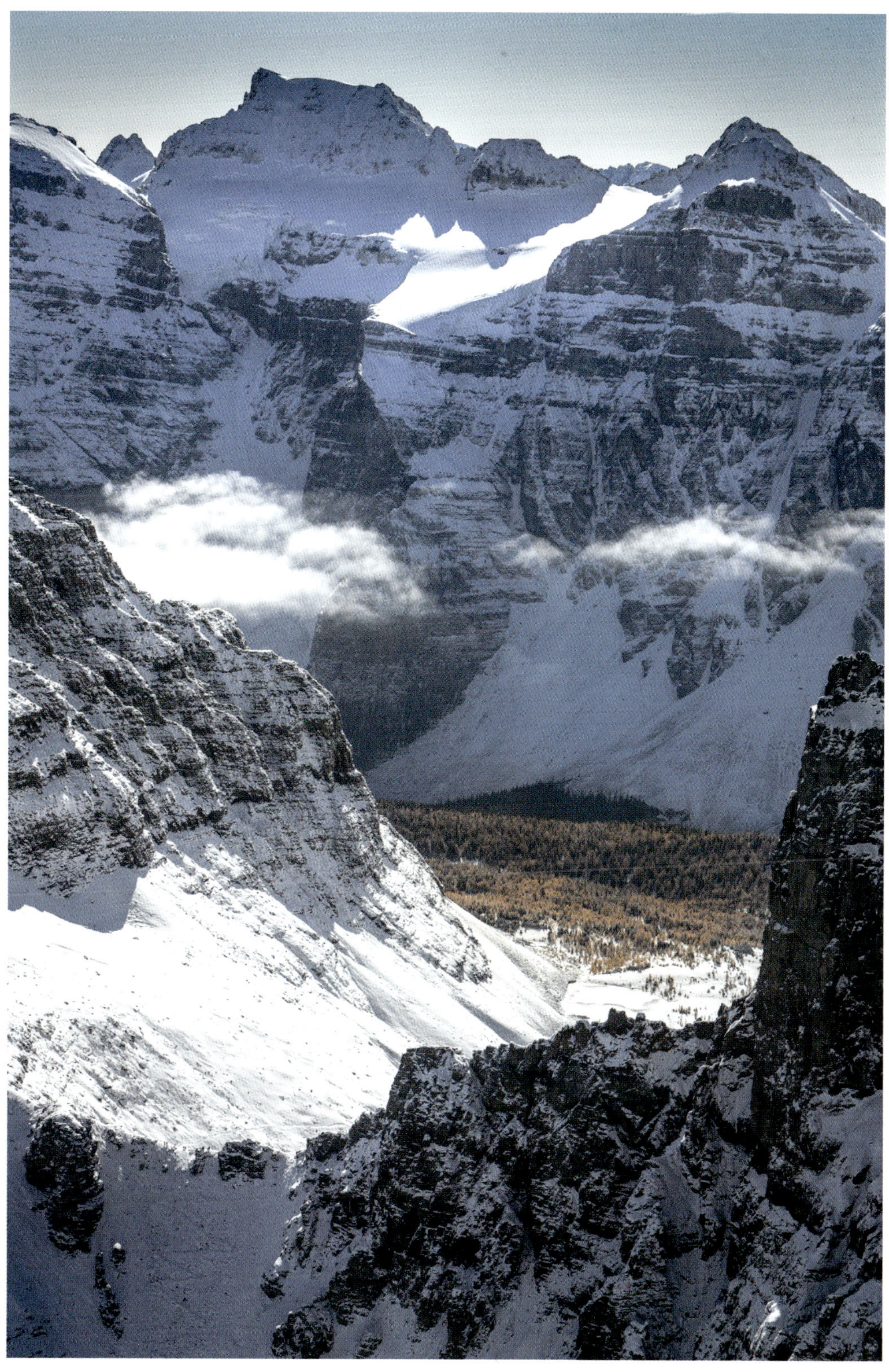

Opposite: Winter tightens its grip on Eiffel Lake as Deltaform Mountain towers above.

Above: An October view of Sentinel Pass, after the first significant snowfall
of the year blankets the Canadian Rockies. Larch Valley and Mount Fay lie beyond.

Overleaf: The horseshoe of peaks surrounding Lake Louise is one of the most recognizable skylines
in the world. Lake Agnes is visible on the far right in this image taken at the height of larch season.

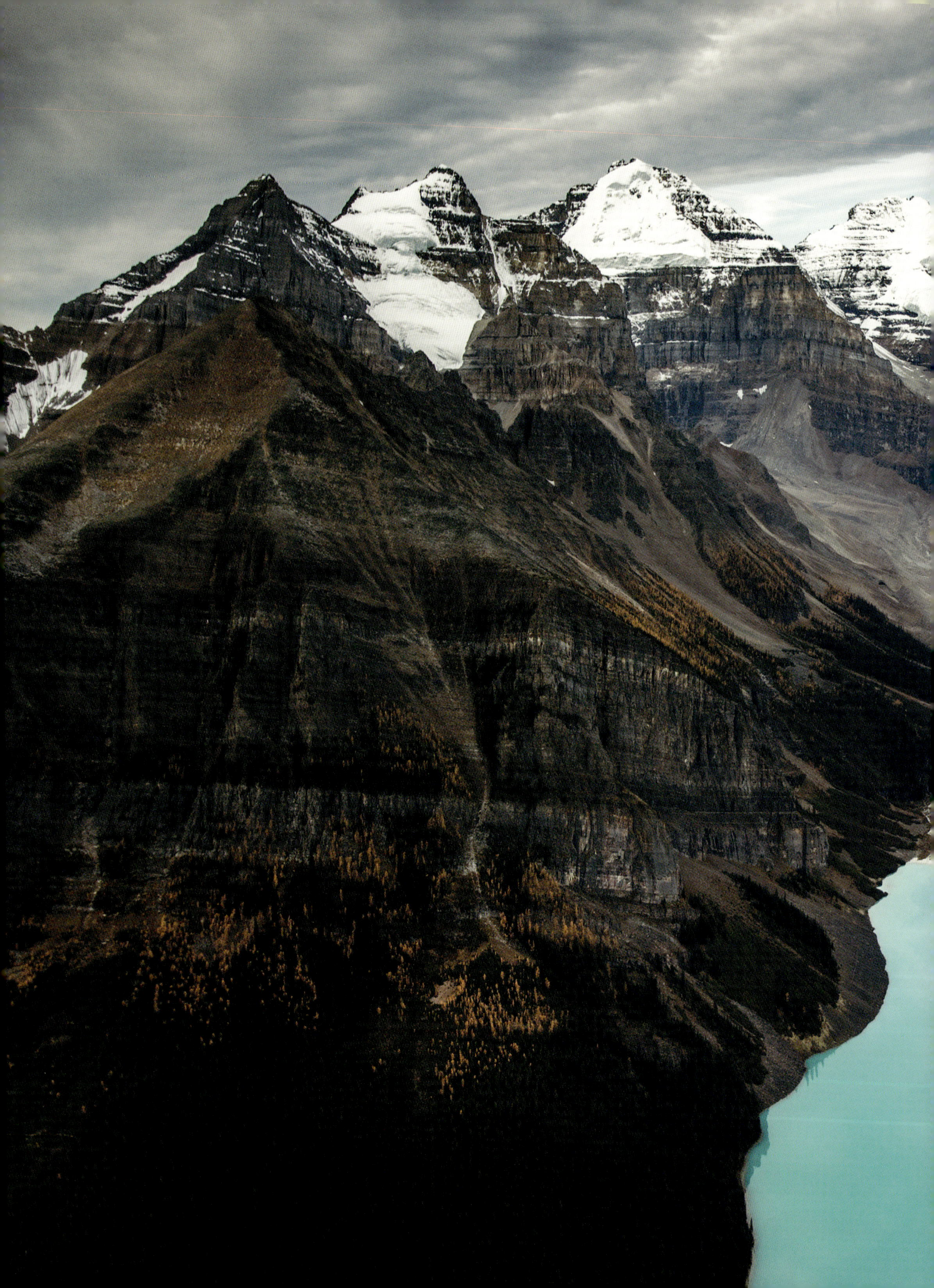

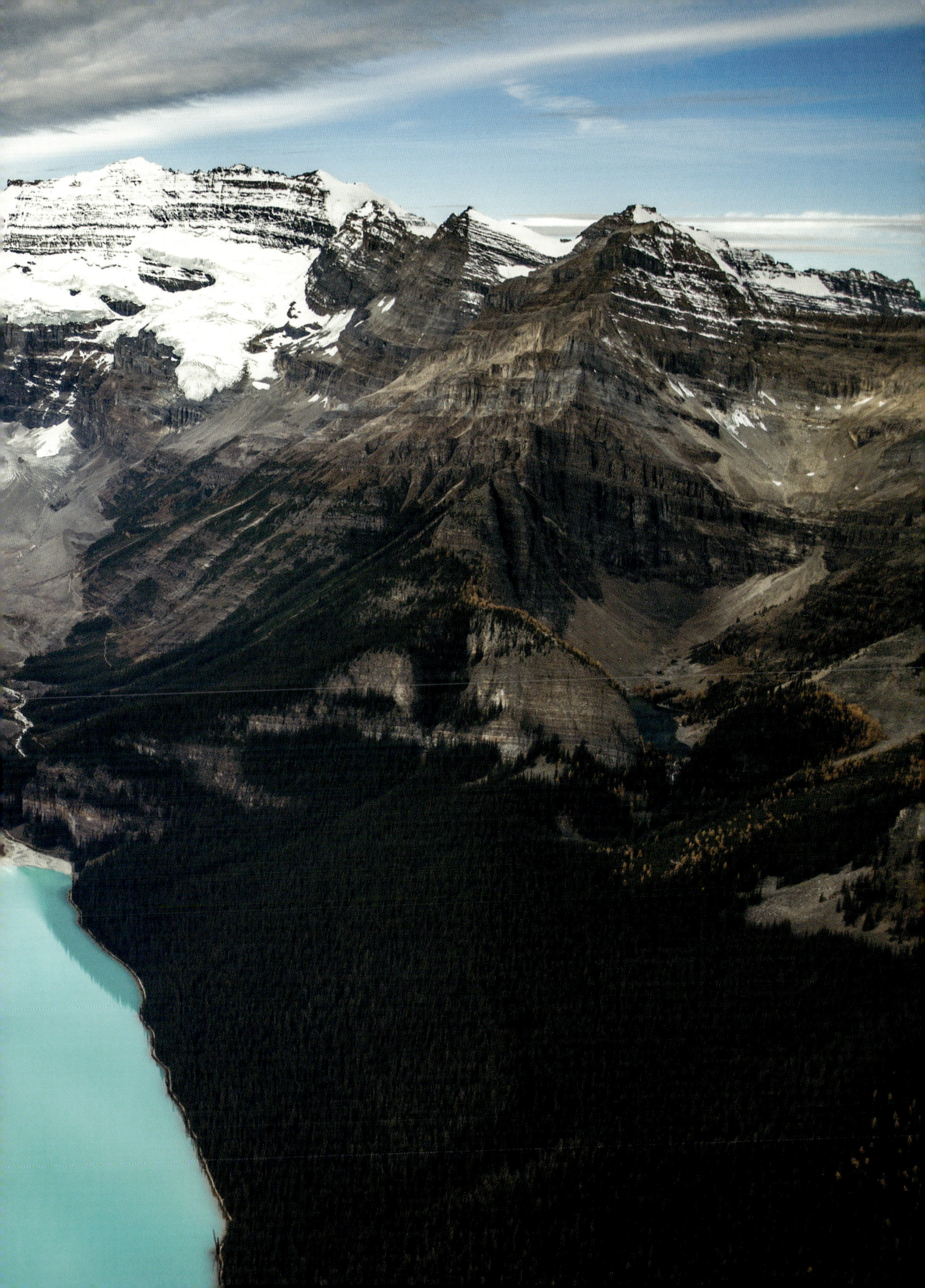

Opposite: This is what the "reverse" view of the iconic Lake Louise shot looks like. Taken from near the top of Mount Victoria, this photograph shows the ski hill beyond the lake, and Mount Douglas at the very back.

Overleaf: The famous trio of emerald-coloured lakes: Louise to the left, Mirror in the centre and Agnes on the right. In the back the jagged skyline is made up of (l–r) Haddo Peak, Mount Aberdeen, Mount Lefroy and Mount Victoria.

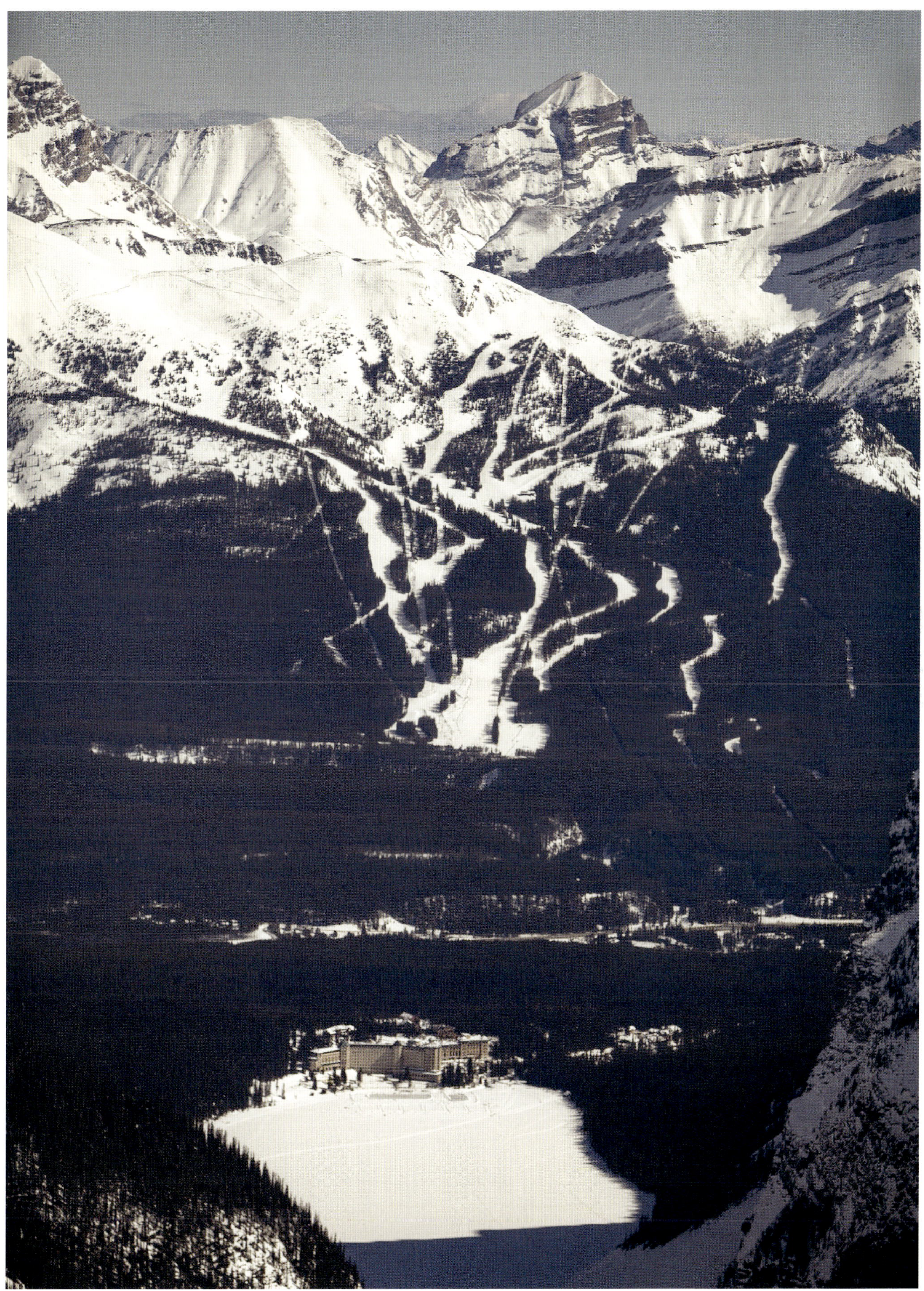

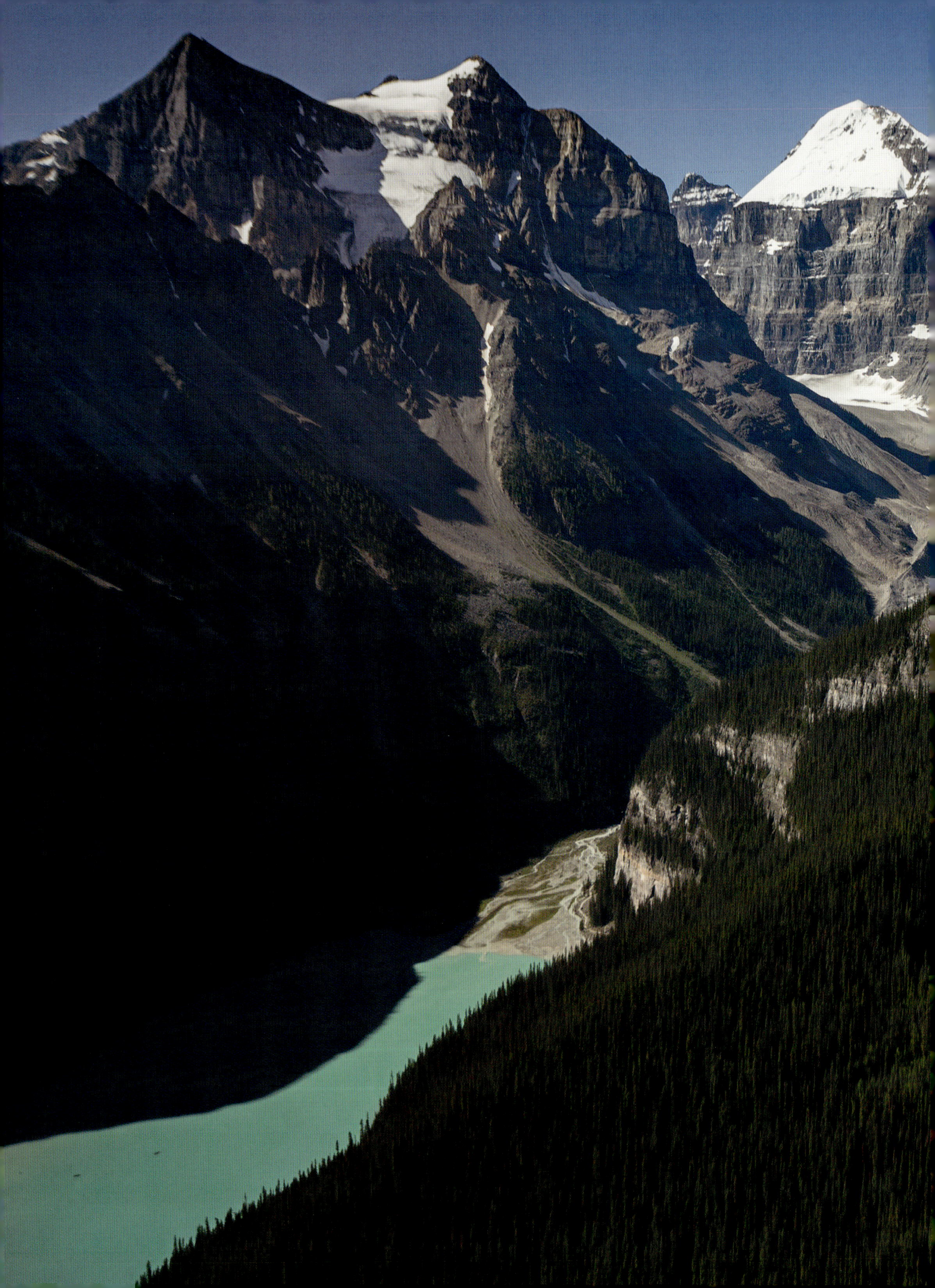

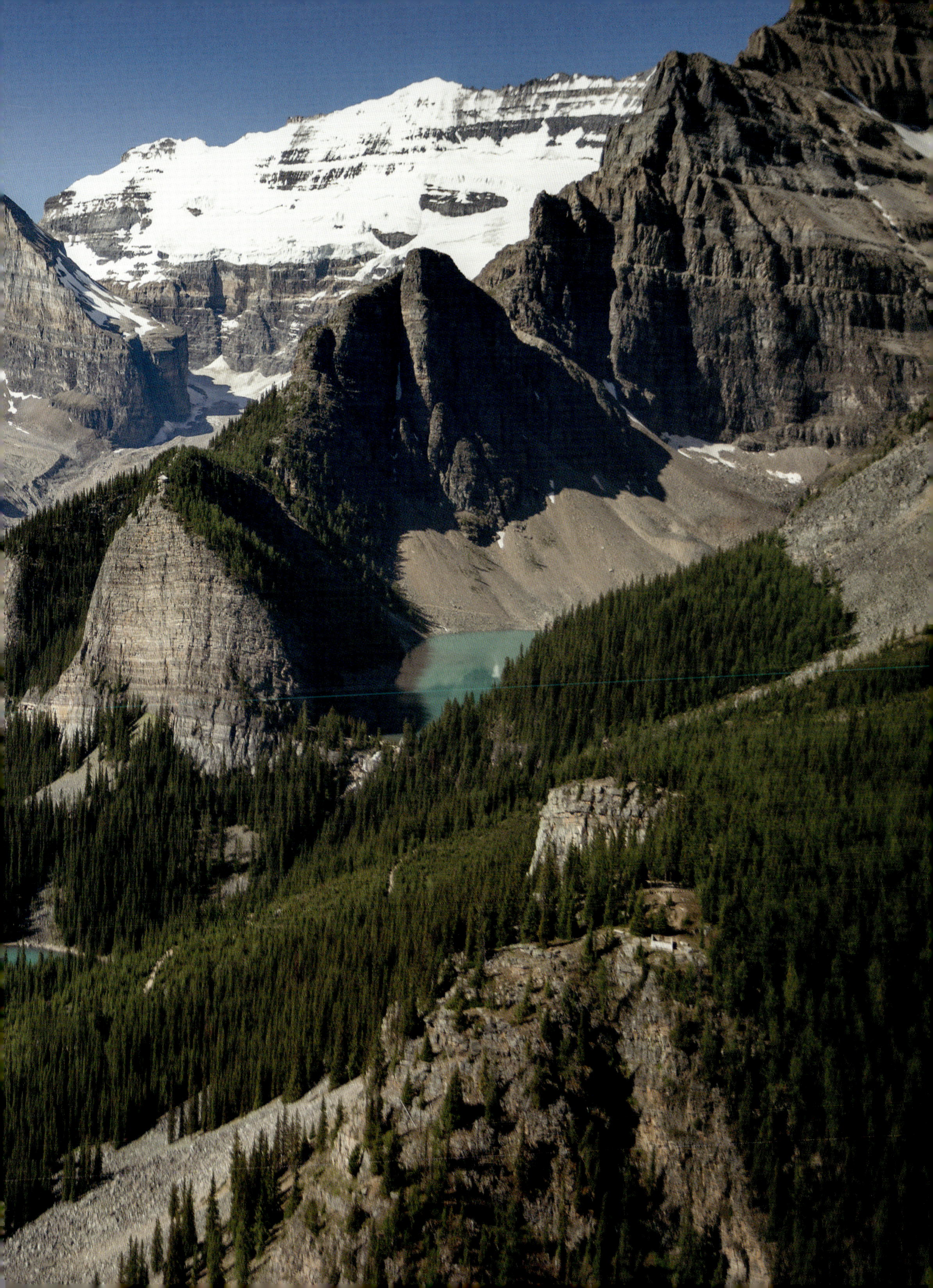

Opposite: Lake Louise just before it freezes, offering one last glimpse at the famous turquoise before winter settles in. The Chateau Lake Louise is visible in the centre.

Overleaf: It may not look that big from the valley bottom, and may have receded considerably, but the hanging glacier that caps Mount Temple is still extremely impressive when viewed up close.

Following spread: The unparalleled setting of Lake Louise, nestled at the foot of the Great Divide. Tiny canoes can be seen floating on the lake.

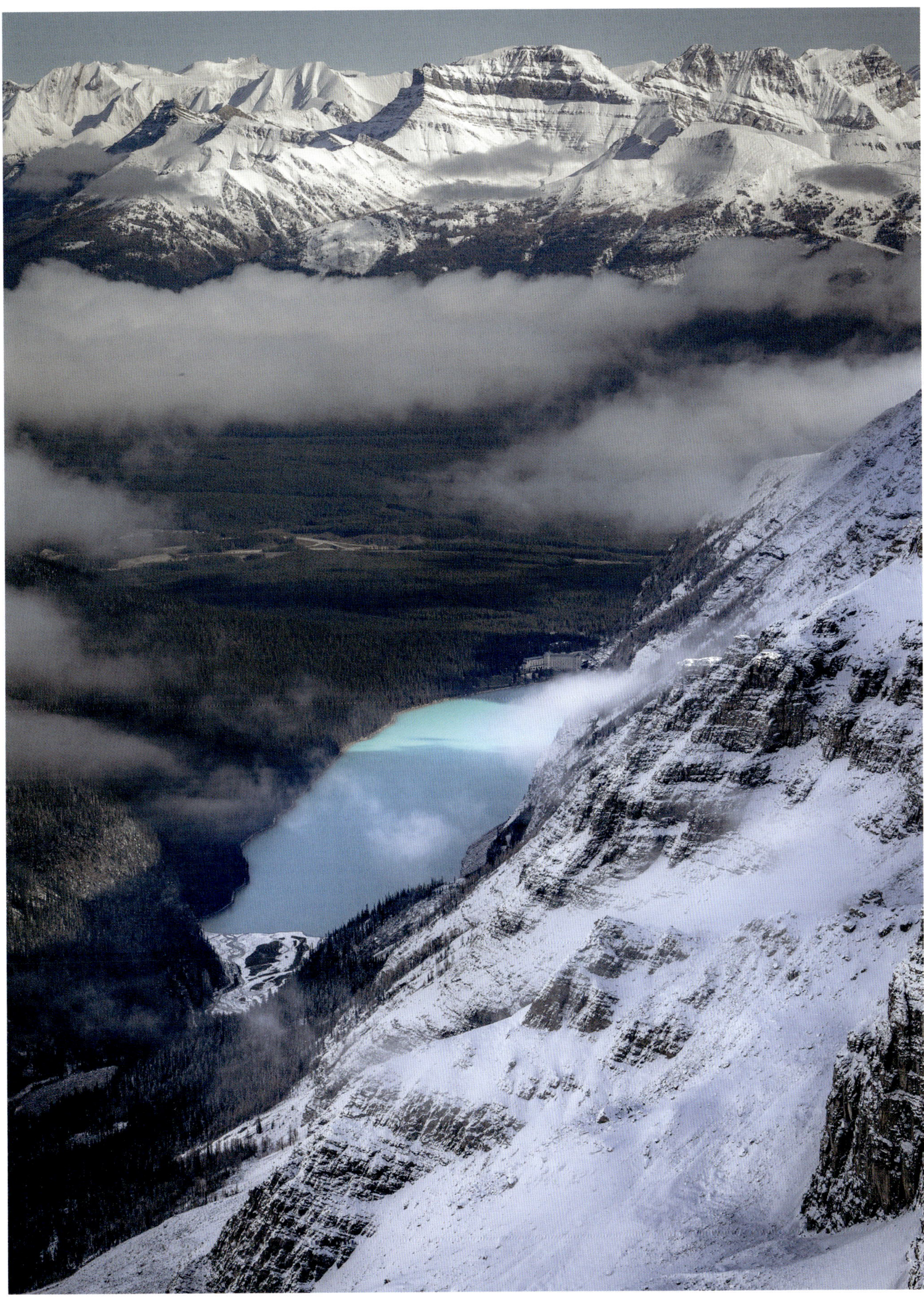

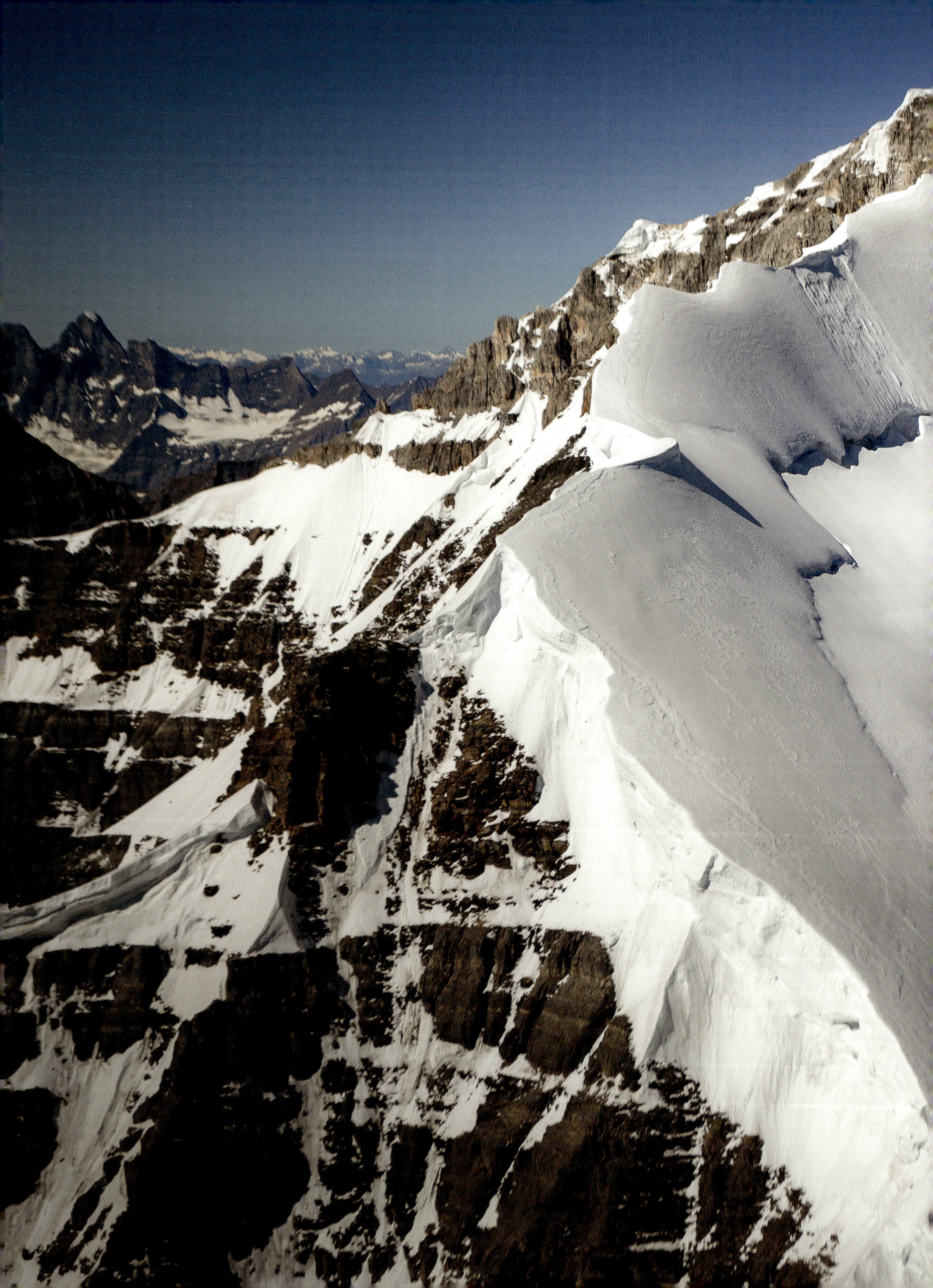

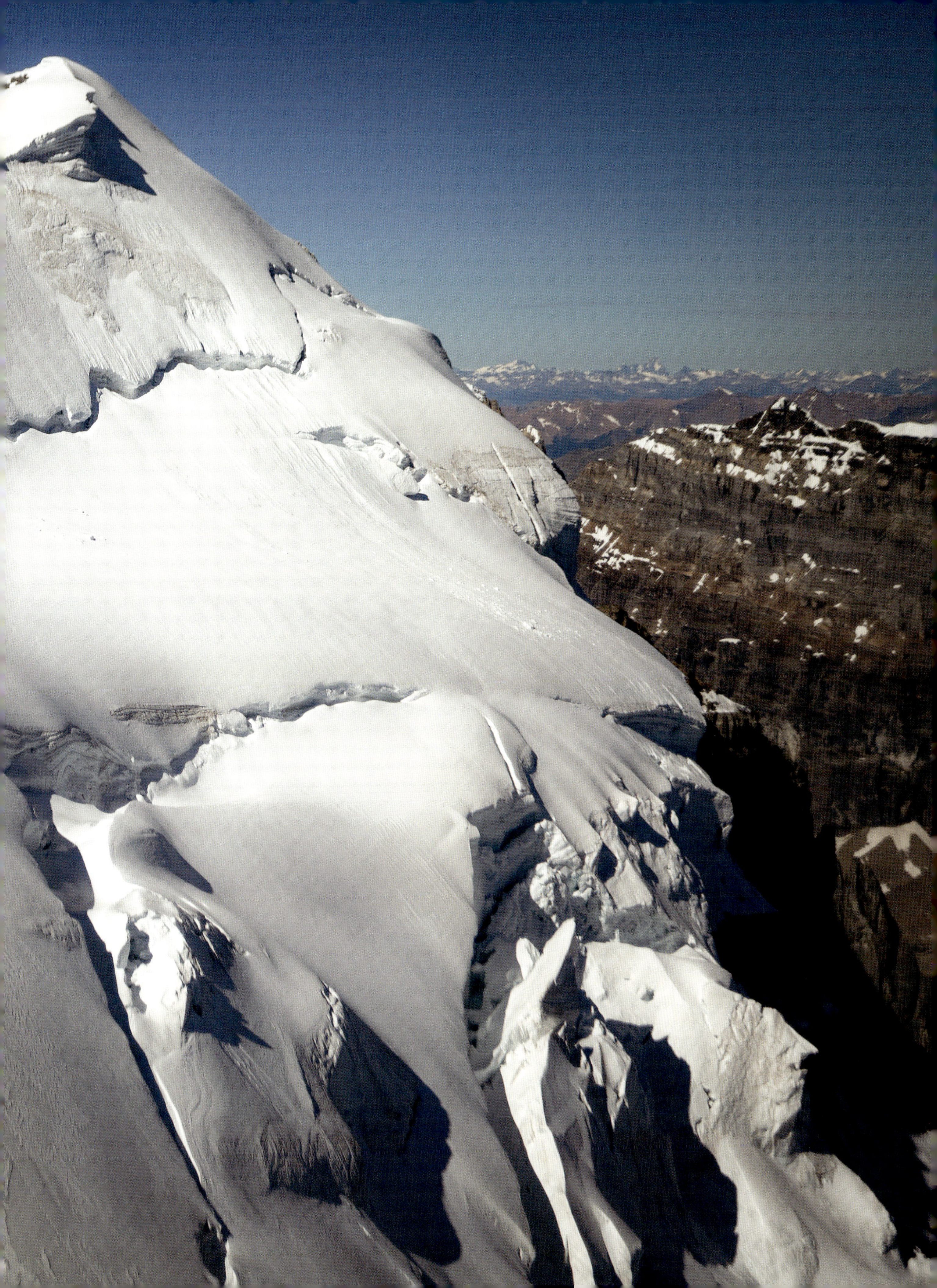

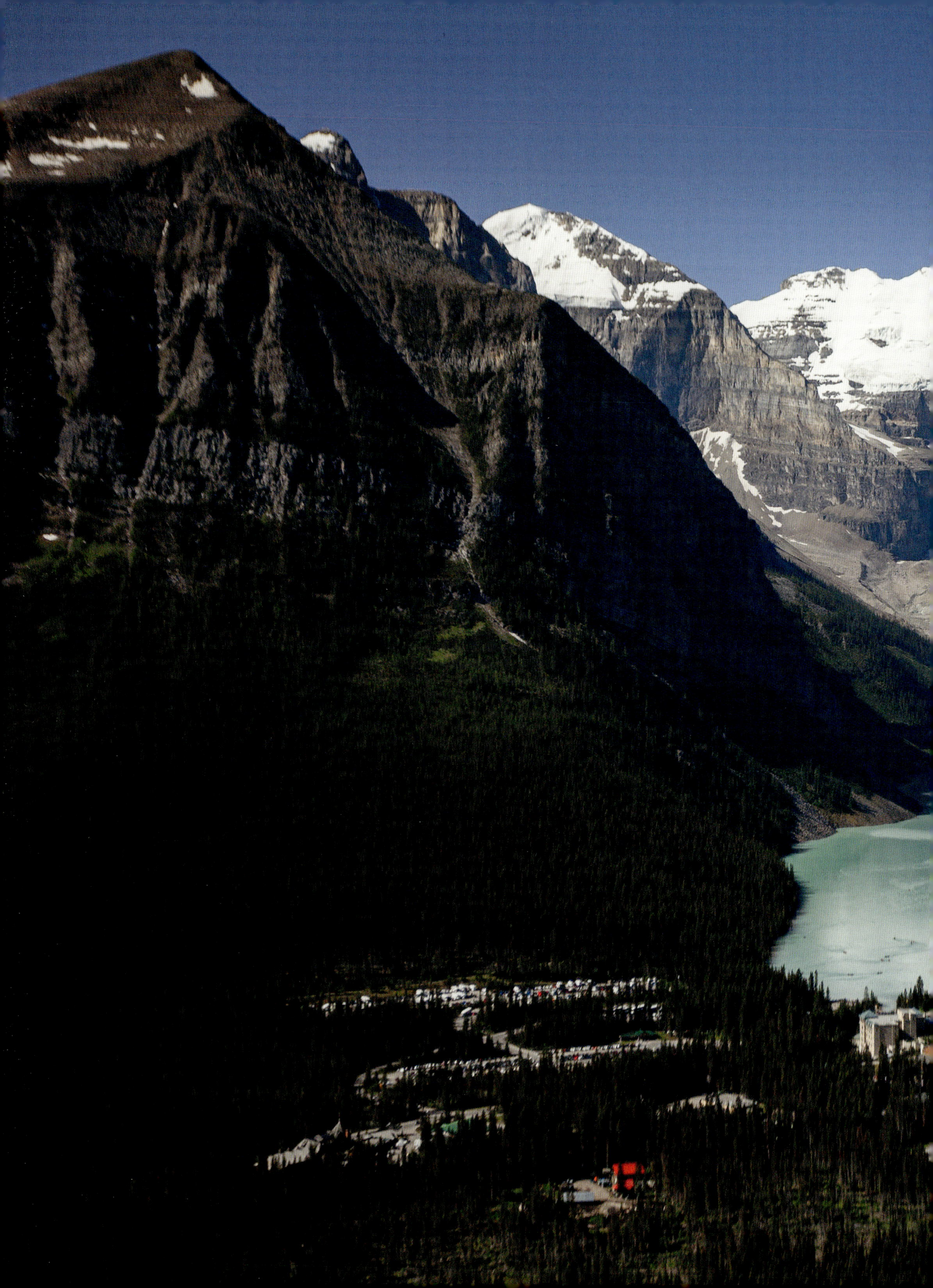

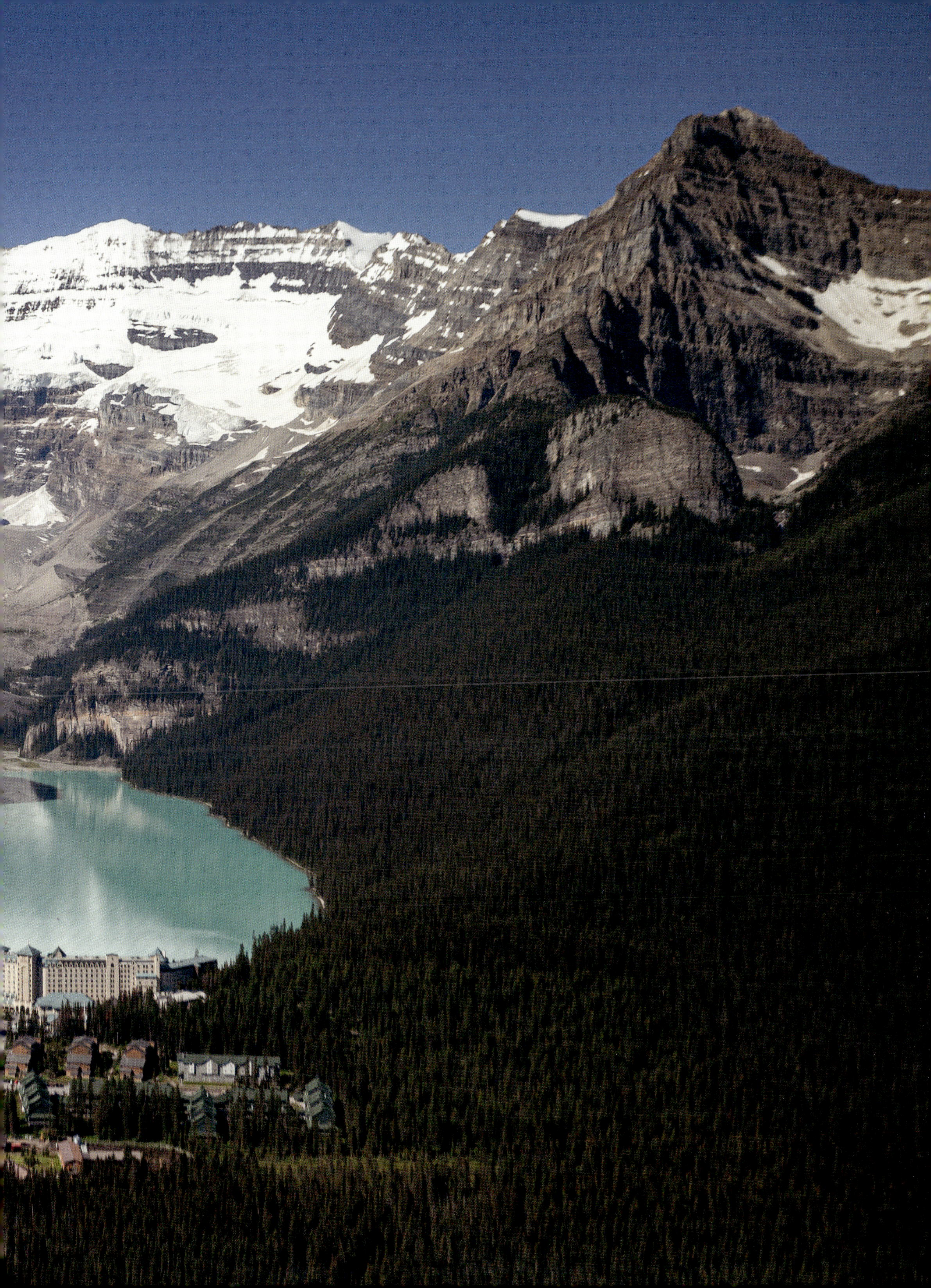

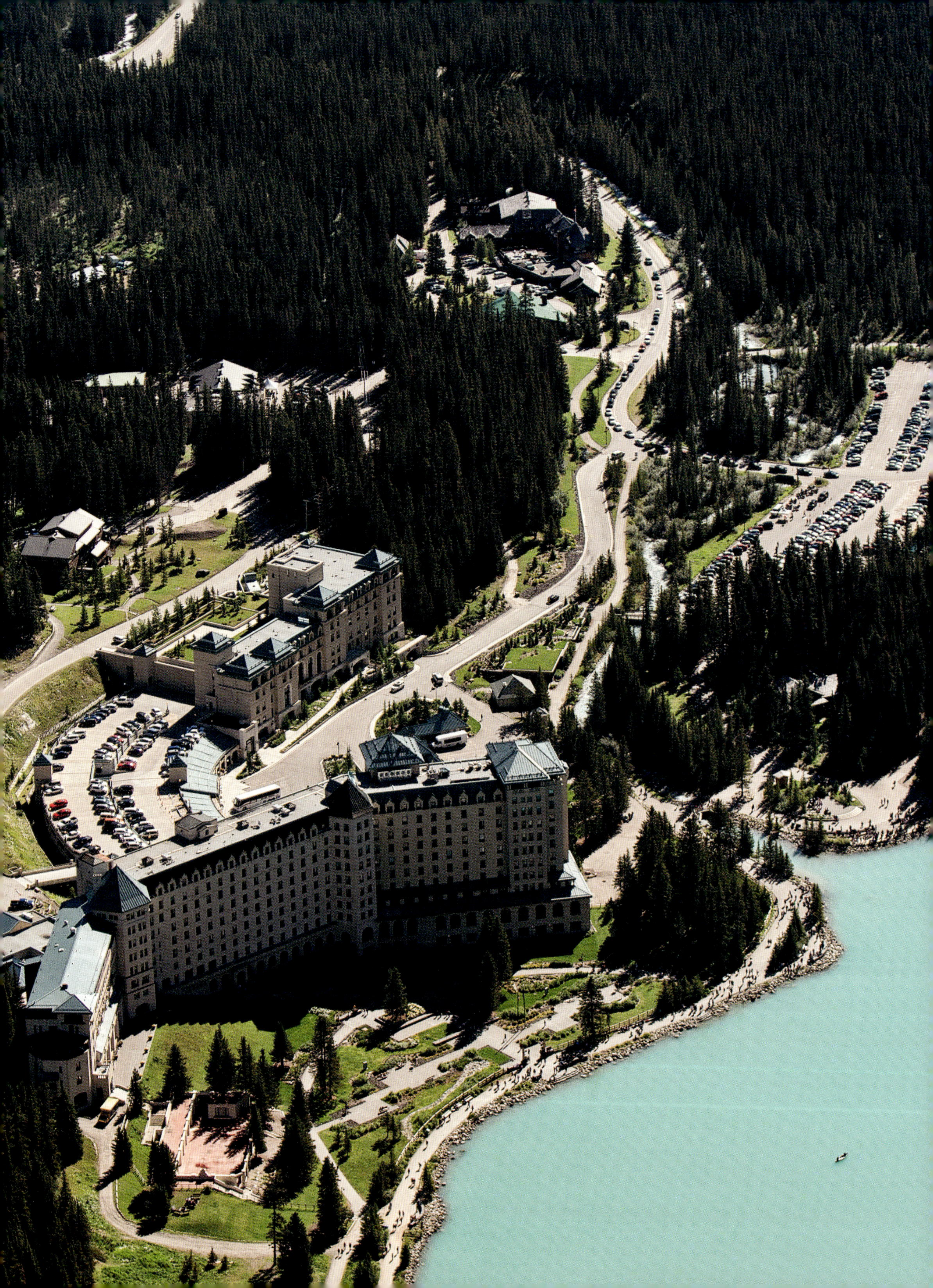

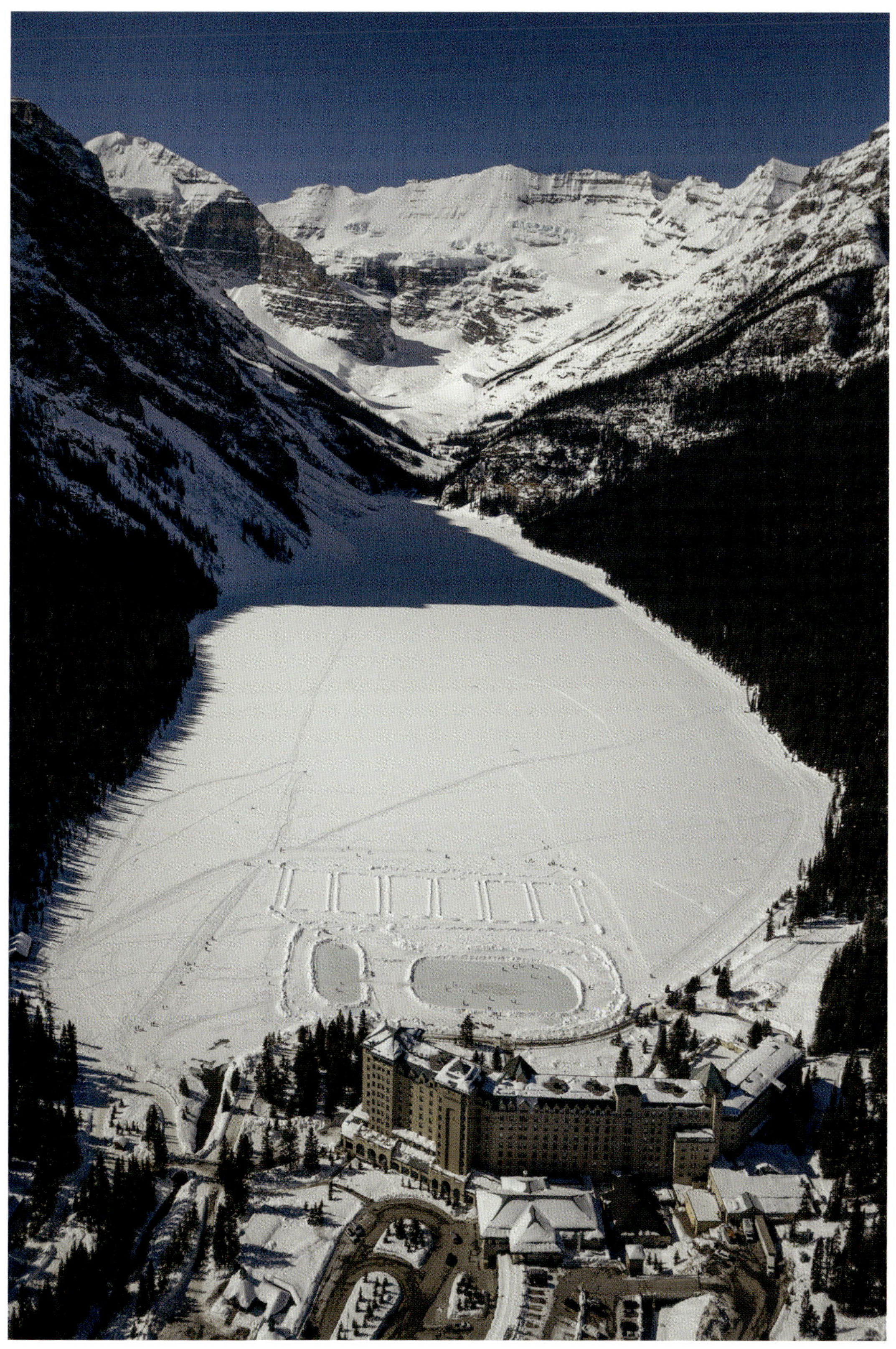

Opposite: This nearly top-down view of Lake Louise showcases the surreal colour of the lake at the height of summer. A canoe is visible on the right.

Above: Lake Louise shortly after the pond hockey tournament in February. In the winter, the ultimate canoe venue turns into one of the world's finest ice-skating rinks.

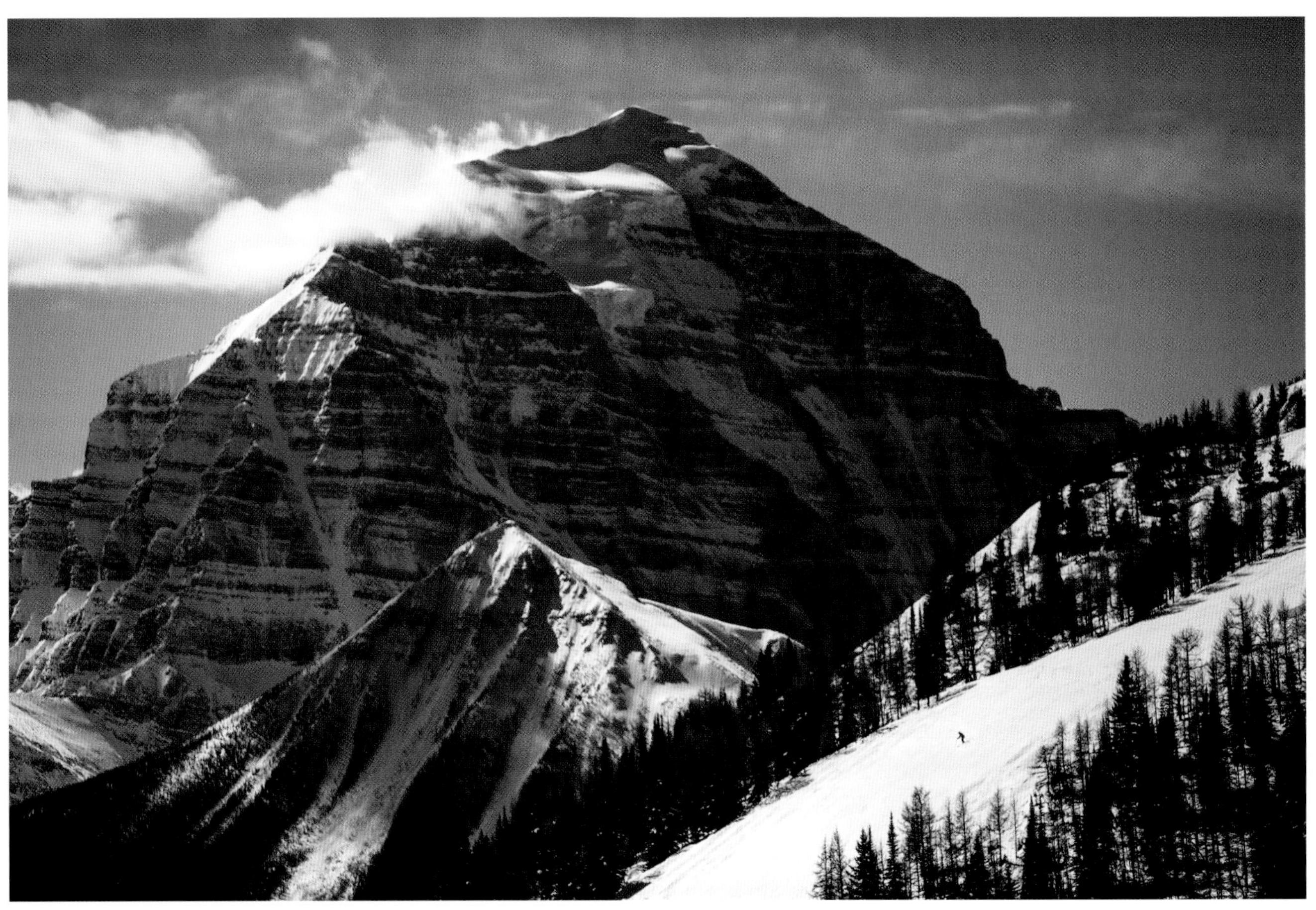

Above: The massive north face of Mount Temple rises above
a lone skier on the slopes of the Lake Louise Ski Resort.

Opposite: The aptly named Top of the World chairlift in Lake Louise
looks out onto an absolutely incredible skyline.

Overleaf: Sentinel Pass, long known as one of the best day hikes in Banff National Park, is dwarfed
by the spire of Pinnacle Mountain. On the left are Minnestimma Lakes and a few of the Ten Peaks,
while on the right of the pass one can spot the trail and impressive Hungabee Mountain in the back.

Following spread: The larch-clad Big Beehive separates Lake Agnes (l) from Lake Louise (r).

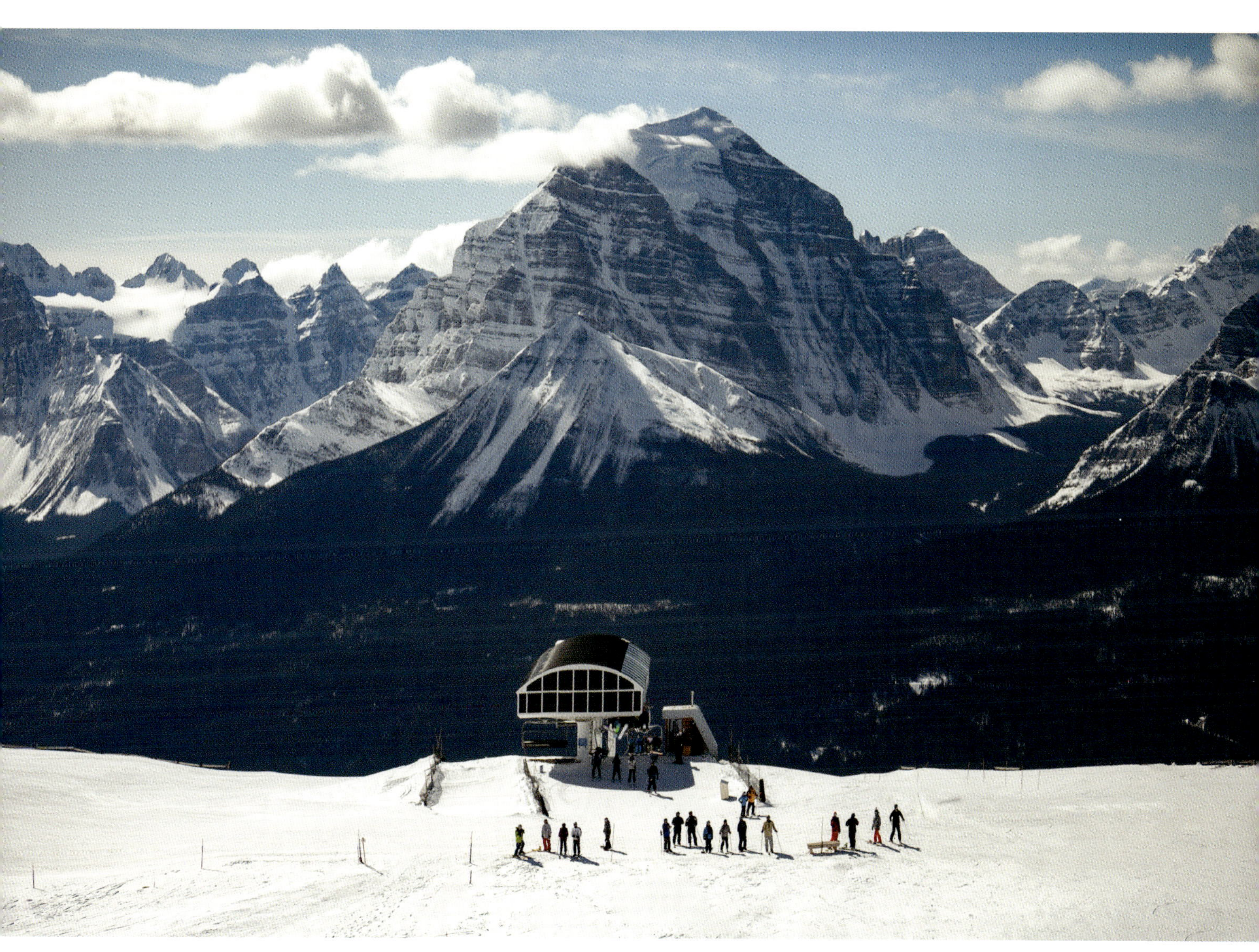

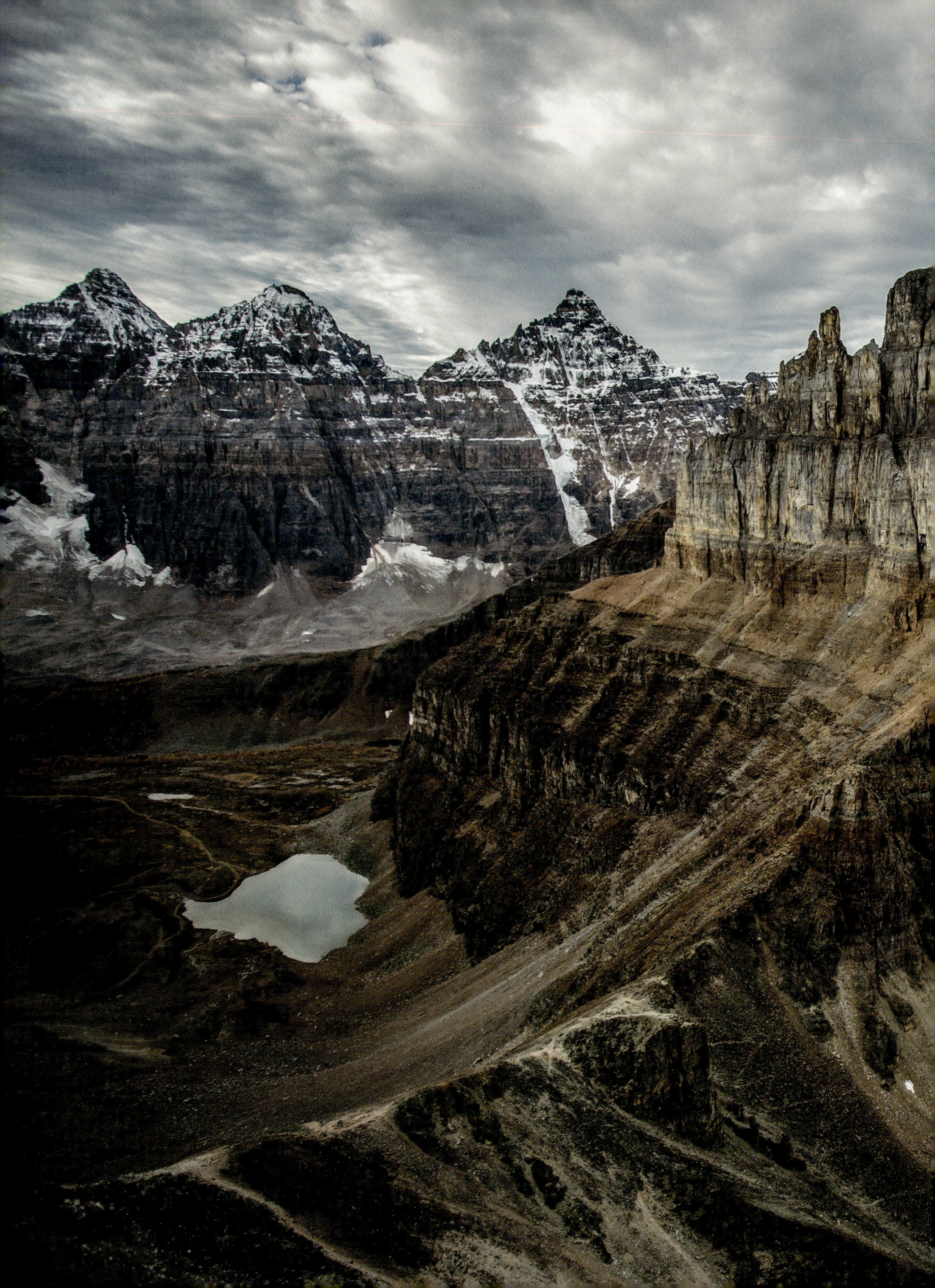

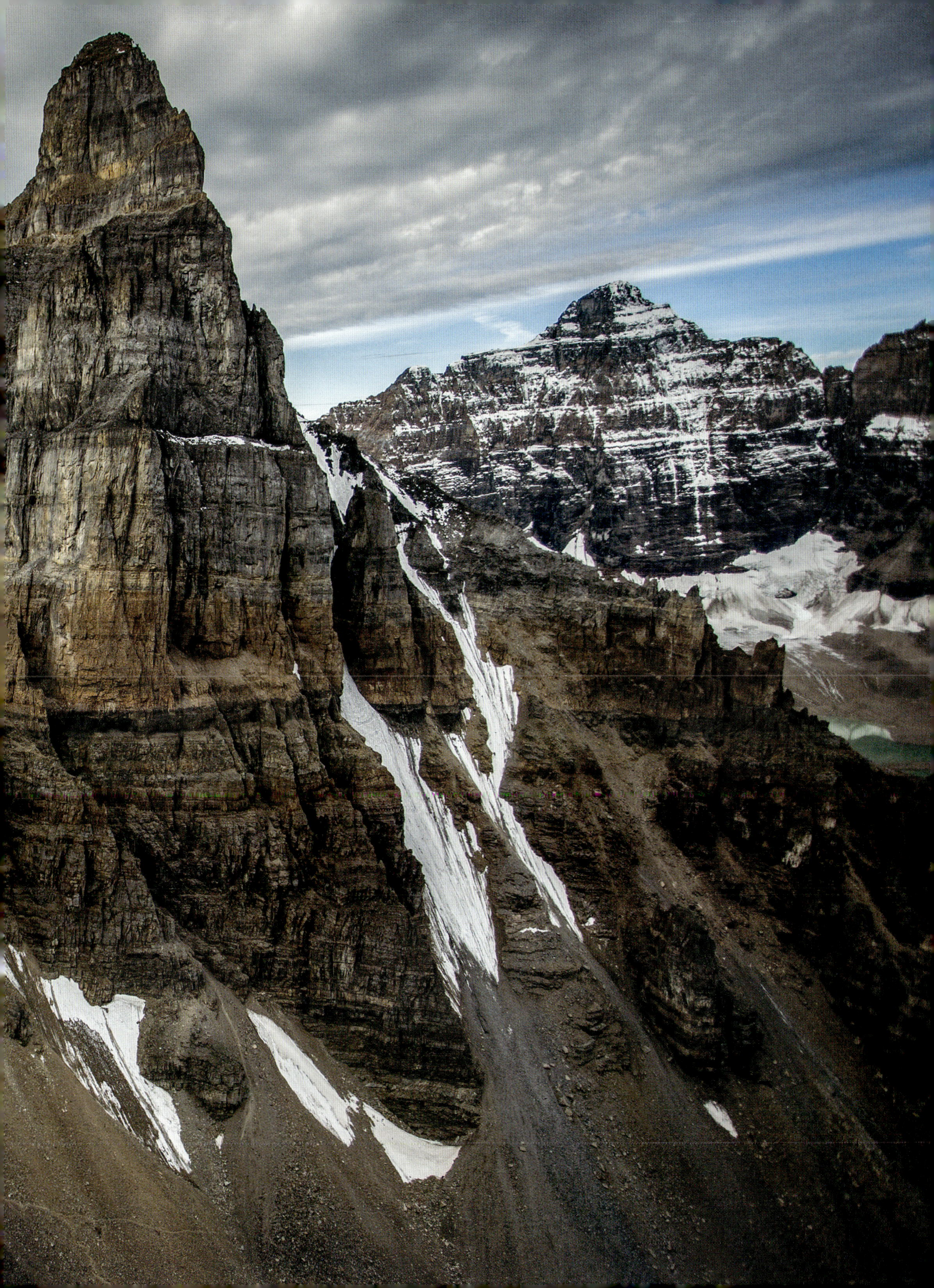

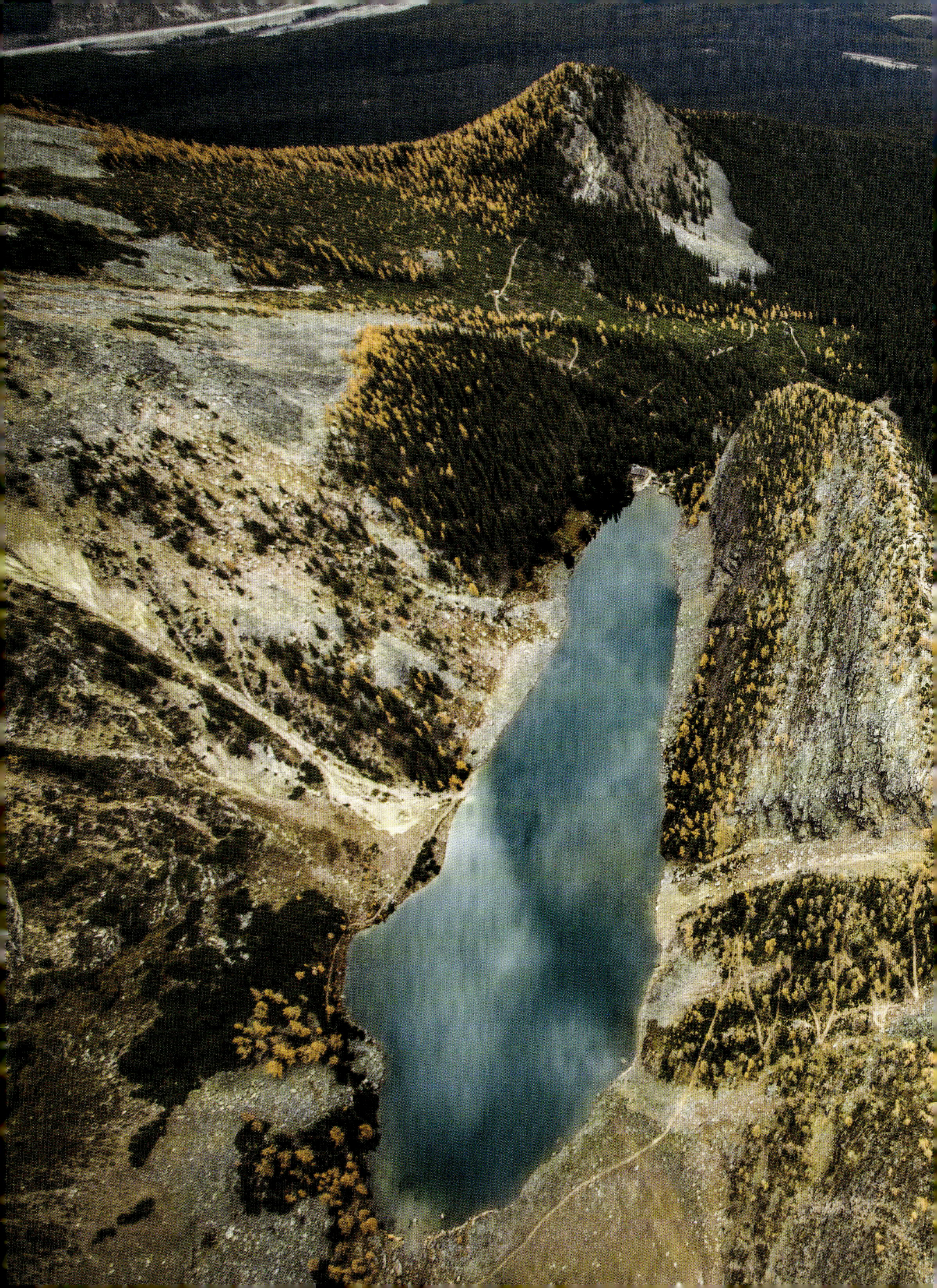

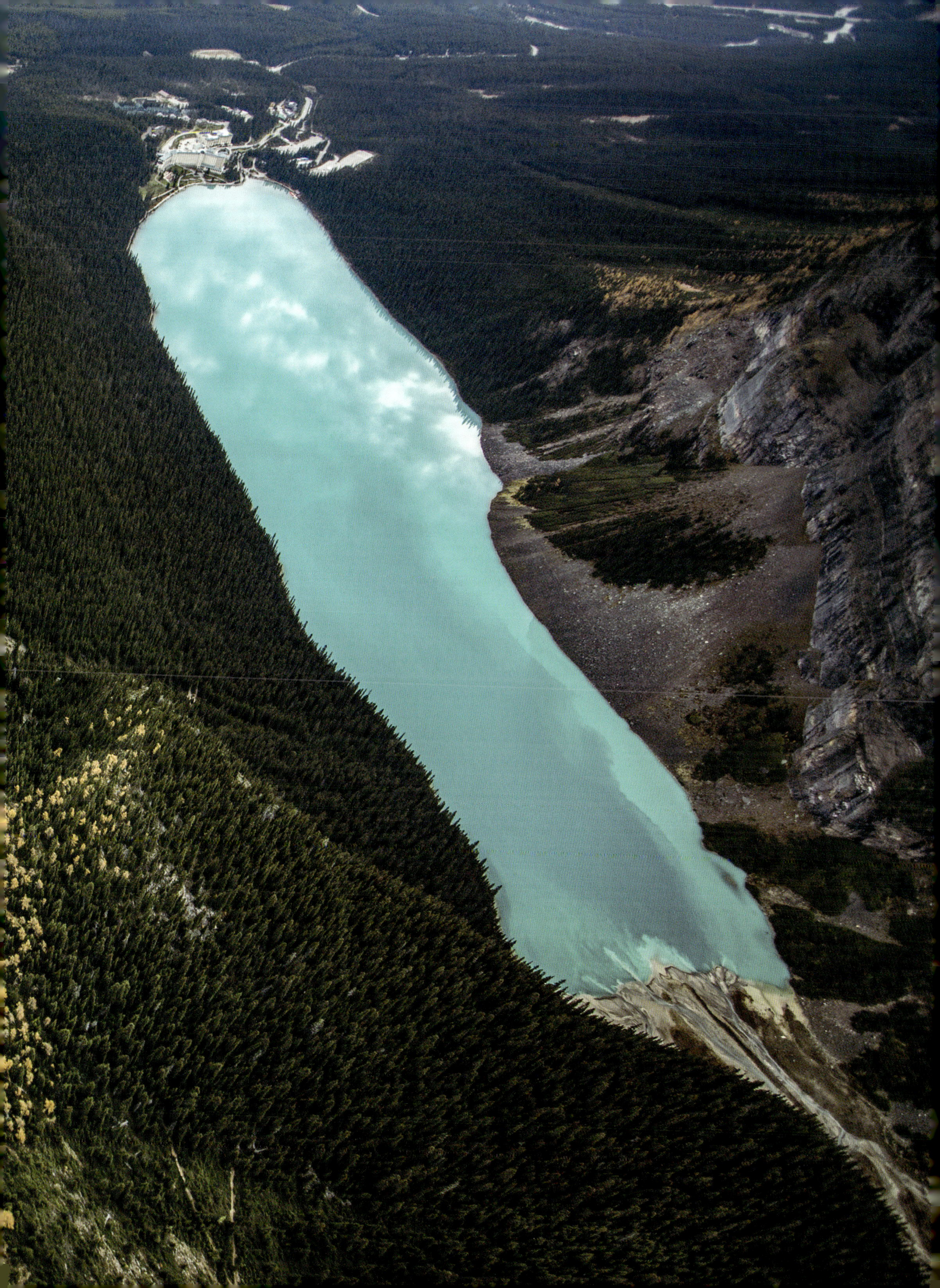

Opposite: Mount Temple rises above an inversion on an October morning.

Overleaf: Rarely visited Temple Lake is tucked under Mount Temple
in this larch-filled view of the Great Divide.

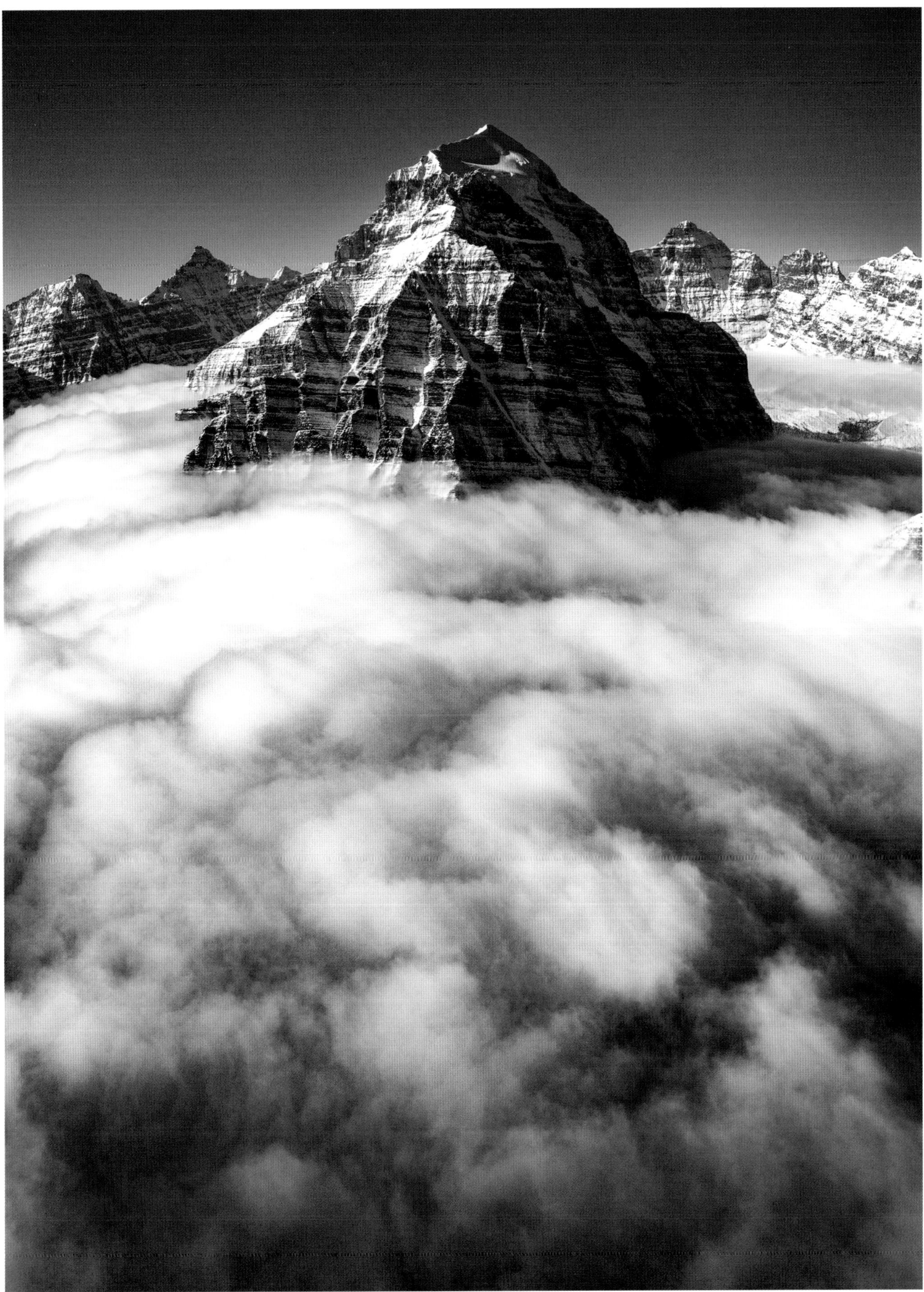

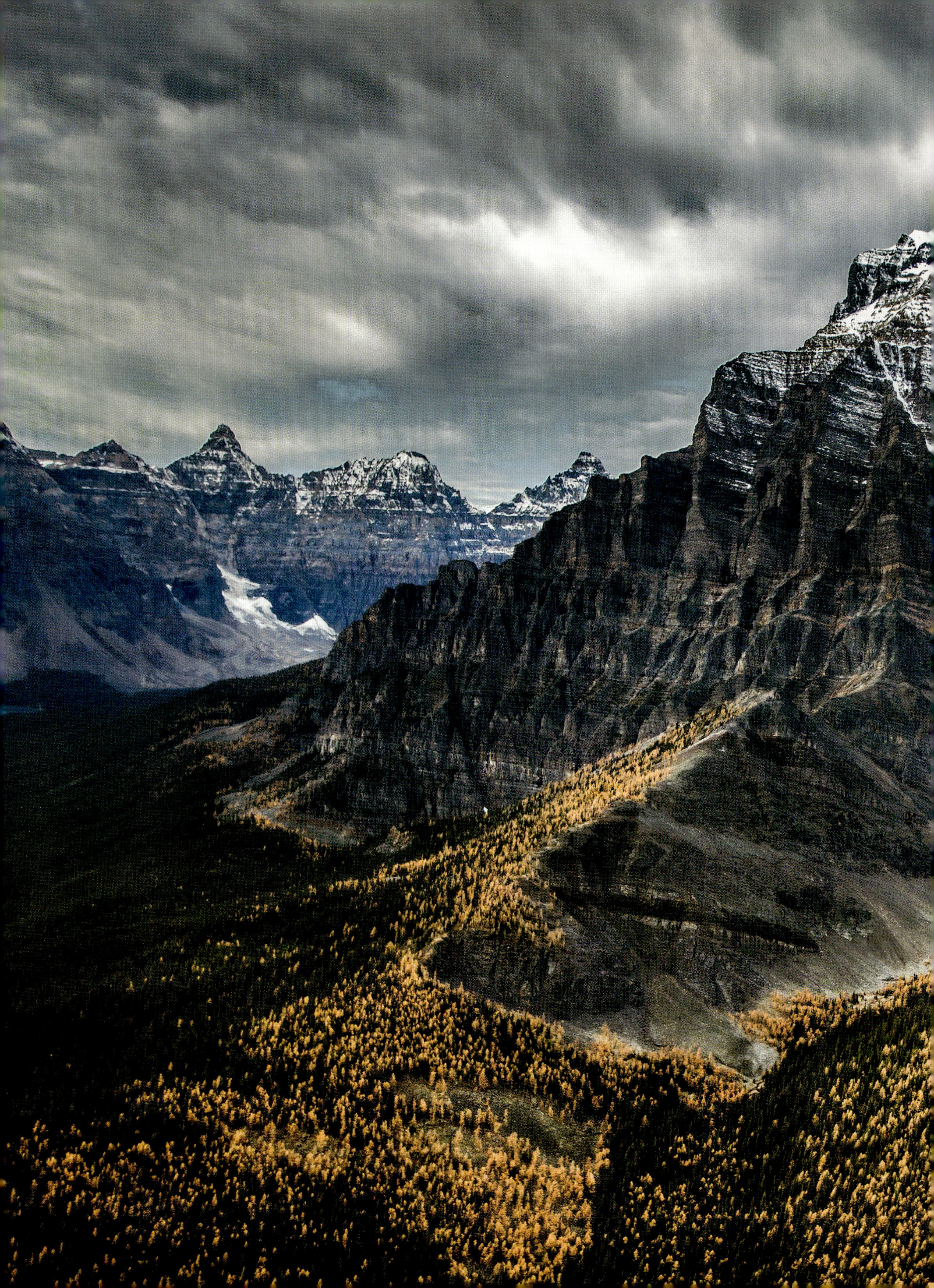

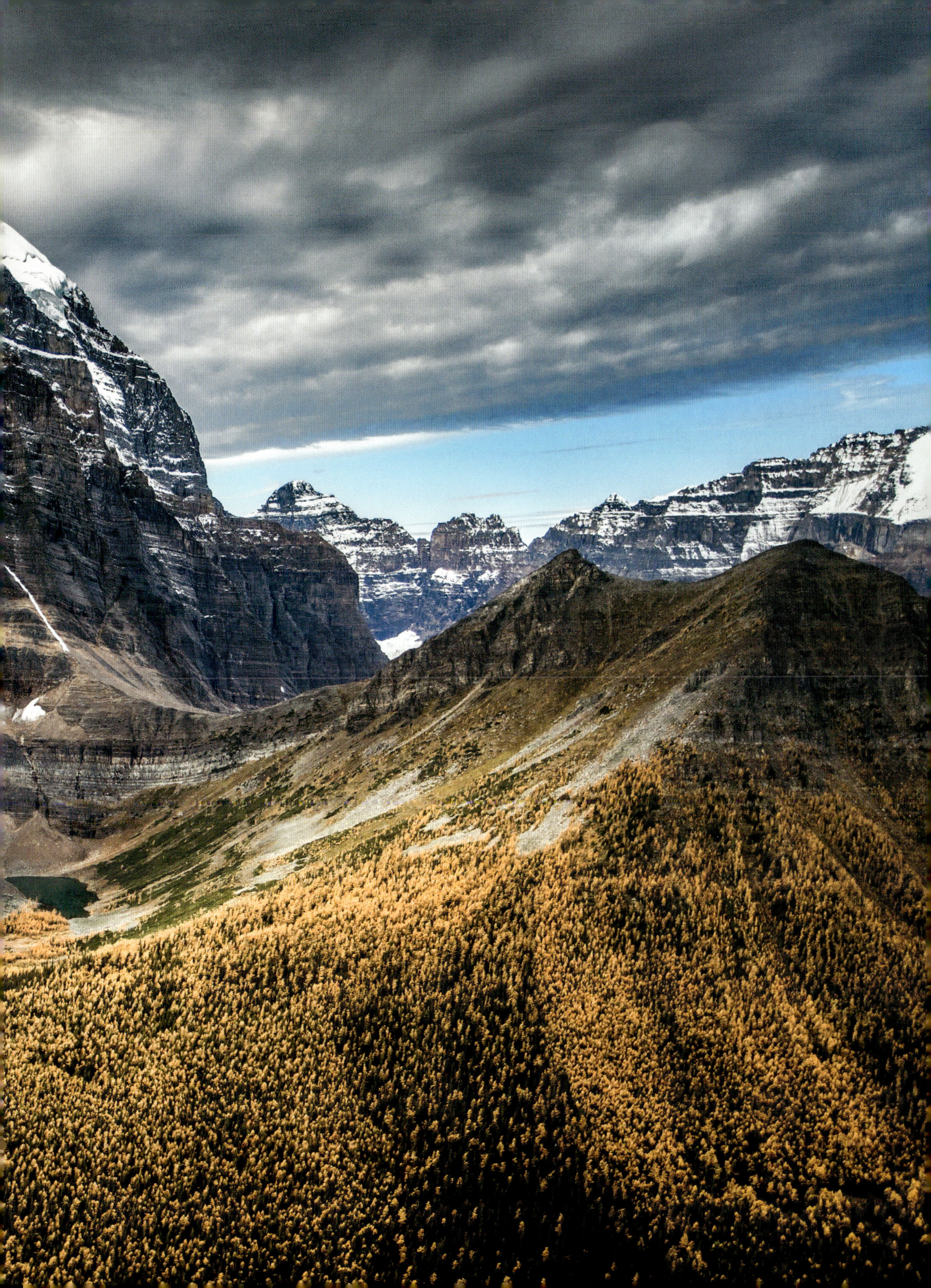

Canada's second-highest building in altitude, and one of its most unlikely, Abbot Pass Hut is perched high in a world of rock and snow between the slopes and glaciers of mounts Lefroy and Victoria.

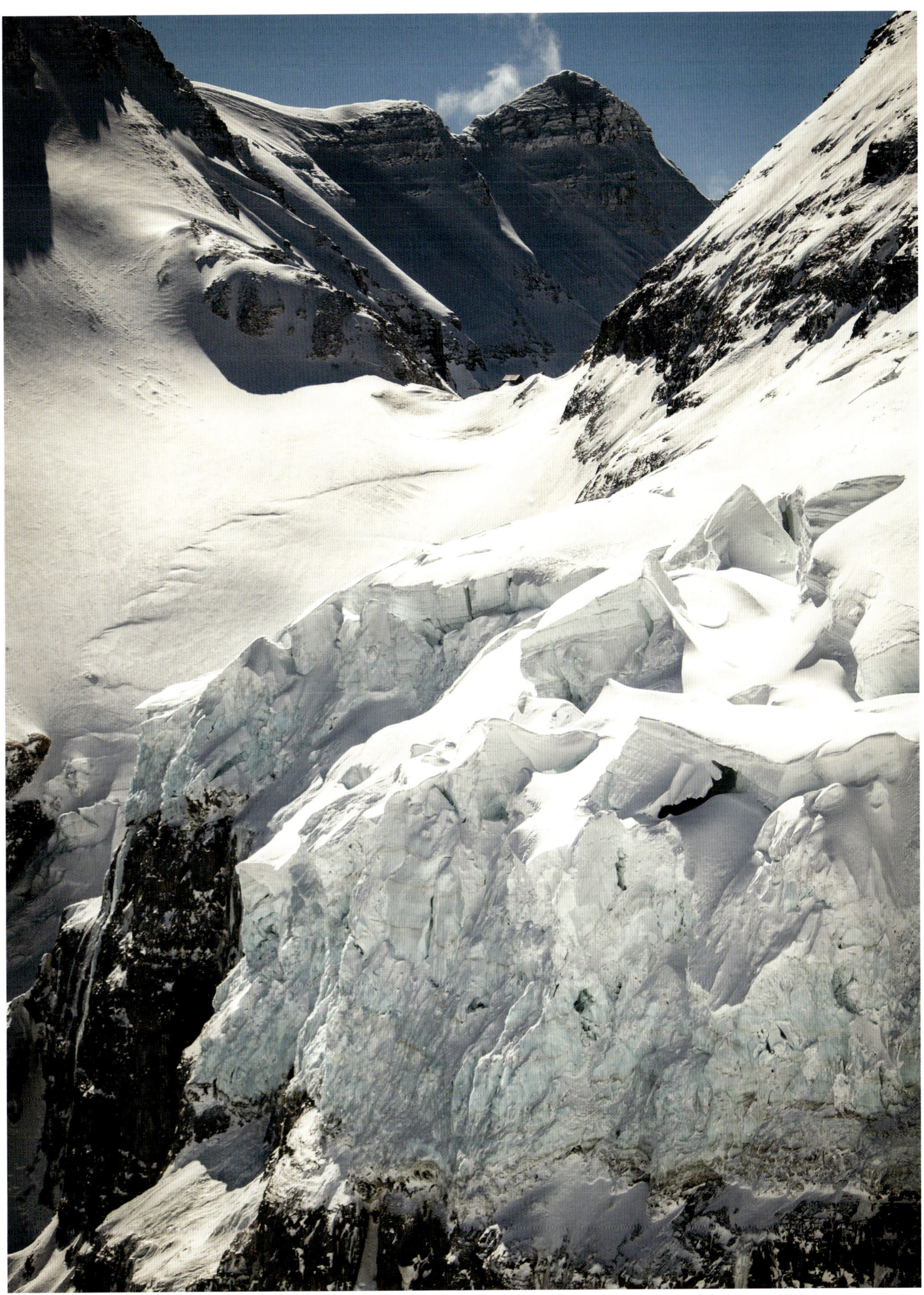

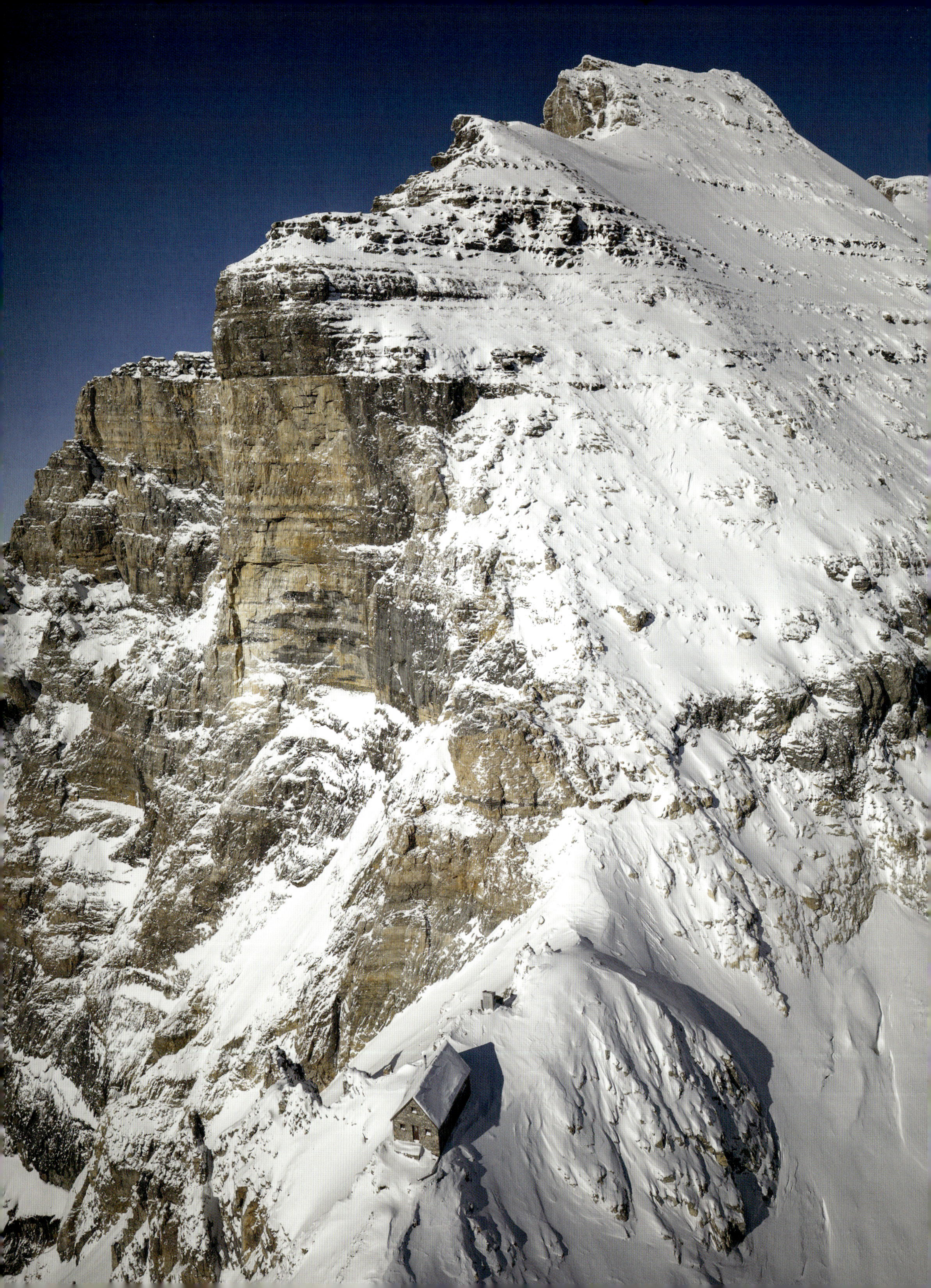

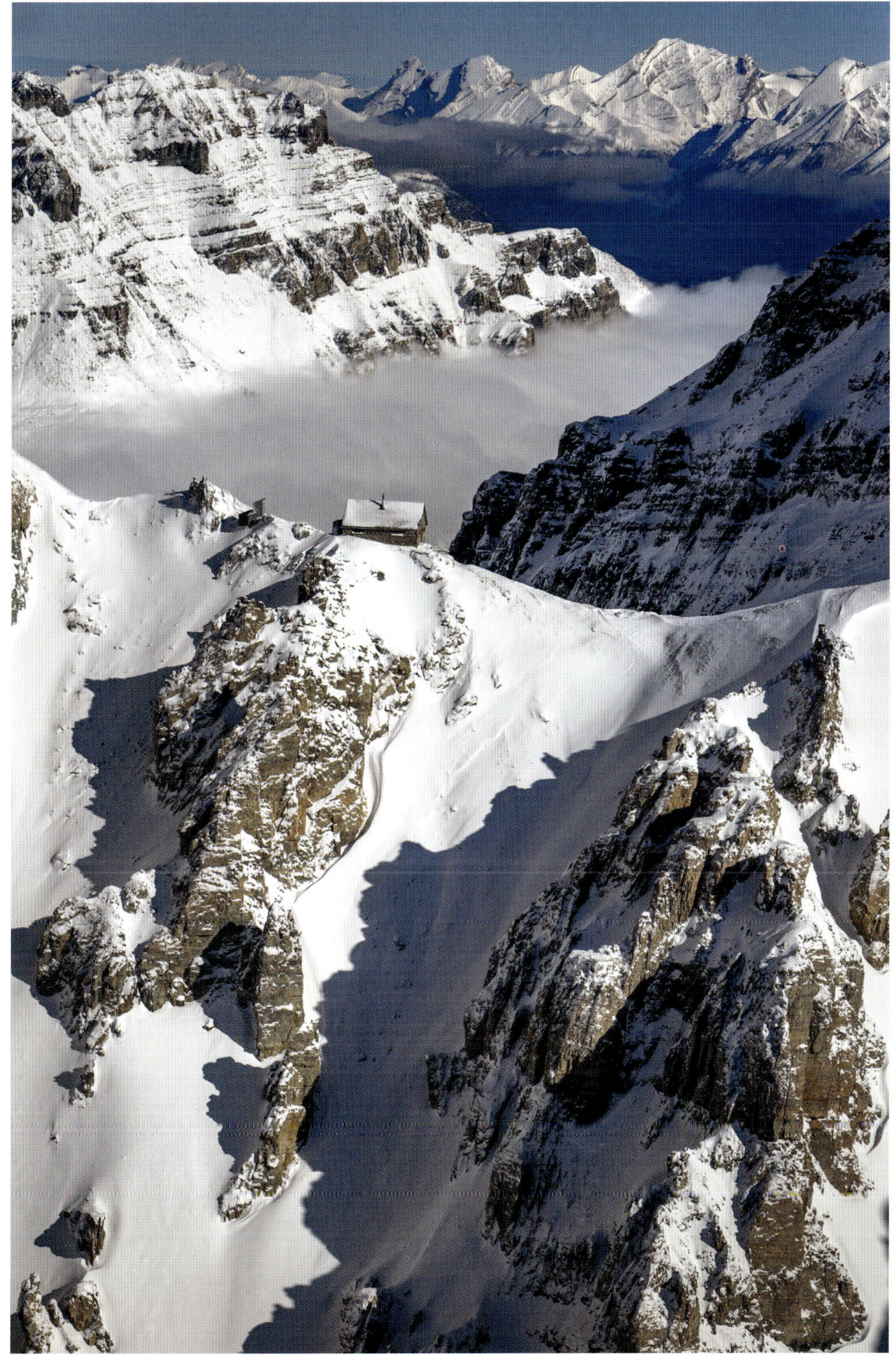

Constructed in 1922 and officially opened in 1923, Abbot Pass Hut was built to safe-house mountaineers after an incident on Mount Lefroy took the life of Philip Stanley Abbot, for whom the pass was named. It was constructed primarily using nearby stones, but all additional materials had to be brought up from Lake Louise. This involved using pack horses to carry supplies up the lower glacier, and then a winch system to get their loads up to the pass. Overall, about two tons of building materials needed to be hauled up to the site to complete the structure.

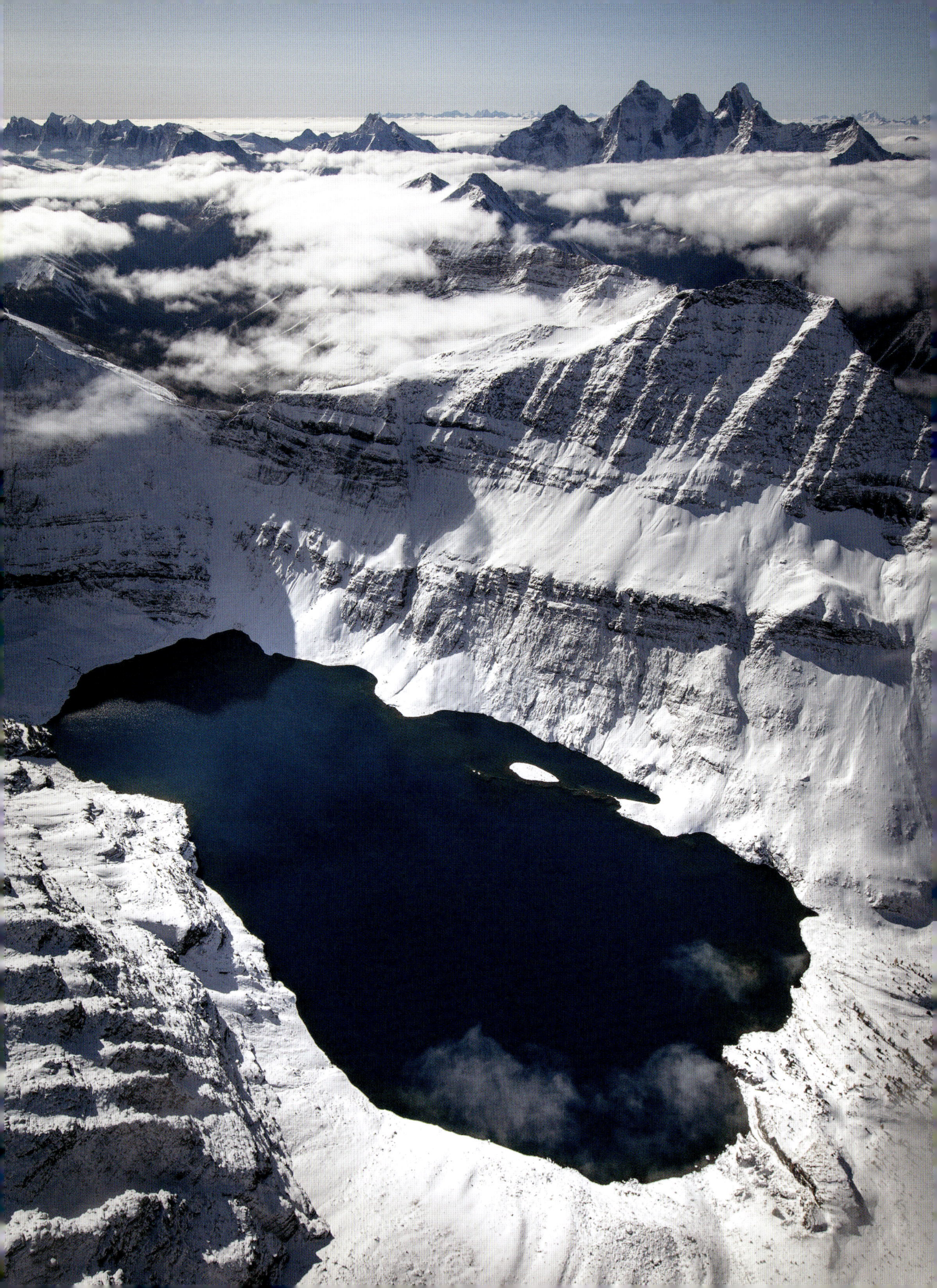

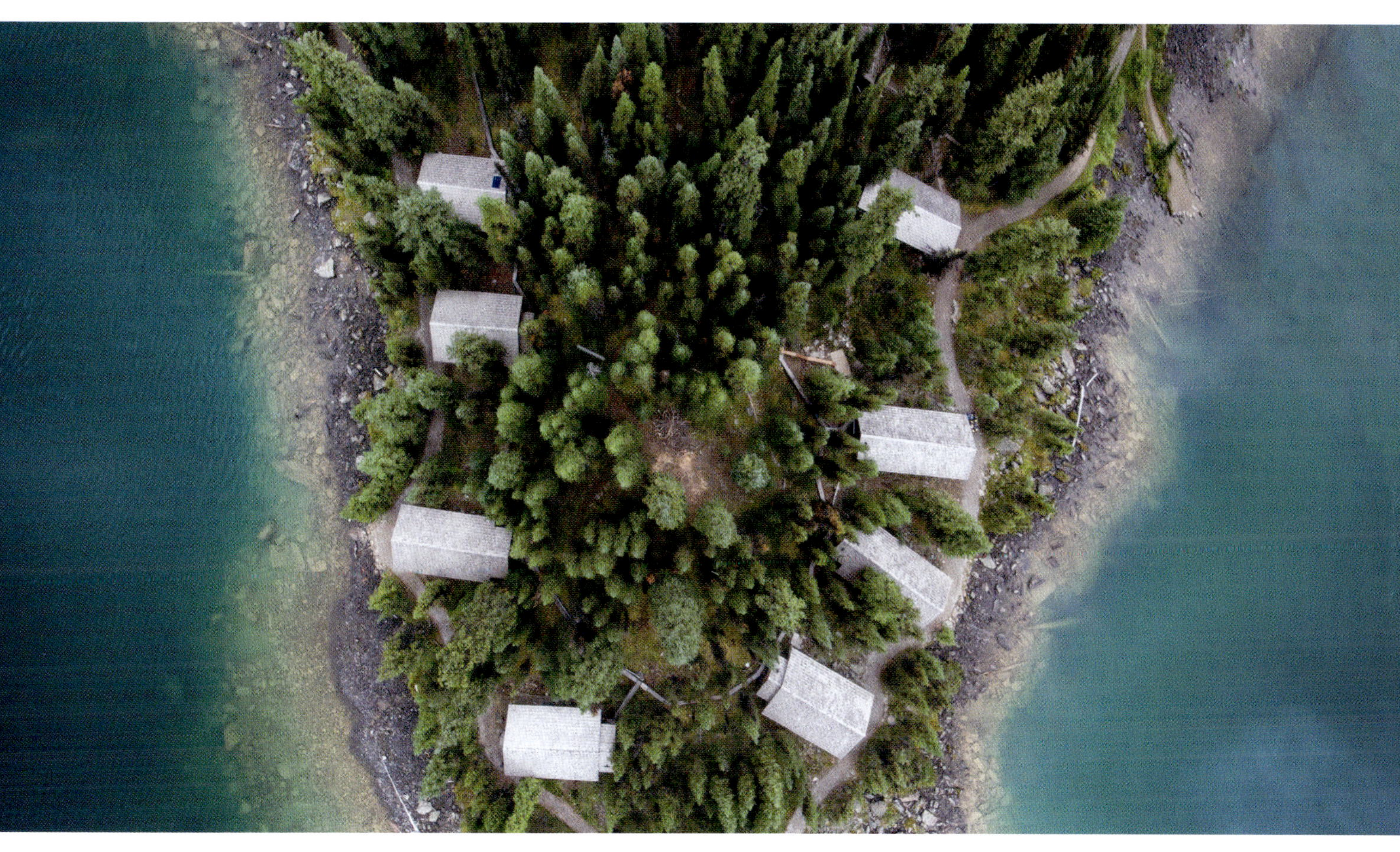

Opposite: Lake McArthur sparkles in the October sunshine.
The mighty Goodsirs stand tall in the background.

Above: The cabins of Lake O'Hara Lodge, one of the most
enchanting places to spend a night in the mountain parks.

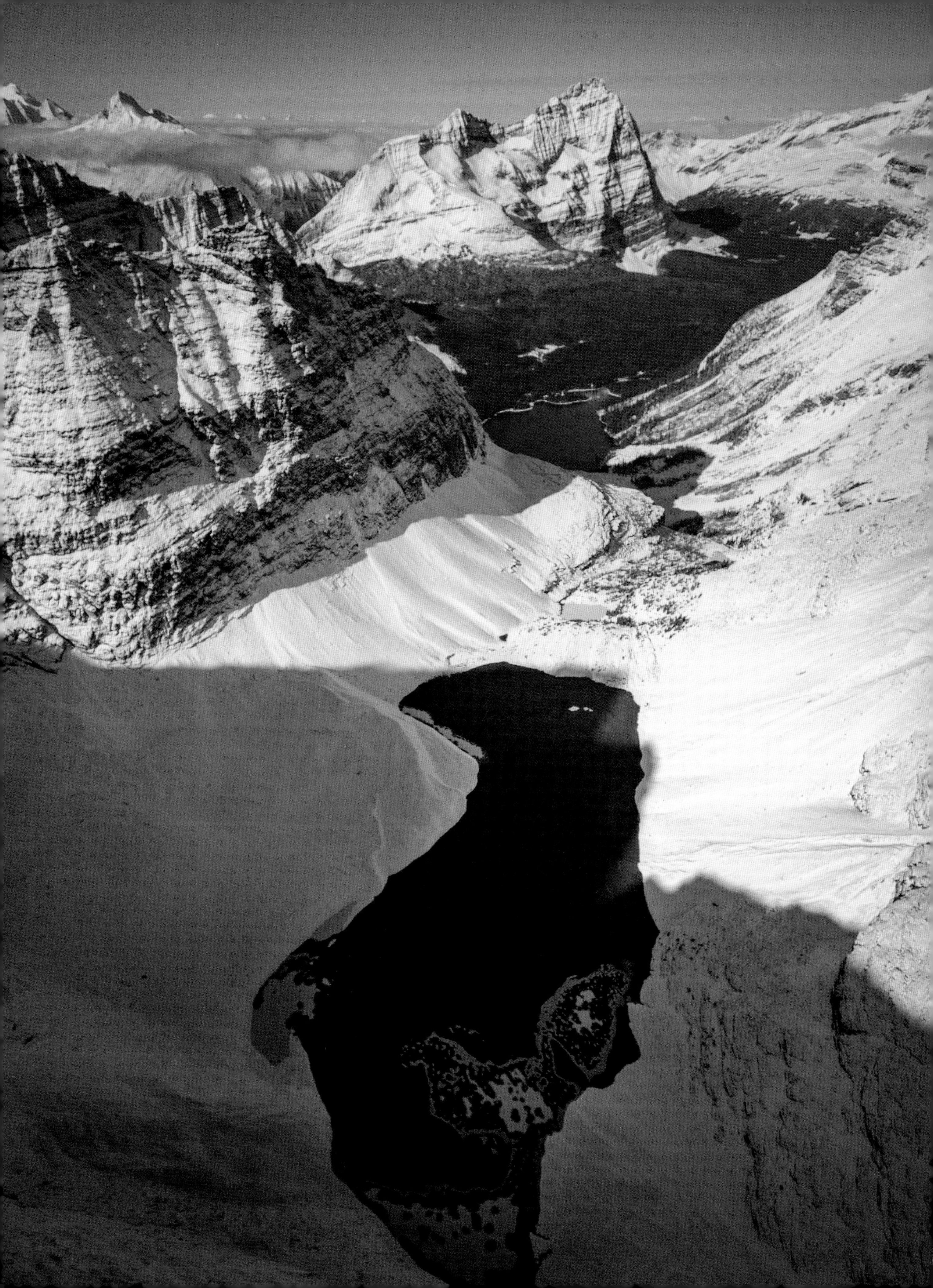

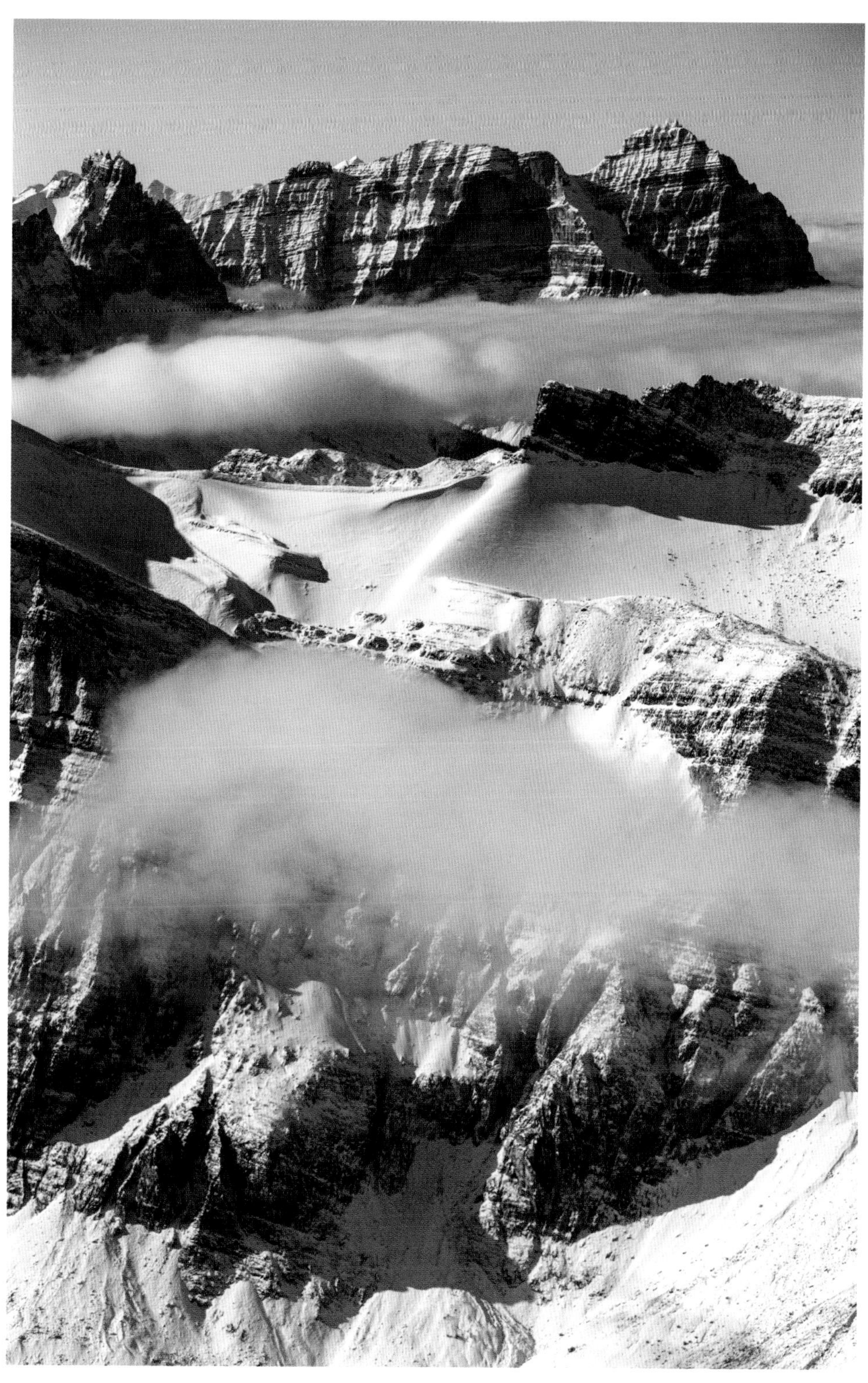

Opposite: Ice forms on Lake Oesa, with Lake O'Hara in the background, 150 metres below. The elegant, larch-skirted peak in the background is Odaray Mountain.

Above: Ranges of Yoho National Park, with Cathedral Crags (l) and immense Mount Stephen (r) rearing their heads at the back.

Overleaf: The Goodsir Towers, the highest peaks in the Ottertail Range, emerge from an early-morning cloud inversion.

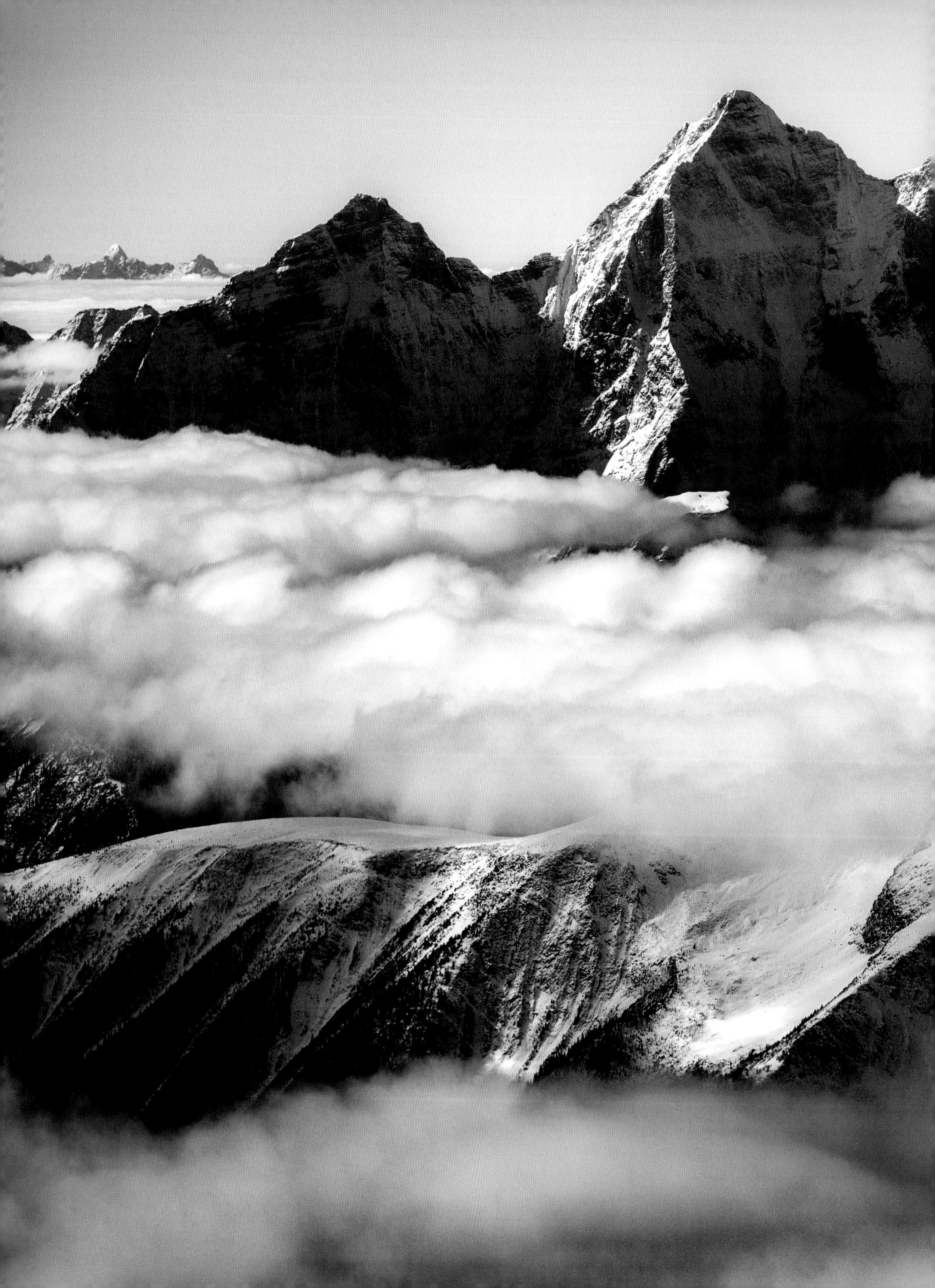

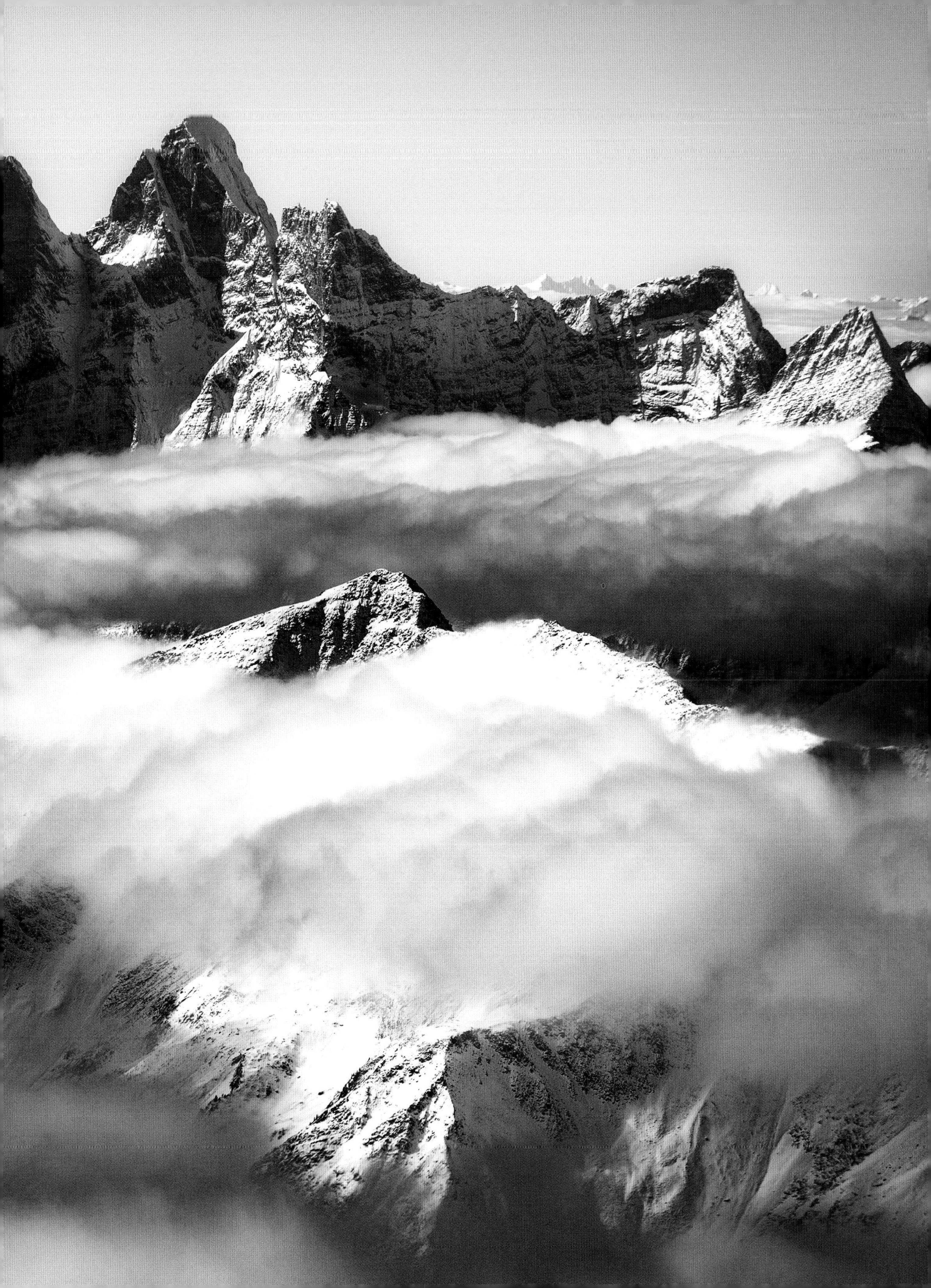

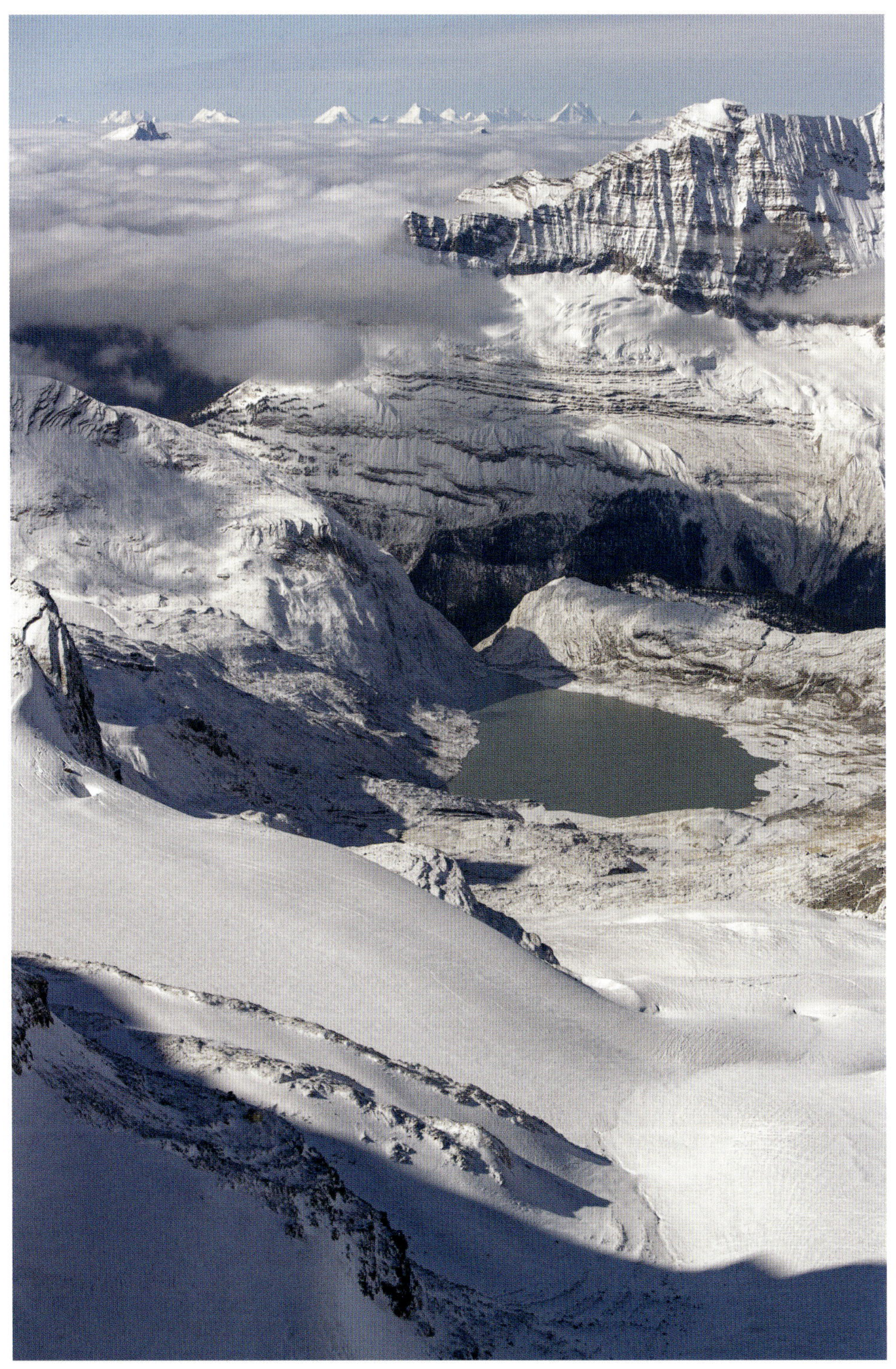

Above: A telephoto view of the unnamed lake that feeds Takakkaw Falls. At the bottom of the frame, on a ridge in the shadows, is the yellow Scott Duncan Hut, the last stopping point along the traverse of the Wapta and Waputik icefields. Across the valley is the Iceline Trail, while the distant peaks lie beyond the Canadian Rockies.

Opposite: The extensive Waputik Icefield covers the lower slopes of Mount Balfour, the highest point in the Wapta/Waputik area, at 3272 metres.

Overleaf: The Kicking Horse River carves its way through the landscape near Field, BC.

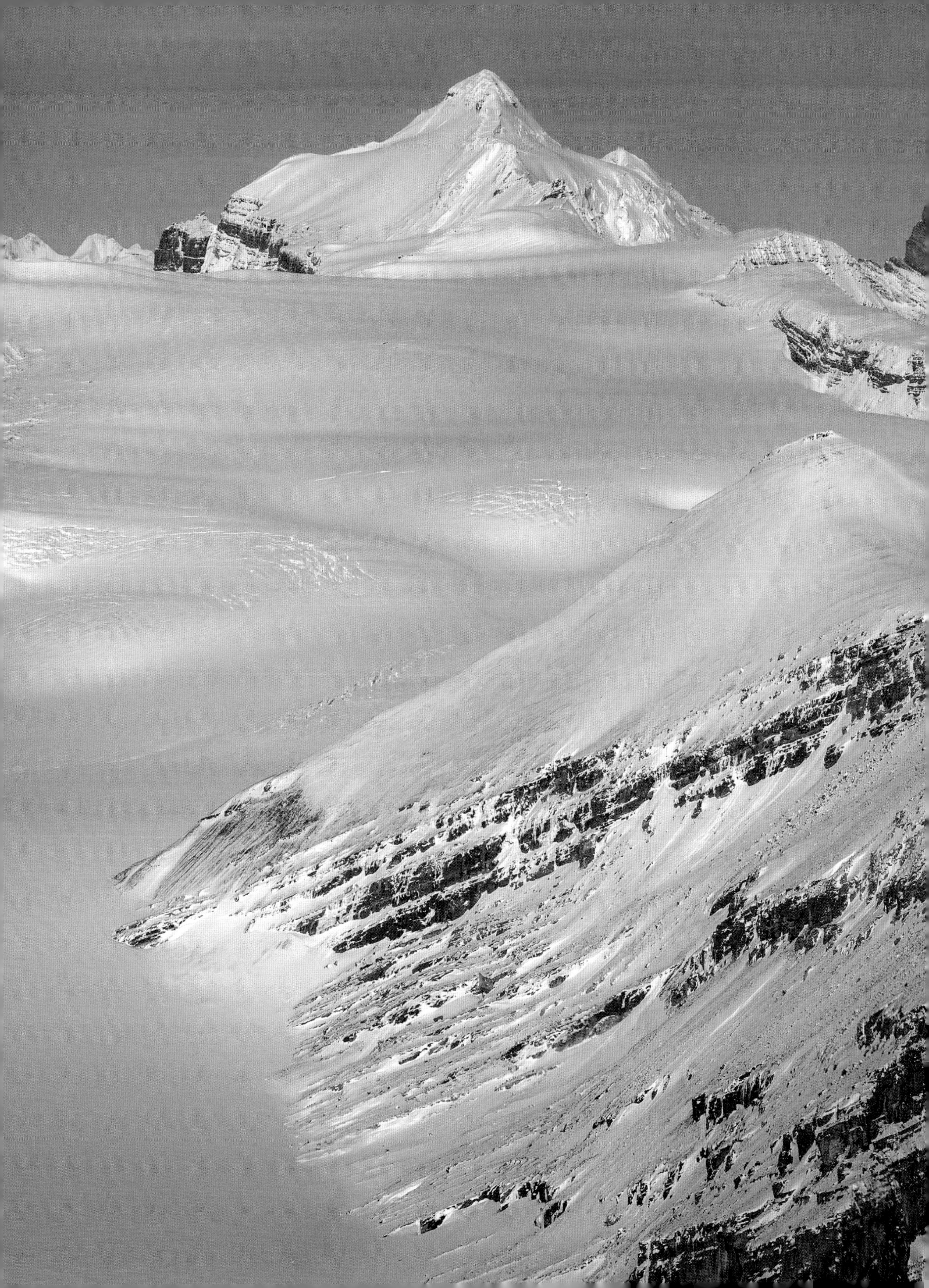

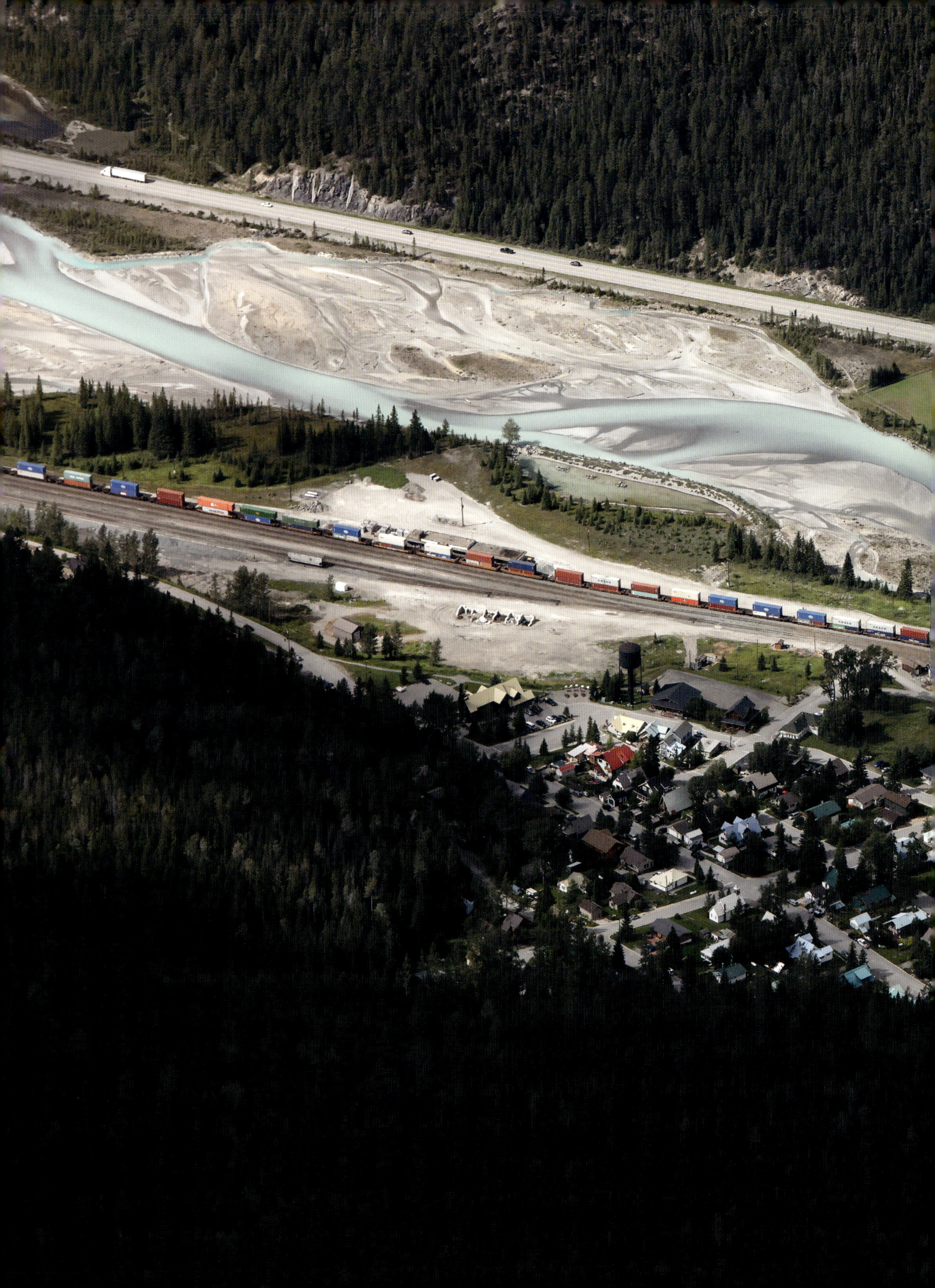

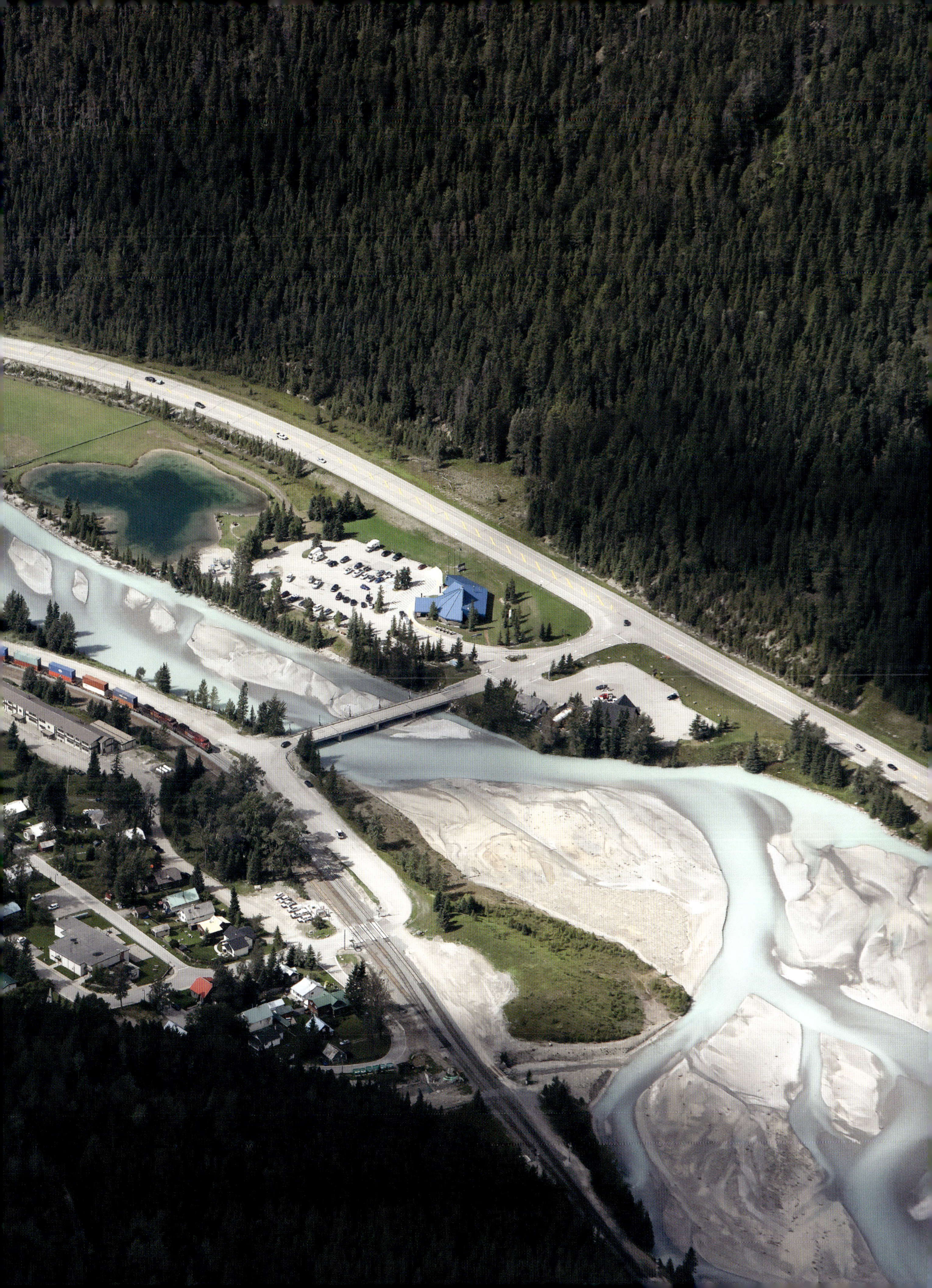

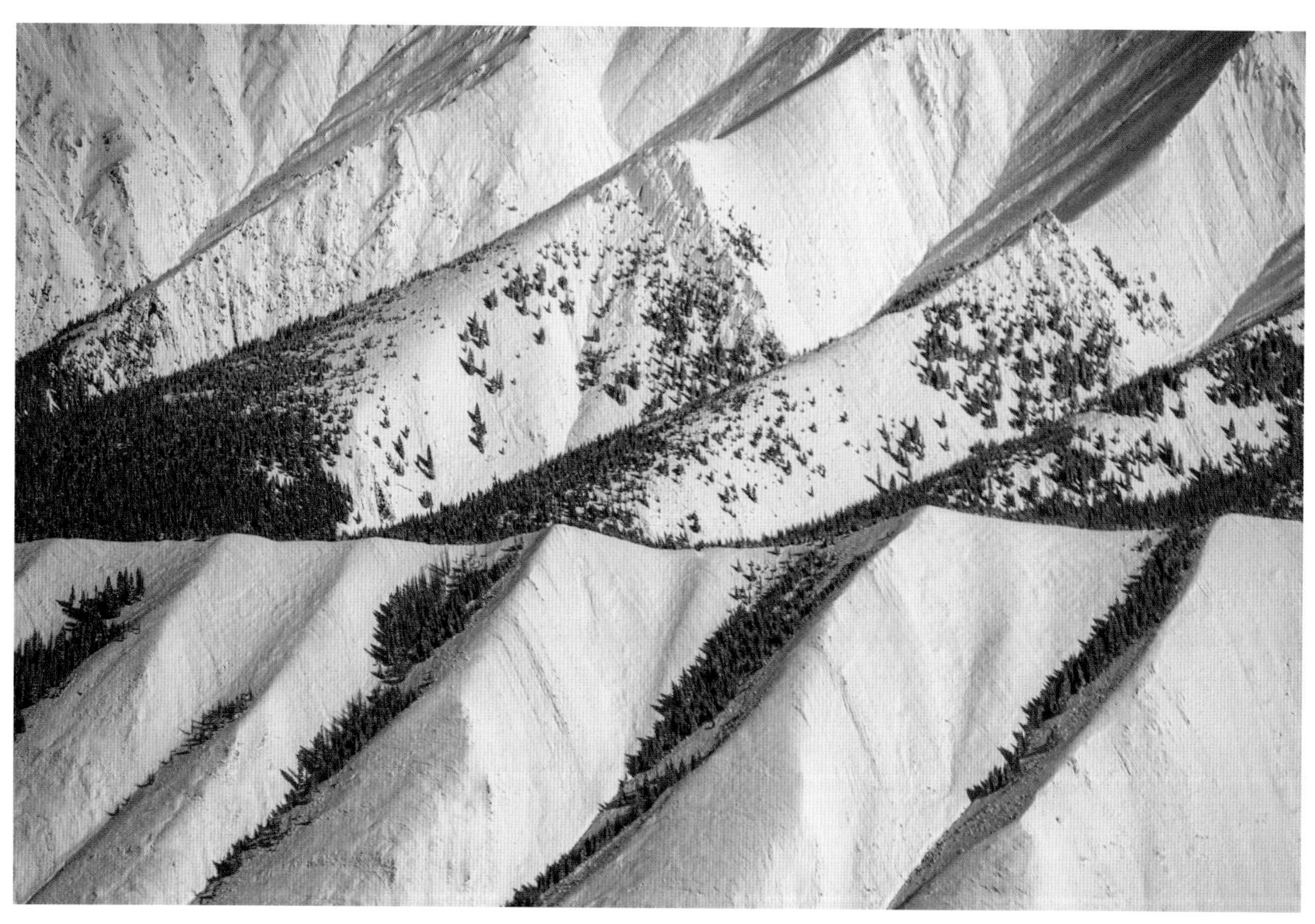

Above: Mountain folds and snow-dusted trees of Kootenay National Park.

Opposite: The up-thrust ranges of Kootenay National Park look like a frozen ocean from the air. Mount Assiniboine is clearly visible 70 kilometres away.

Overleaf: The rarely seen west side of Moraine Lake's Ten Peaks, with (l–r) Neptuak, Deltaform, Tuzo and Allen, plus the broad pyramid of Mount Temple near the centre.

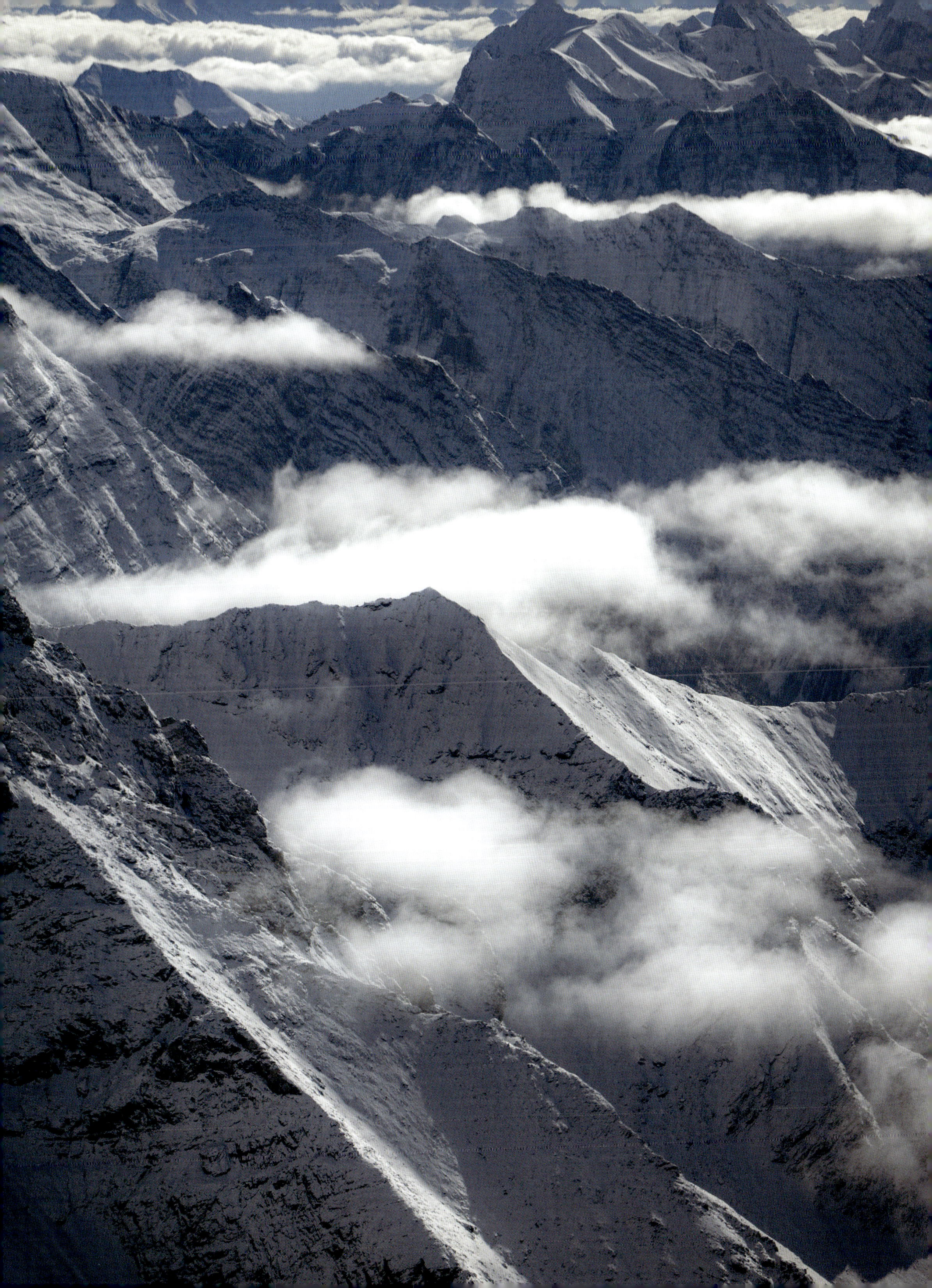

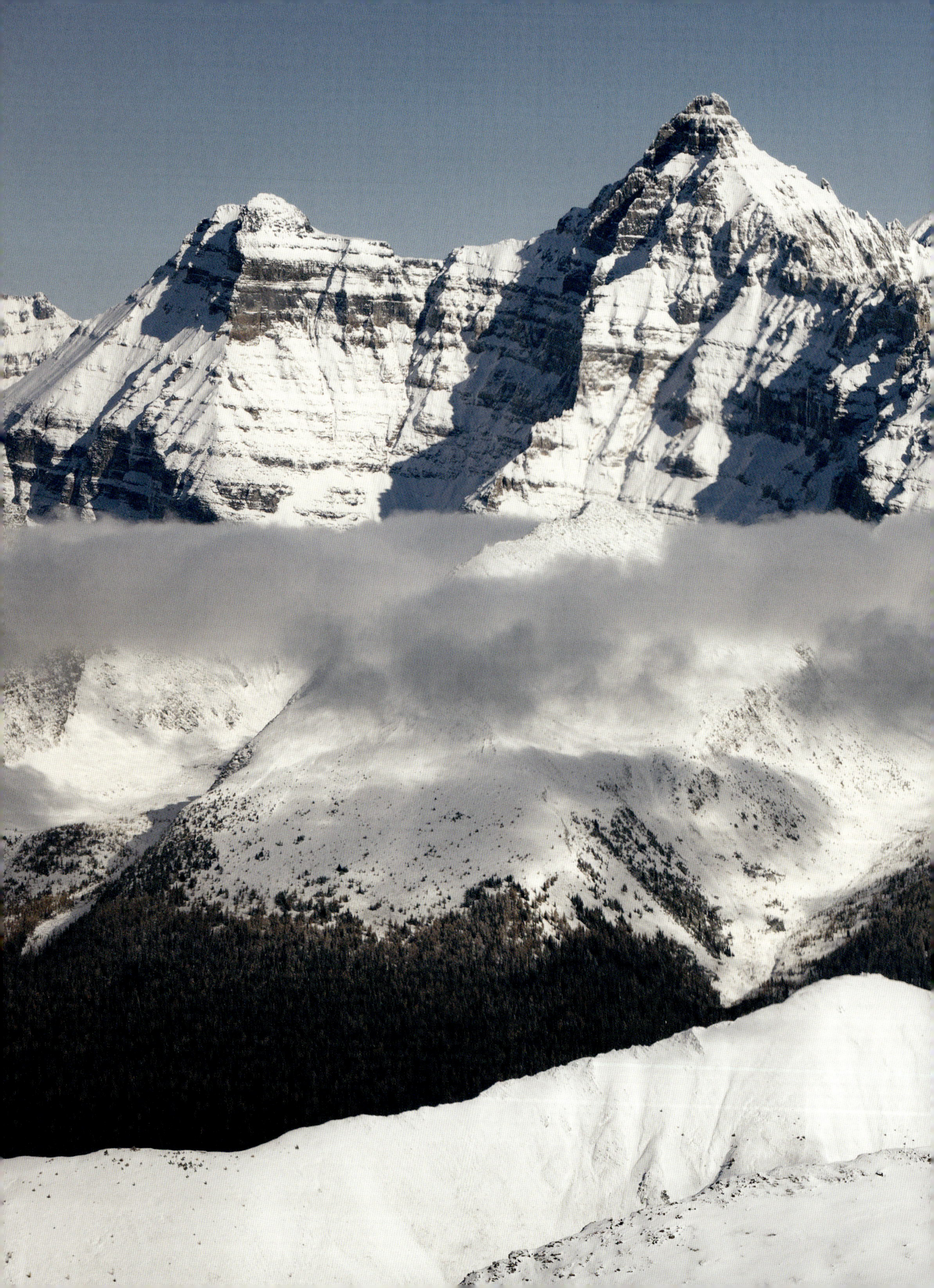

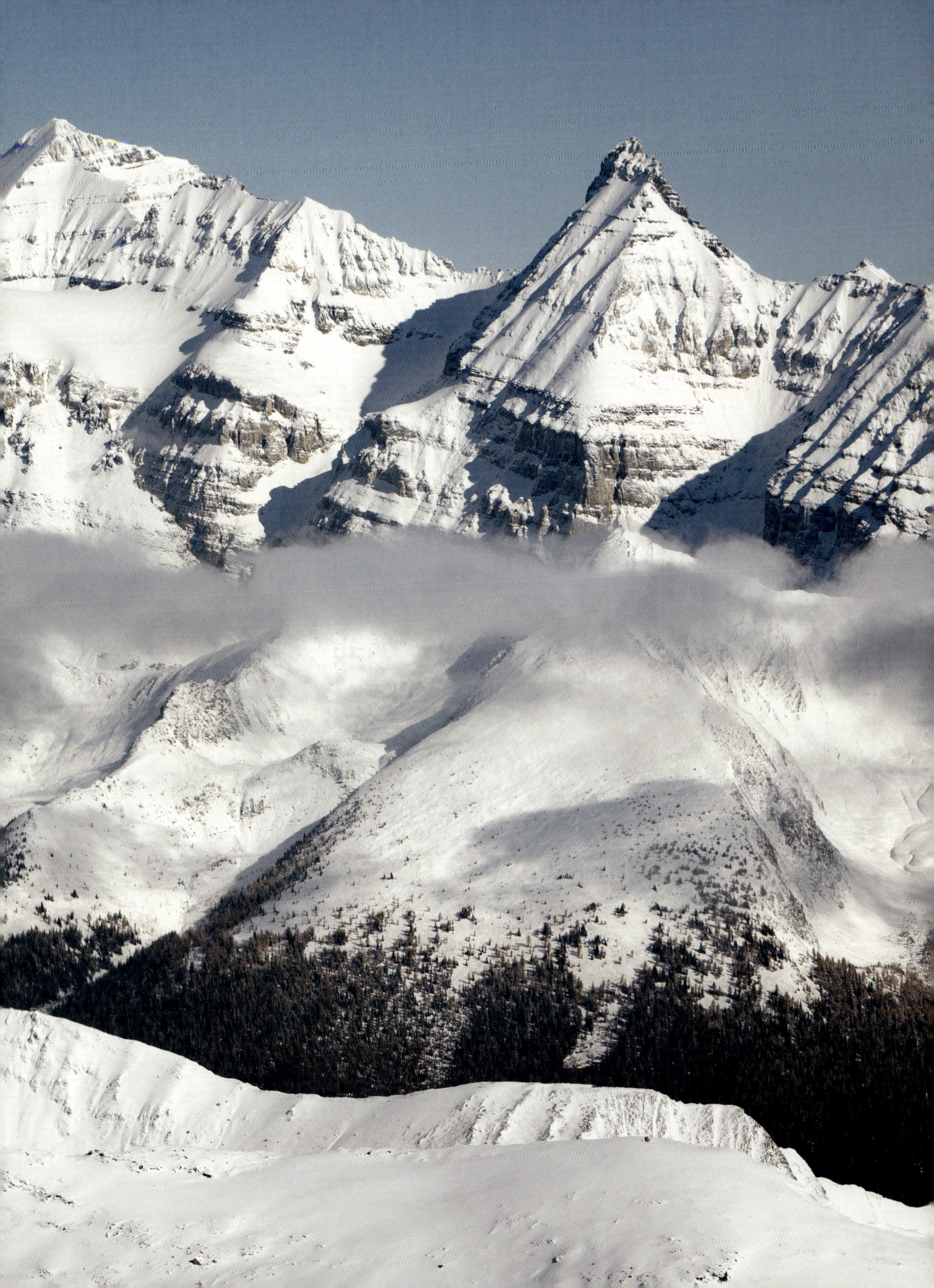

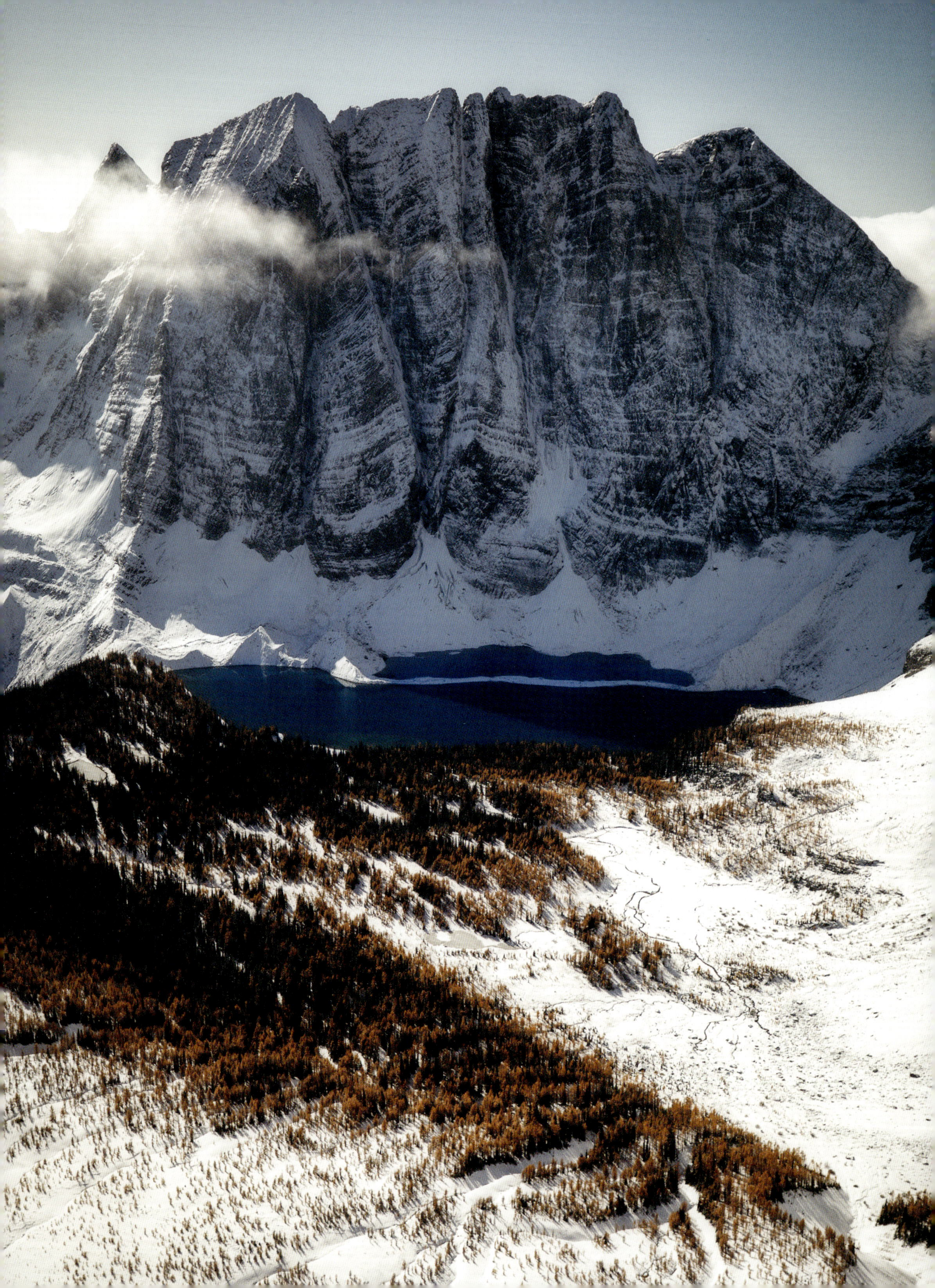

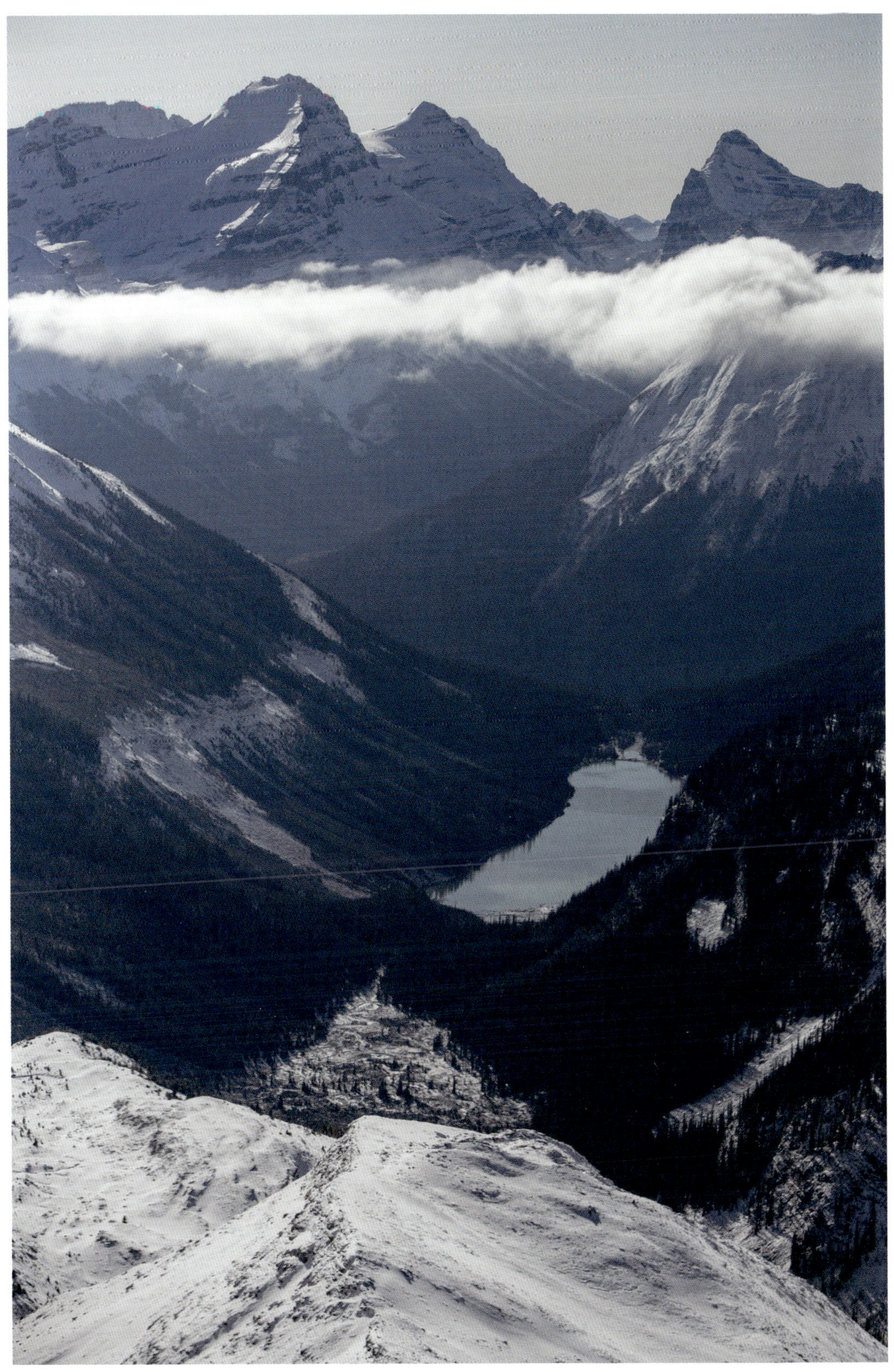

Opposite: Floe Lake and Floe Peak make for a most scenic combination
as fall and winter overlap in Kootenay National Park.

Above: Peaceful Sherbrooke Lake on a misty morning in the
mountains. Across the way is the valley of Lake O'Hara.

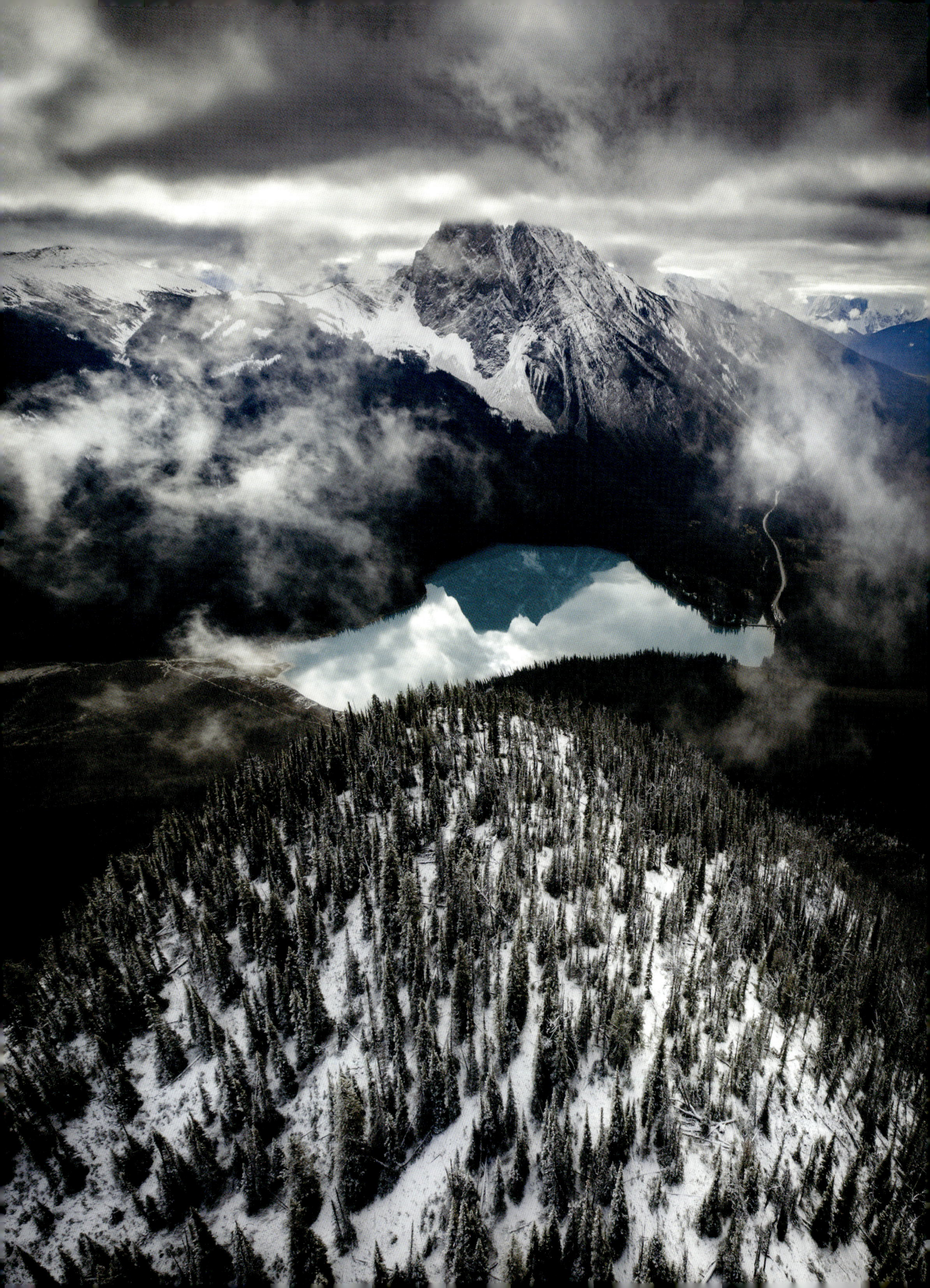

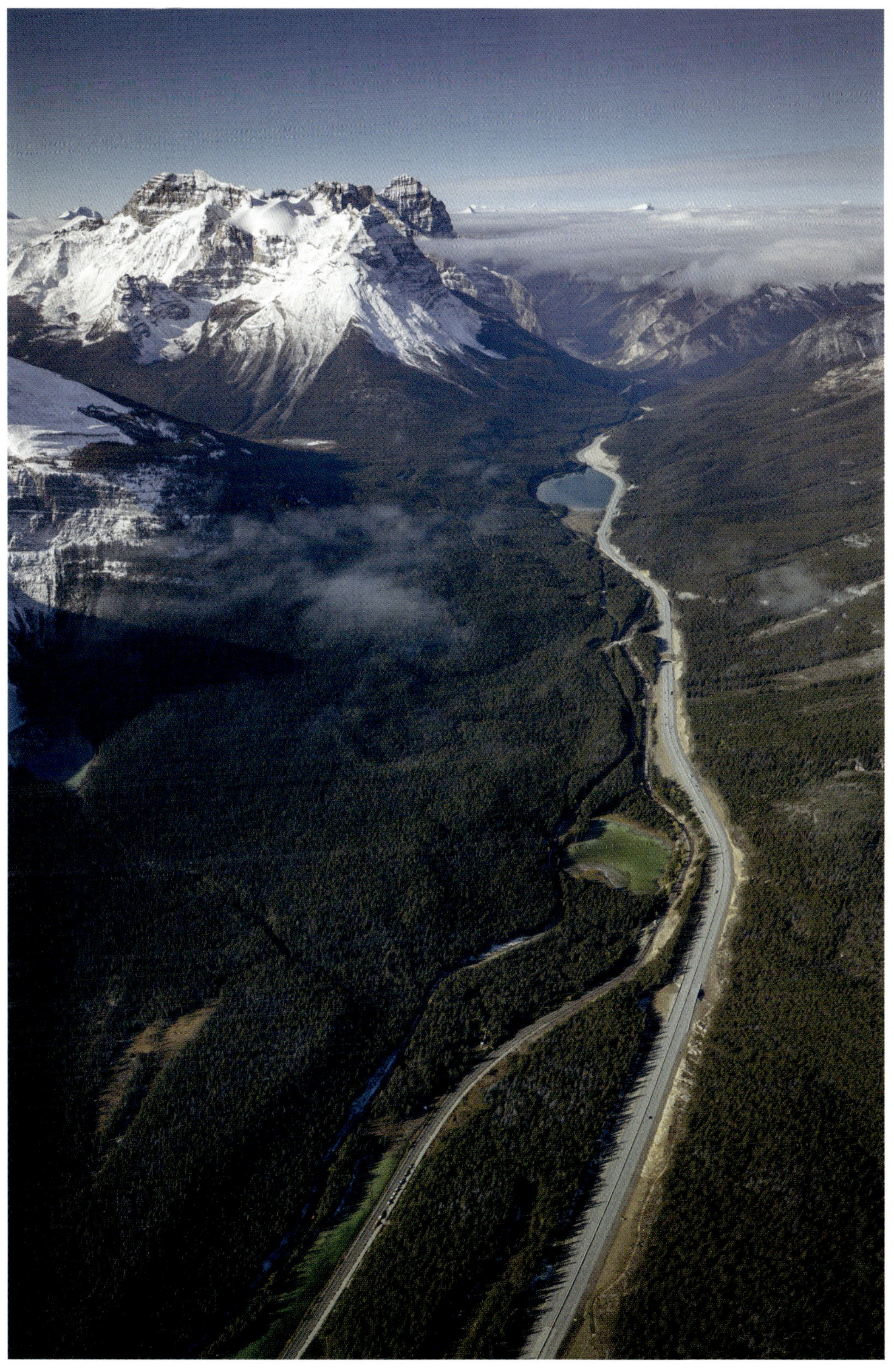

Opposite: Only the reflection reveals the peaks of Mount Burgess in this shot of Emerald Lake.

Above: The Trans-Canada Highway links Alberta and British Columbia at Kicking Horse Pass. Summit Lake is visible at the very bottom of the image, next to the railway tracks. Sink and Wapta lakes are also visible a little farther along the highway.

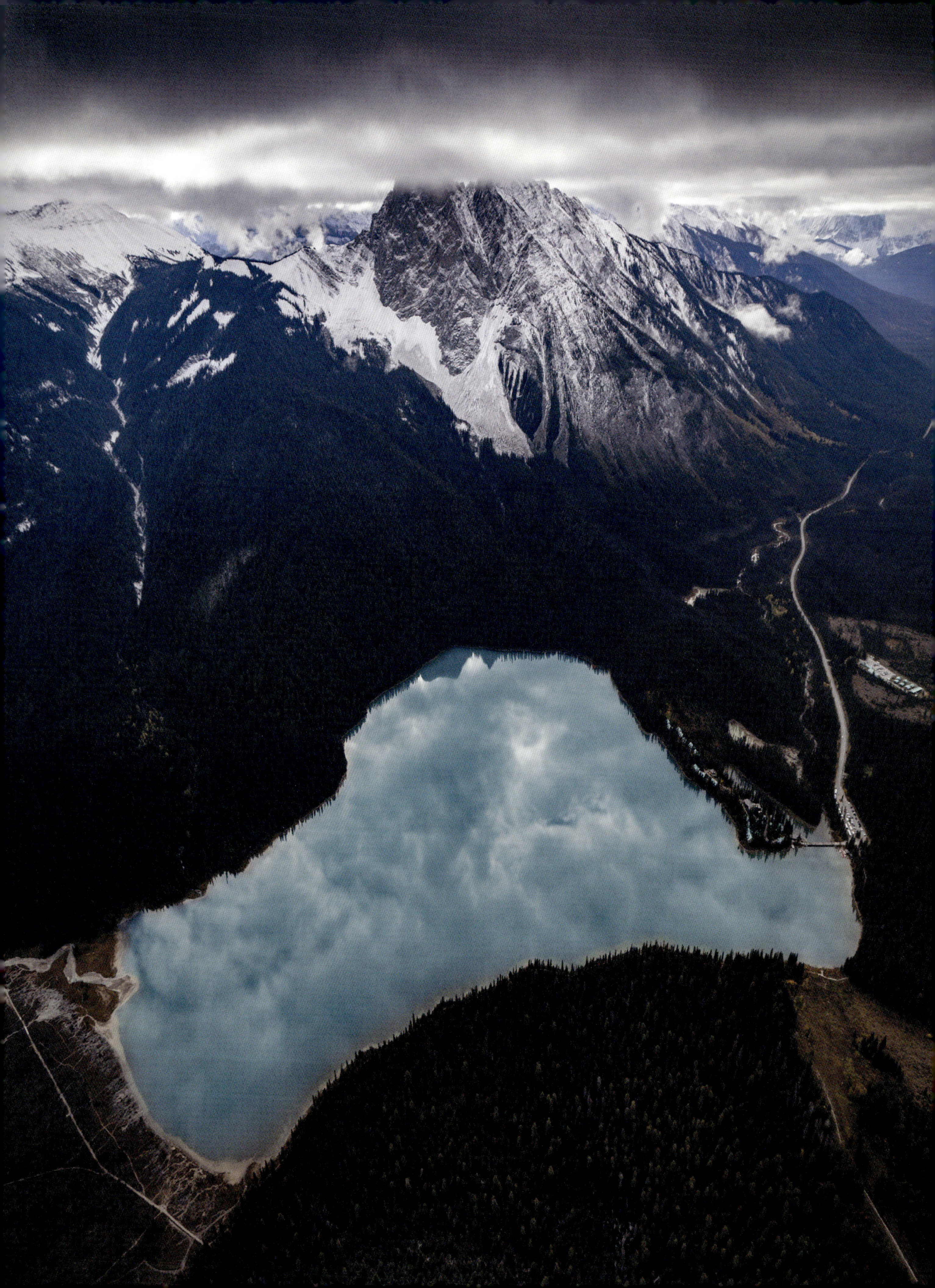

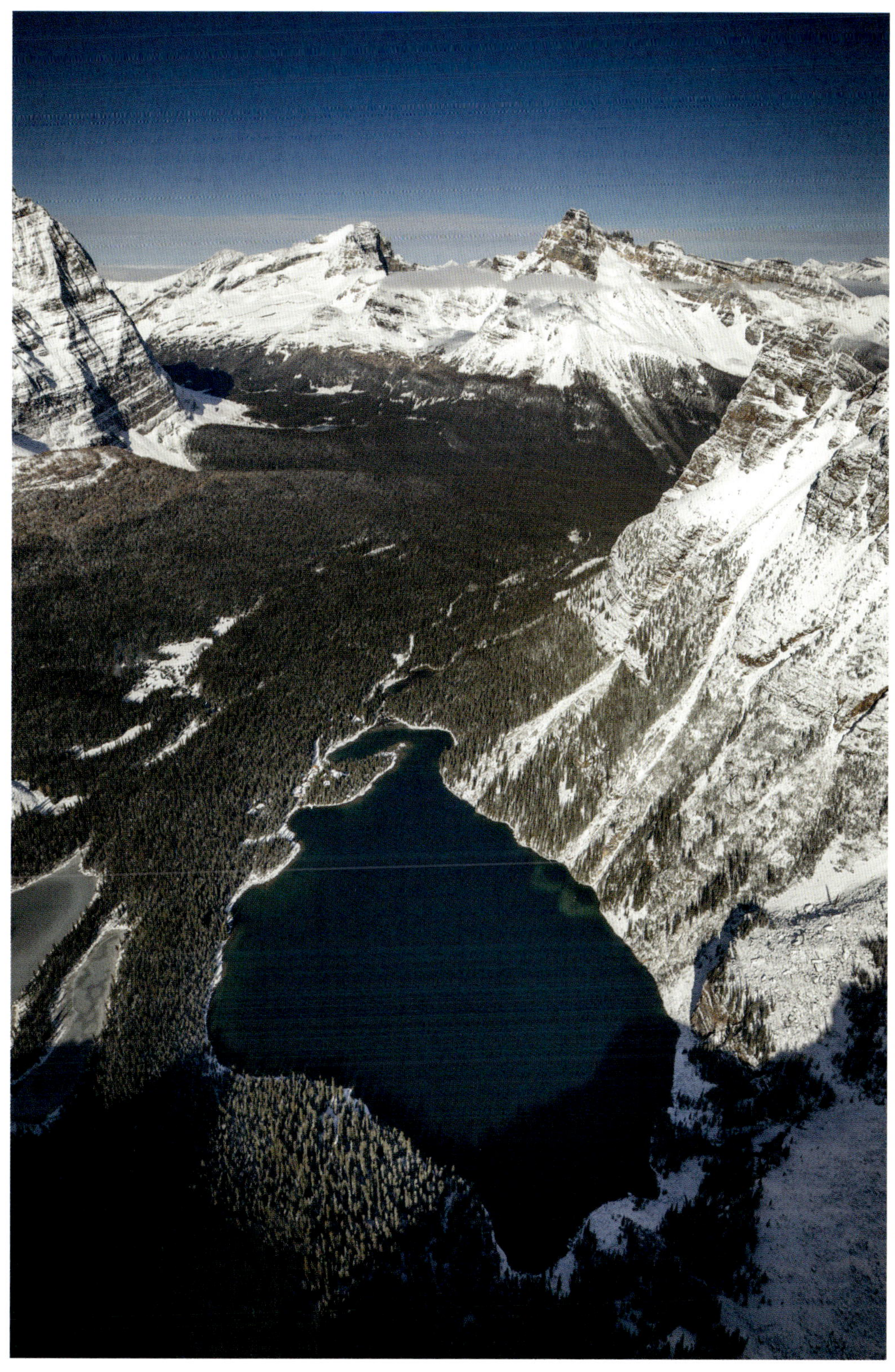

Opposite: Emerald Lake Lodge lies on the south edge of its namesake lake at the base of Mount Burgess.

Above: Legendary Lake O'Hara on a perfect fall morning. Mount Stephen and Cathedral Mountain form the backdrop.

Overleaf: Often dubbed "the most beautiful road in the world," the Icefields Parkway winds past the hulking mass of Mount Wilson in northern Banff National Park.

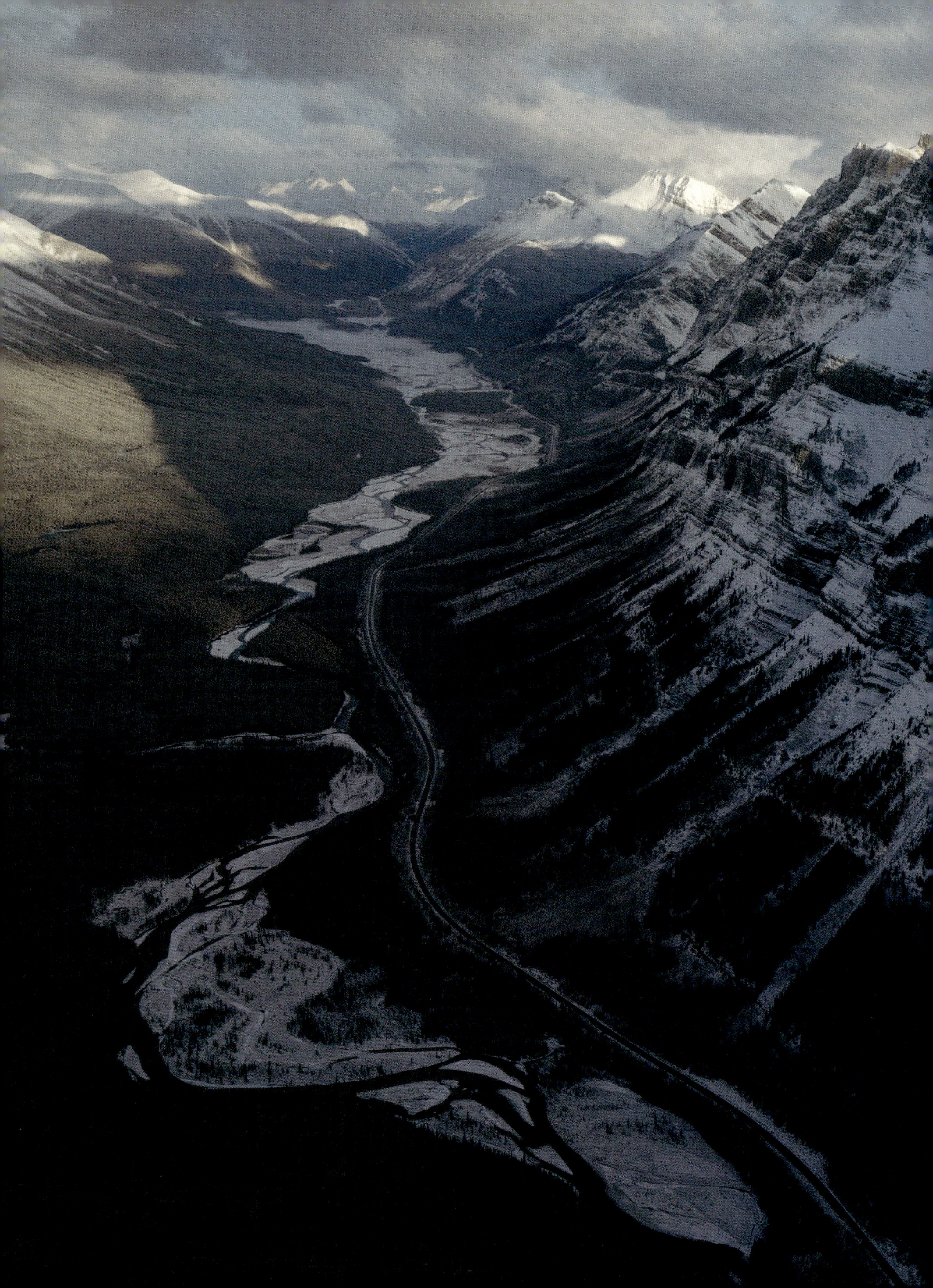

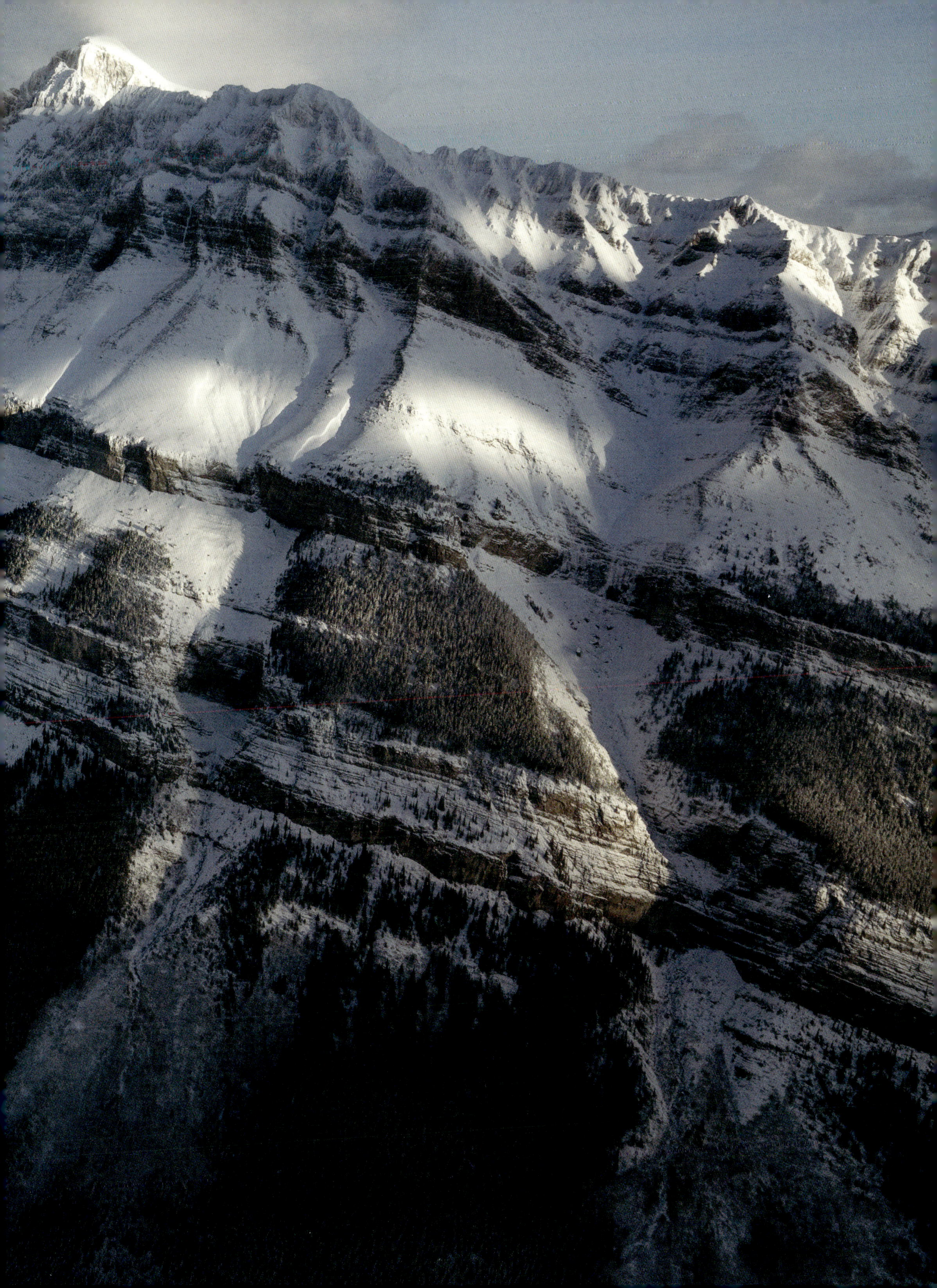

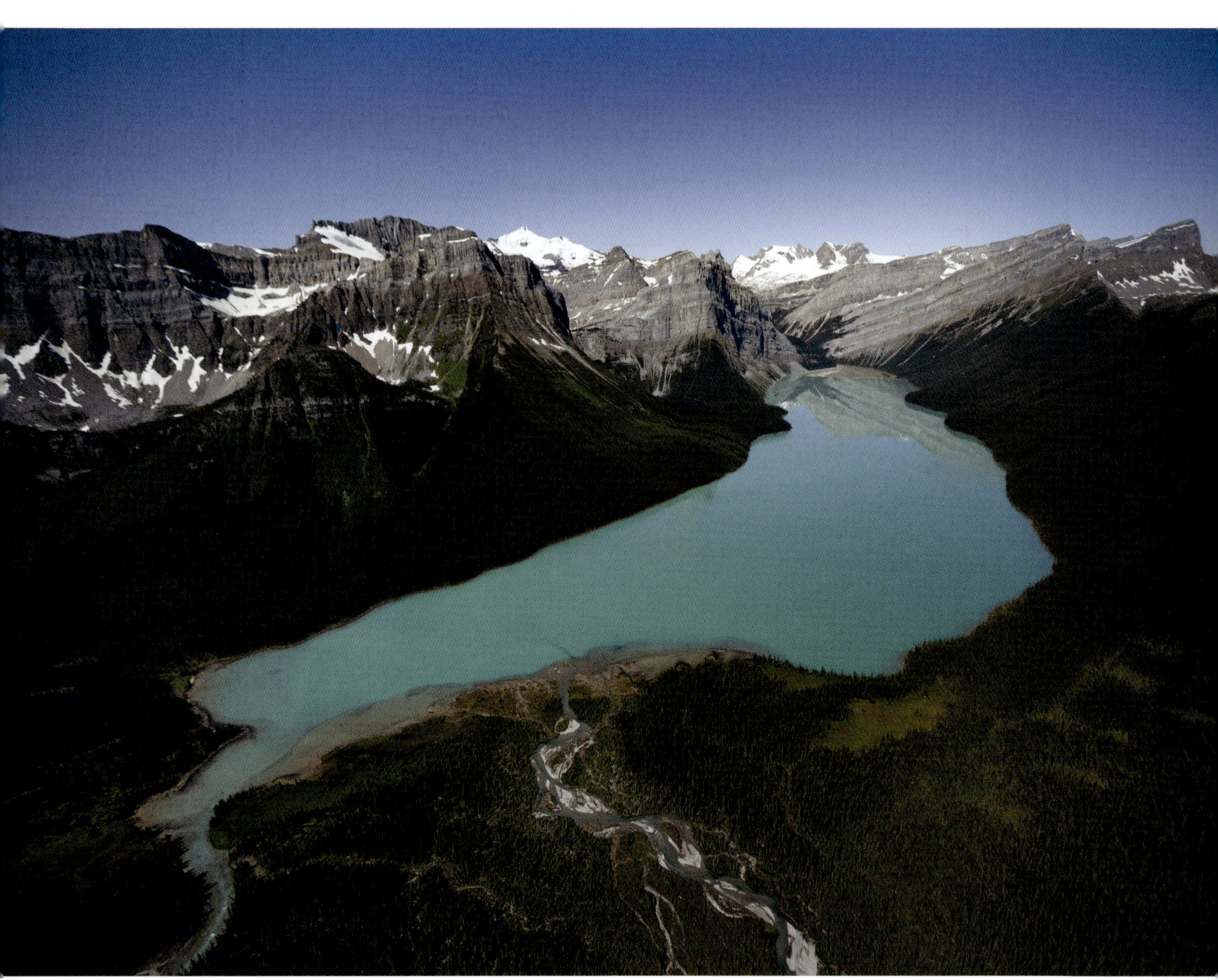

Opposite: Summertime at Hector Lake. Mount Balfour, the edge of the Wapta Icefield and Margaret Lake are visible in the distance.

Overleaf: One of the most beautiful of the mountain lakes along the Icefields Parkway, Bow Lake is pictured here with Crowfoot Mountain (l), the red-roofed Num-Ti-Jah Lodge and the Bow Glacier feeding into a small basin above a waterfall. These are the headwaters of the Bow River, which will carve its way towards Lake Louise, Banff, then Canmore and into the Prairies beyond before eventually feeding into Hudson Bay.

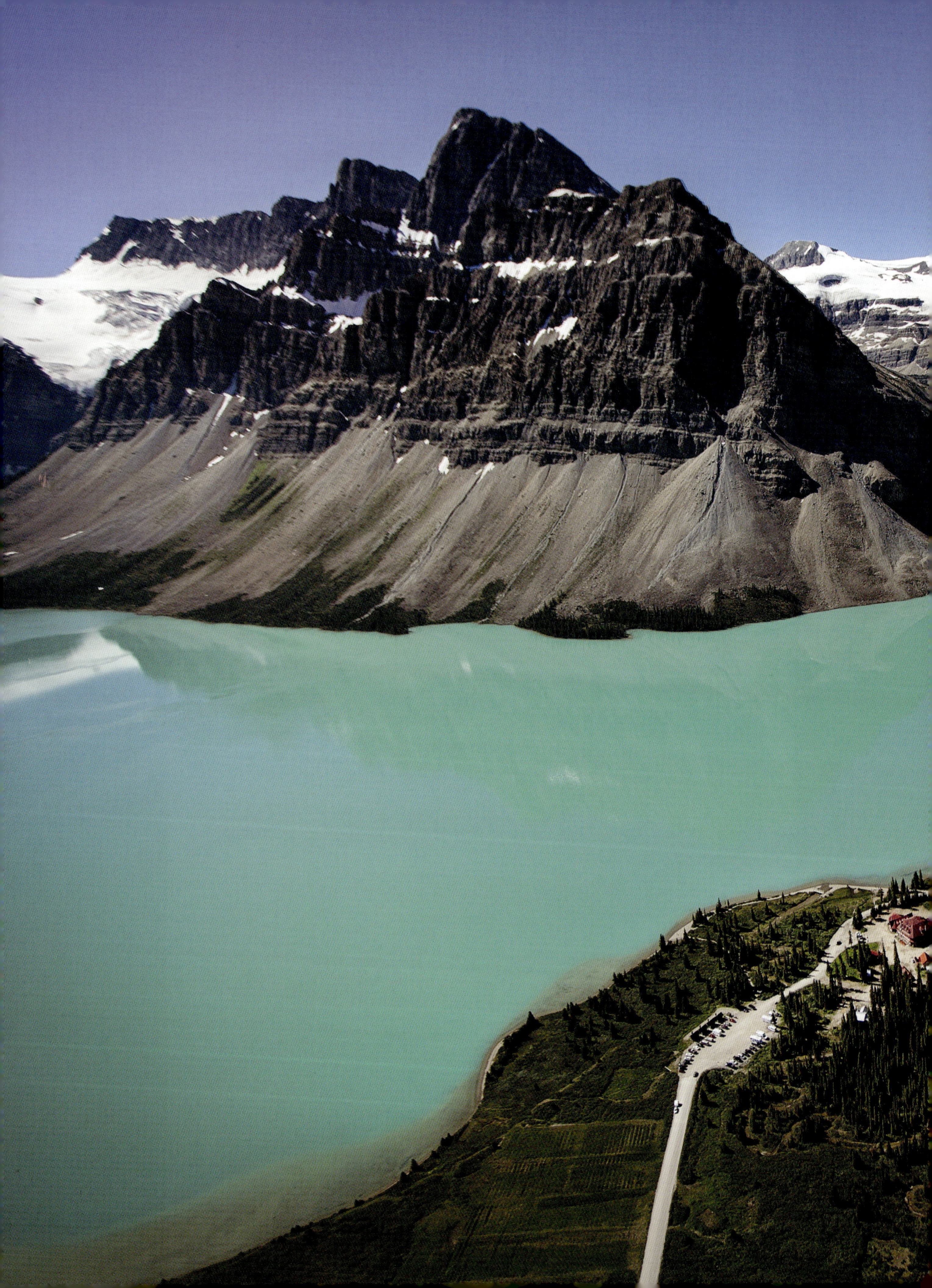

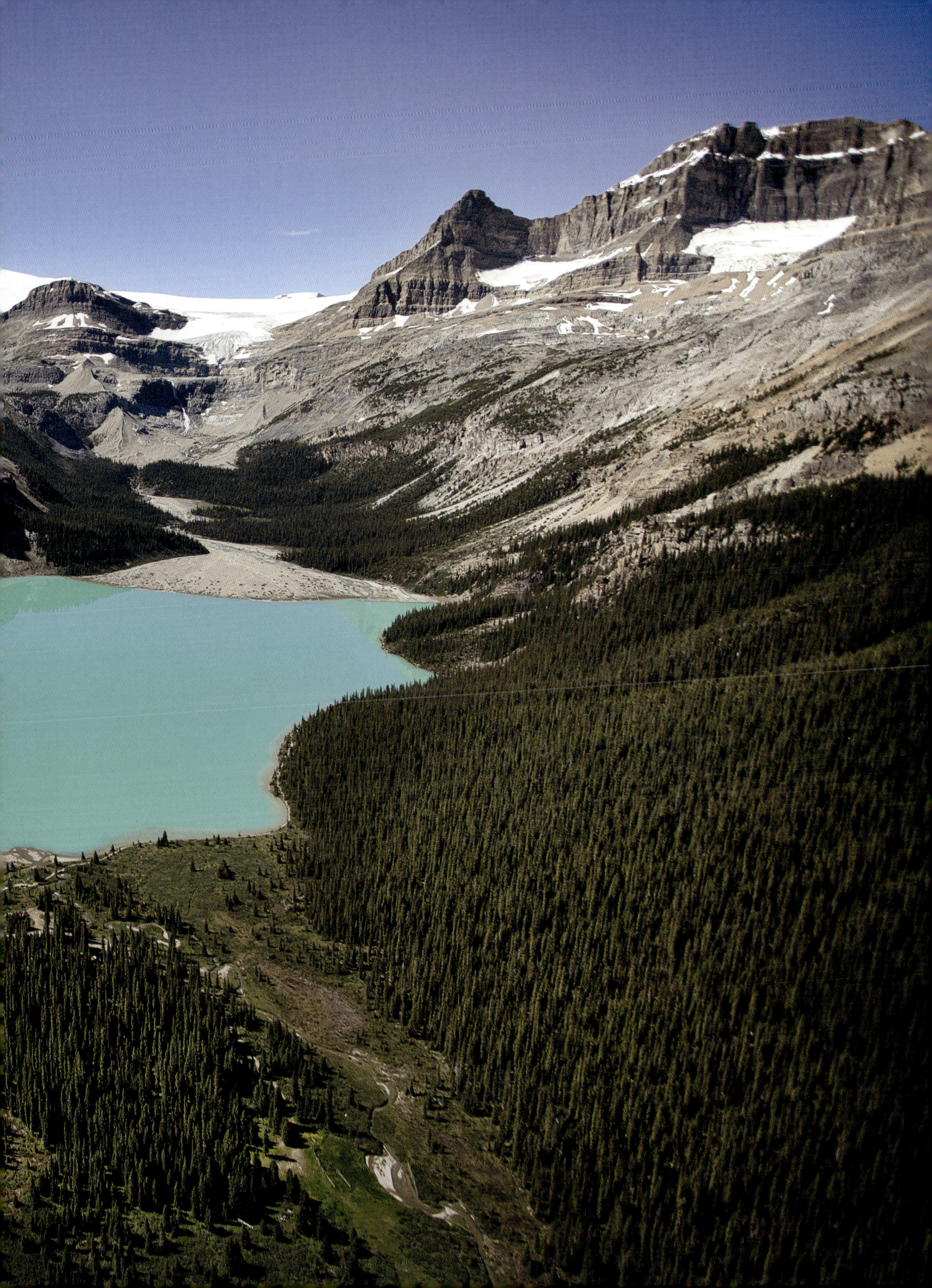

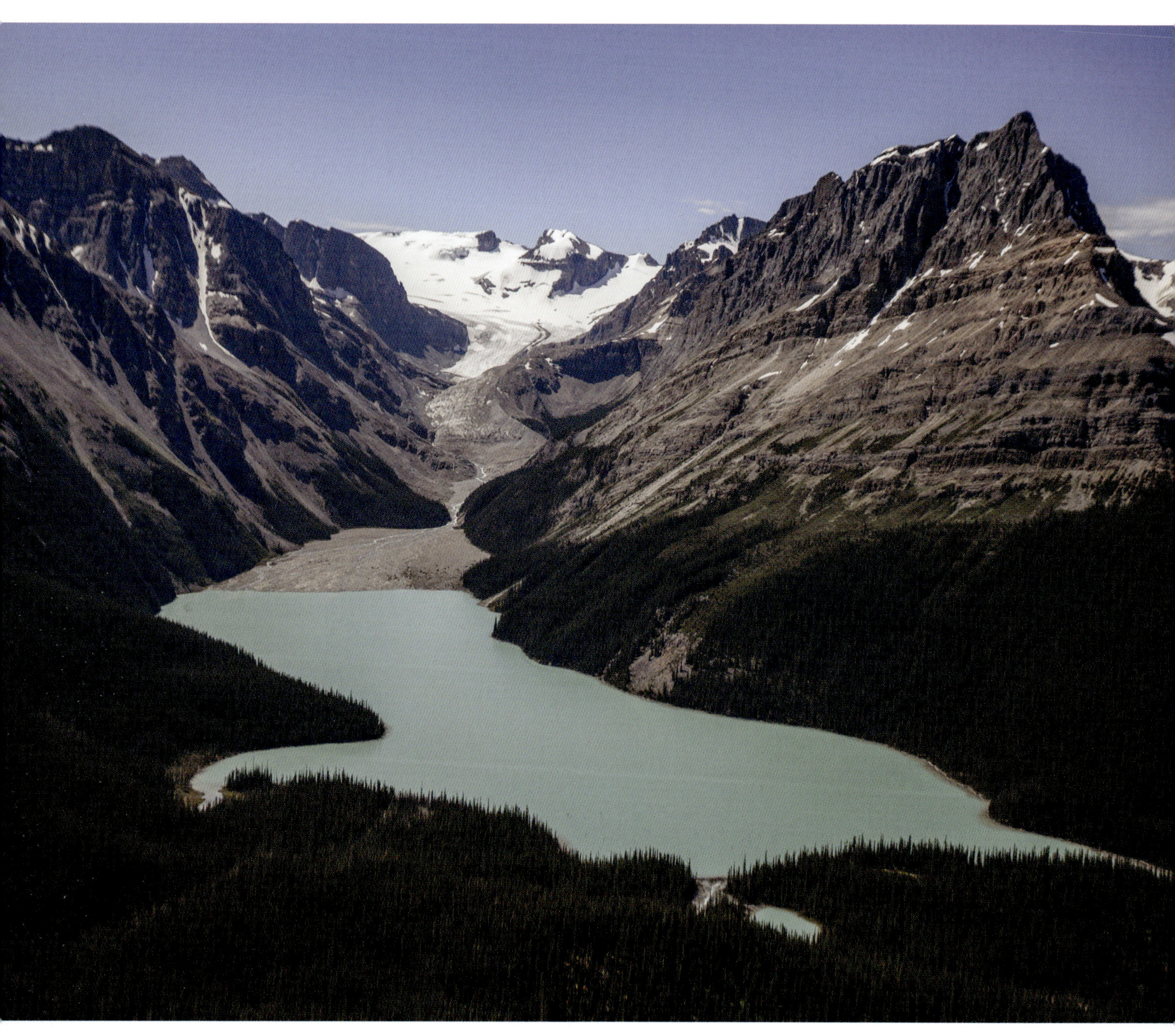

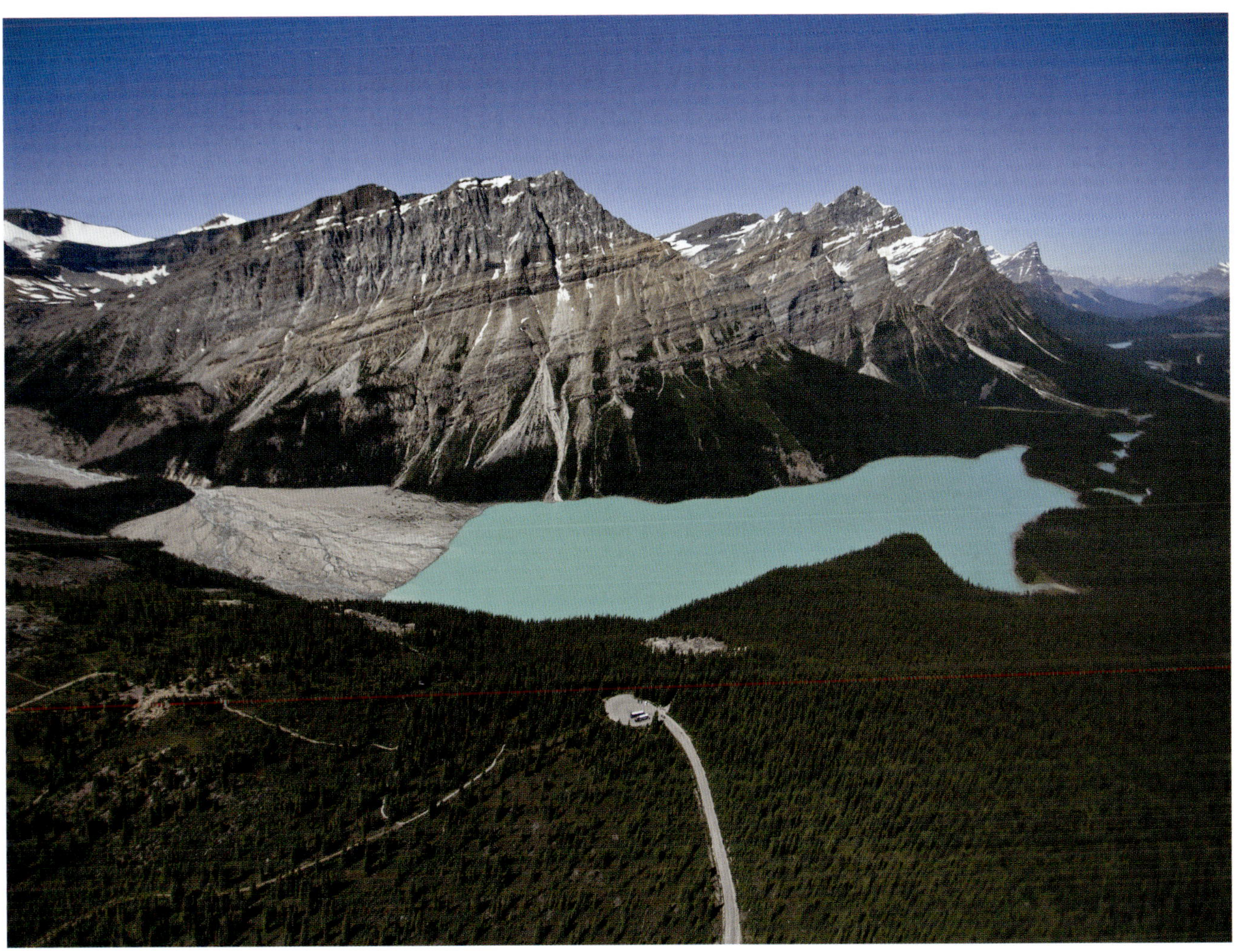

Opposite: The famous Peyto Lake as viewed from the north, with the ever-shrinking Peyto Glacier and Wapta Icefield beyond.

Above: Peyto Lake at the height of summer. The upper parking lot is visible at the bottom of the frame. Caldron Peak, Mount Patterson and pointy Mount Chephren form the skyline.

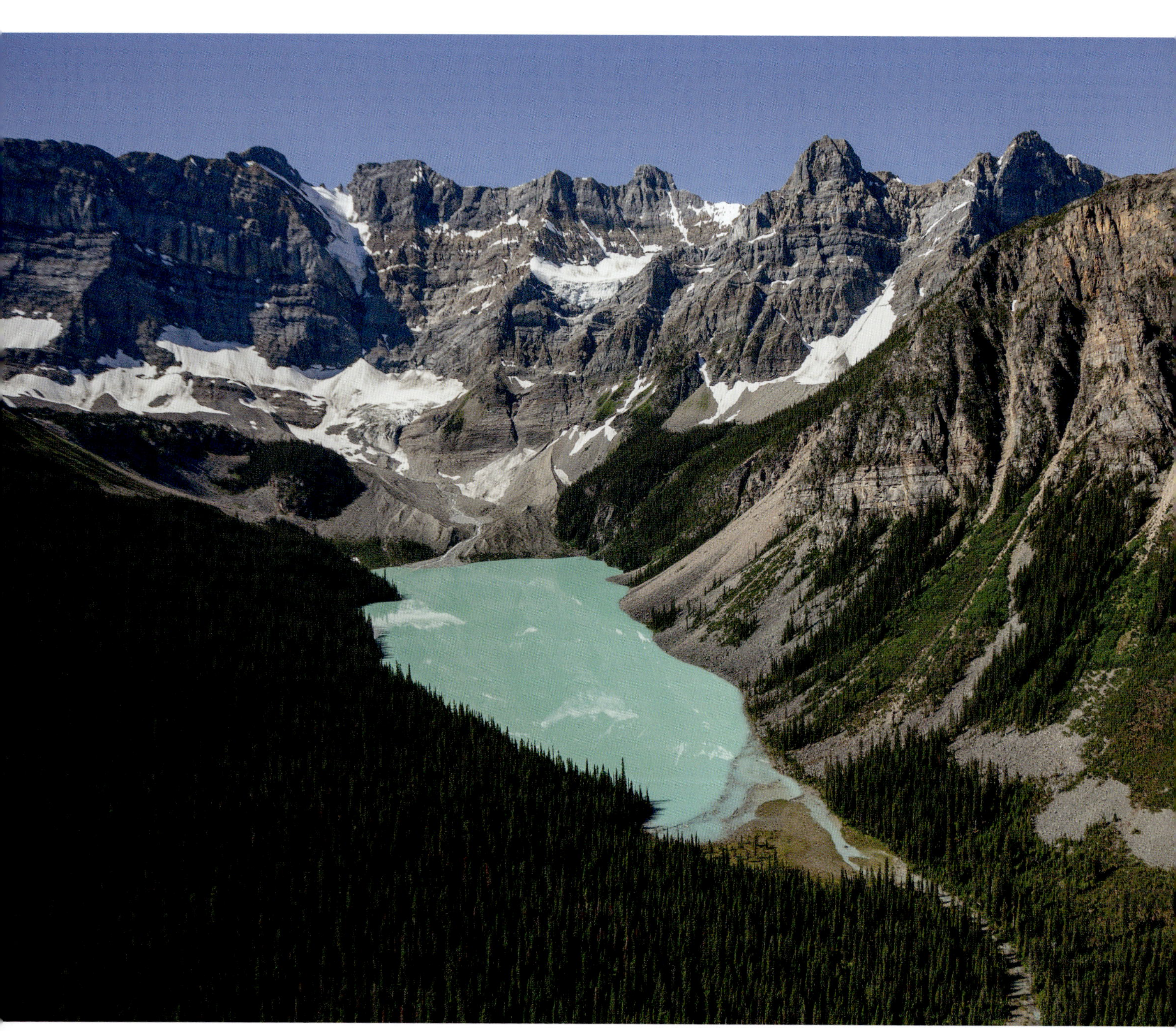

Opposite: Cirque Lake with the glacier-clad ramparts of the Great Divide rising beyond.

Overleaf: The Waterfowl Lakes campground is located in one of the most idyllic spots in Banff National Park, right between the two lakes.

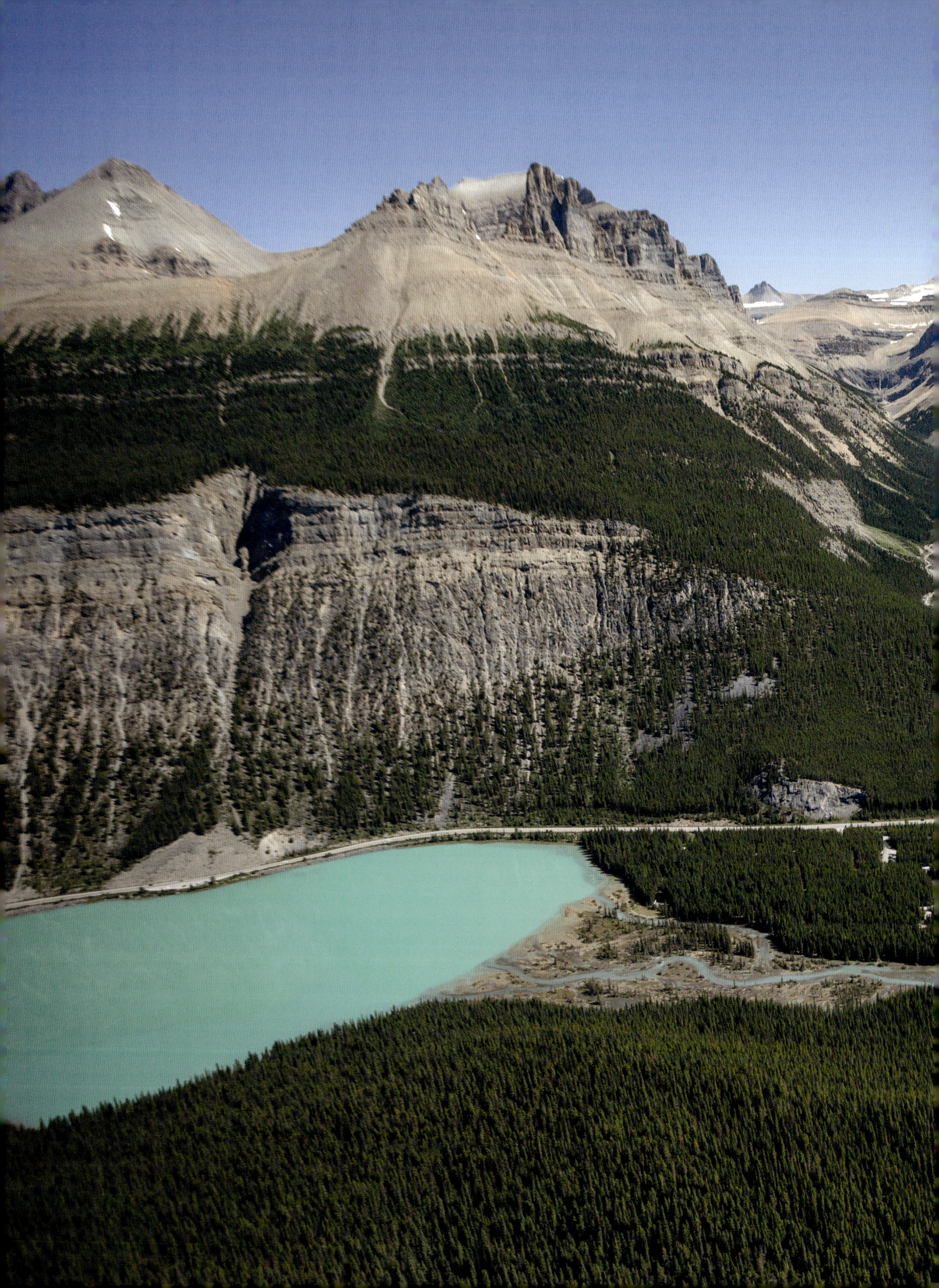

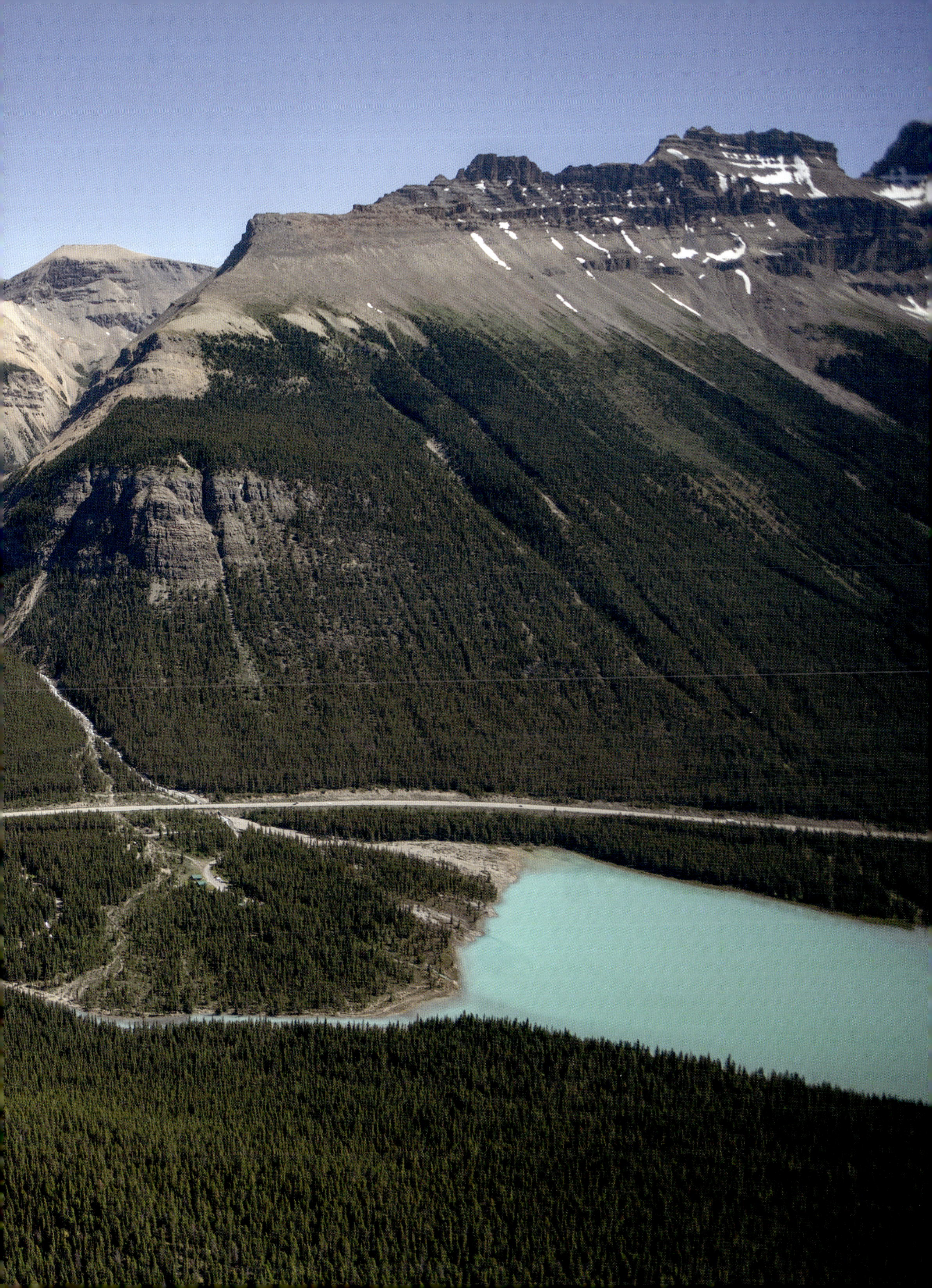

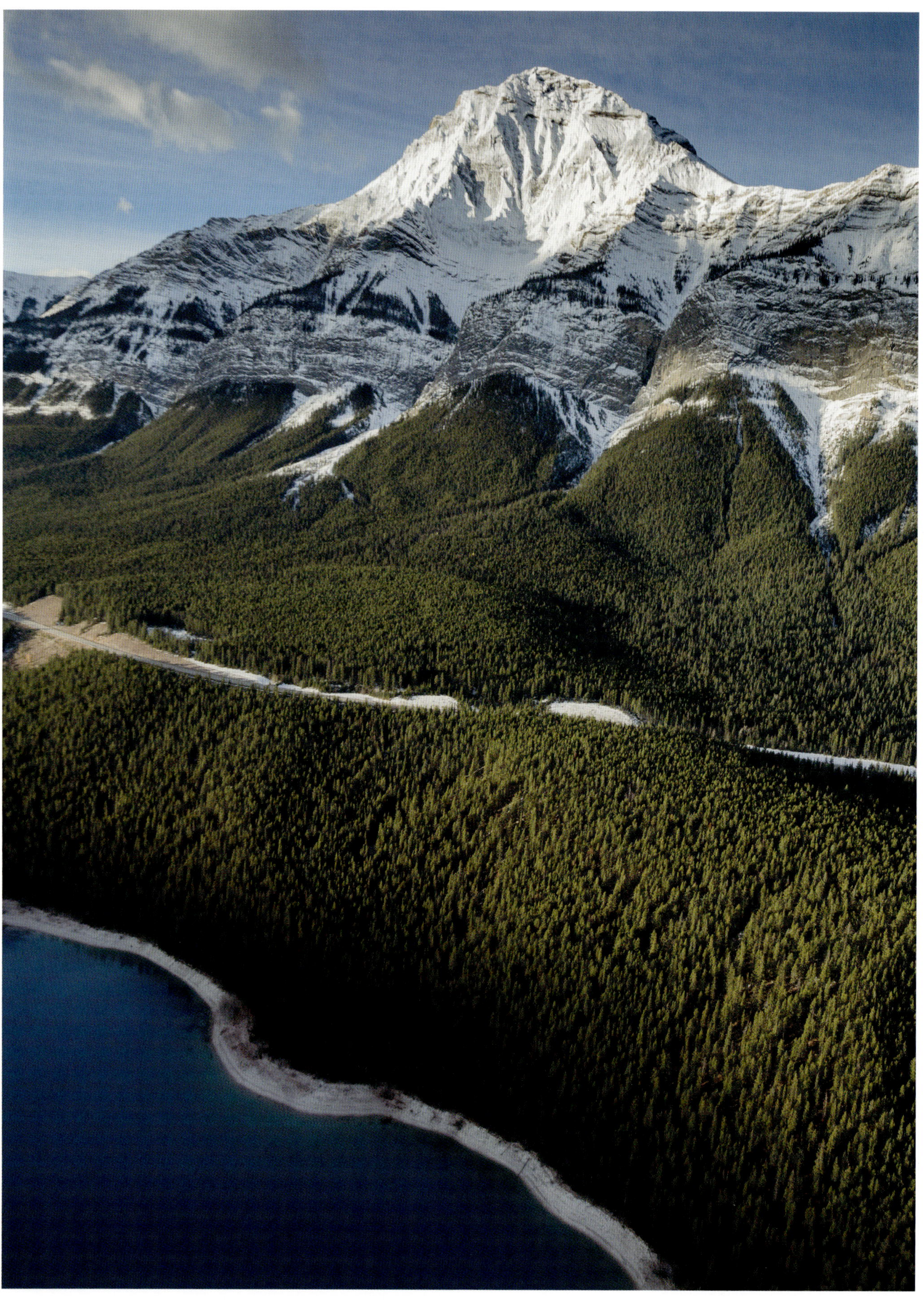

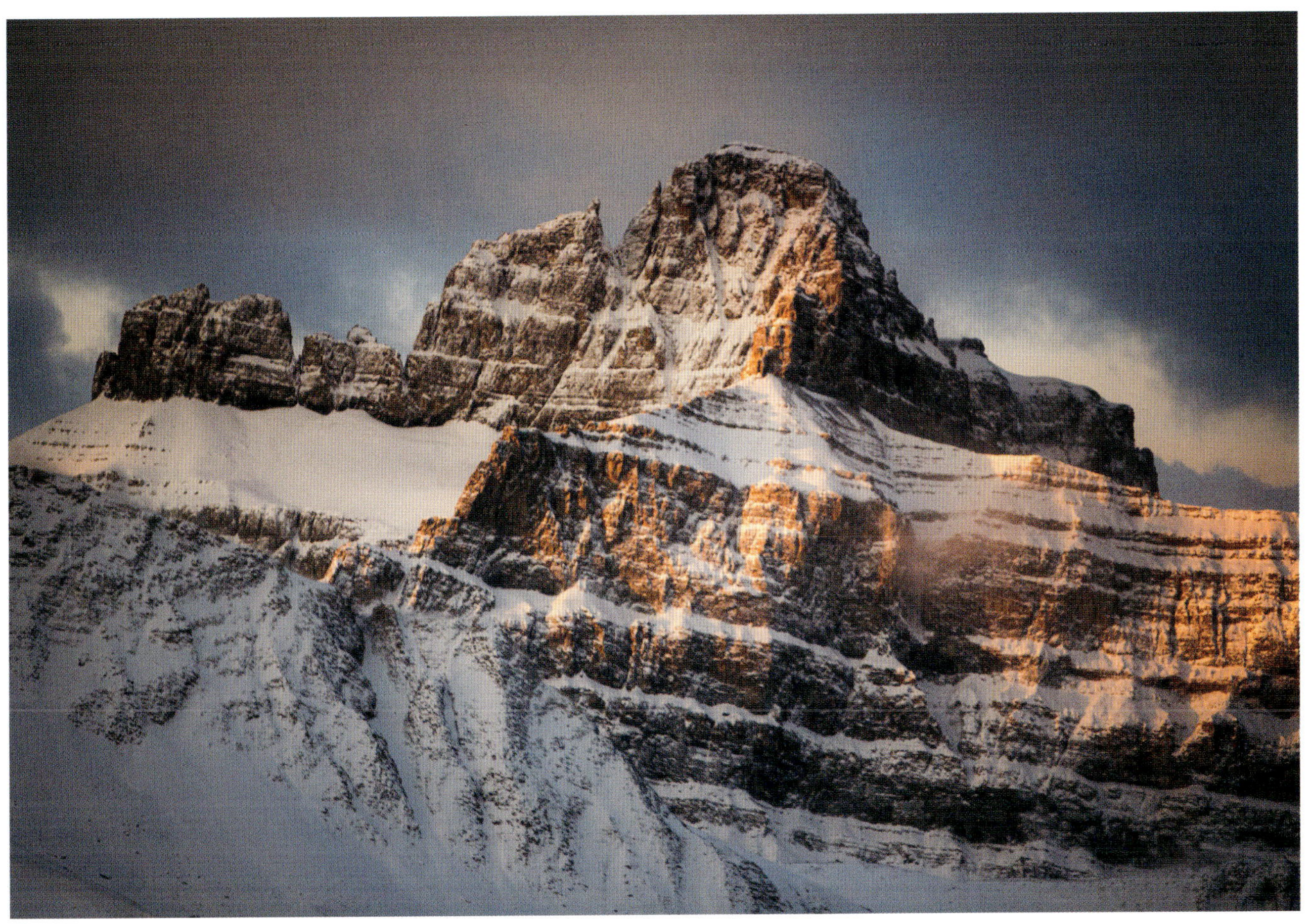

Opposite: The David Thompson Highway cuts through the forests of the Abraham Lake area,
just east of Banff National Park, on an October morning.
Above, Elliott Peak already has its winter look.

Above: First light on the chiselled peaks of the White Goat Wilderness,
just on the edge of Banff National Park.

Overleaf: Exquisite light on Mount Cline and the quartzite towers of Mount Wilson.

Following spread: First rays of sun on the cliffs of Minster Mountain,
near the eastern edge of Banff National Park.

Final spread: Light and snow dance along the ridges of David Thompson country
on a dynamic, windy morning near Banff National Park.

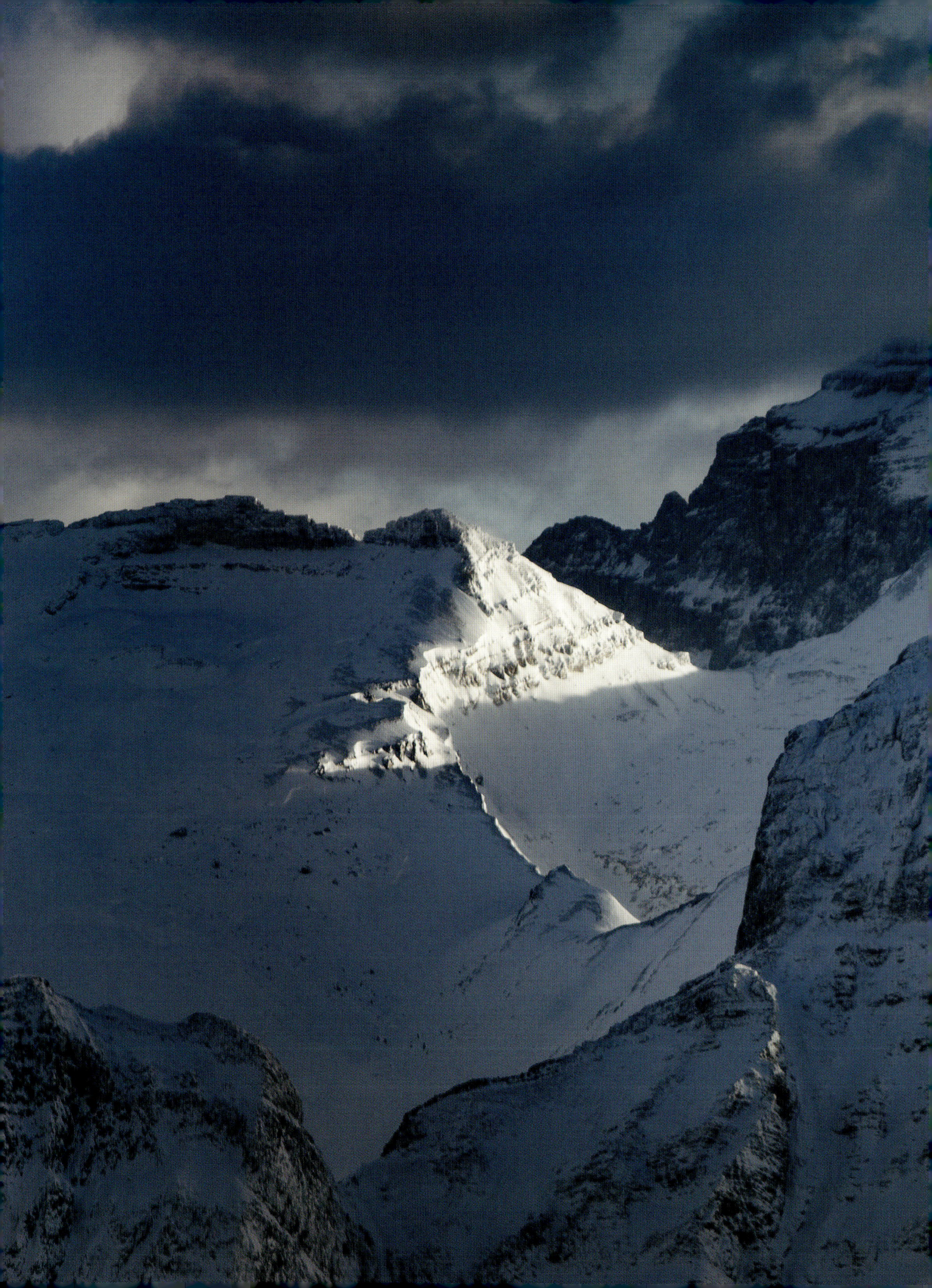

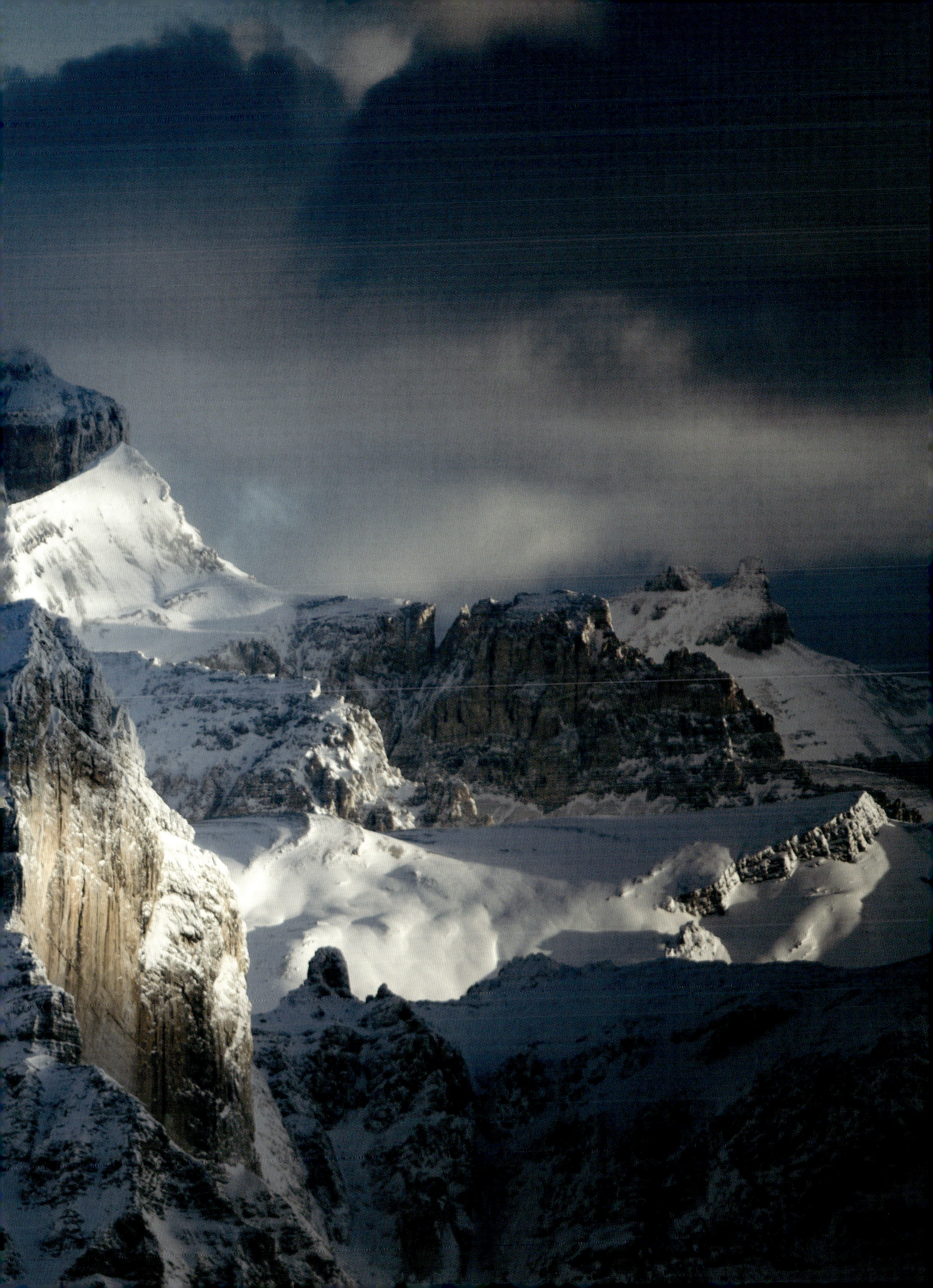

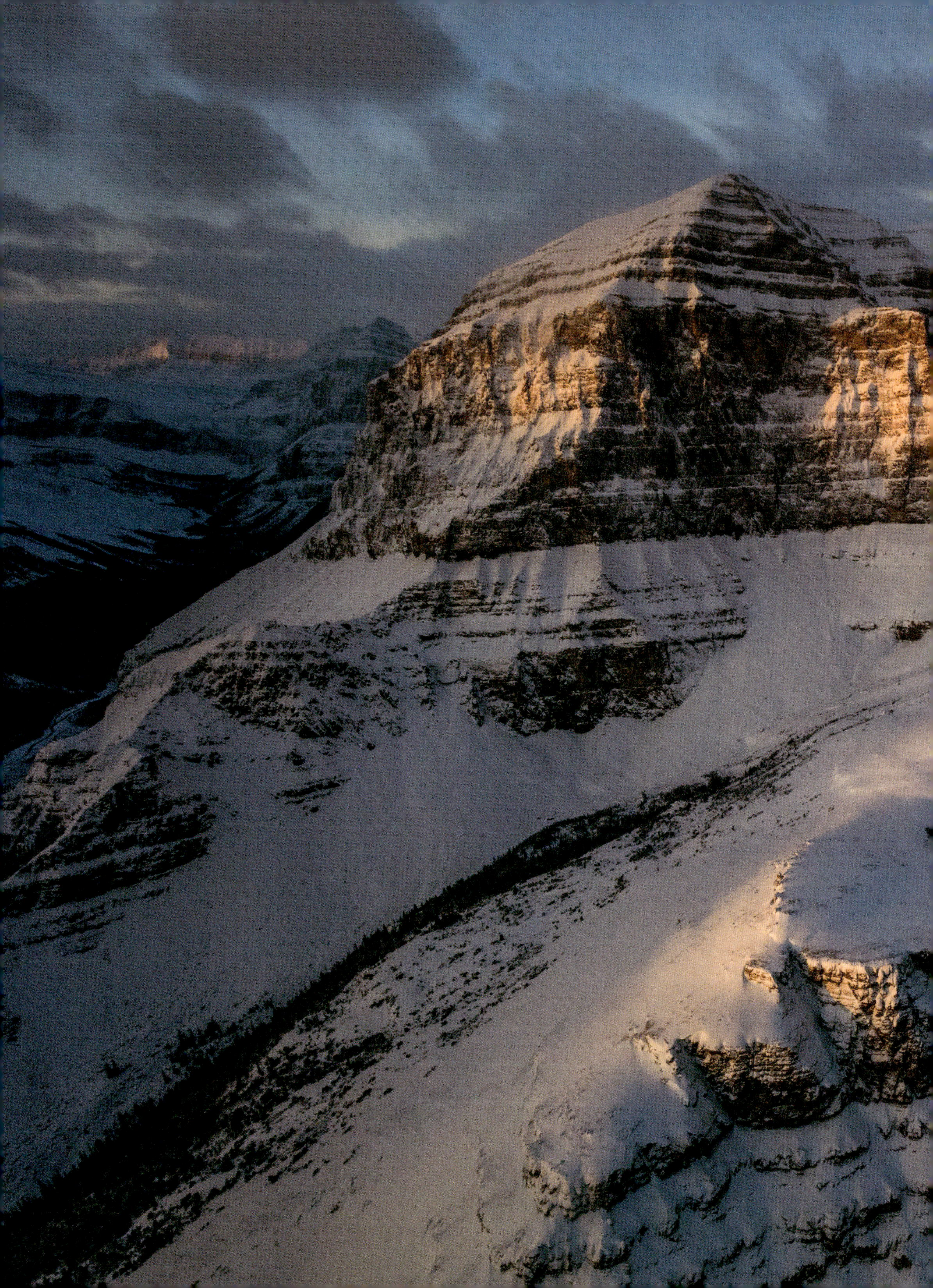

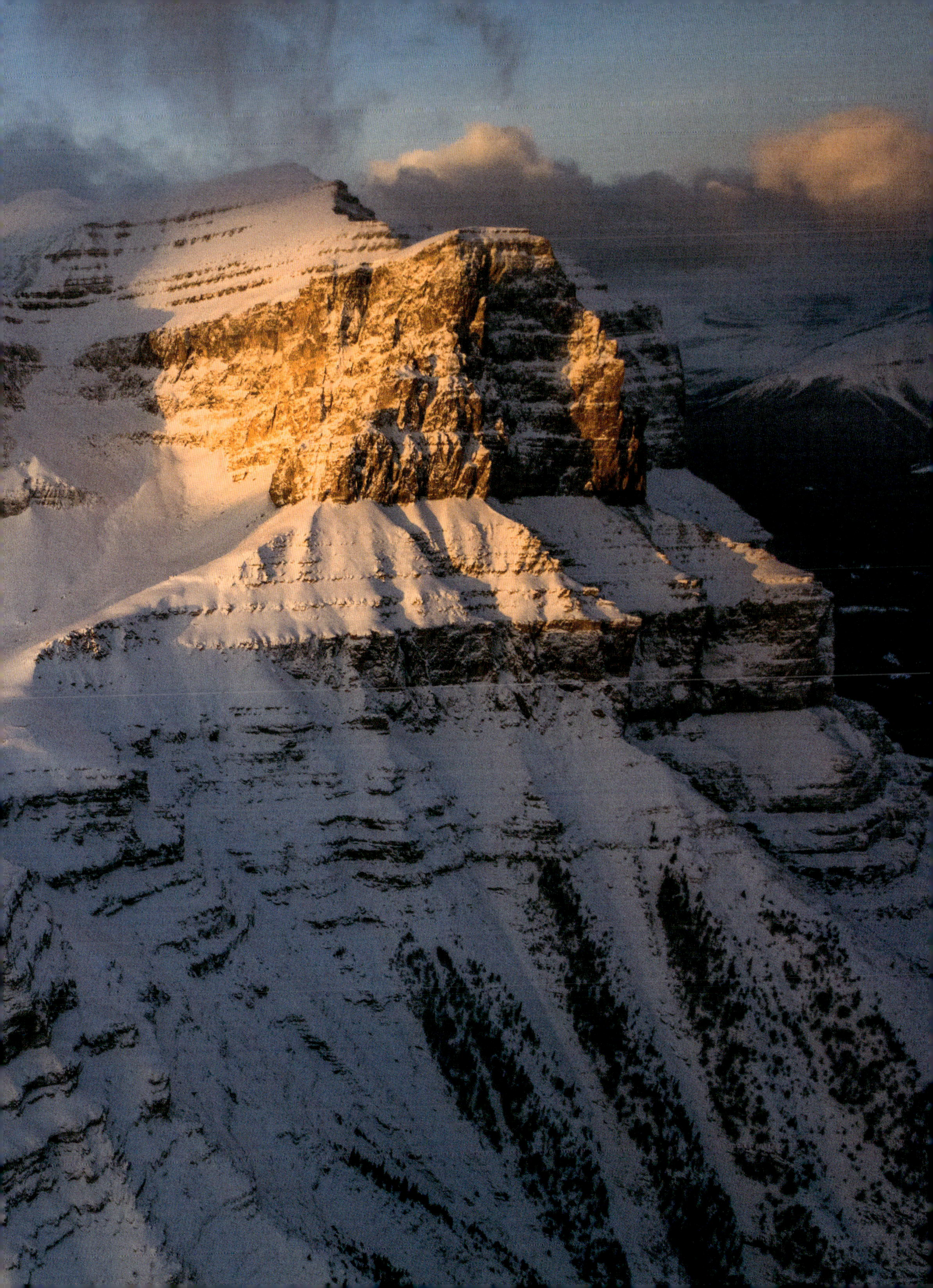

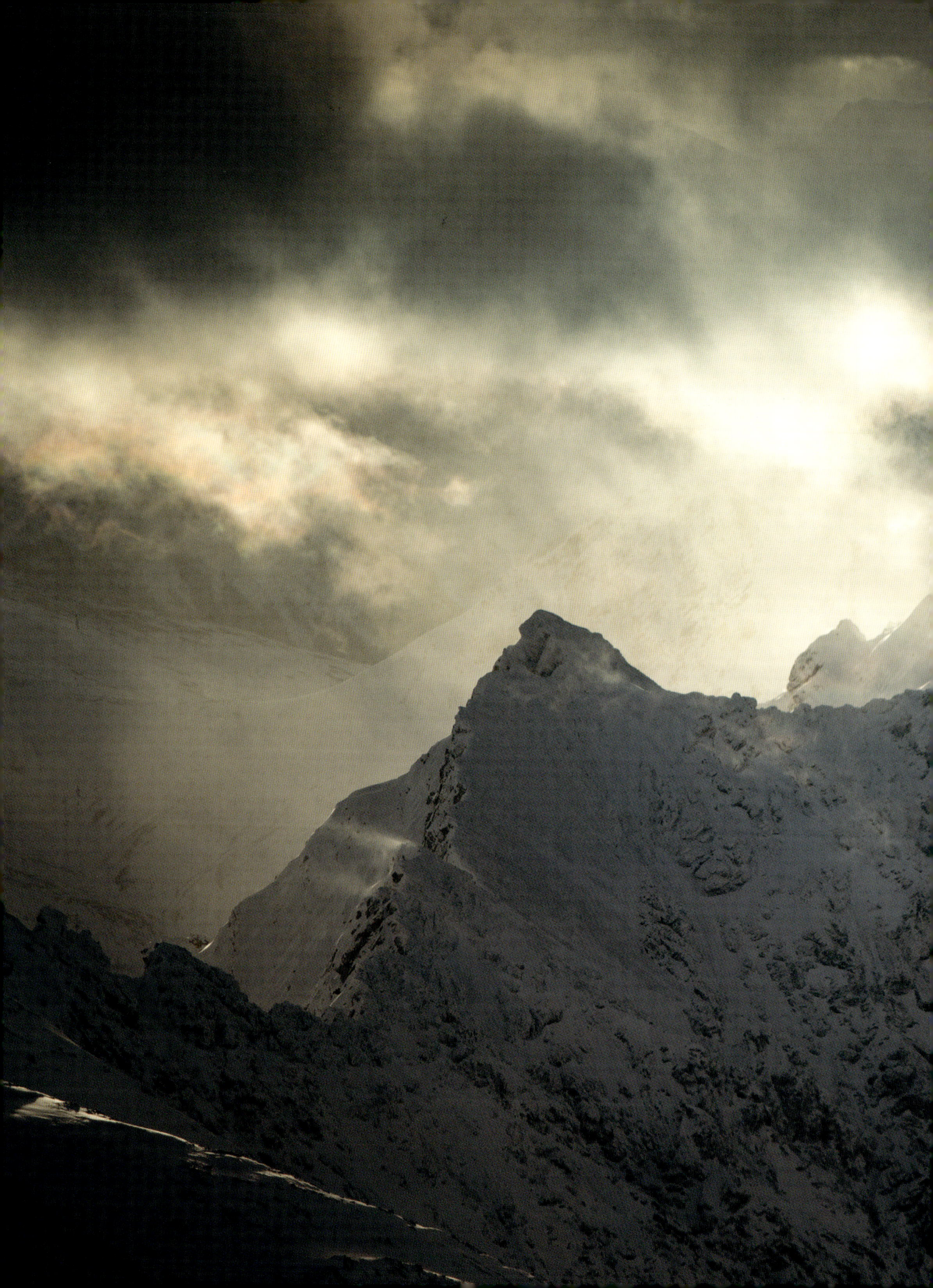

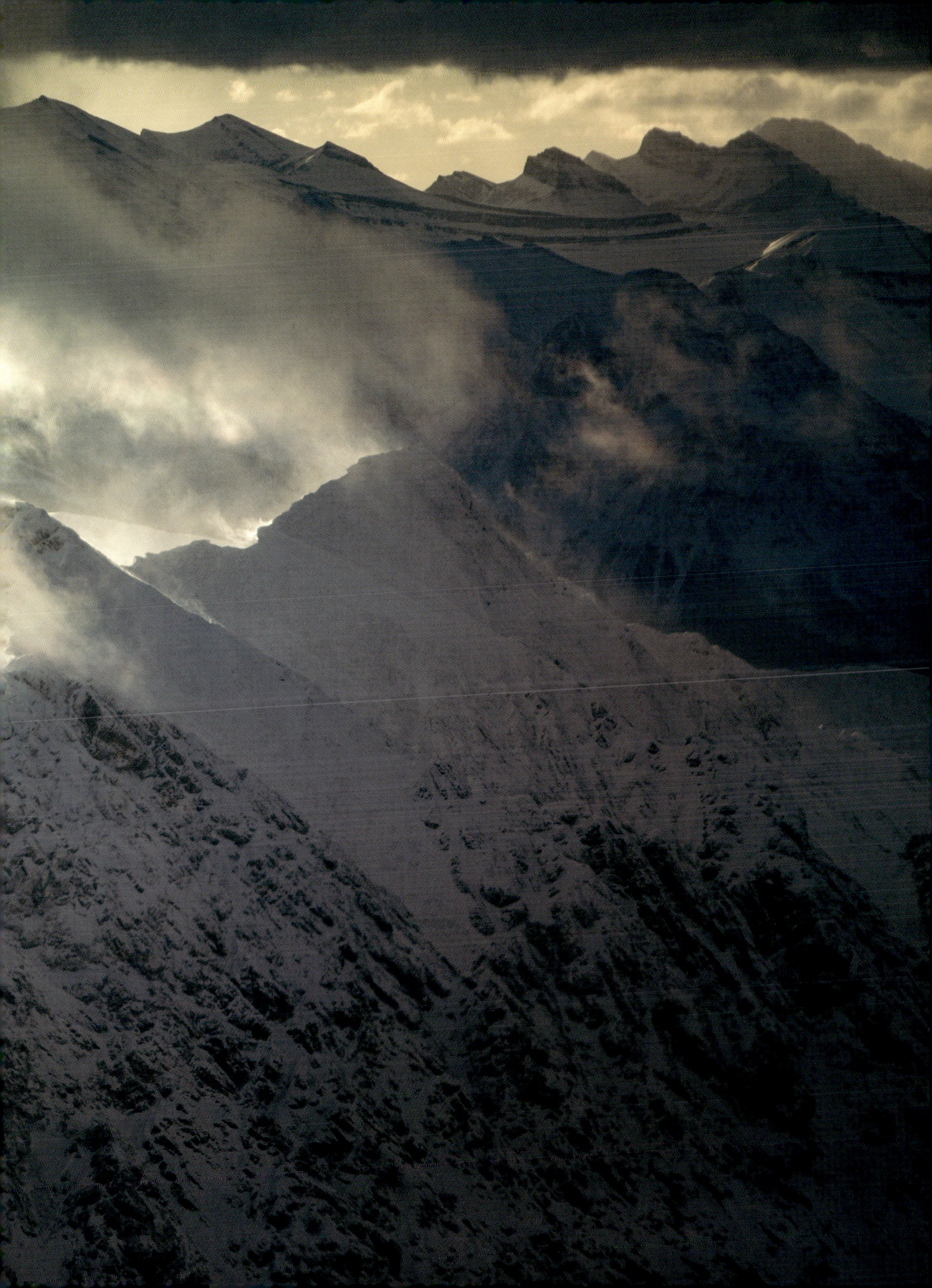

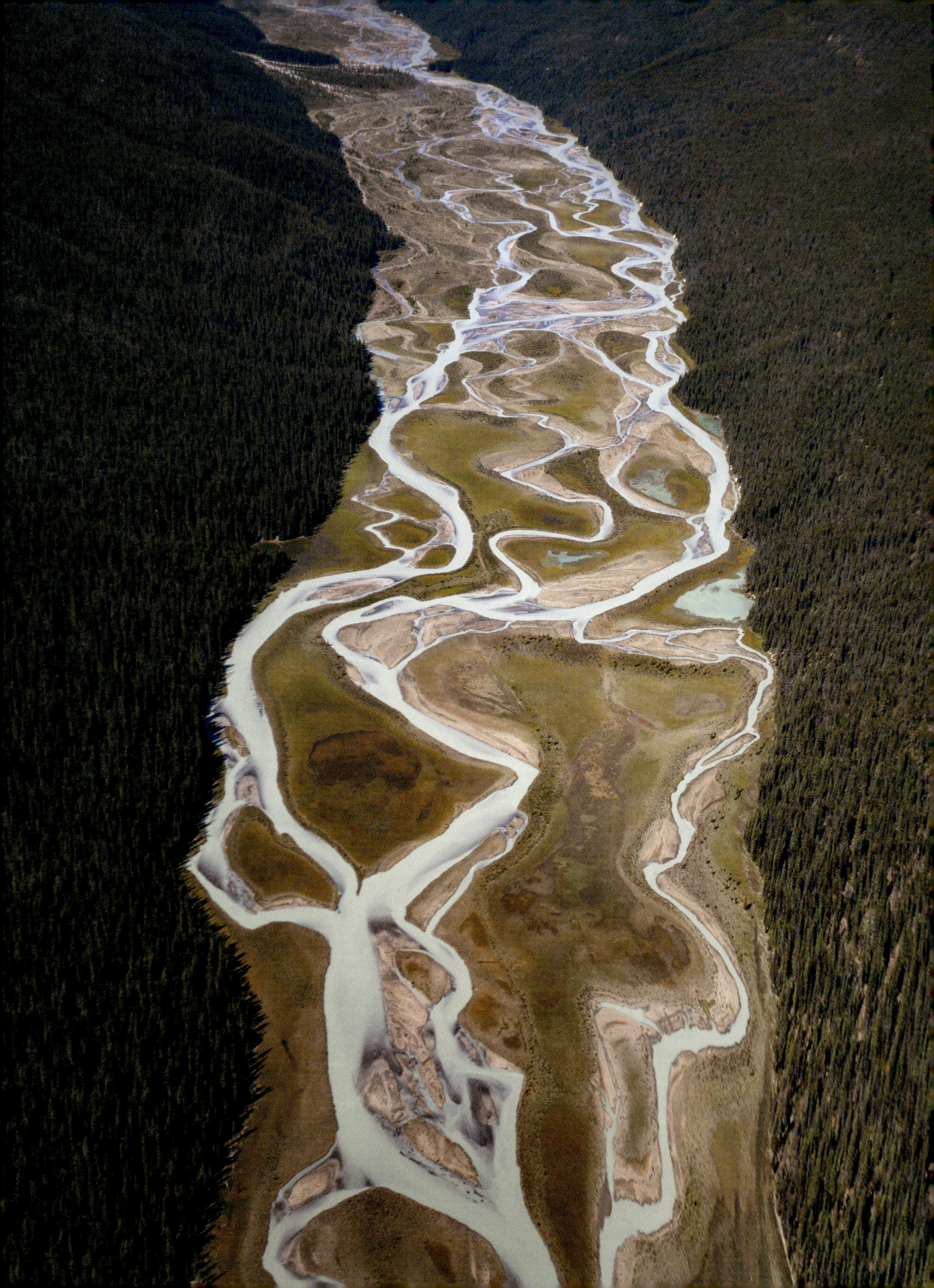

Opposite: North Saskatchewan River braids, near Glacier Lake.

Overleaf: A moody day at Glacier Lake,
a large backcountry lake of western Banff National Park.

Following spread: Morning light on the highlands of the Rampart Creek area,
northern Banff National Park.

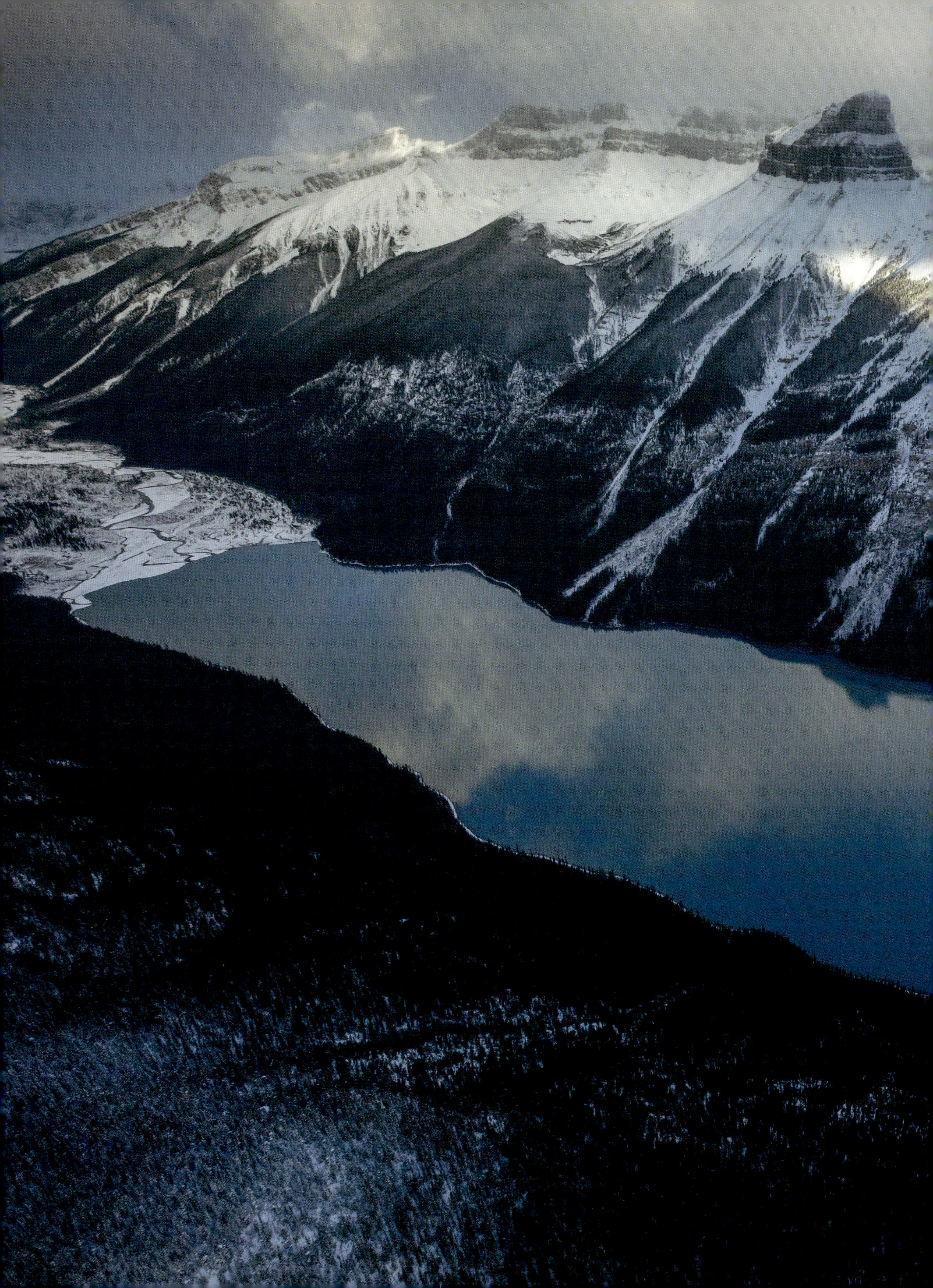

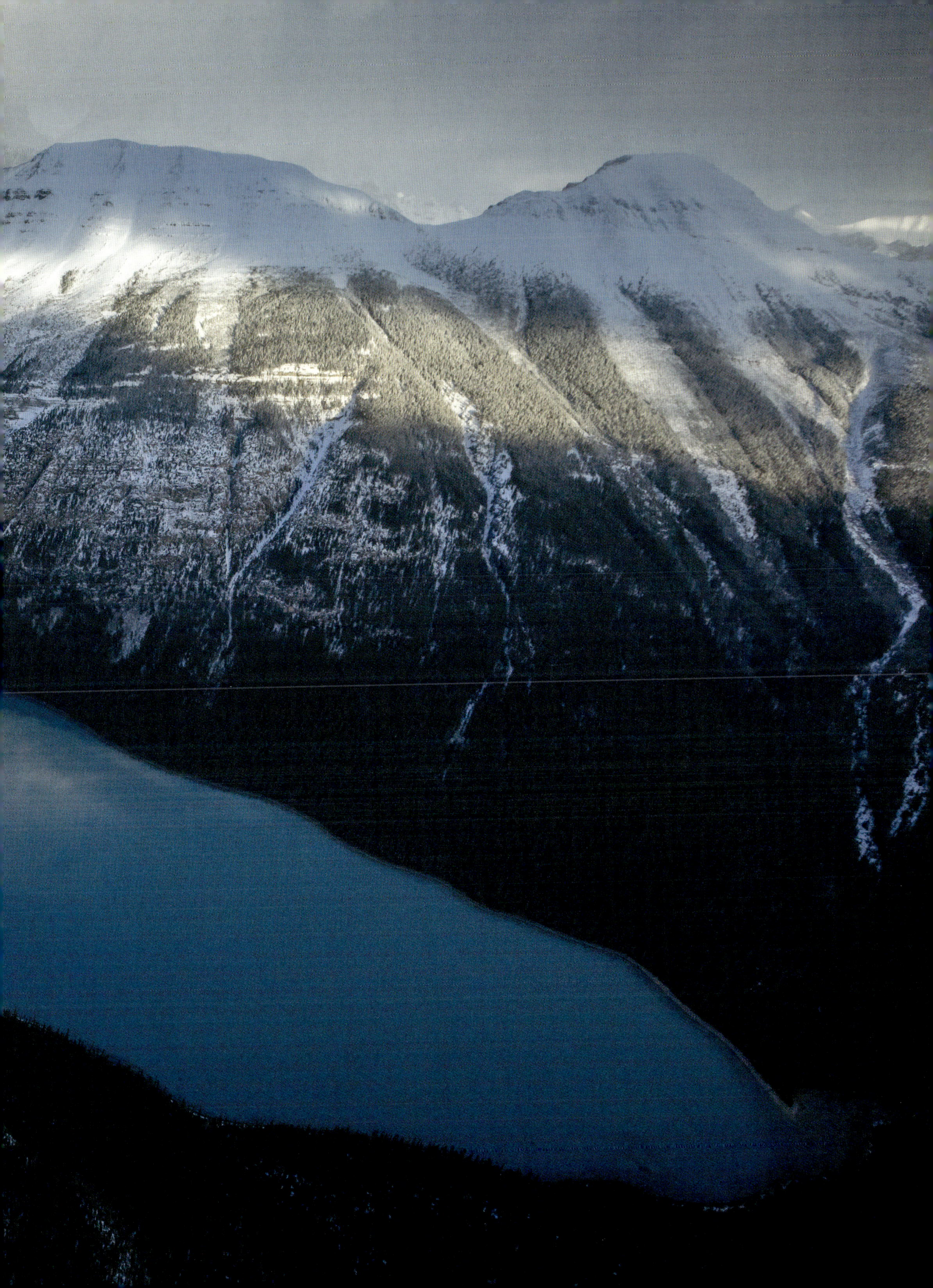

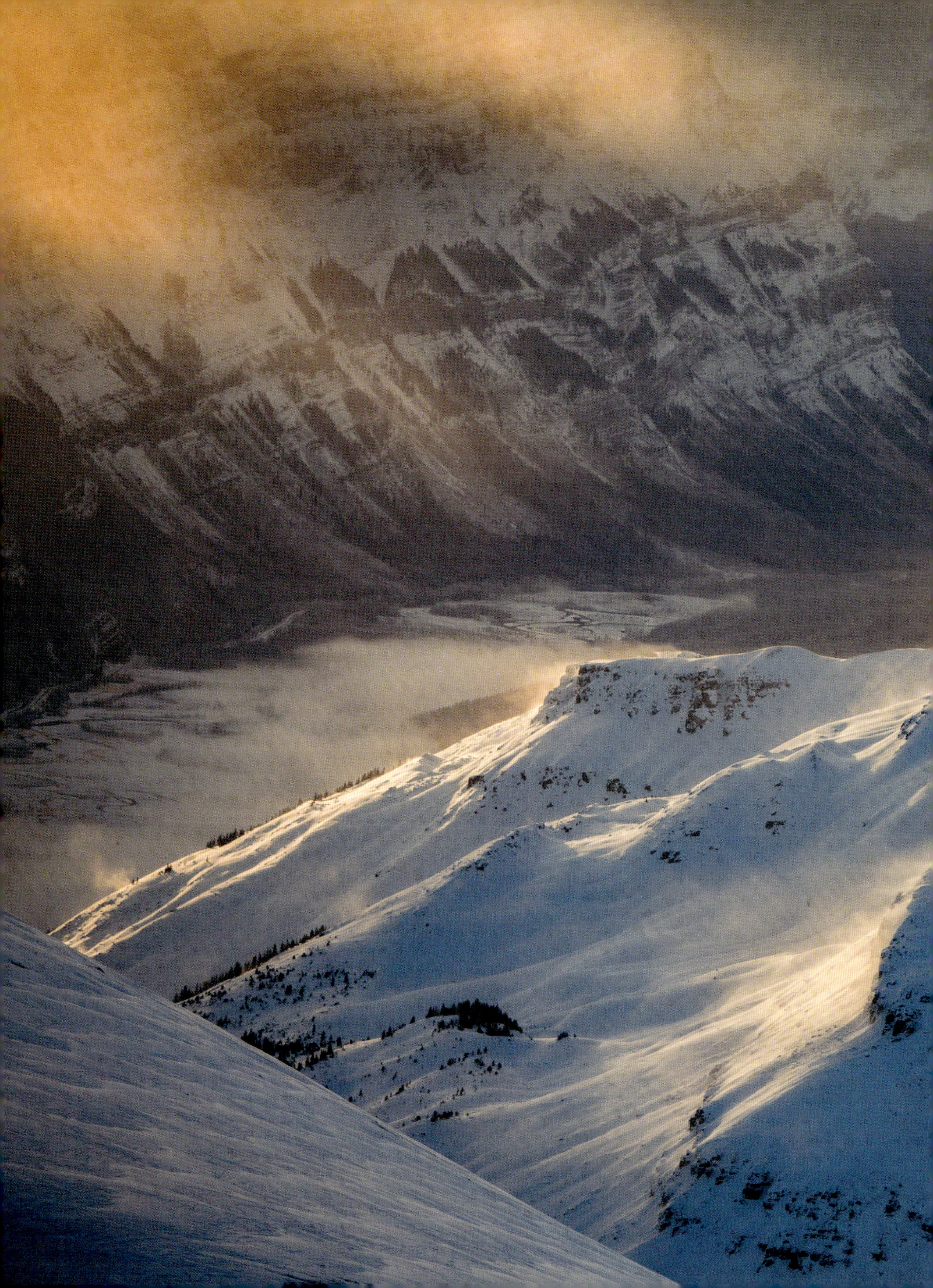

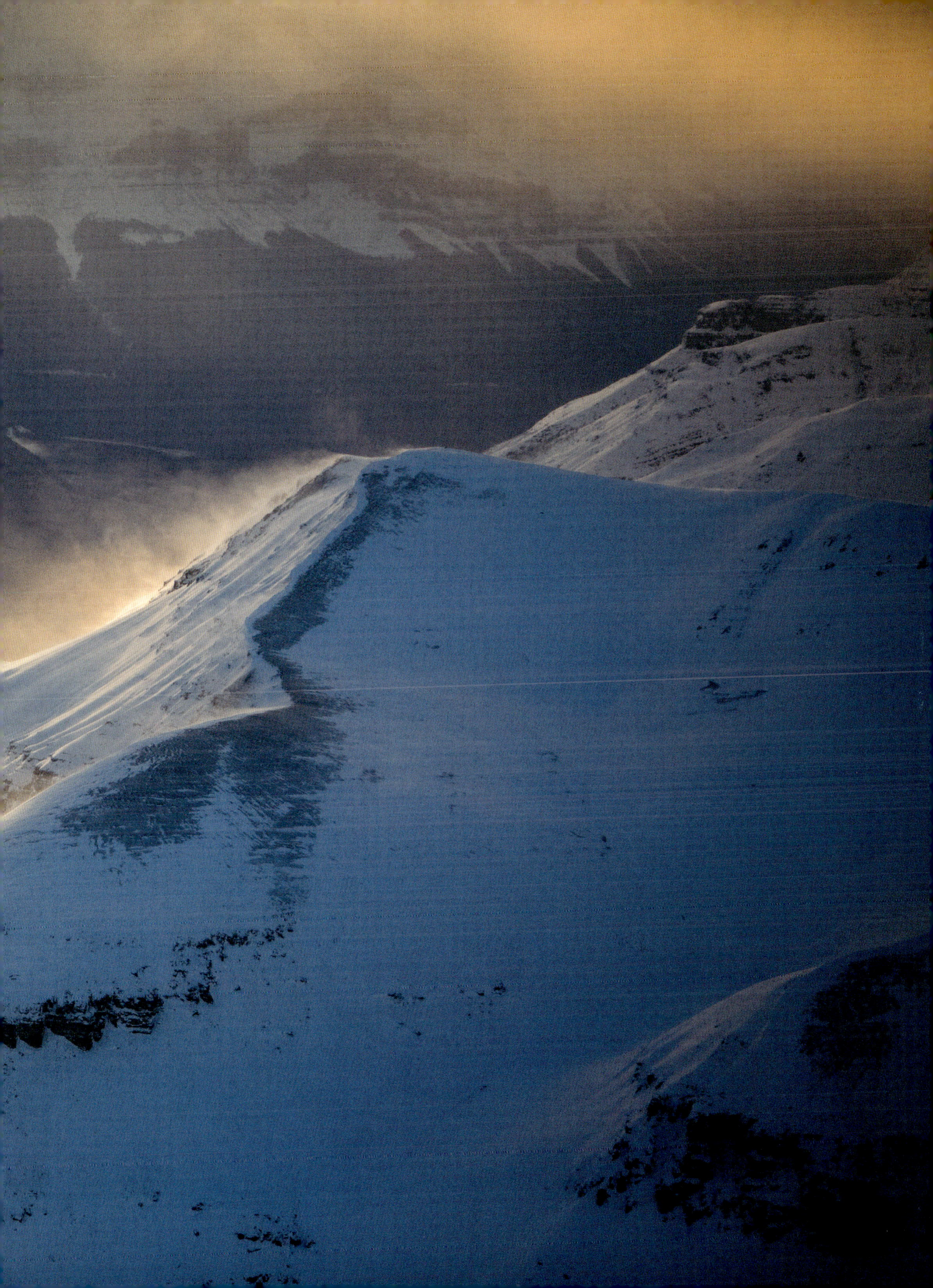

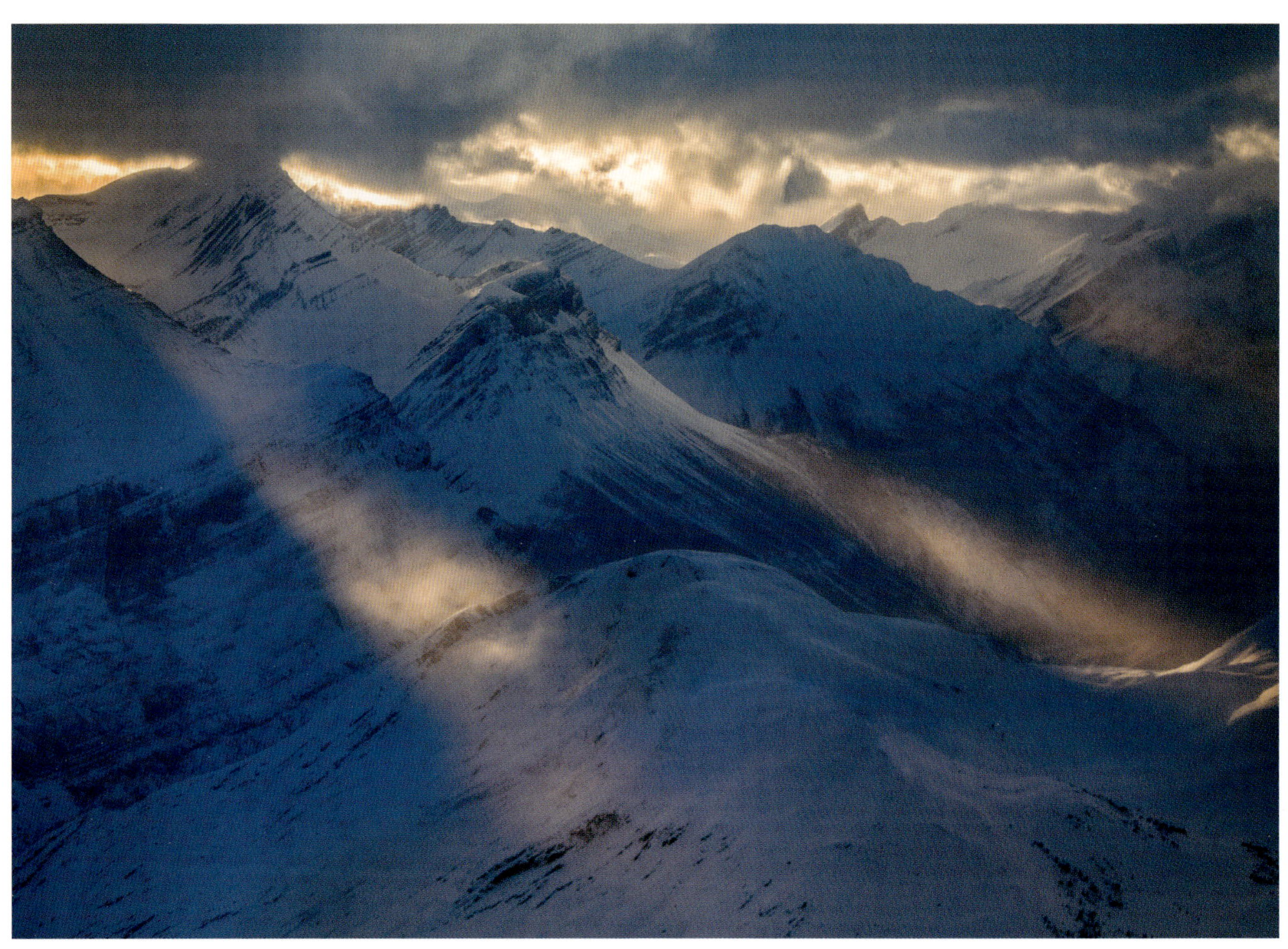

Above: First light spills over Mount Coleman on a dreamy morning flight over the main ranges.

Opposite: Winter closes in on beautiful Coleman Lake, in northern Banff National Park.

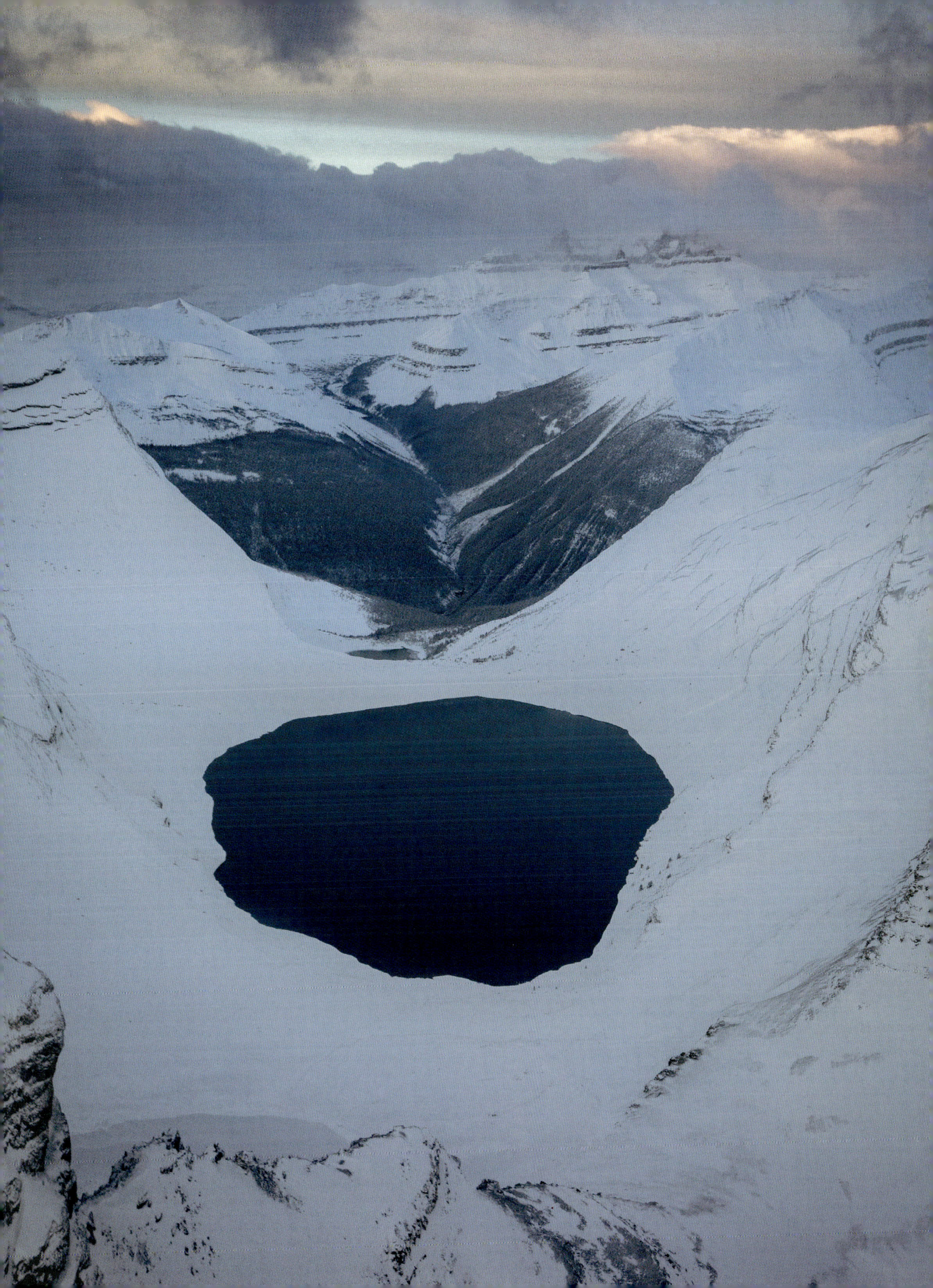

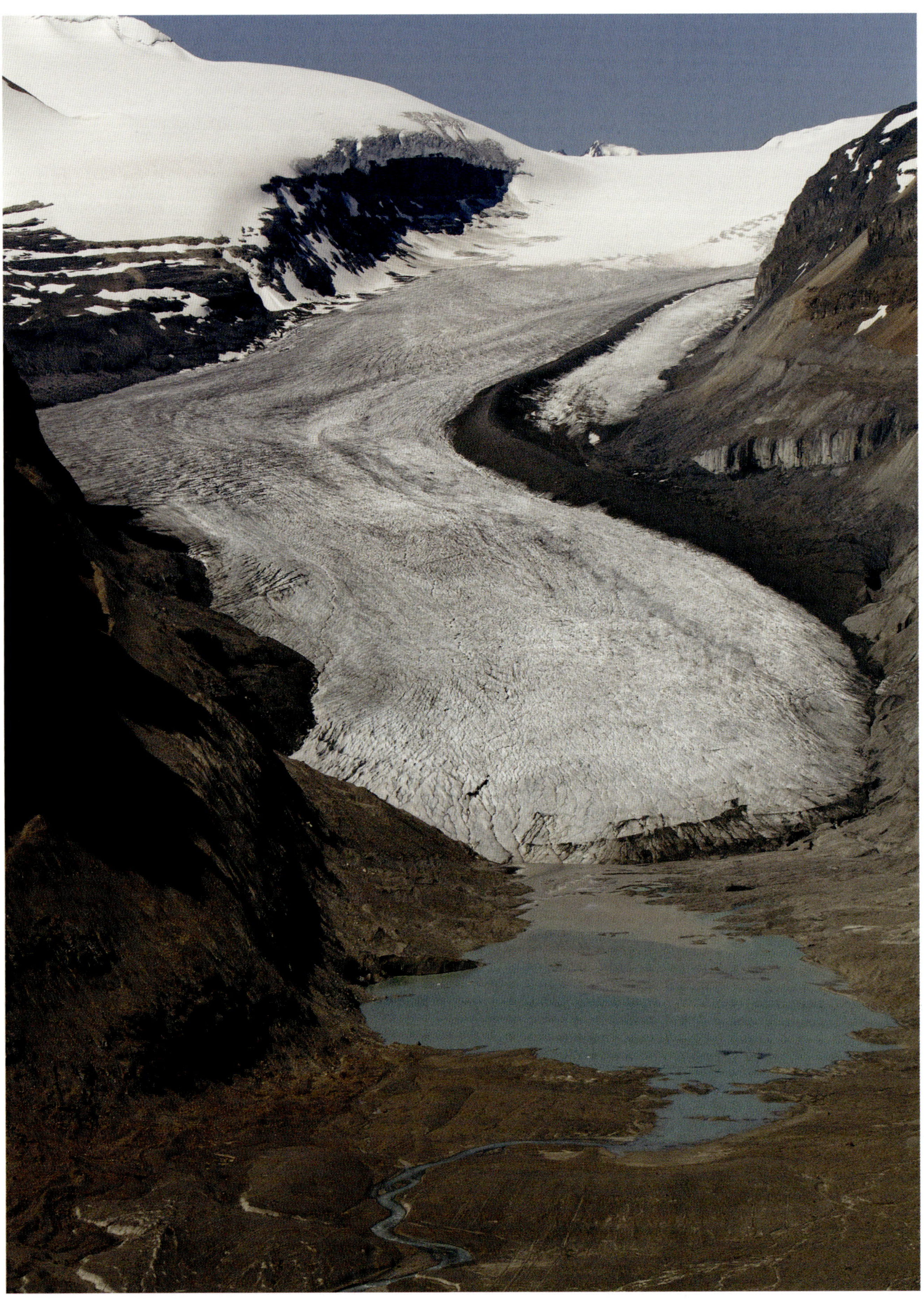

Opposite: The Saskatchewan Glacier carves its way down from the Columbia Icefield and
has retreated considerably in recent years. Its meltwater lake is constantly growing.

Overleaf: The Columbia Icefield Discovery Centre, with the famous Athabasca Glacier cascading down
from the Columbia Icefield on the right. Mount Athabasca is the prominent peak on the left.

Following spread: Looking downhill from above the Athabasca Glacier,
one gets a fabulous view of its intricate crevasse fields.

Final spread: Ice Explorers on the Athabasca Glacier, Jasper National Park.

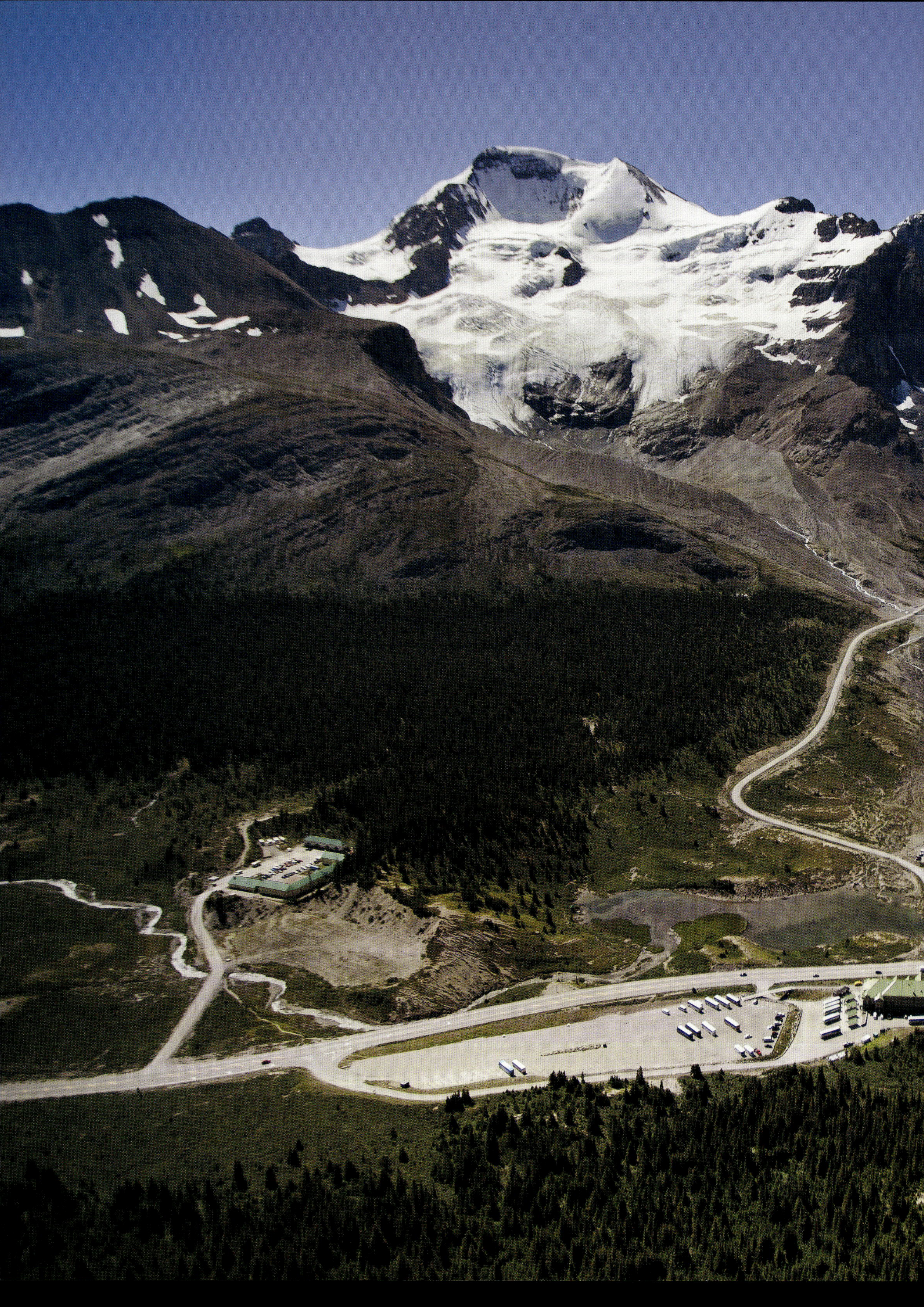

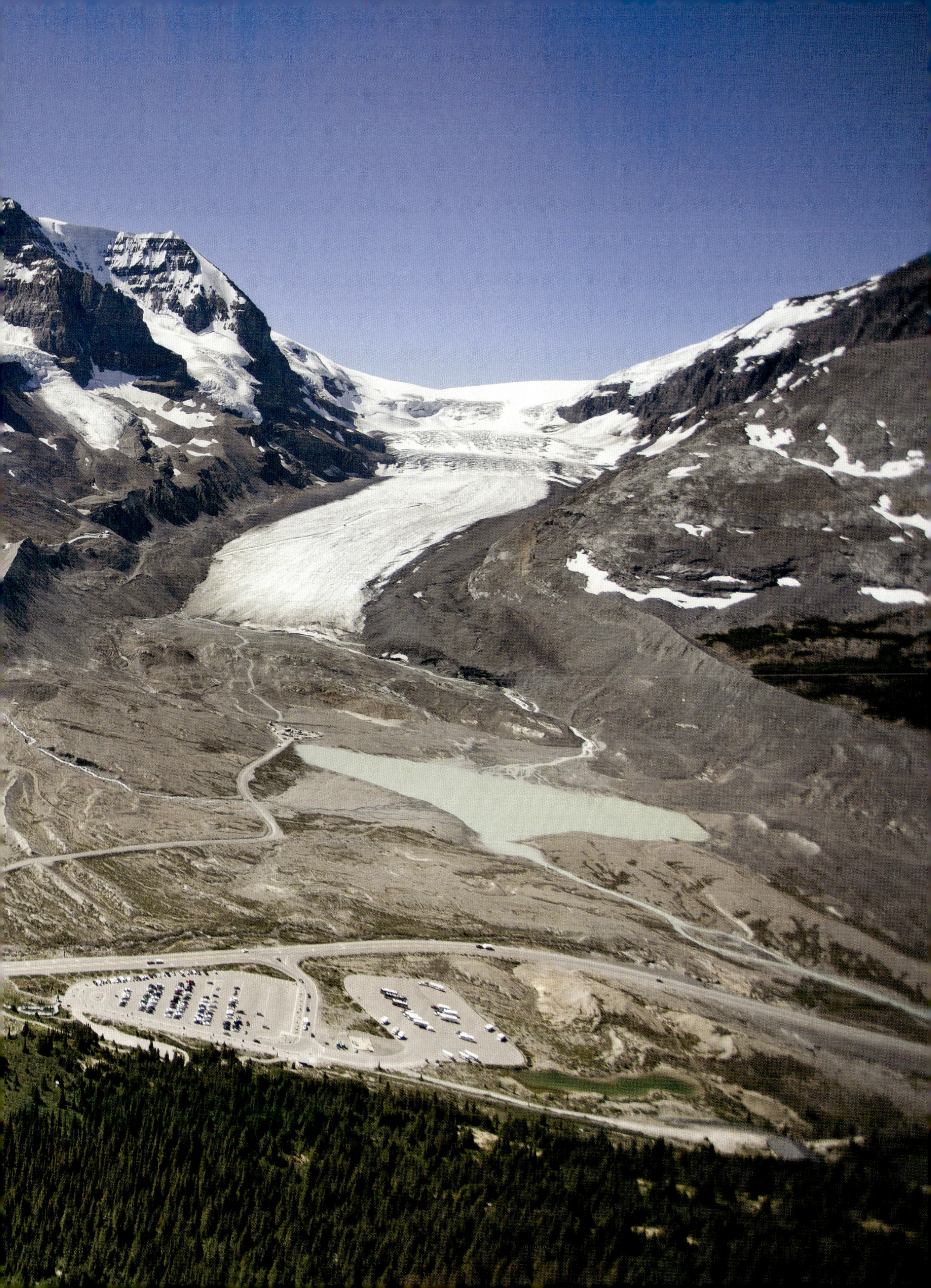

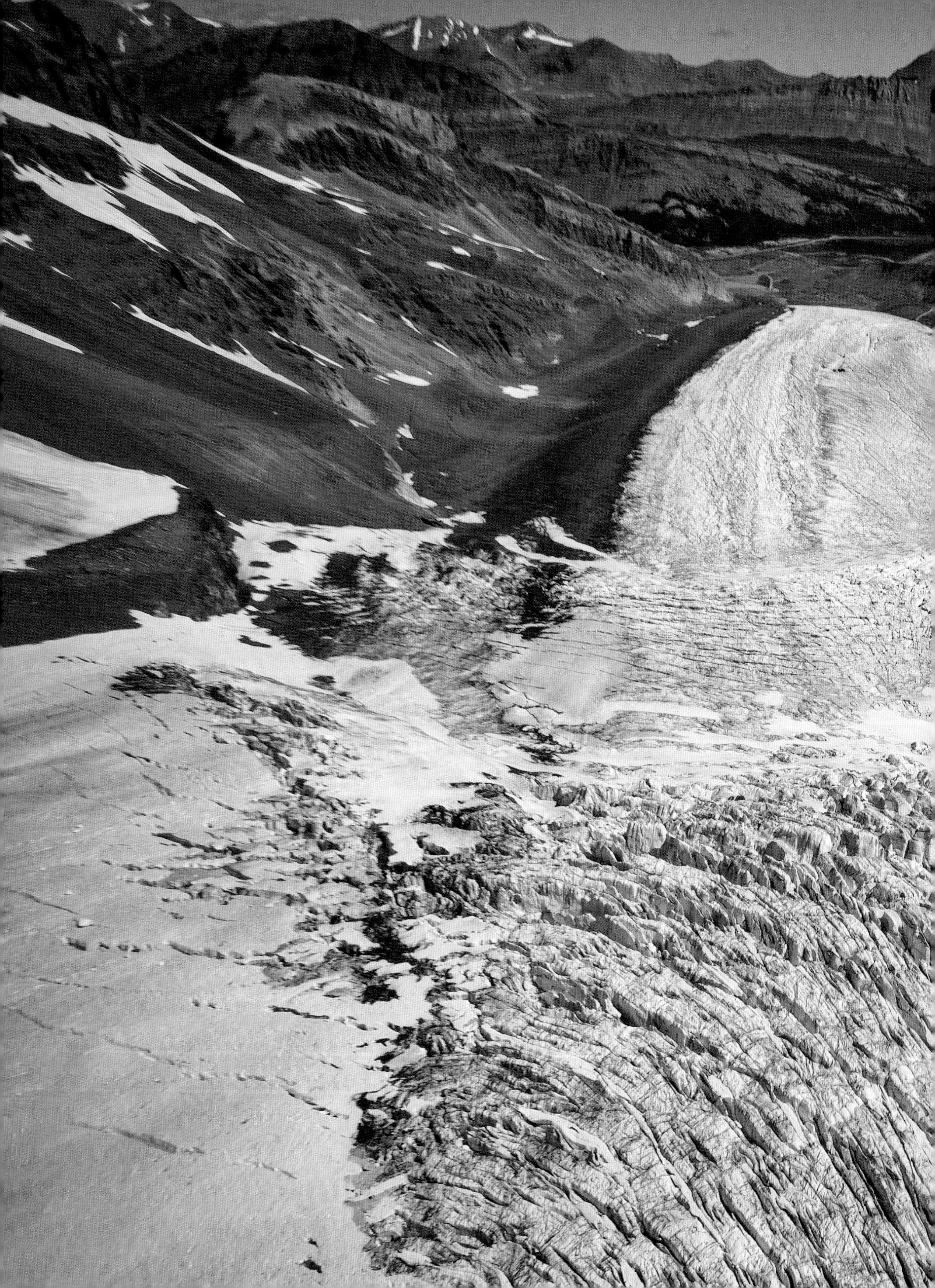

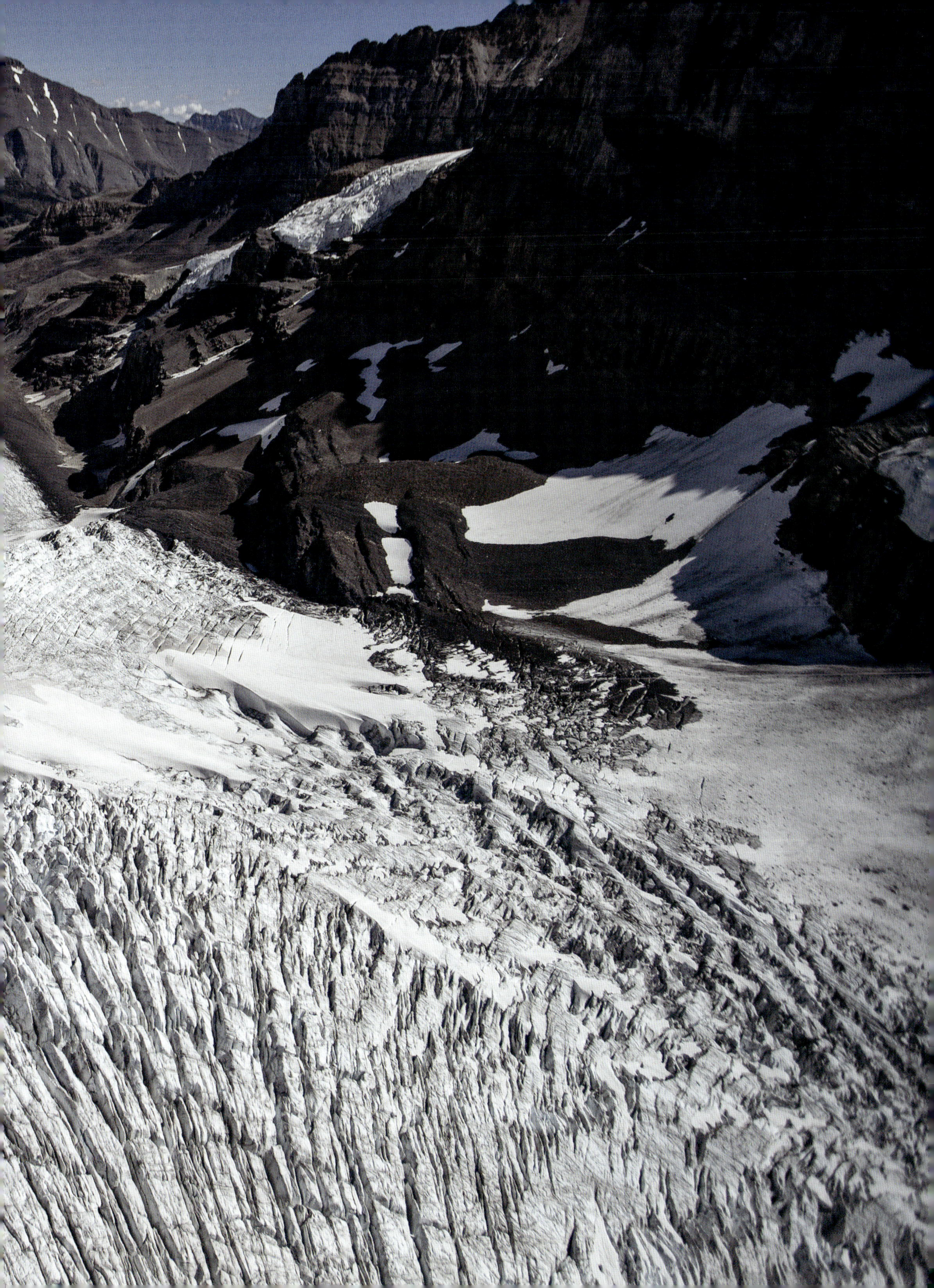

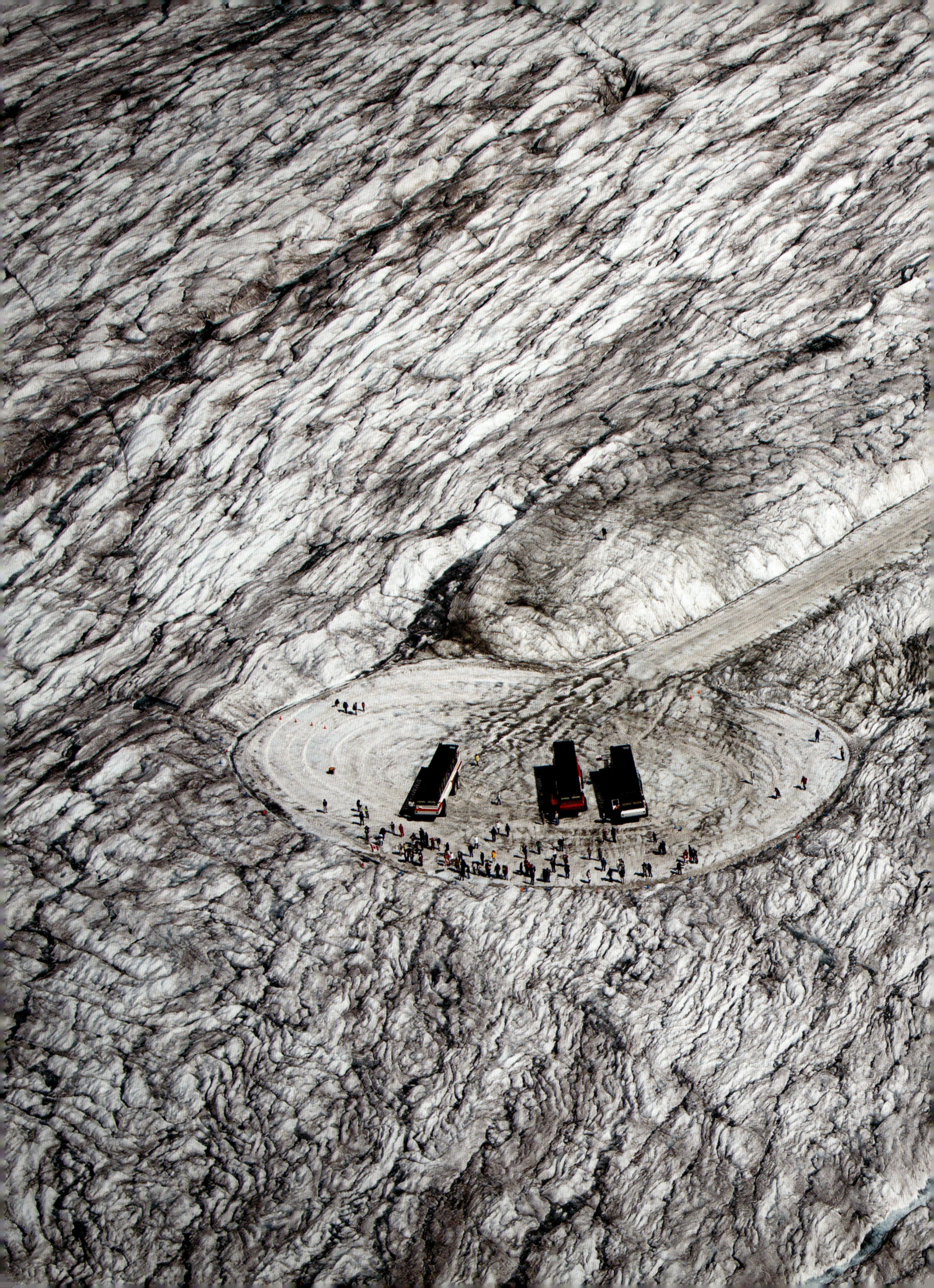

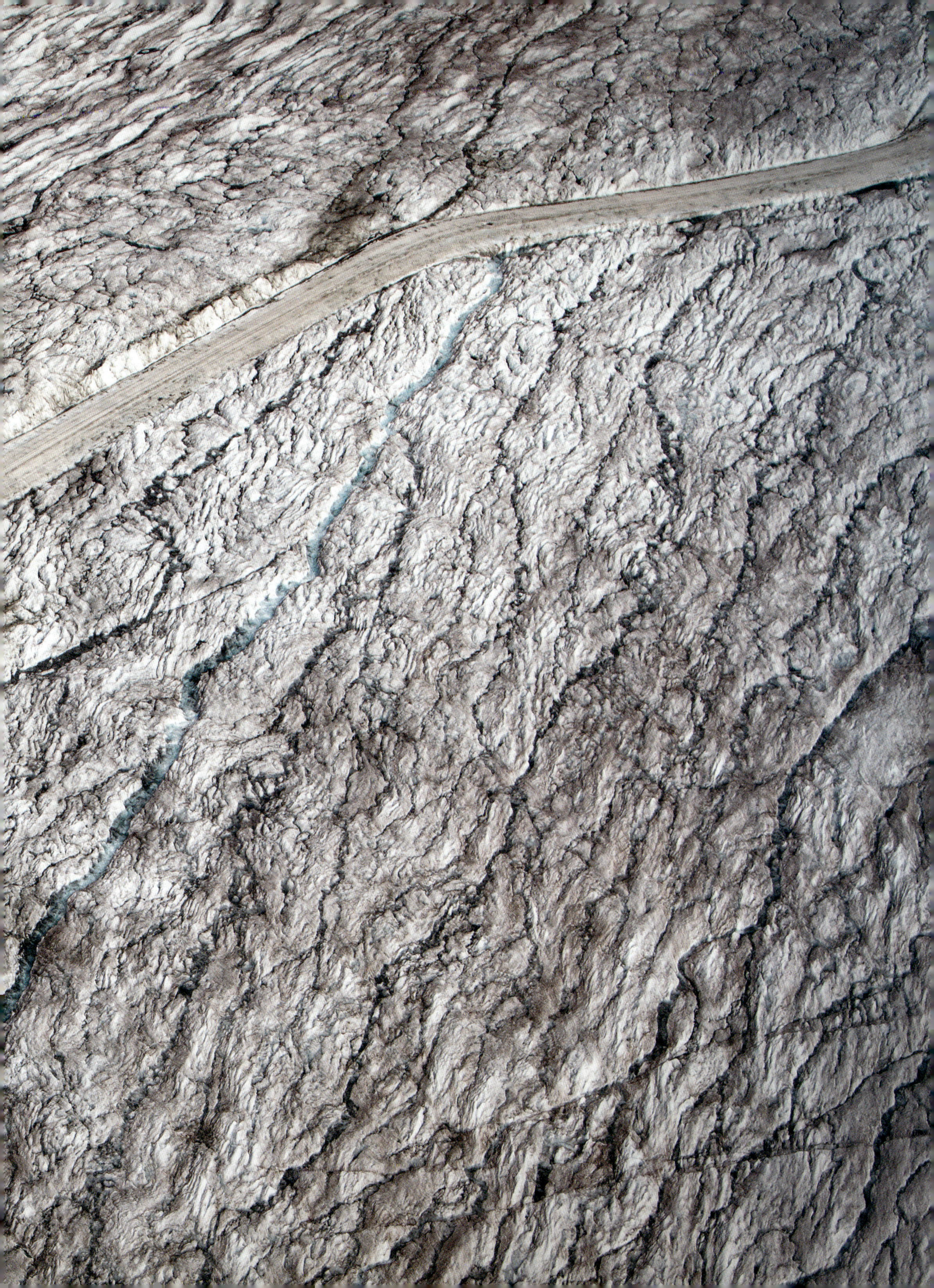

The Athabasca River emerges out of the tall ranges of the Great Divide.
Mount Quincy and Blackfriars Peak are visible in the background.

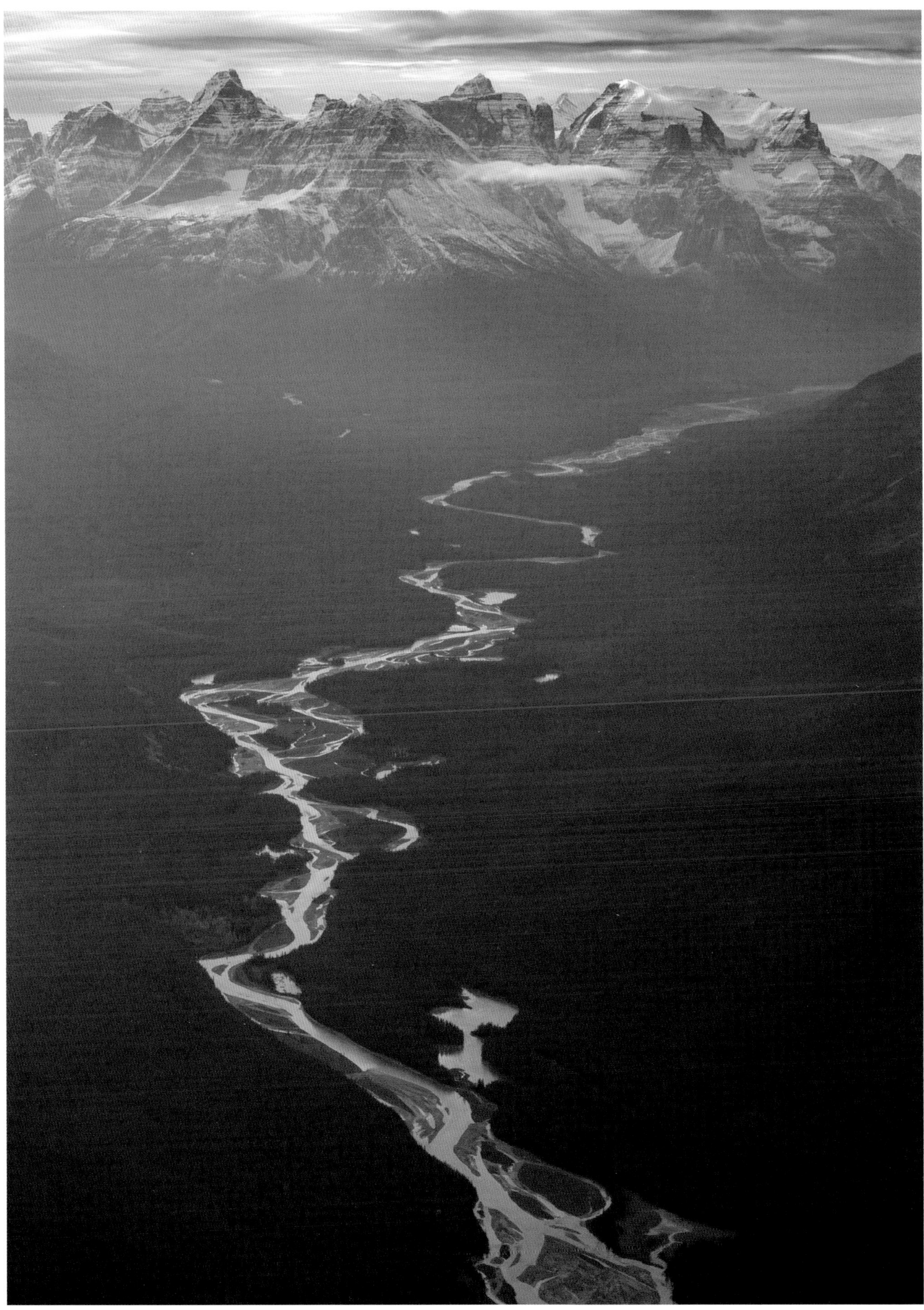

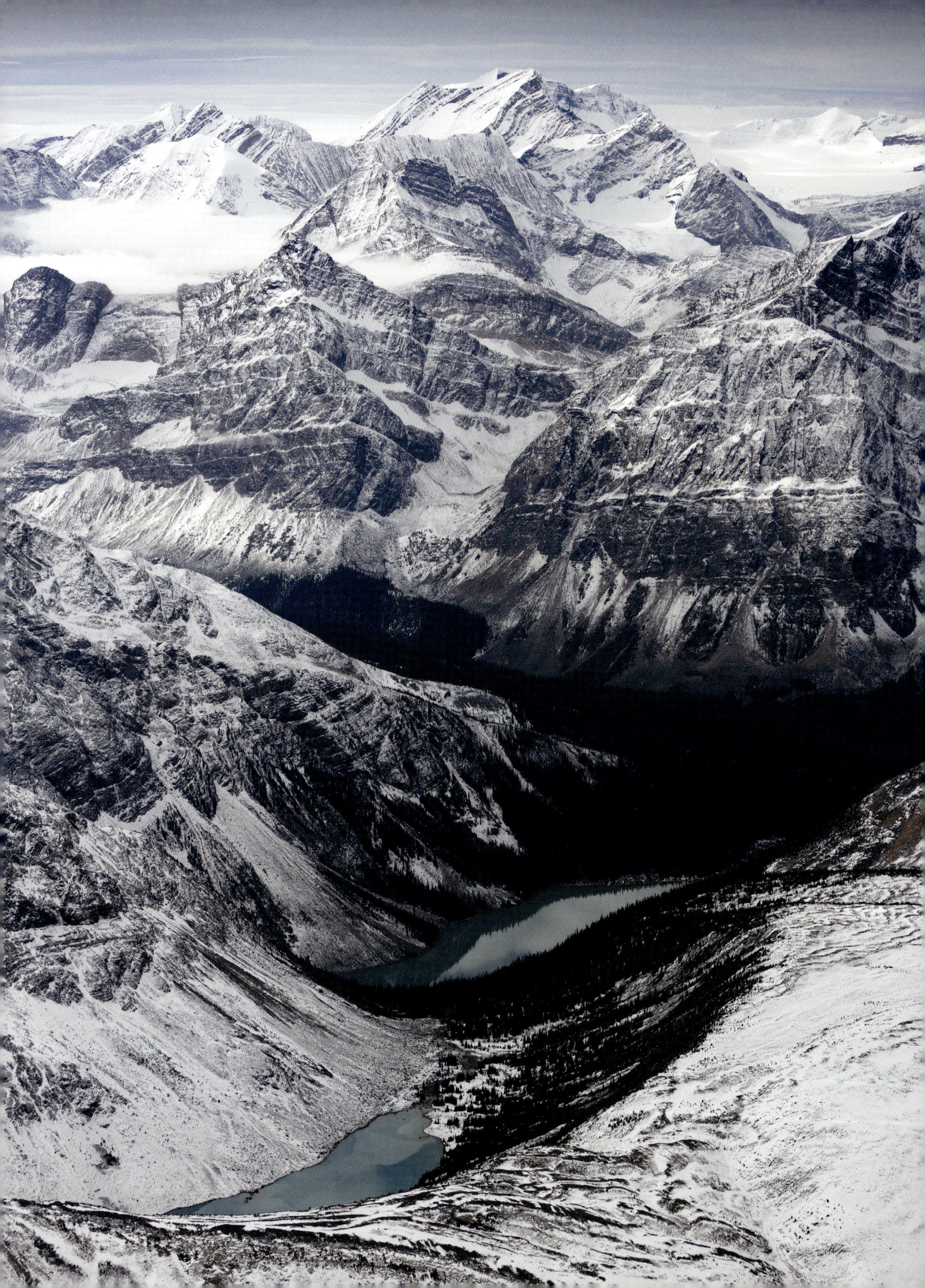

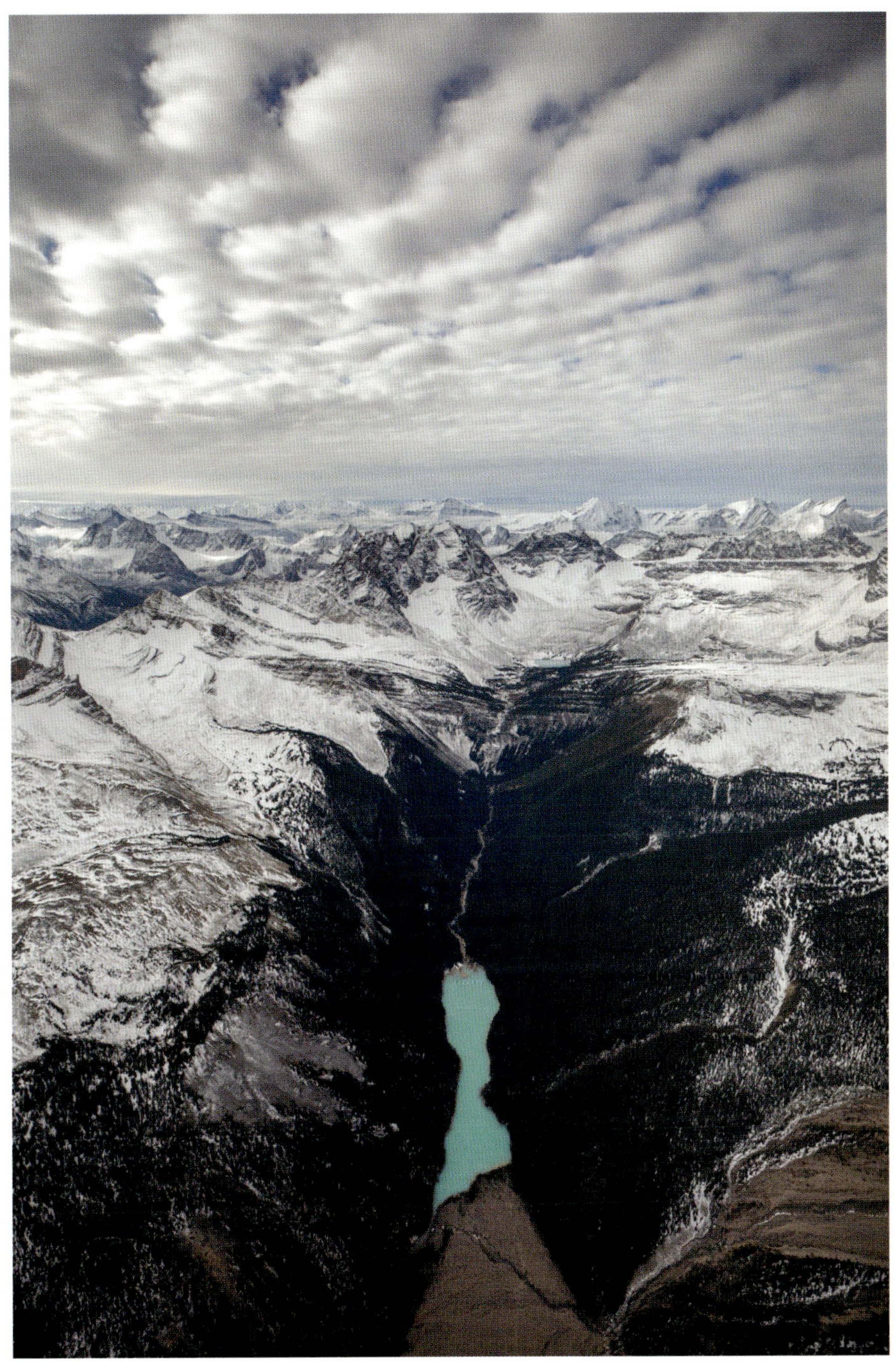

Opposite: Two unnamed lakes of the upper Divergence Creek Valley
add a splash of colour to this snowy scene in Jasper National Park.

Above: Fryatt Lake is a true gem of the Jasper backcountry.

Following spread: Fortress Lake is the centrepiece of Hamber Provincial Park. One interesting note about
Fortress Lake is that it is believed to have drained underground towards the Chaba to the east at times,
while at other times (including now) it drains into the Wood River to the west. The Alberta–BC provincial
boundary lies between the river and the lake. The Hooker Icefield is visible on the far right of the image.

Final spread: The setting of the Fortress Lake Wilderness Retreat is straight out of
a dream, surrounded by turquoise waters and the mighty Chisel Peak.

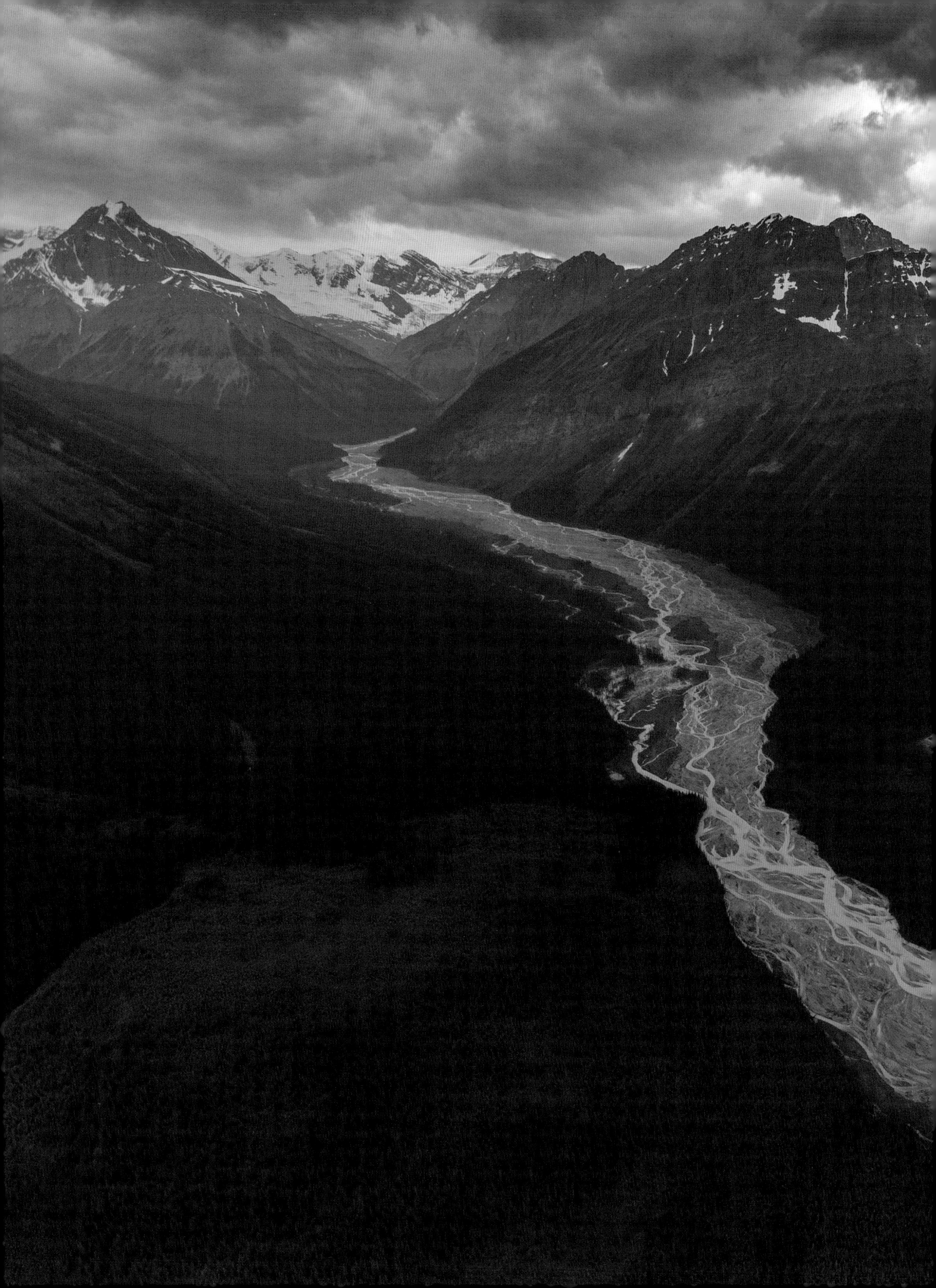

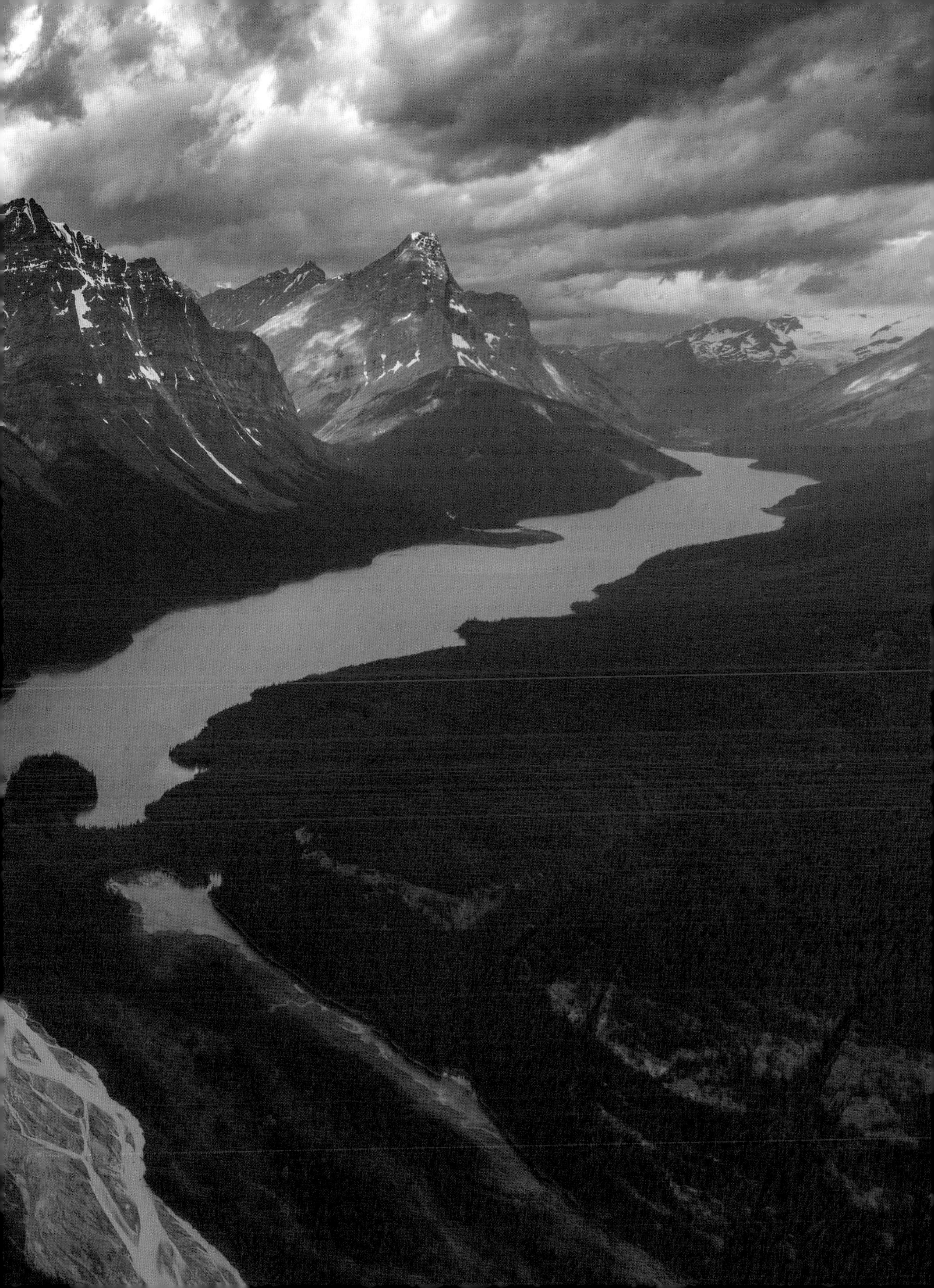

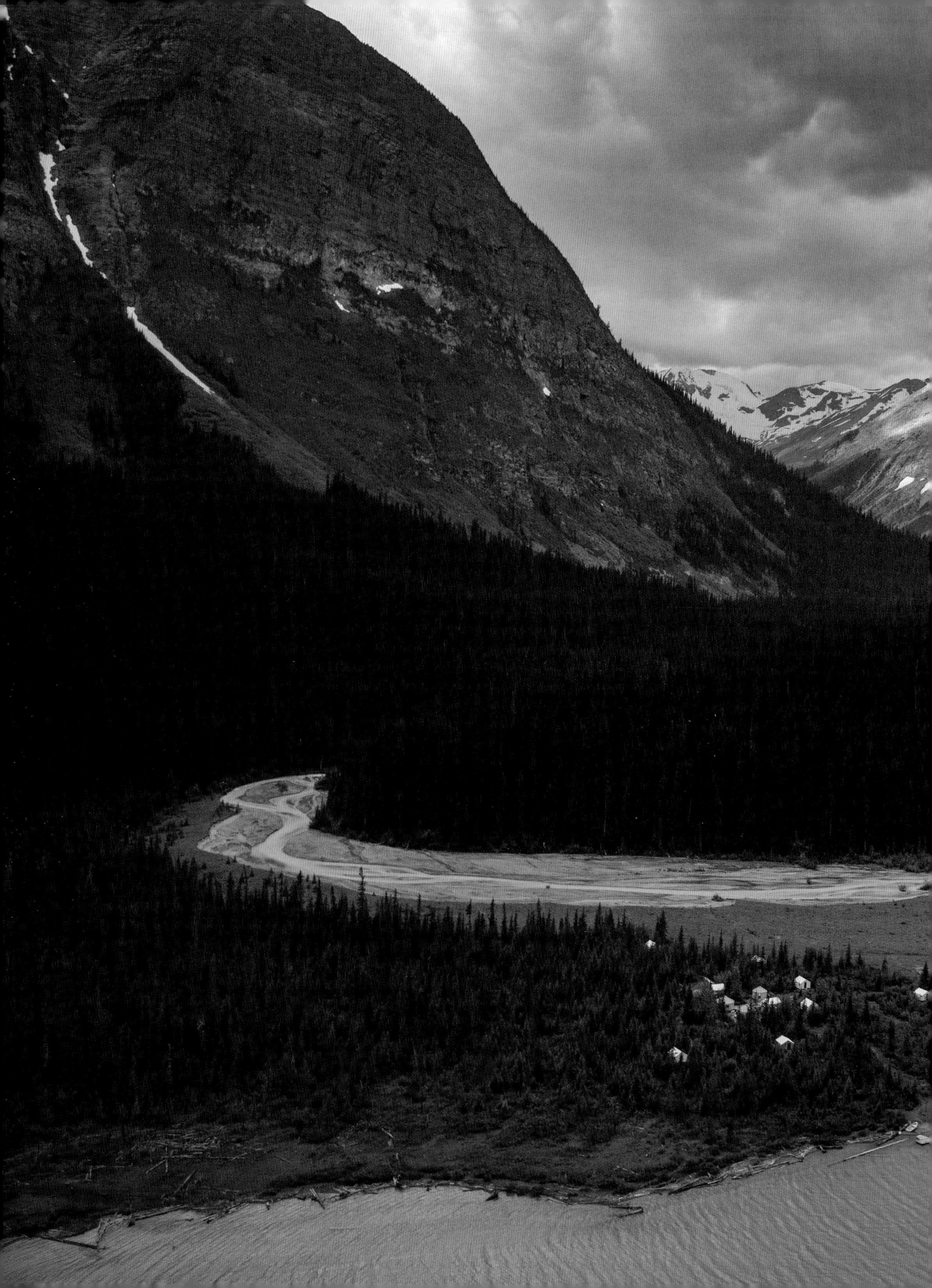

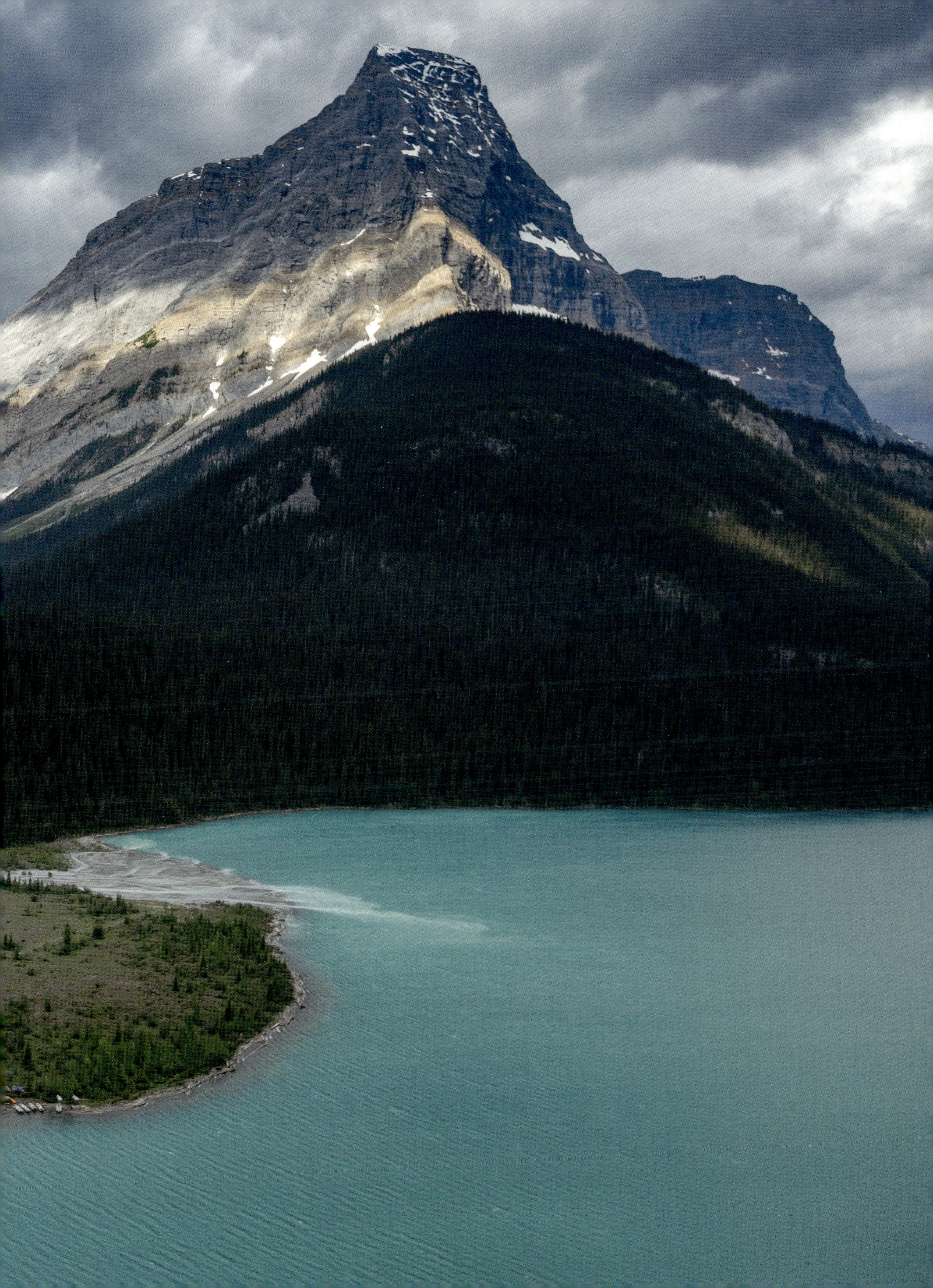

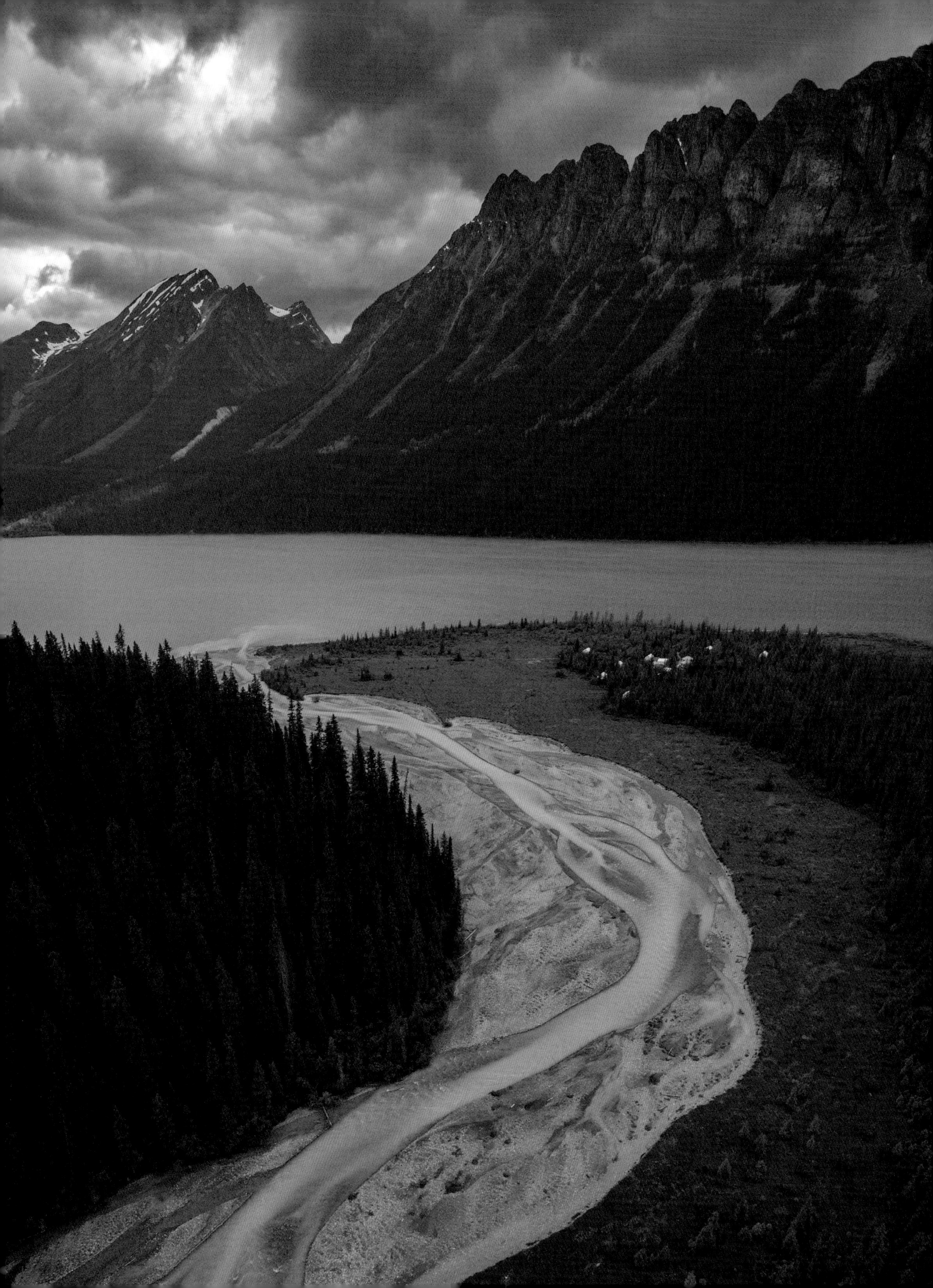

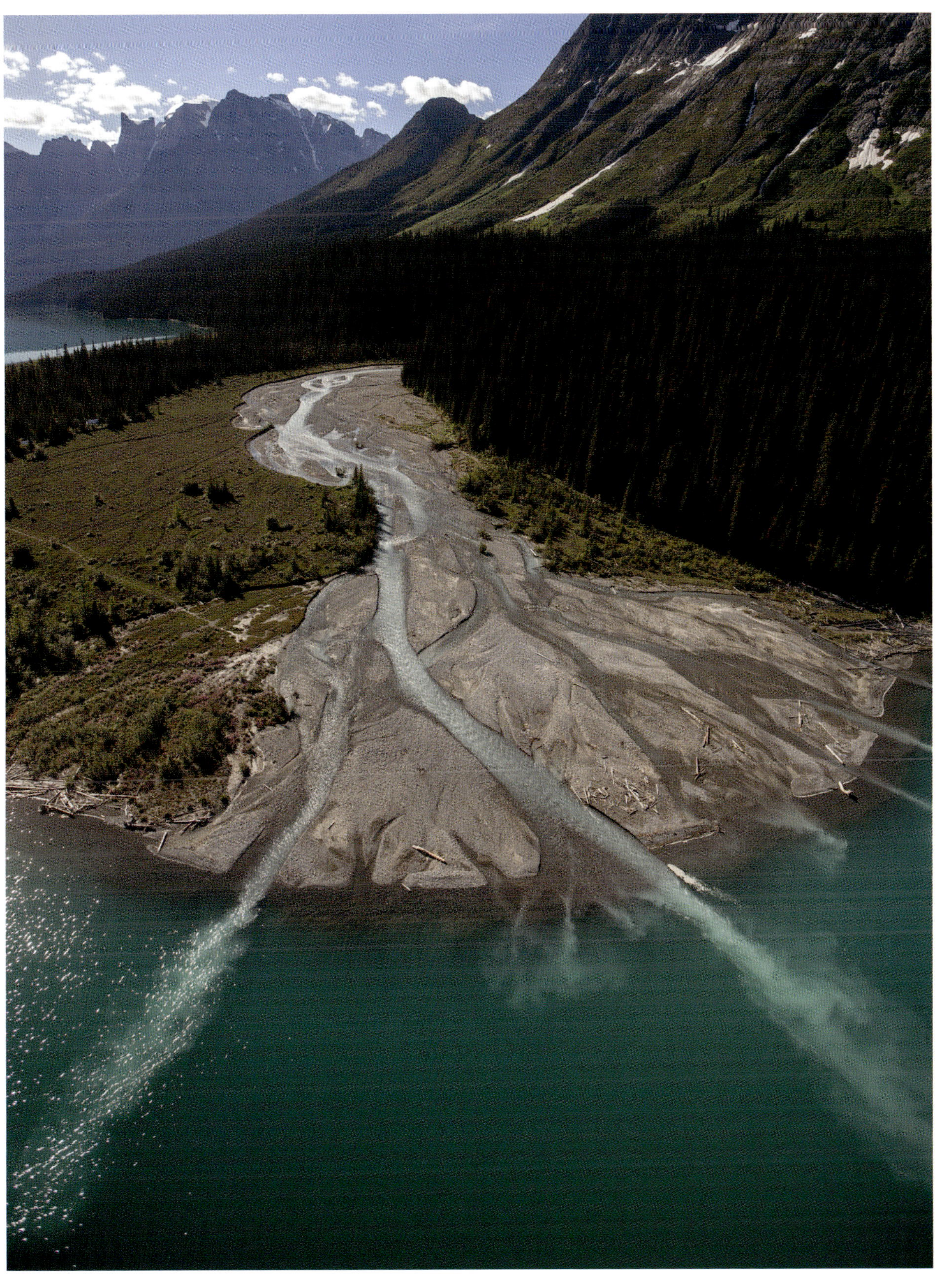

Opposite: Chisel Creek empties into Fortress Lake on a moody day in Hamber Provincial Park.

Above: Plumes of silt appear where Chisel Creek enters Fortress Lake.
The suspended silt gives the lake its stunning colour.

The cabins of the Fortress Lake Wilderness Retreat are scattered on the delta
where Chisel Creek meets Fortress Lake. Chisel Peak stands tall to the southwest.
In the distance are beautiful Serenity Mountain and the Hooker Icefield.

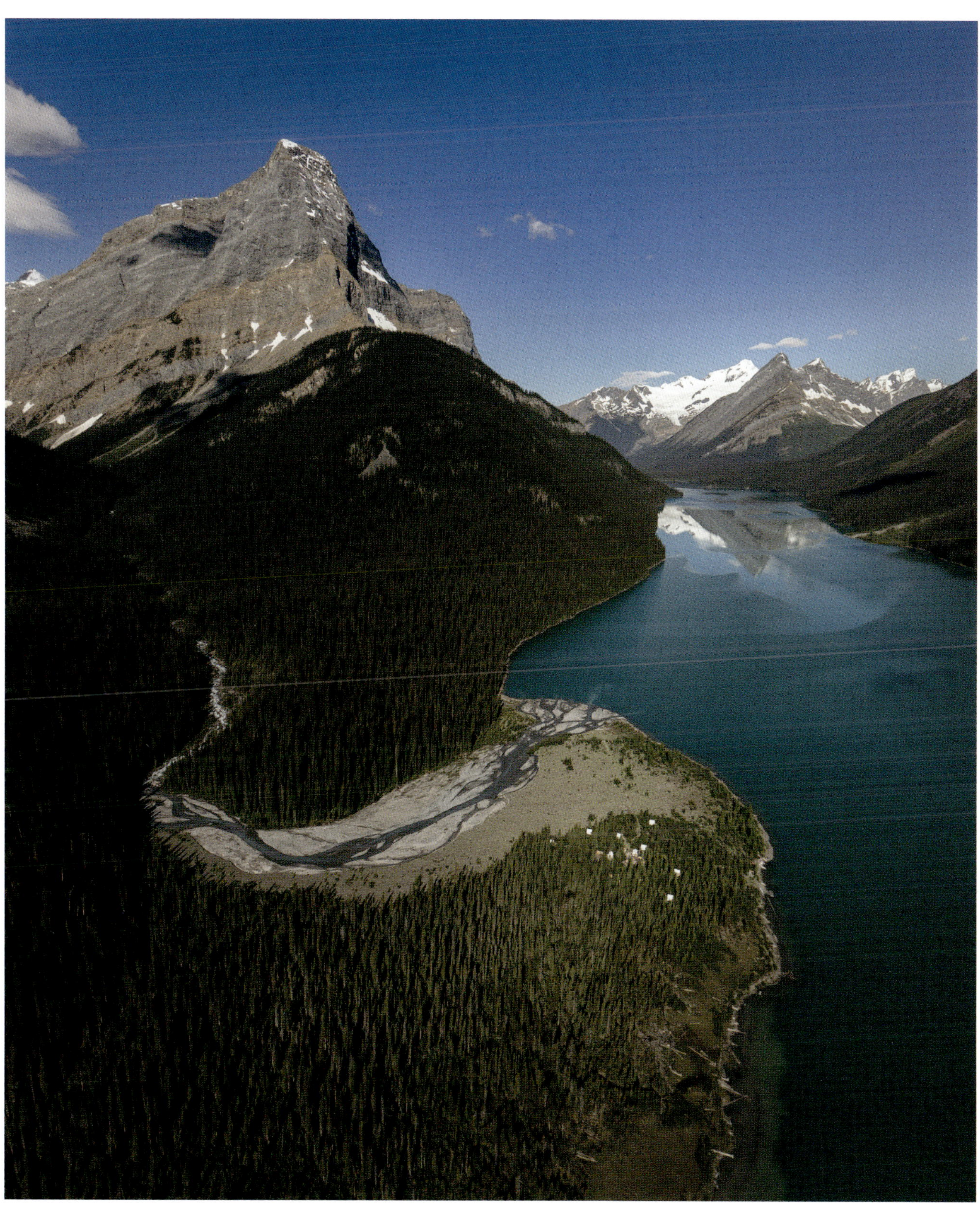

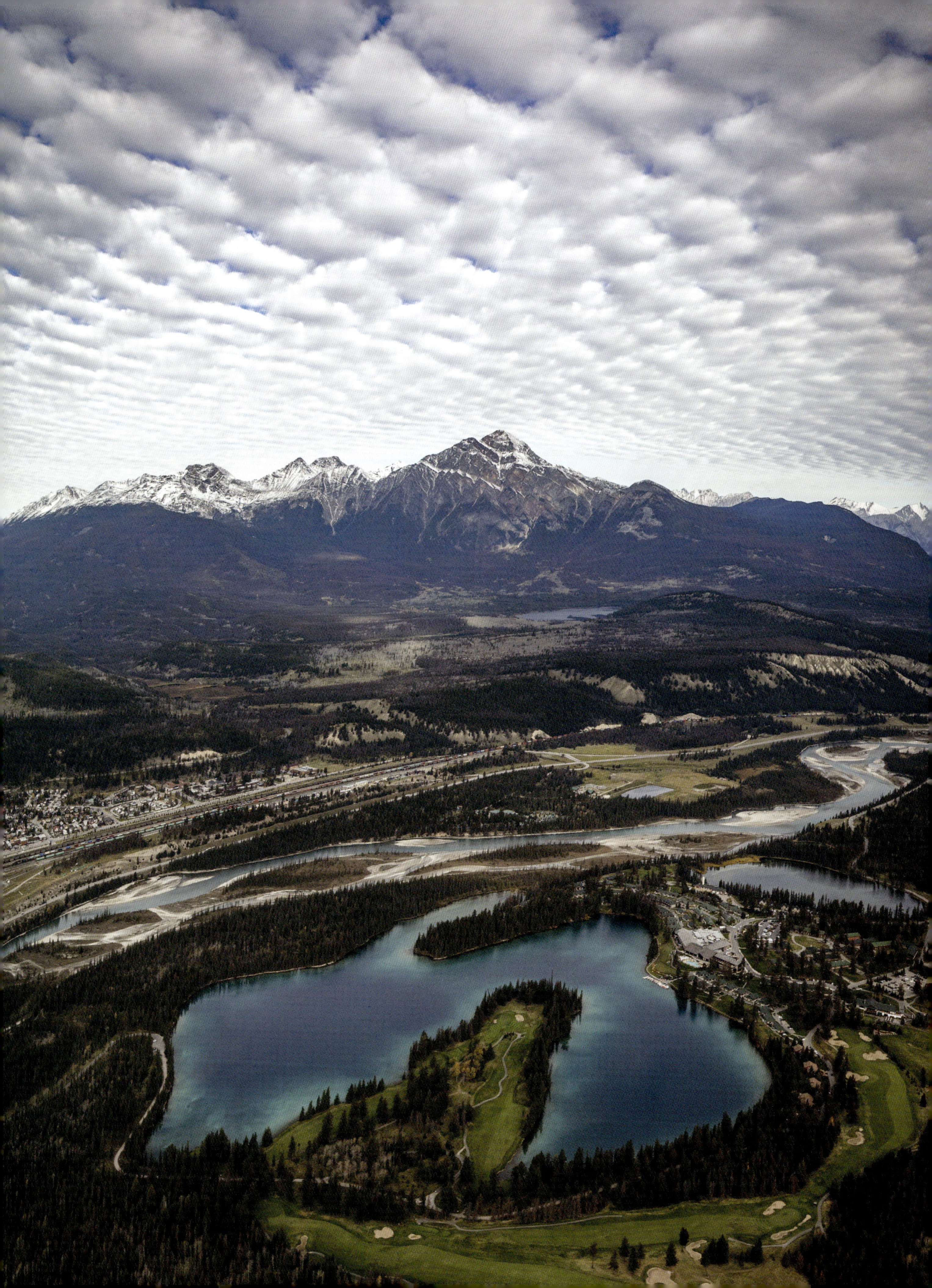

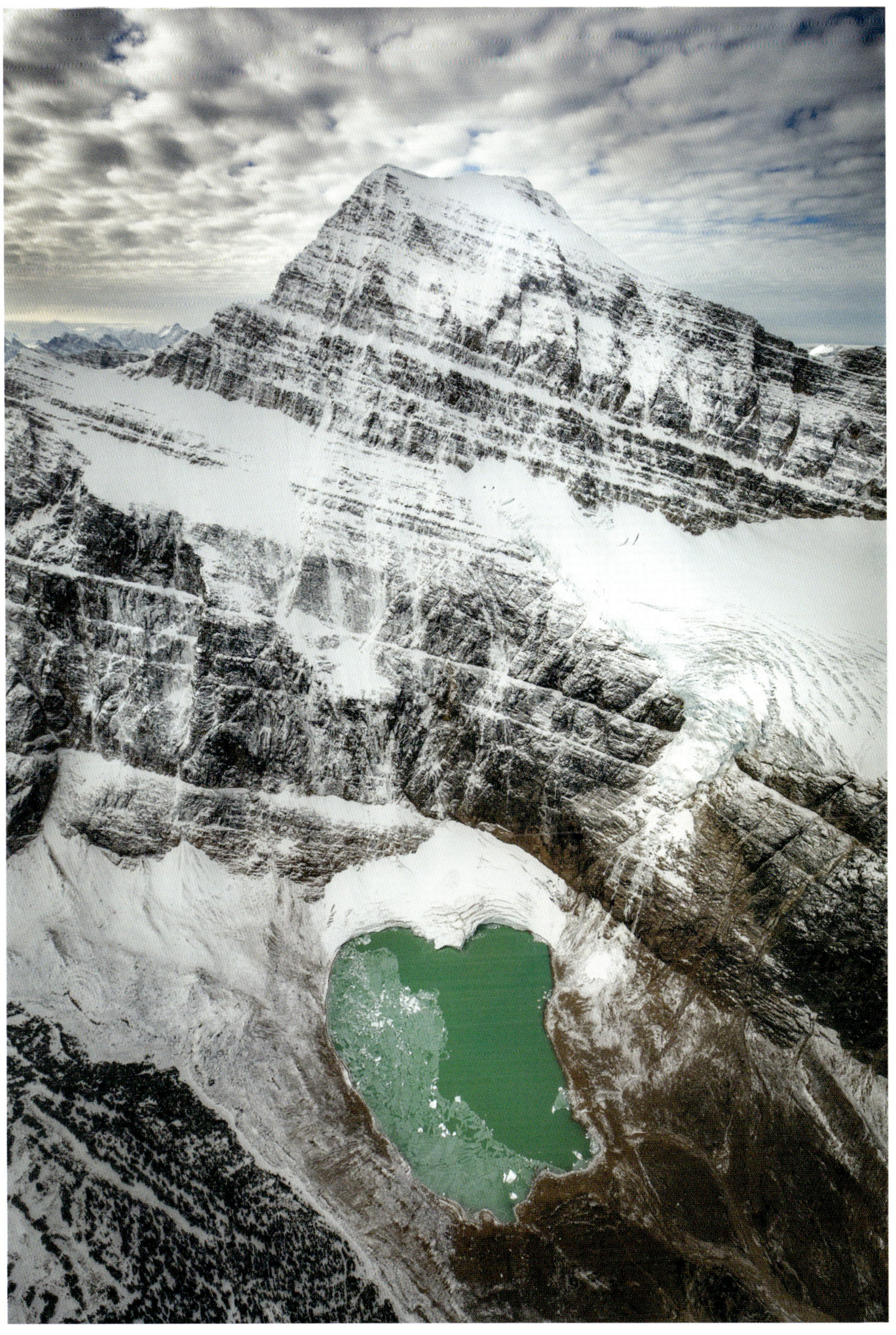

Opposite: The Fairmont Jasper Park Lodge and golf course encircles Lac Beauvert in Jasper National Park. Pyramid Mountain stands in the distance.

Above: The Angel Glacier on Mount Edith Cavell crumbles into Cavell Pond, leaving icebergs floating in the green water.

Opposite: The aptly named, snow-dusted Chevron Mountain
rises out of the Jasper backcountry.

Overleaf: The notable peaks of the Ramparts stand tall
over the Tonquin Valley and Amethyst Lakes.

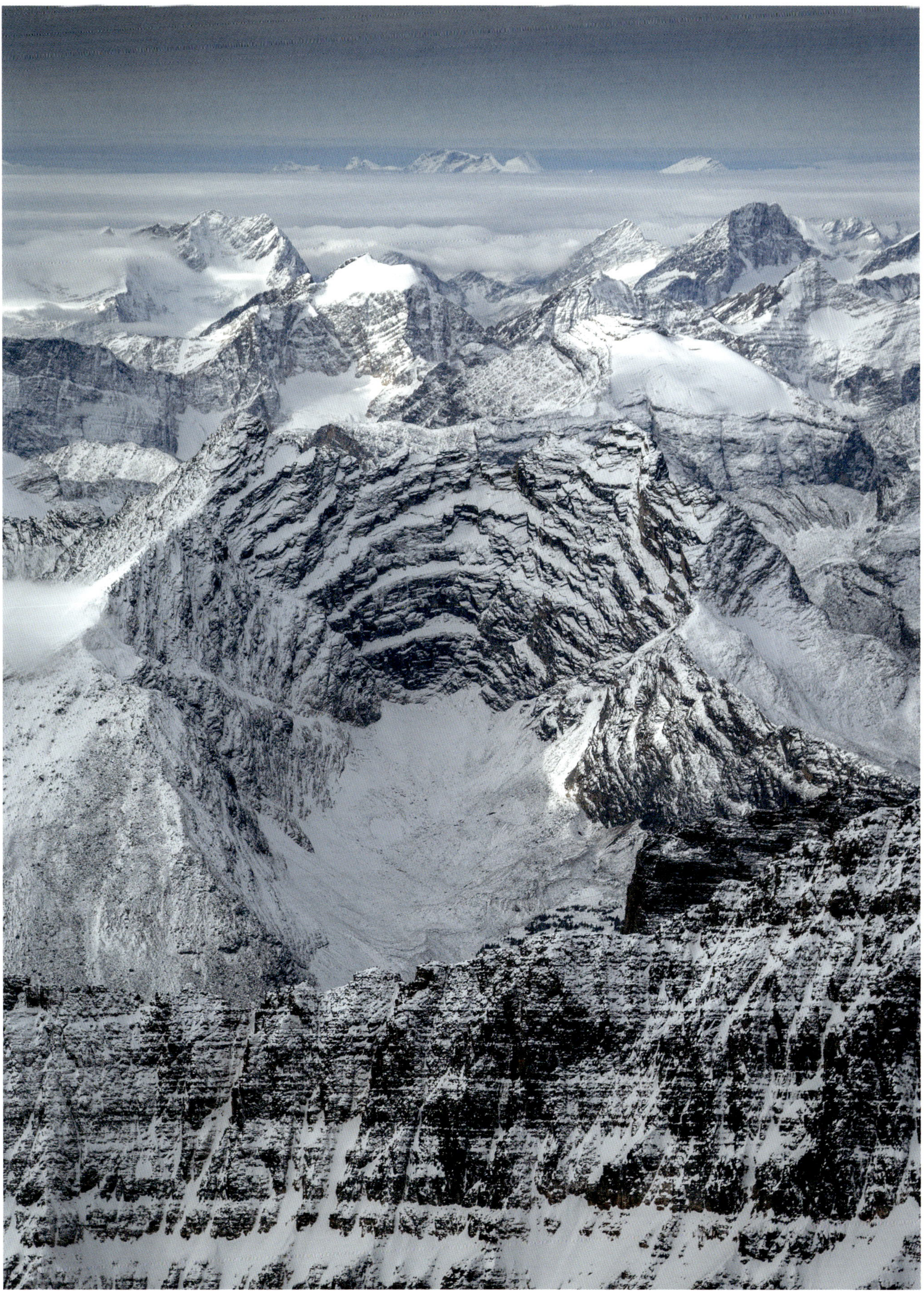

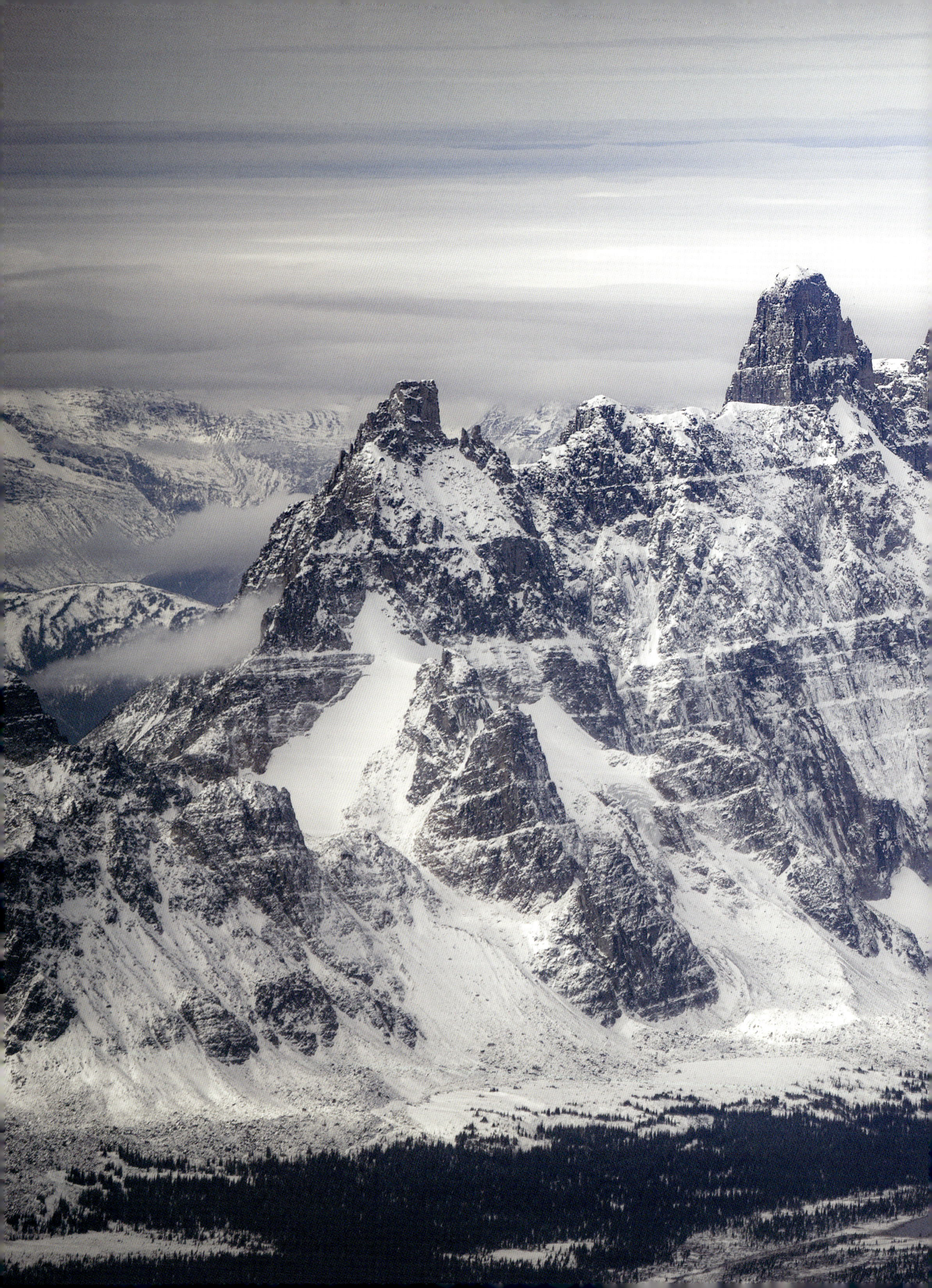

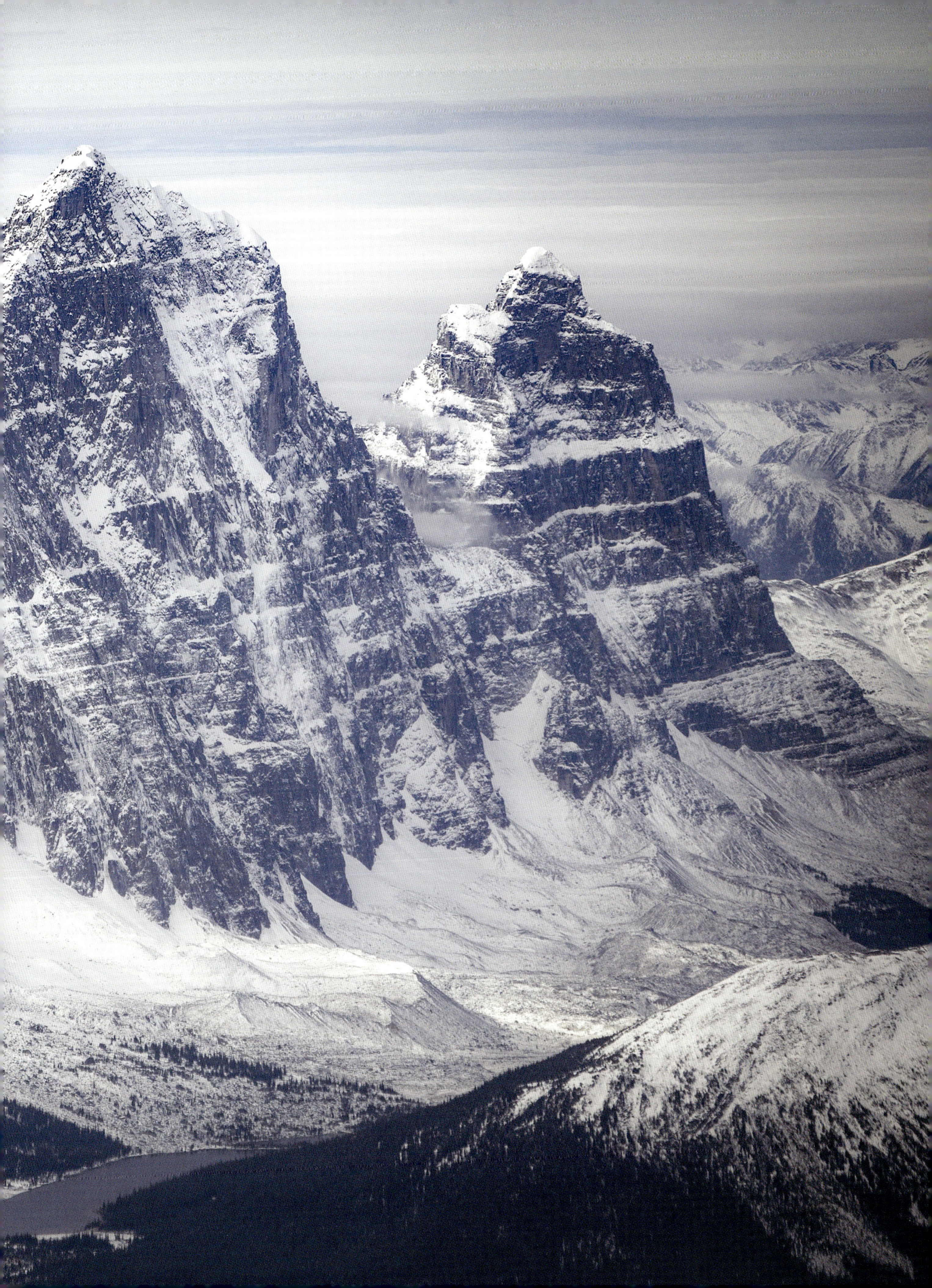

Opposite: Striking Lake Columbia sits below the massive north face
of Mount Columbia, the highest peak in Alberta, on the left.
Its neighbour to the right is Mount King Edward.

Overleaf: The Columbia Glacier tumbles down from the Columbia Icefield
into the lake of the same name, on a stunning summer day
in Jasper National Park. Note the ogives (darker bands) on the glacier.
On the far left, in the distance, is Mount Bryce.

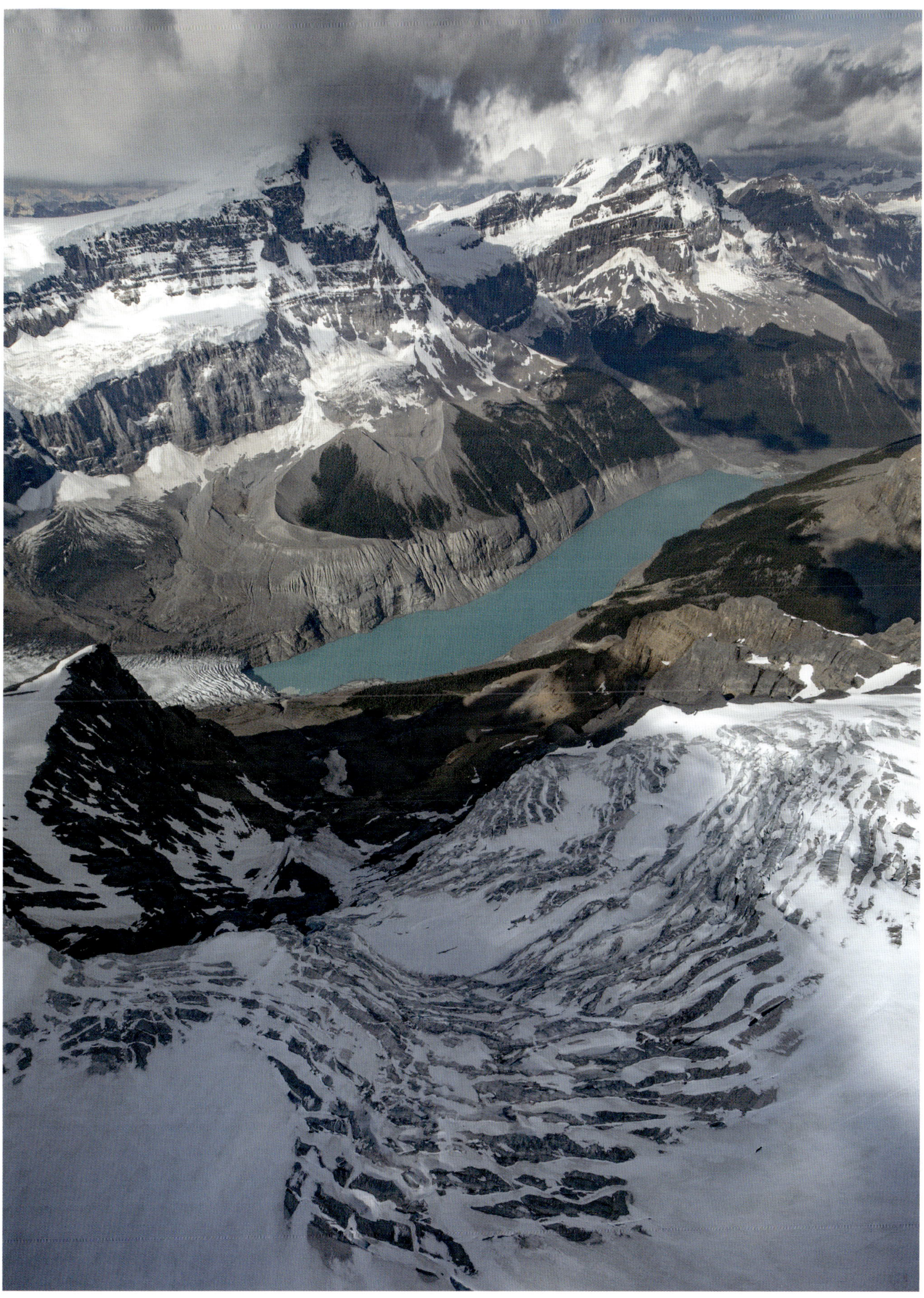

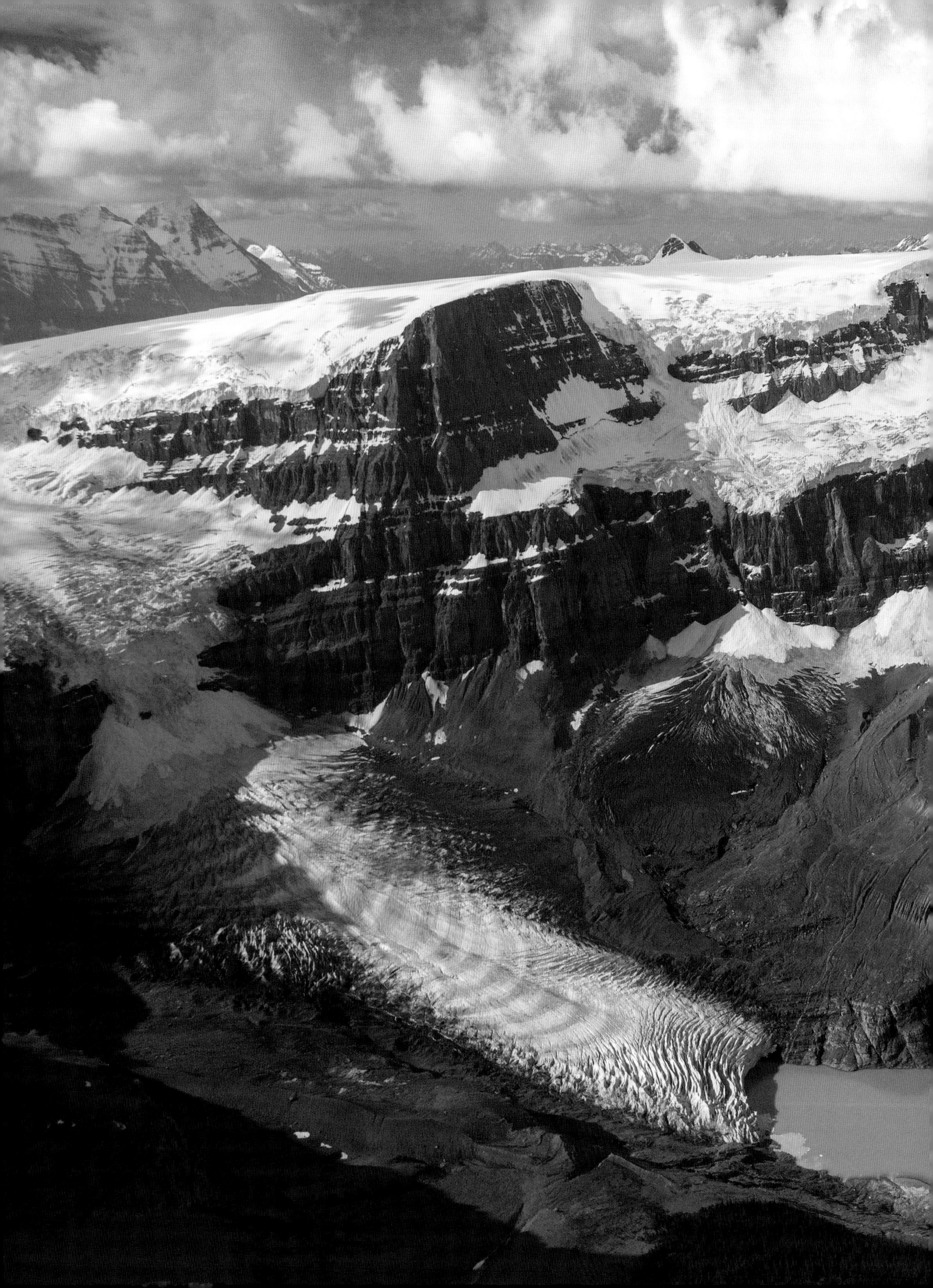

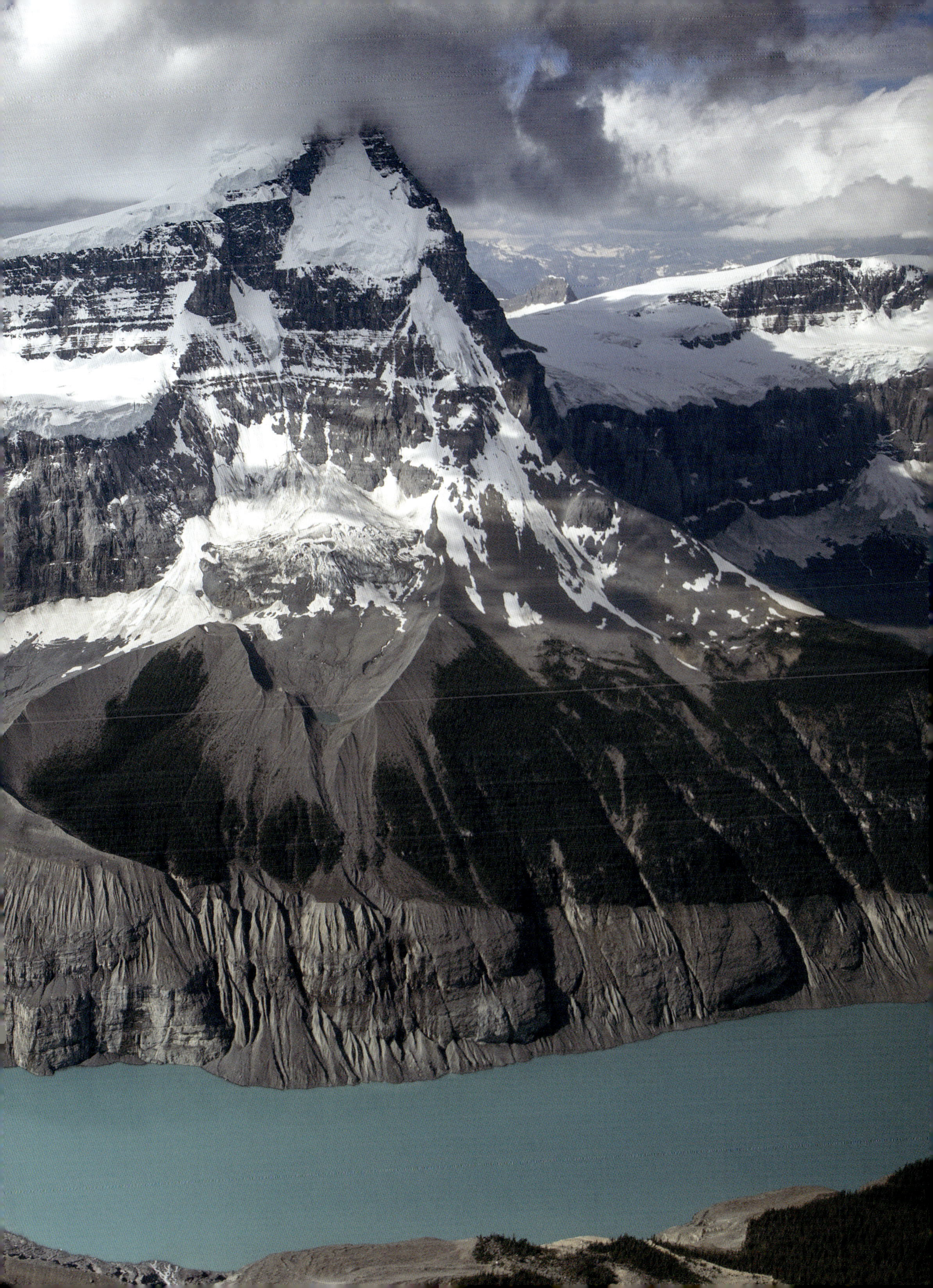

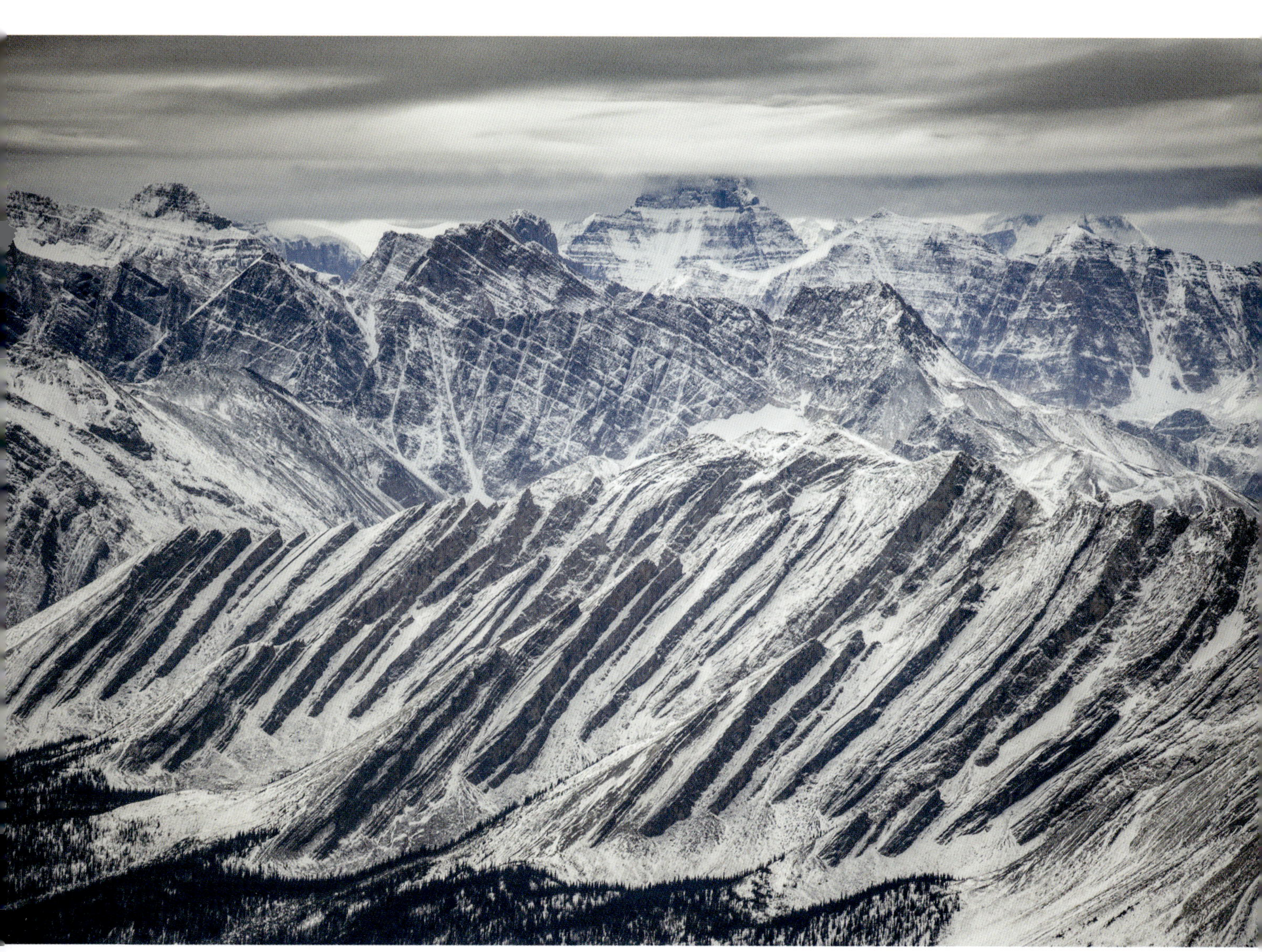

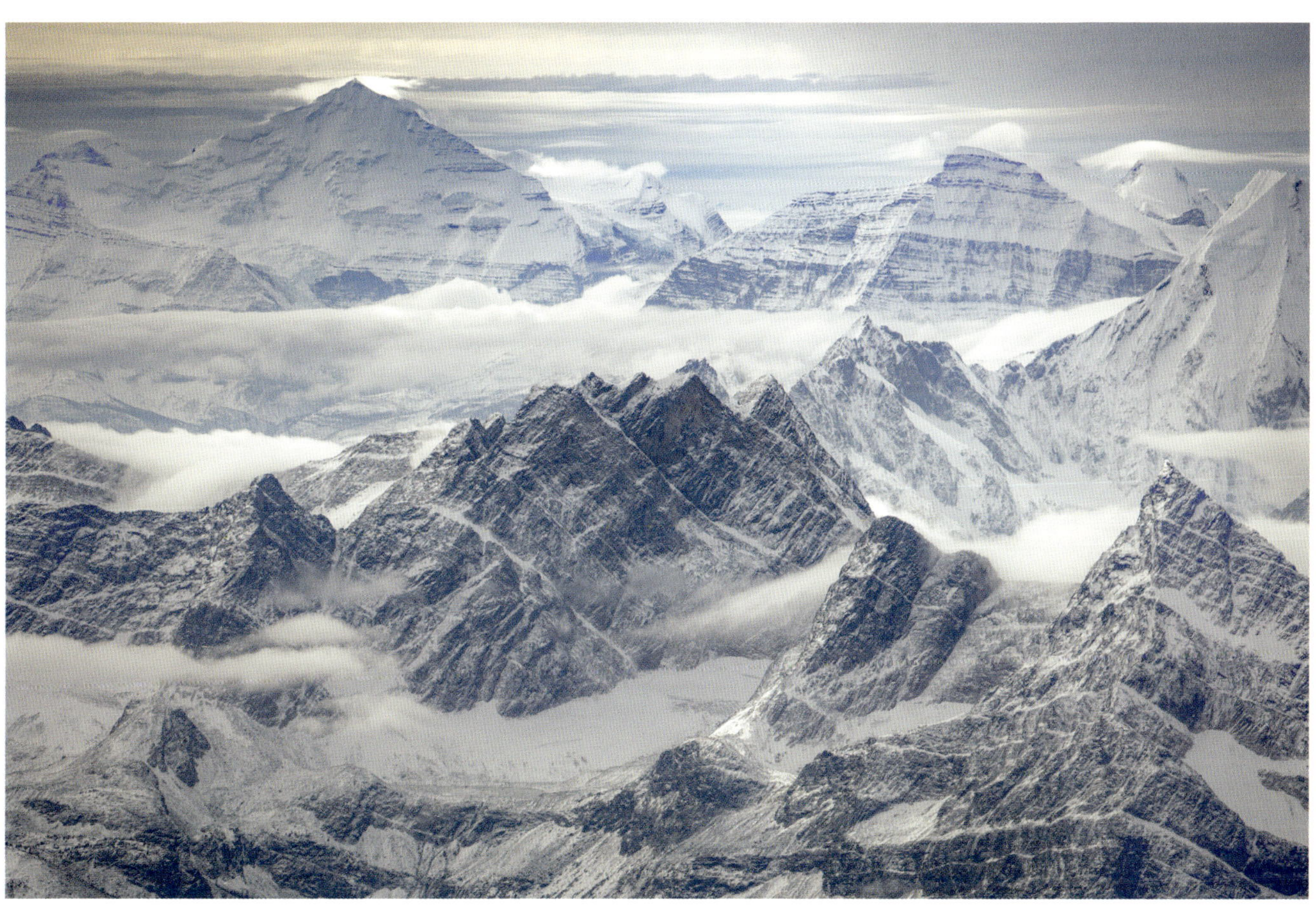

Opposite: Mount Alberta, with its head in the clouds. The dusting of snow
reveals patterns and rock layers that are otherwise less prominent.

Above: The monstrous pyramid of Mount Clemenceau, fourth highest peak in the Canadian Rockies,
emerges head and shoulders above the other ranges of Jasper National Park.

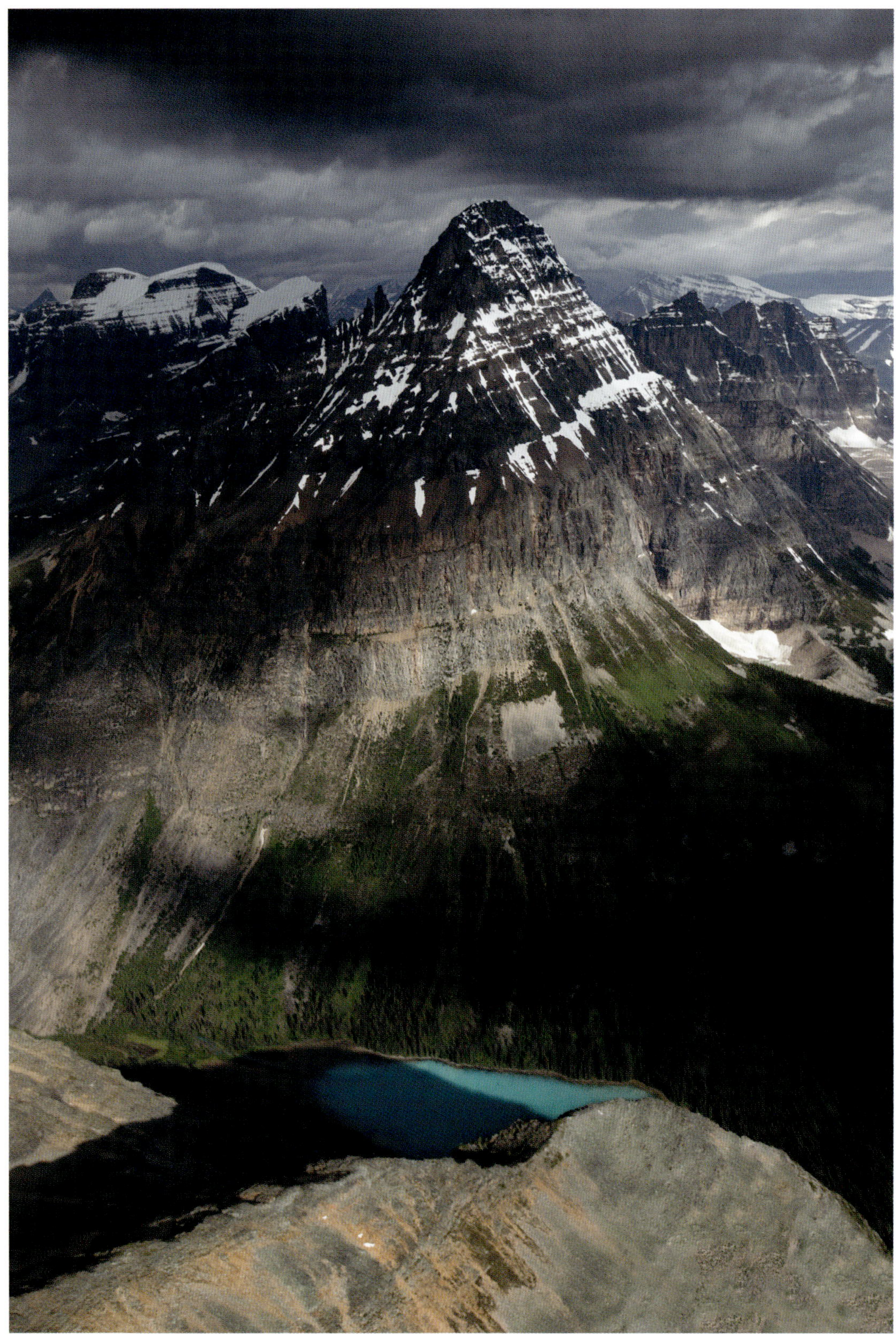

Above: Horn-shaped Blackfriars Peak and an unnamed lake are painted
in beautiful light during a summer flight to Hamber Provincial Park.

Opposite: Mount Alberta is known in the mountaineering world as the most difficult
peak to climb in the Canadian Rockies. This is the "easy" east side.

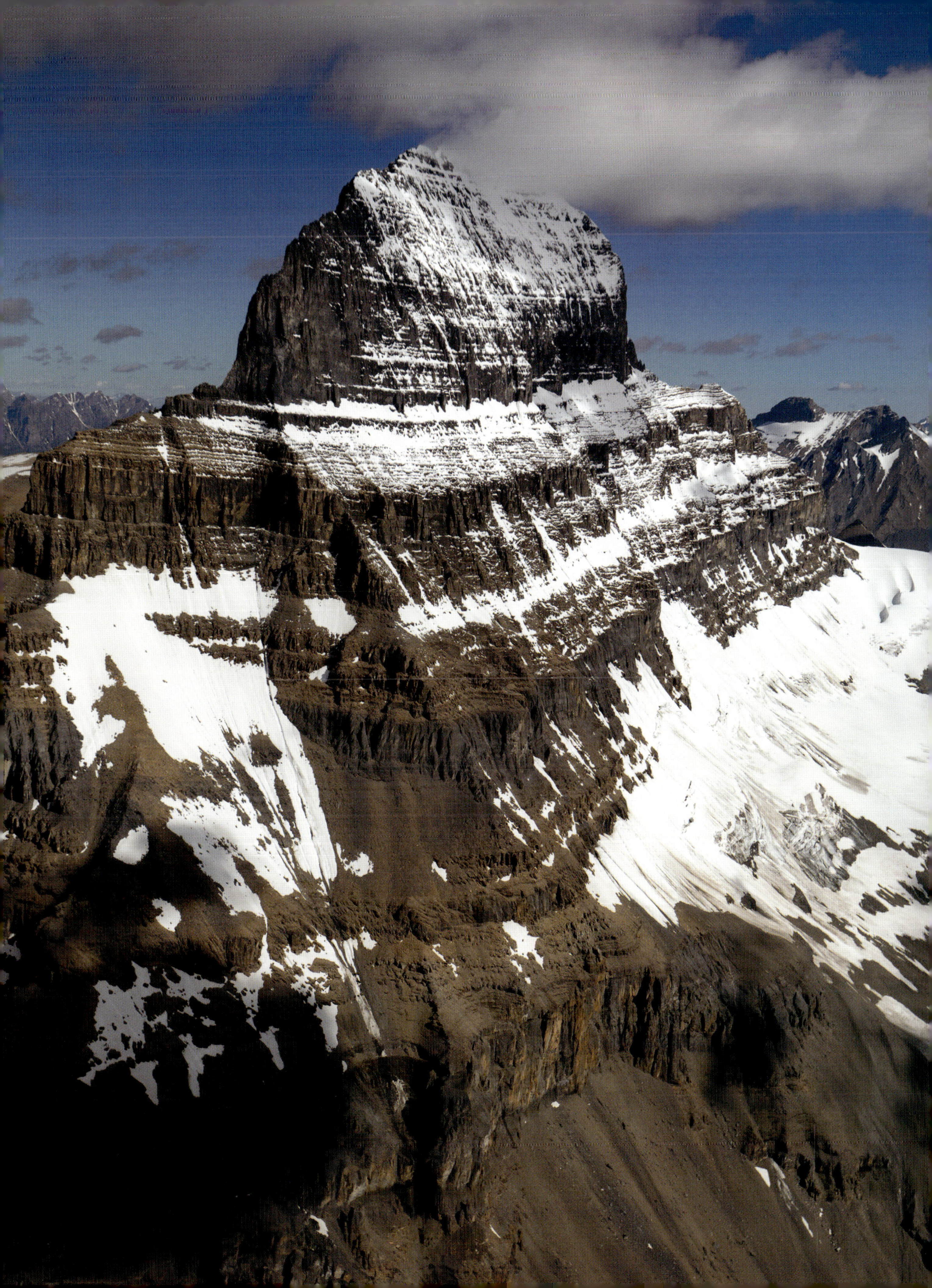

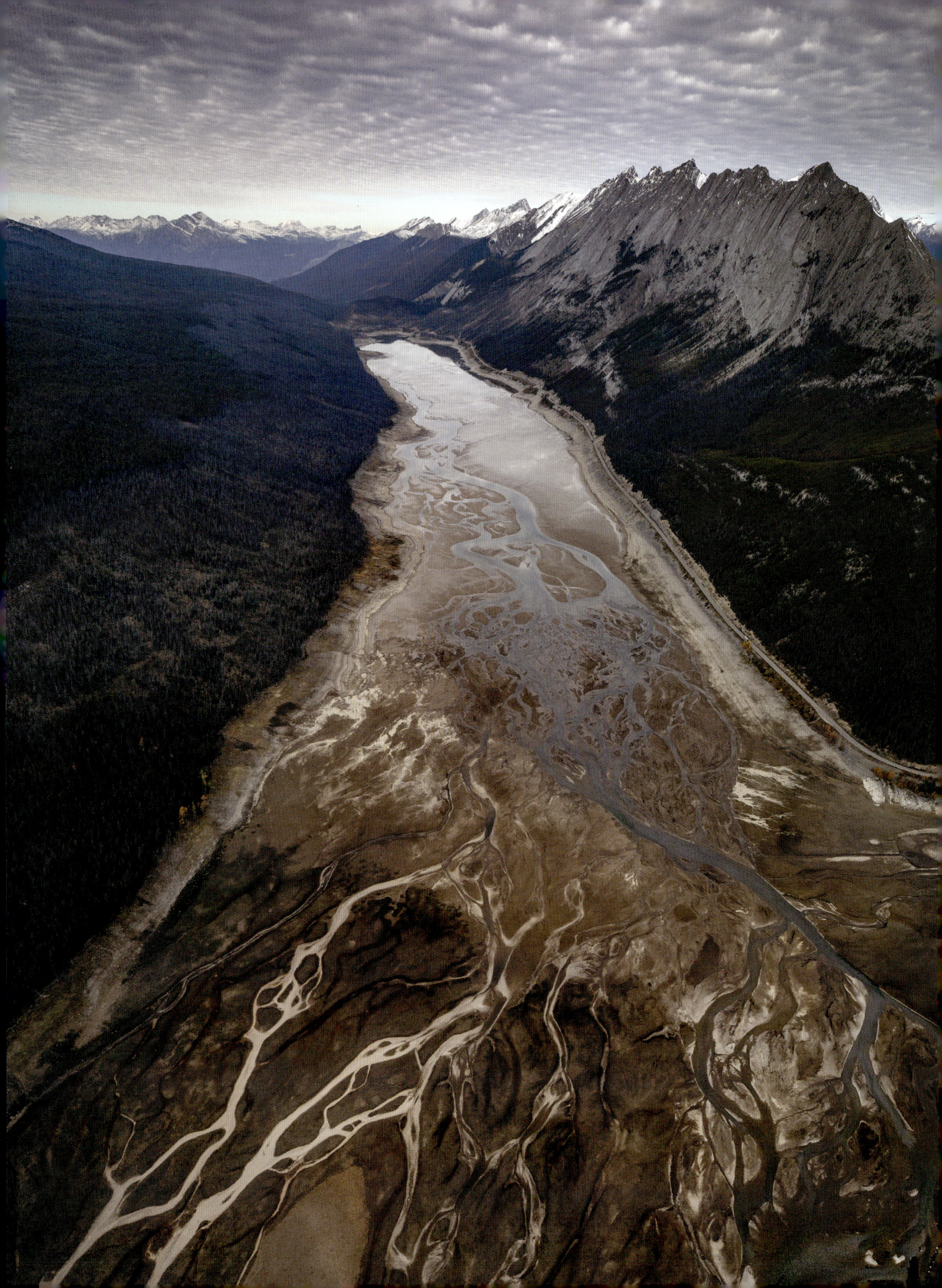

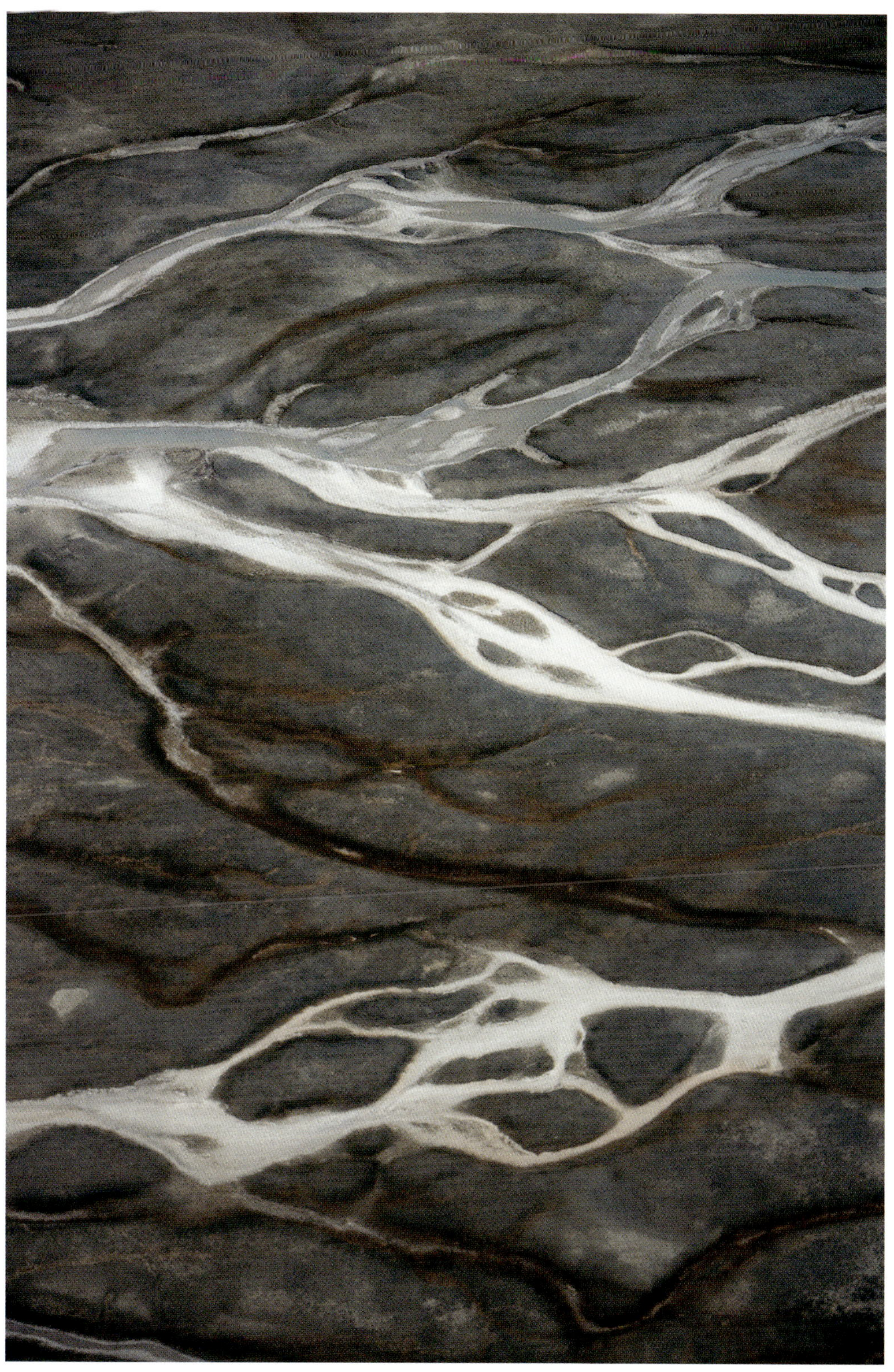

Opposite: Intricate patterns grace the south end of Medicine Lake.

Above: Abstract flow structures on the bed of Medicine Lake. A unique feature on the Jasper landscape, this lake fills up with glacial meltwater in the summer. In fall and winter the lake dissipates through sinkholes out the bottom, leaving behind mere pools connected by streams.

Overleaf: Waterways make patterns in Medicine Lake.

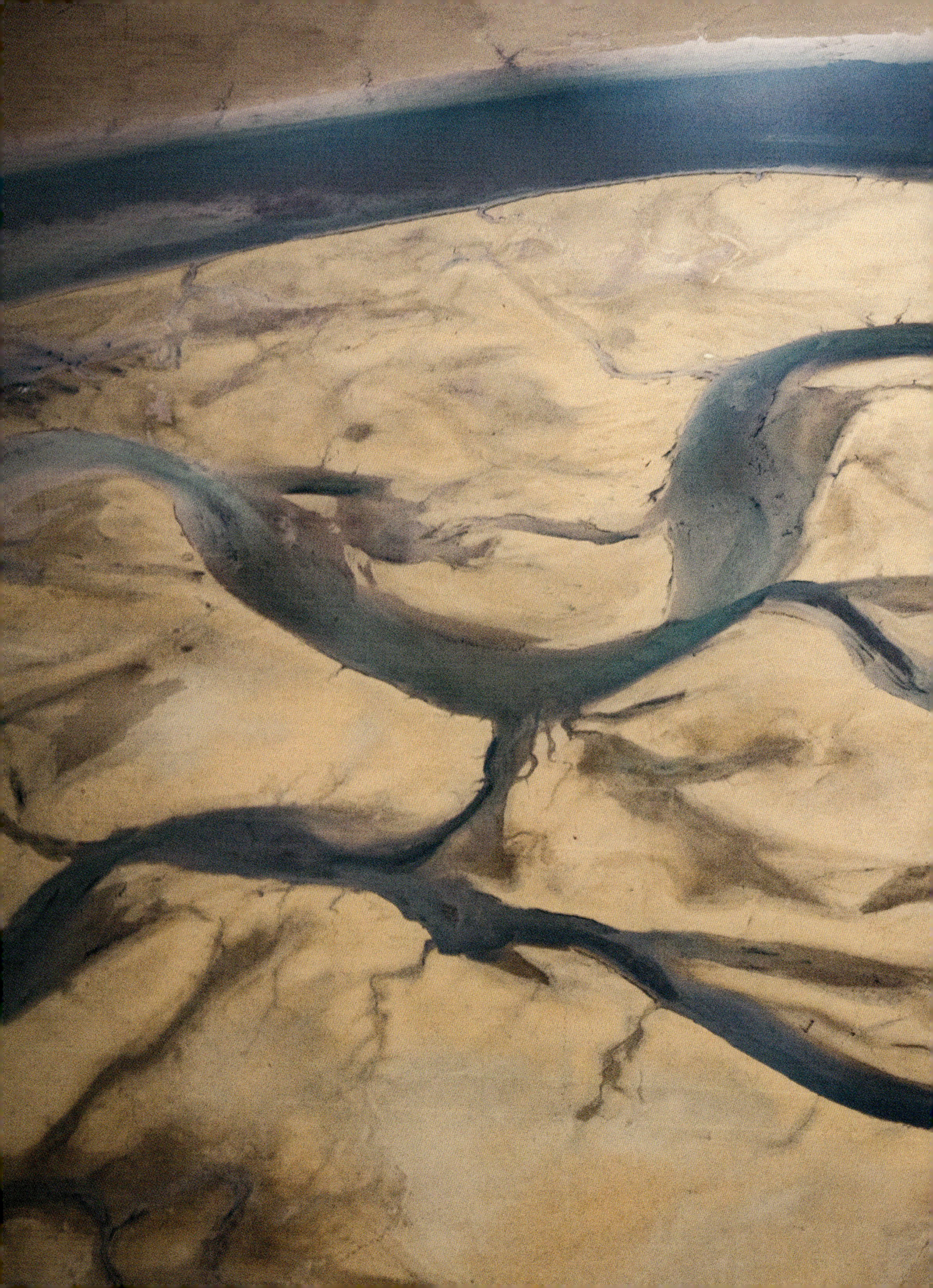

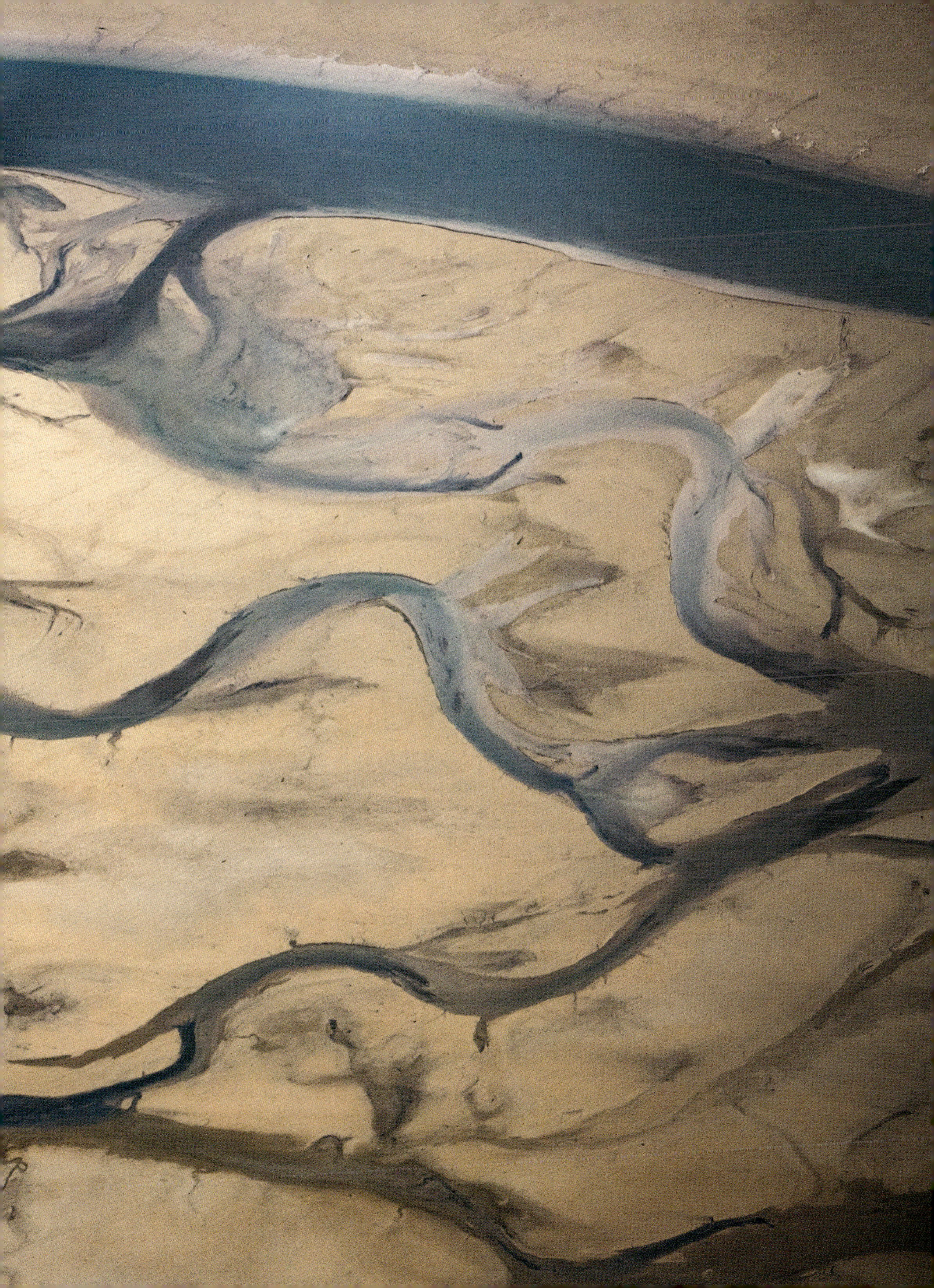

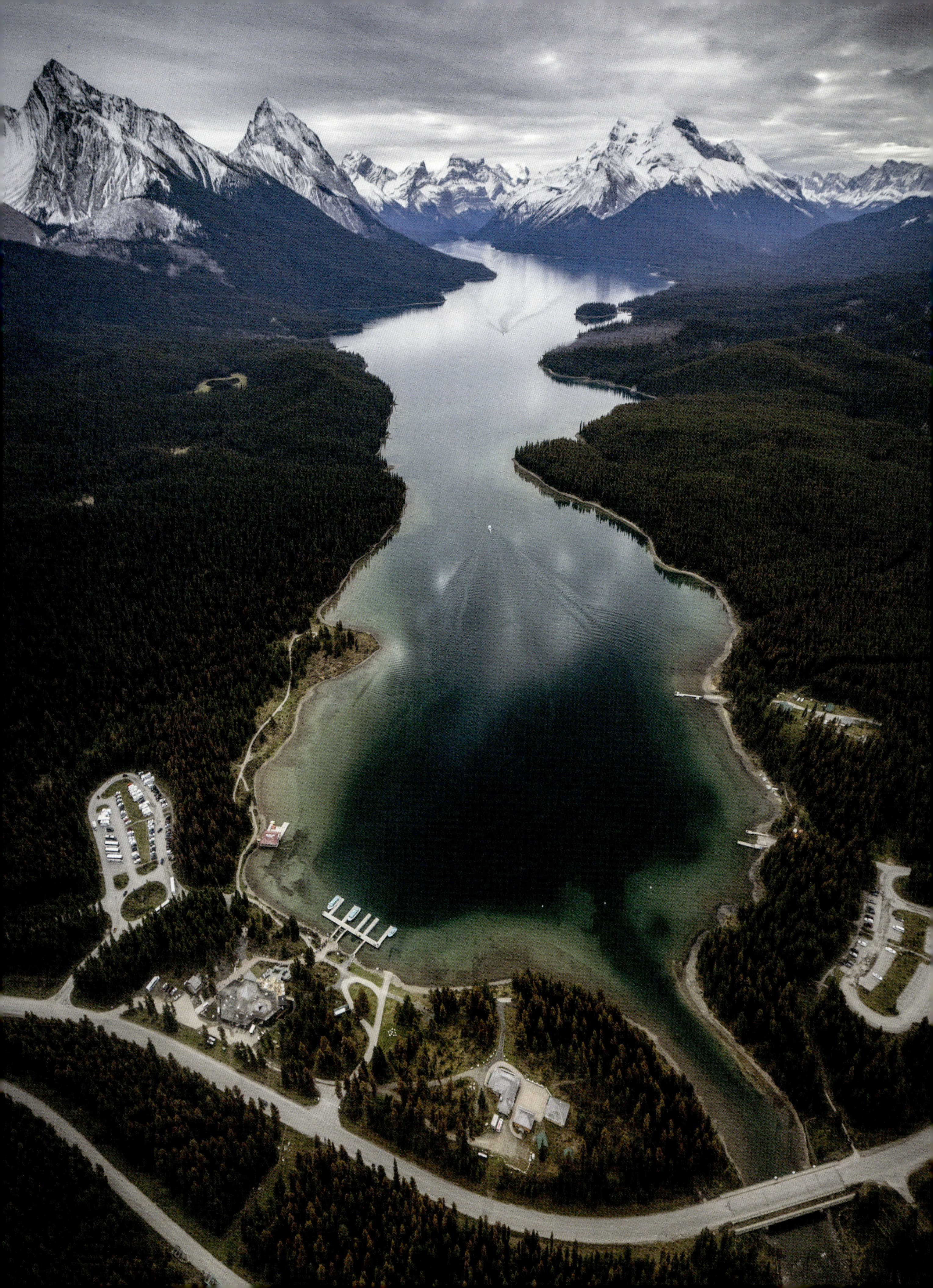

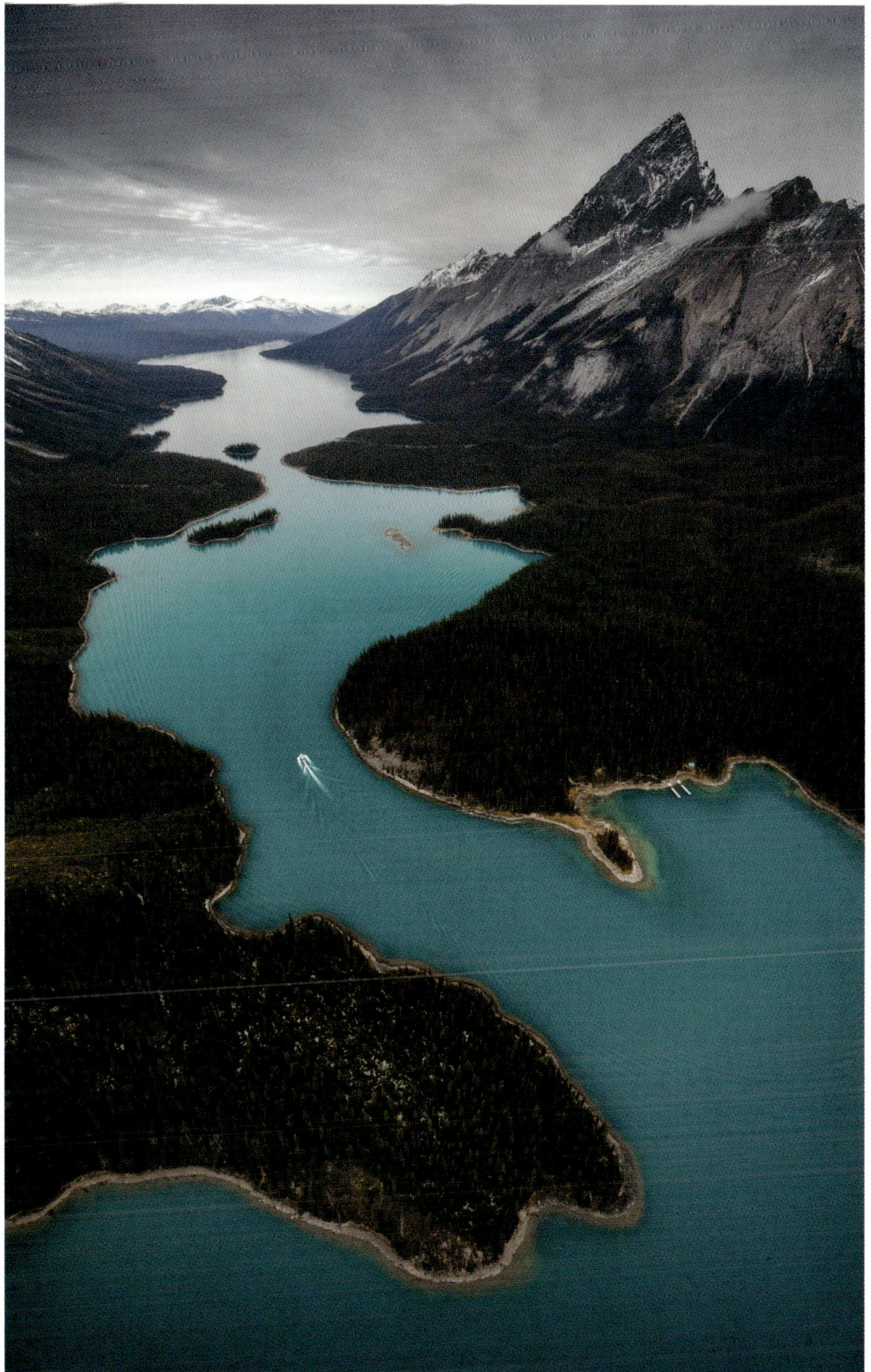

Opposite: Looking south along Maligne Lake, by anyone's account
one of the most gorgeous bodies of water in the Canadian Rockies.

Above: Looking north along Maligne Lake and its narrows. Spirit Island is visible as a peninsula
near the centre of the image, while triangular Samson Peak dominates the skies in the distance.
As this image demonstrates, for much of the year Spirit Island isn't an island
when lake levels are low but rather a peninsula.

Overleaf: A boat cruises up Maligne Lake, just past Spirit Island. Seen from the shore,
the view of Spirit Island and Maligne Lake is one of the most photographed in the Canadian Rockies.

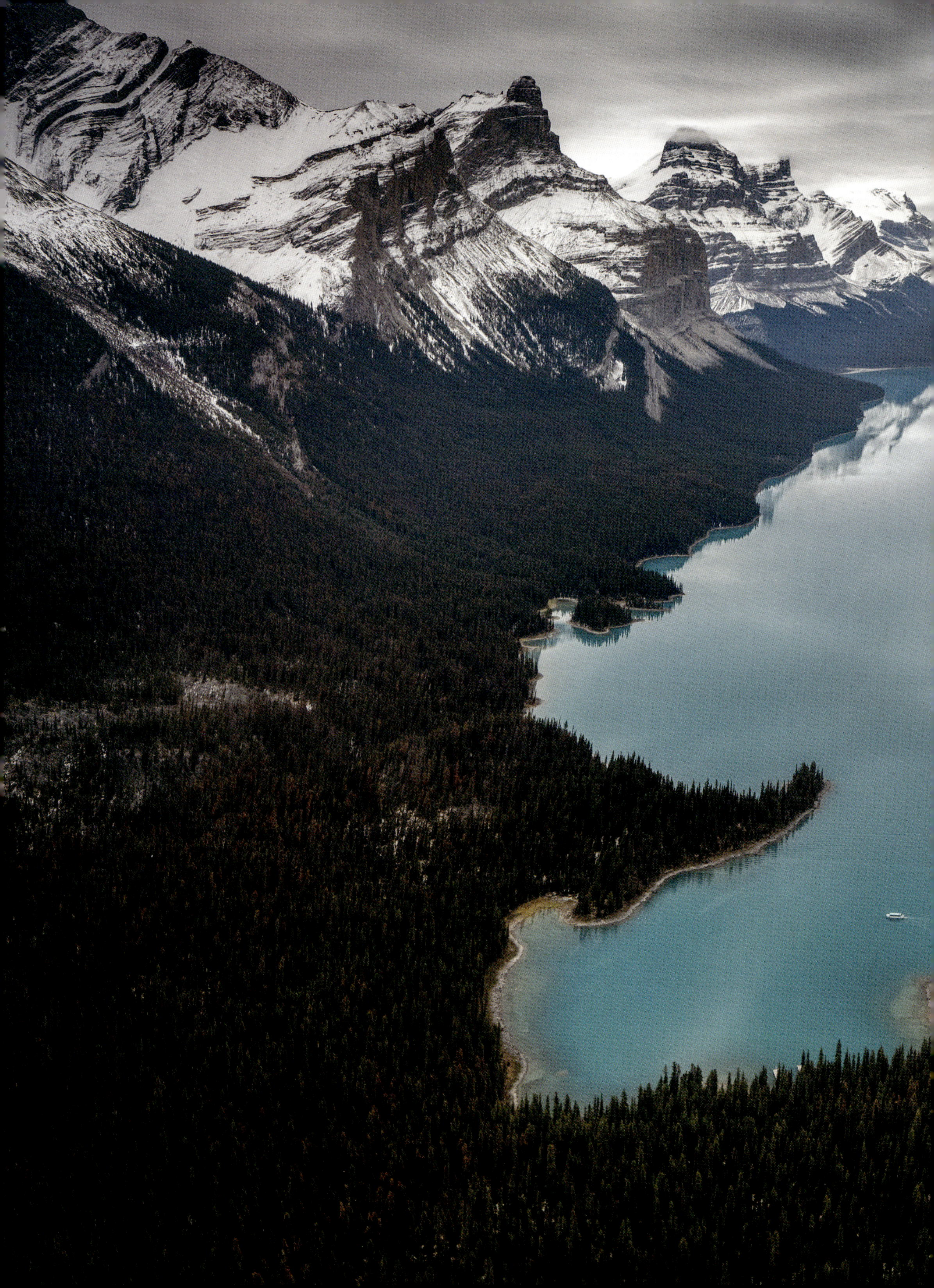

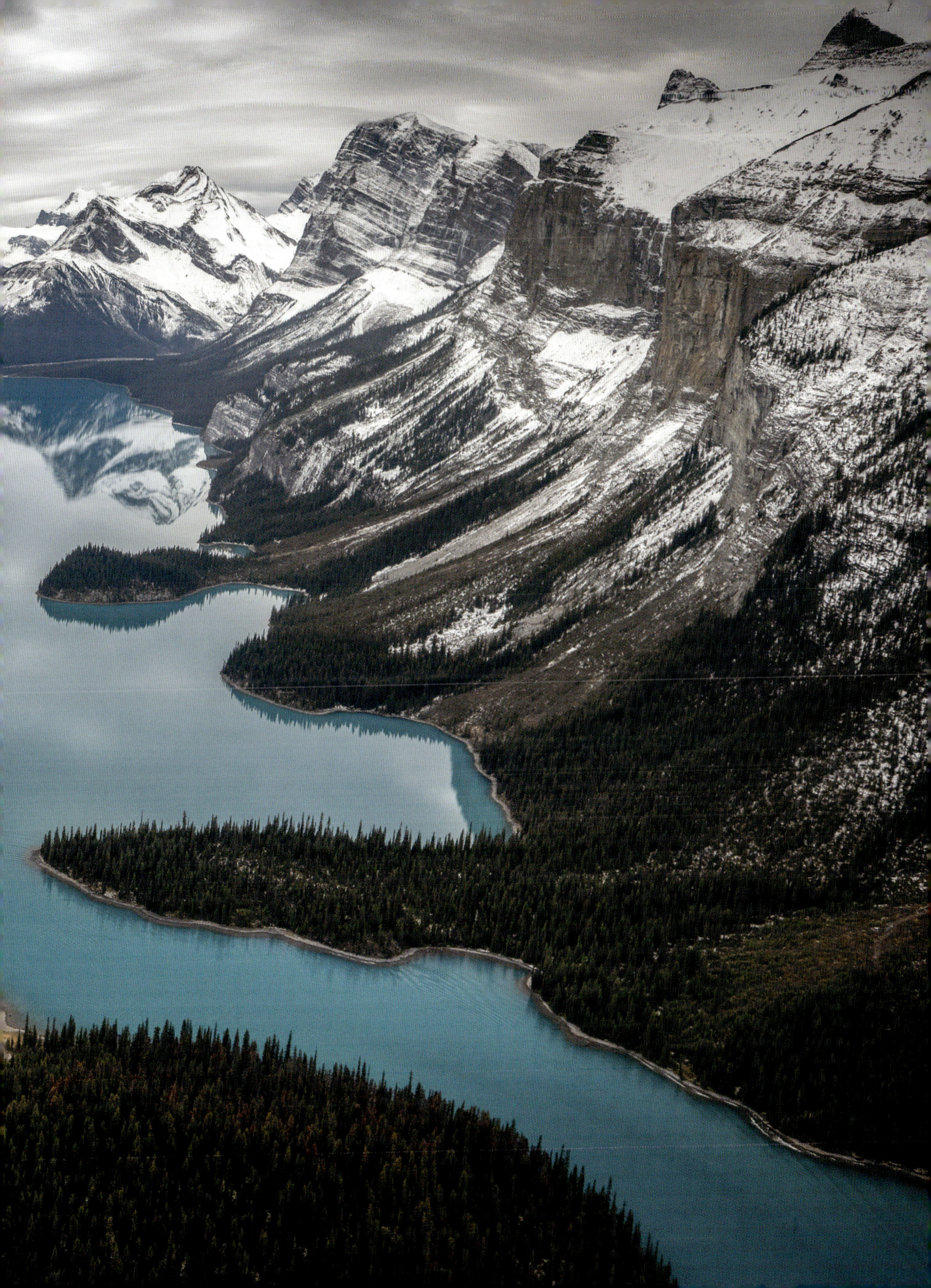

Opposite: On any clear day in Jasper National Park,
the striking shape of Mount Robson to the northwest steals the show.

Overleaf: This image shows much of the Berg Lake Trail, one of the finest hikes
in the world. The adventure starts near Kinney Lake over on the right, and then
follows the waterway past Emperor Falls (bottom left) to emerge in the basin
where Mist and Berg lakes sit. Massive Mount Robson looks down on all the action.

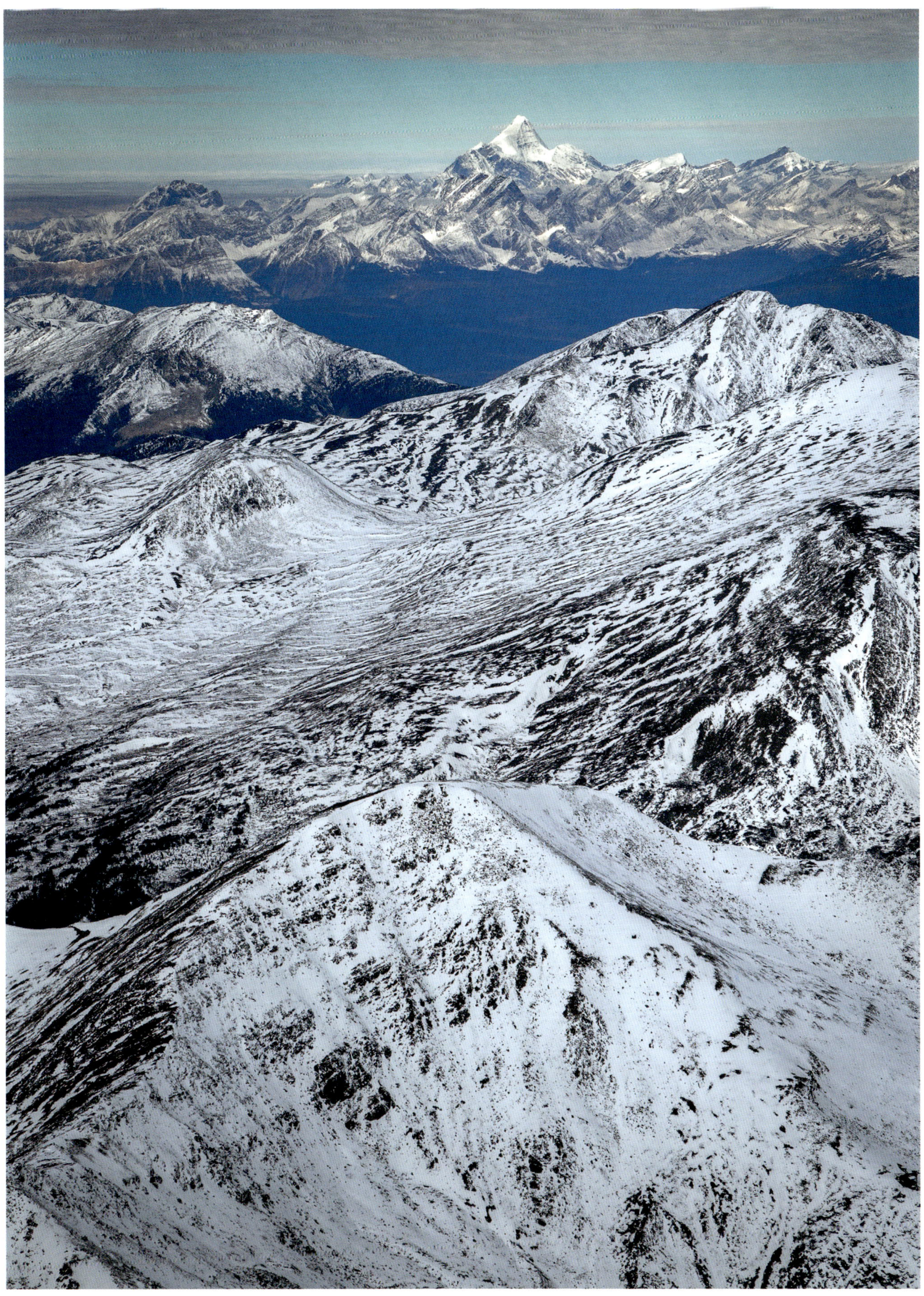

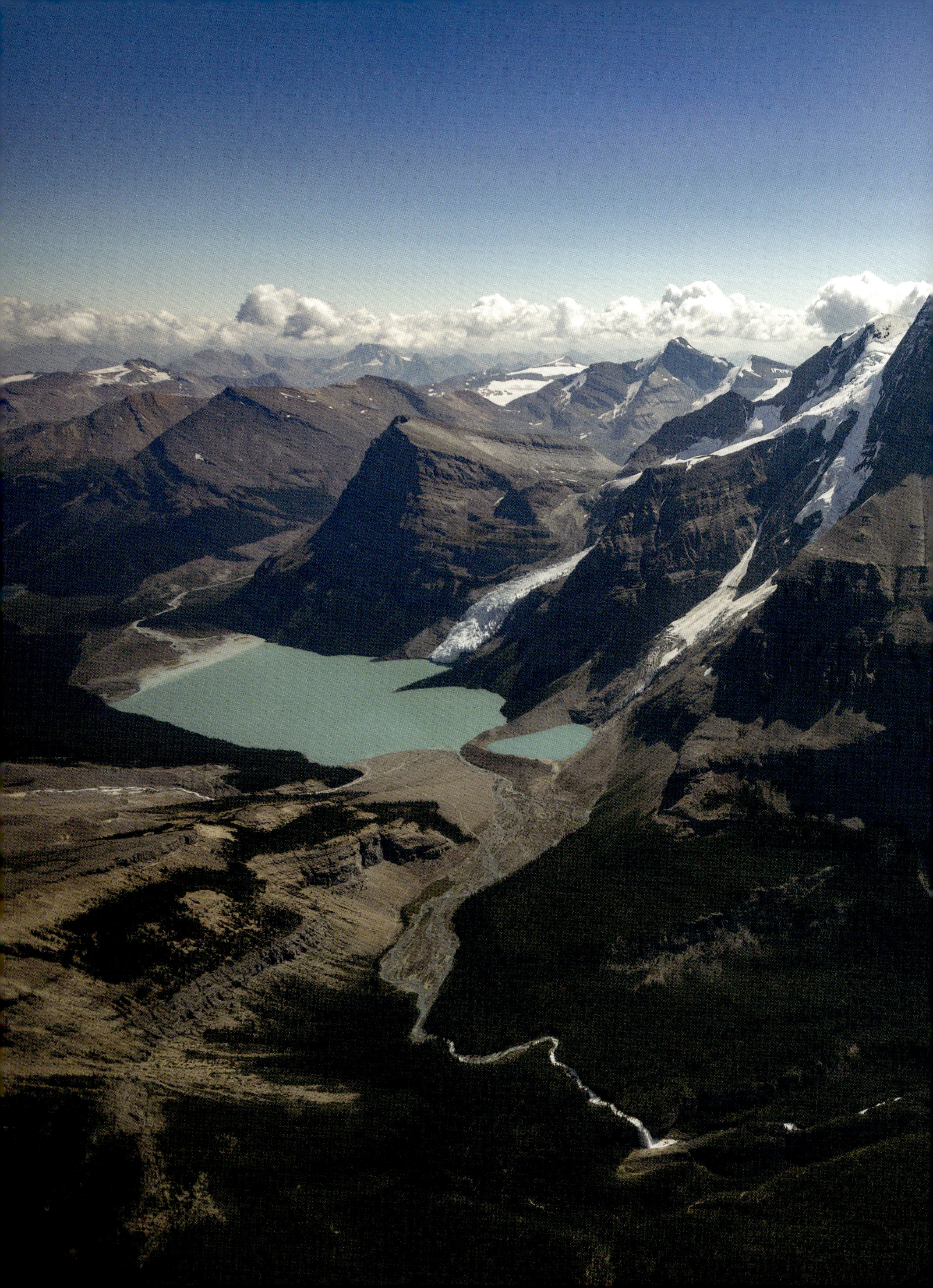

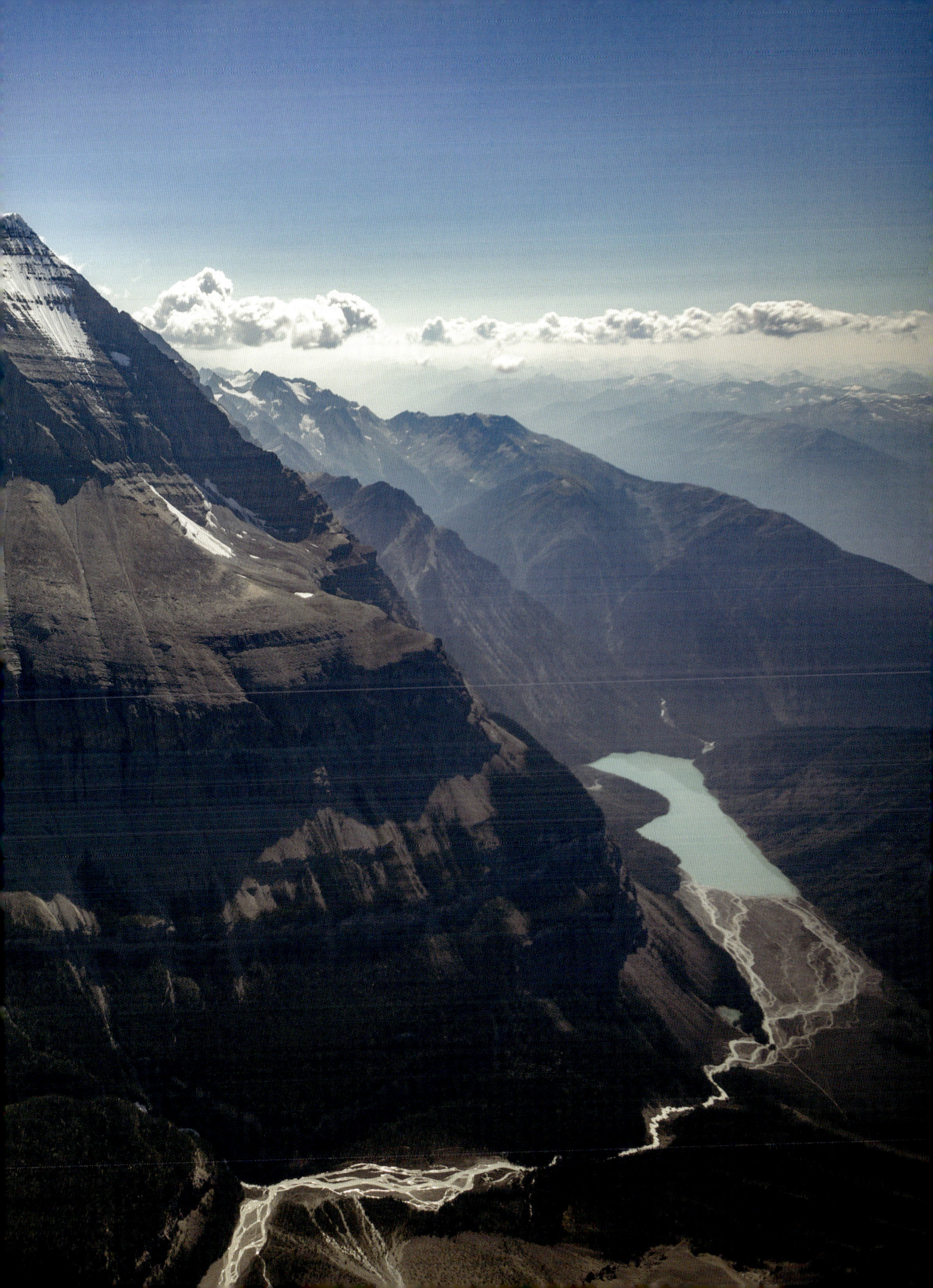

Opposite: The north face of Mount Robson reflects the sunlight in this image taken above greenish Hargreaves Lake. Berg and Mist lakes are visible in the shadows.

Overleaf: The moon sets between White Pyramid and Mount Phillips.
Below are the Hargreaves Glacier and its namesake lake.

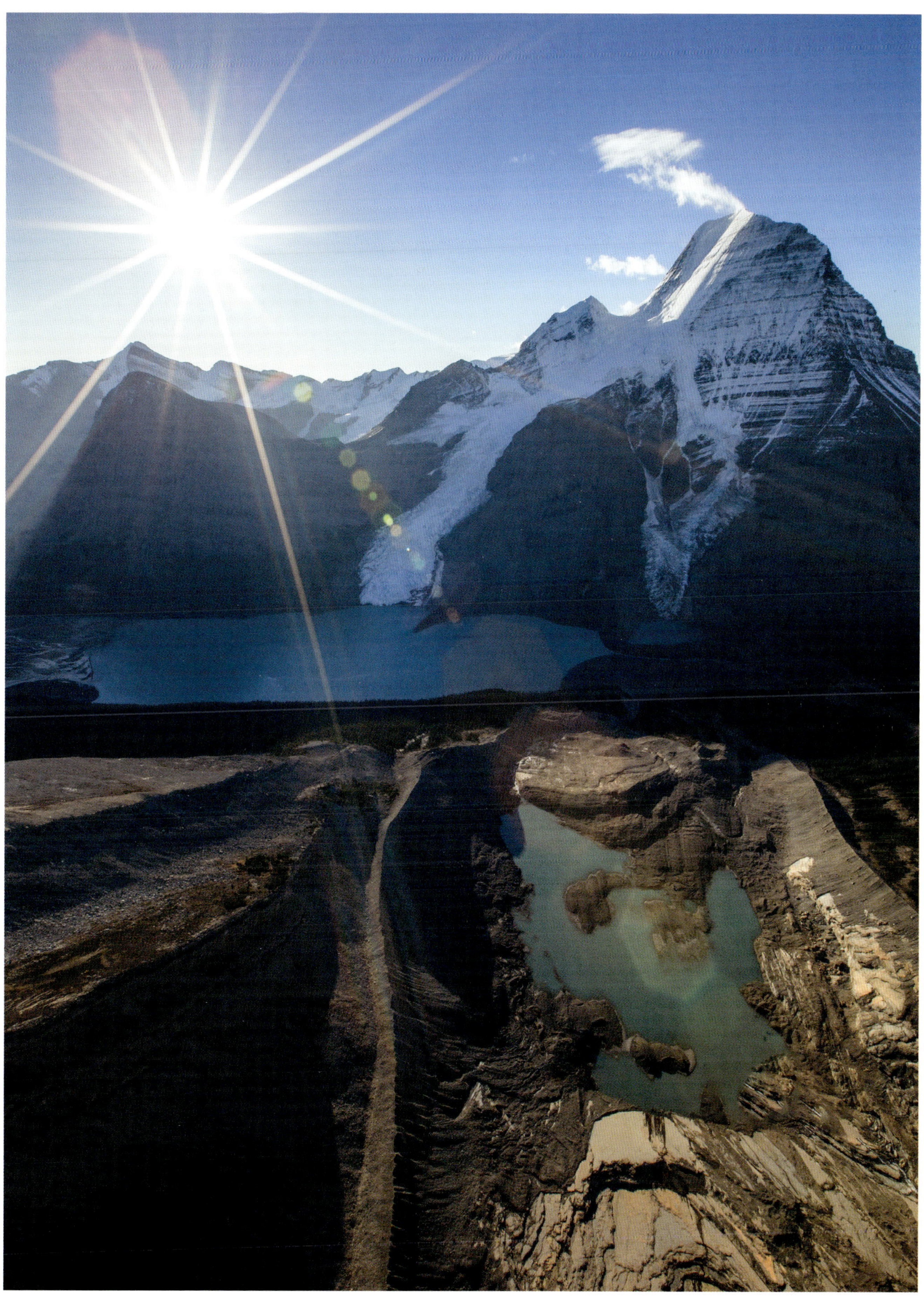

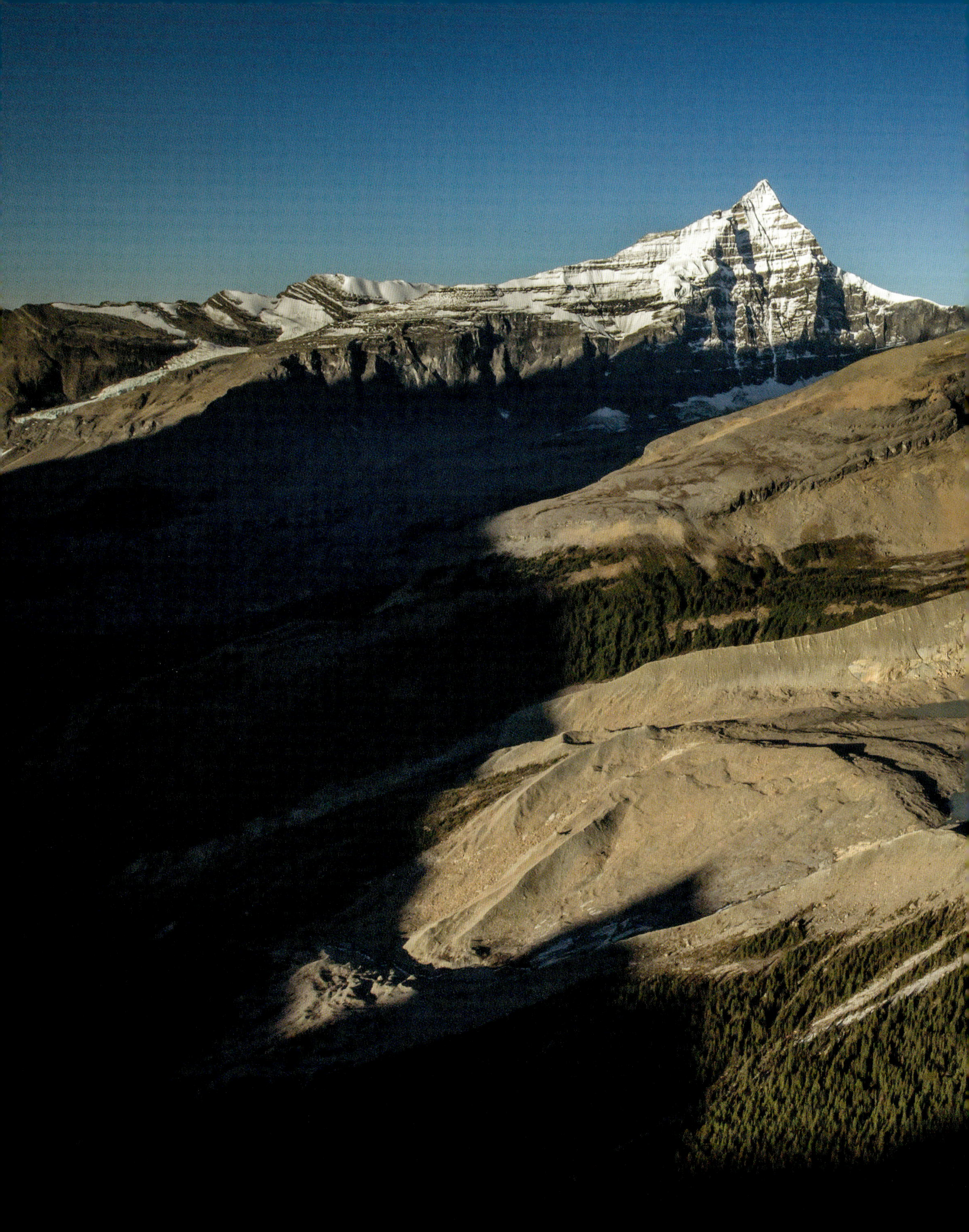

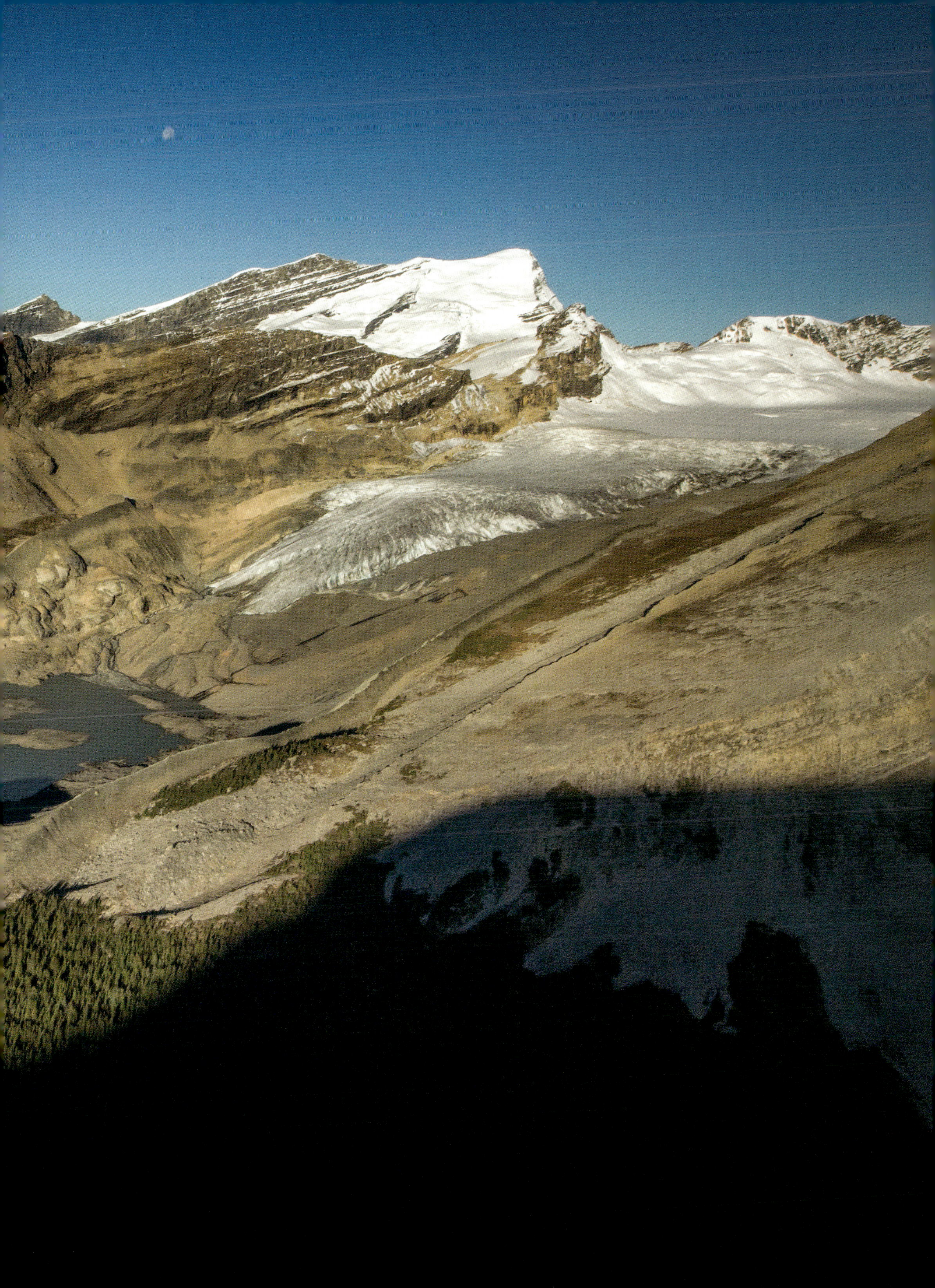

Opposite: The Emperor Ridge on Mount Robson is one of the most famous climbing routes on the highest peak in the Canadian Rockies. The mountain, which stands tall at 3954 metres, is unofficially called Cloud Cap Mountain after the cloud that frequently forms over the summit, thankfully not on this glorious day flying over it. Mount Robson was first known to Indigenous peoples as Yuh-hai-has-kun (The Mountain of the Spiral Road).

Overleaf: The triangular shadow of Mount Robson creeps toward other glaciated giants of the area: (l–r) White Pyramid, Mount Longstaff and Mount Phillips.

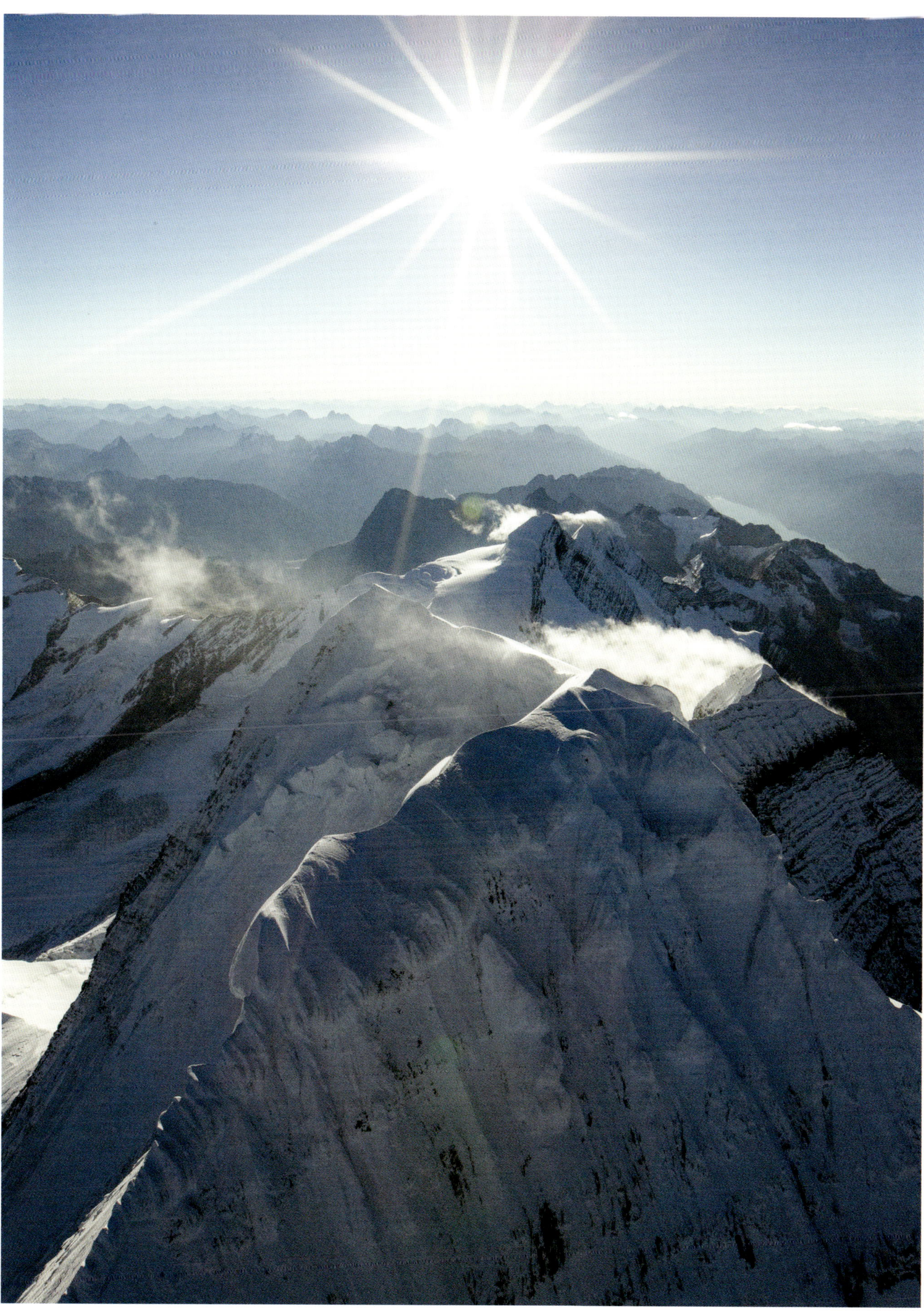

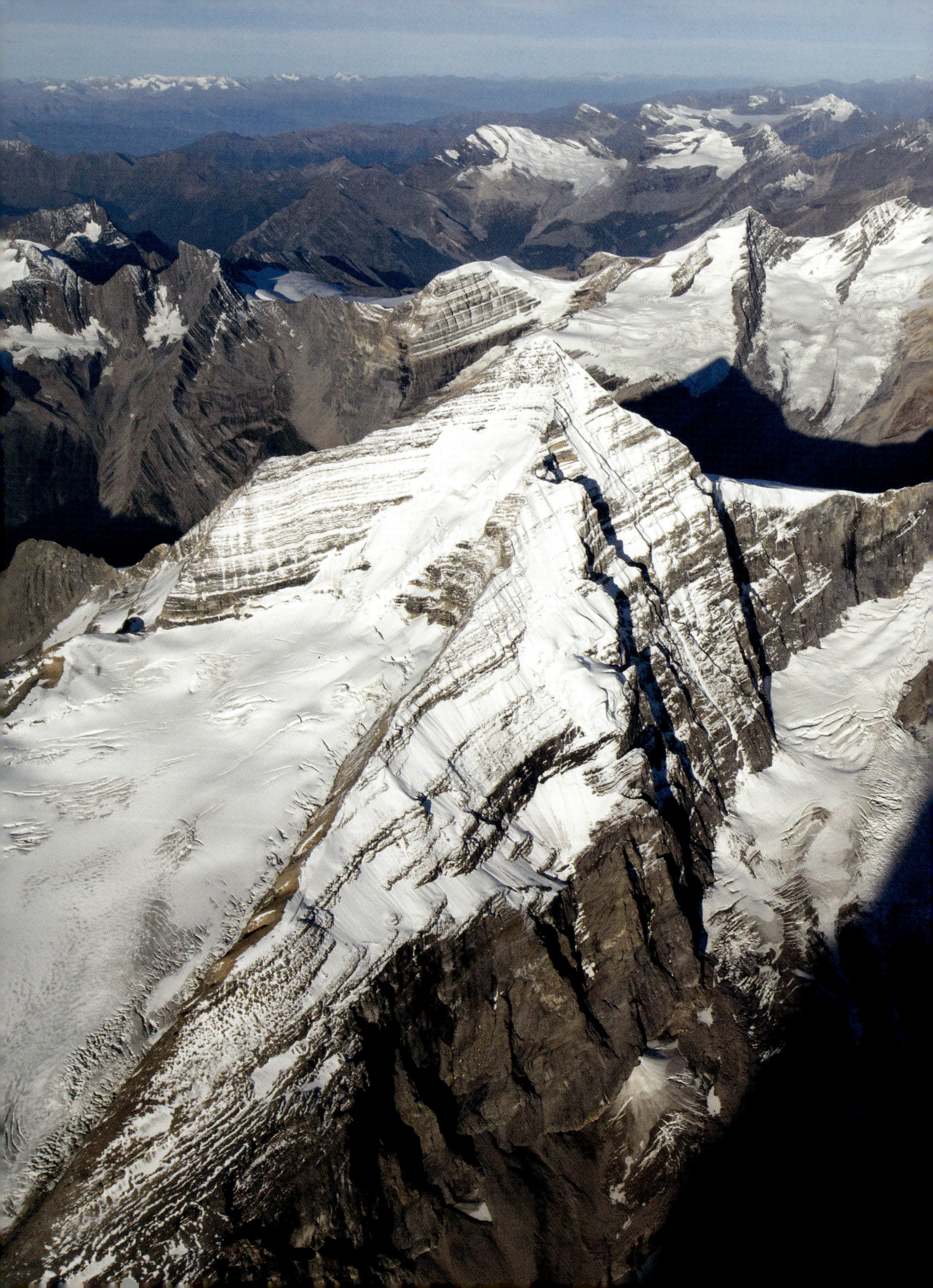

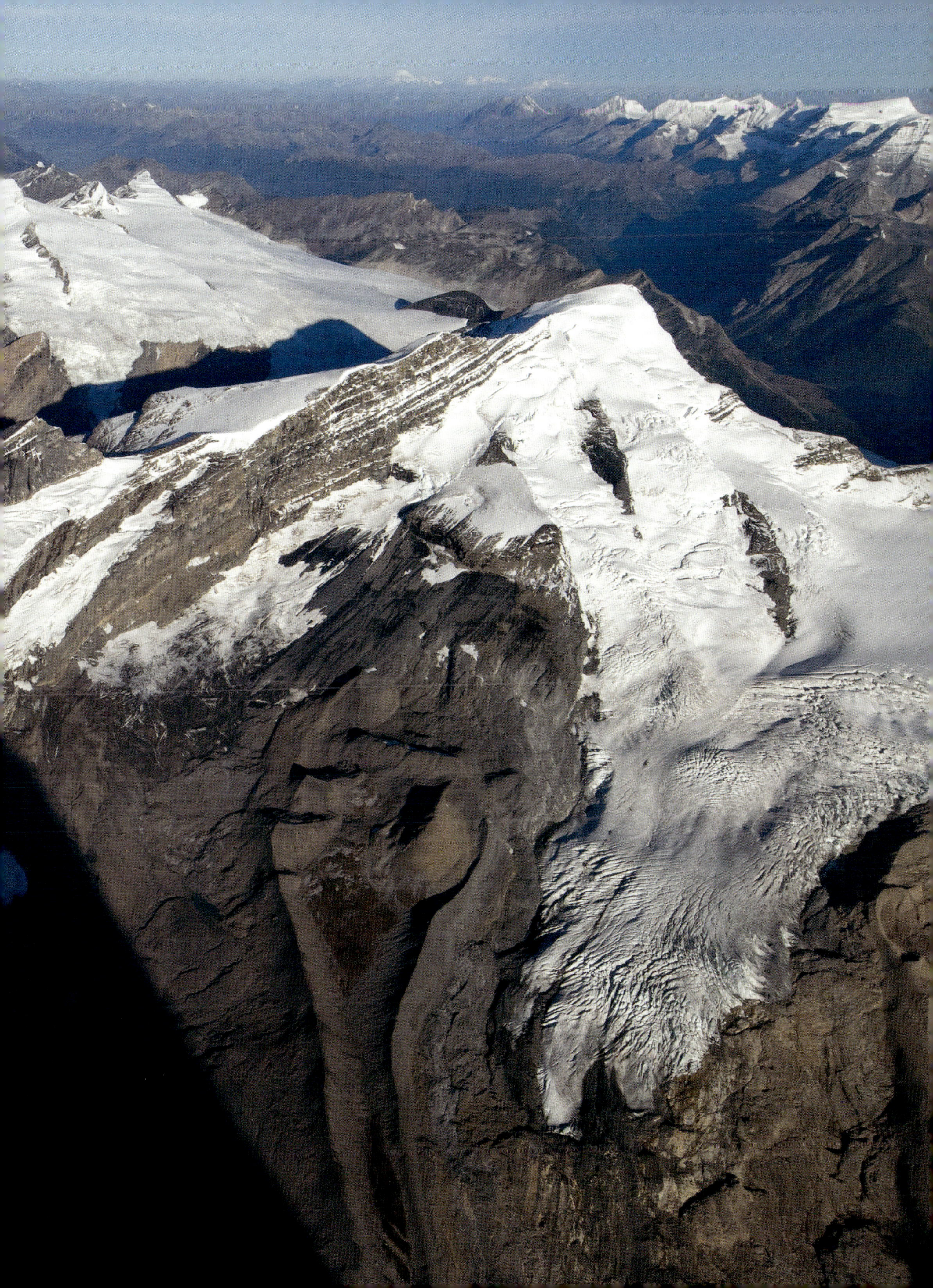

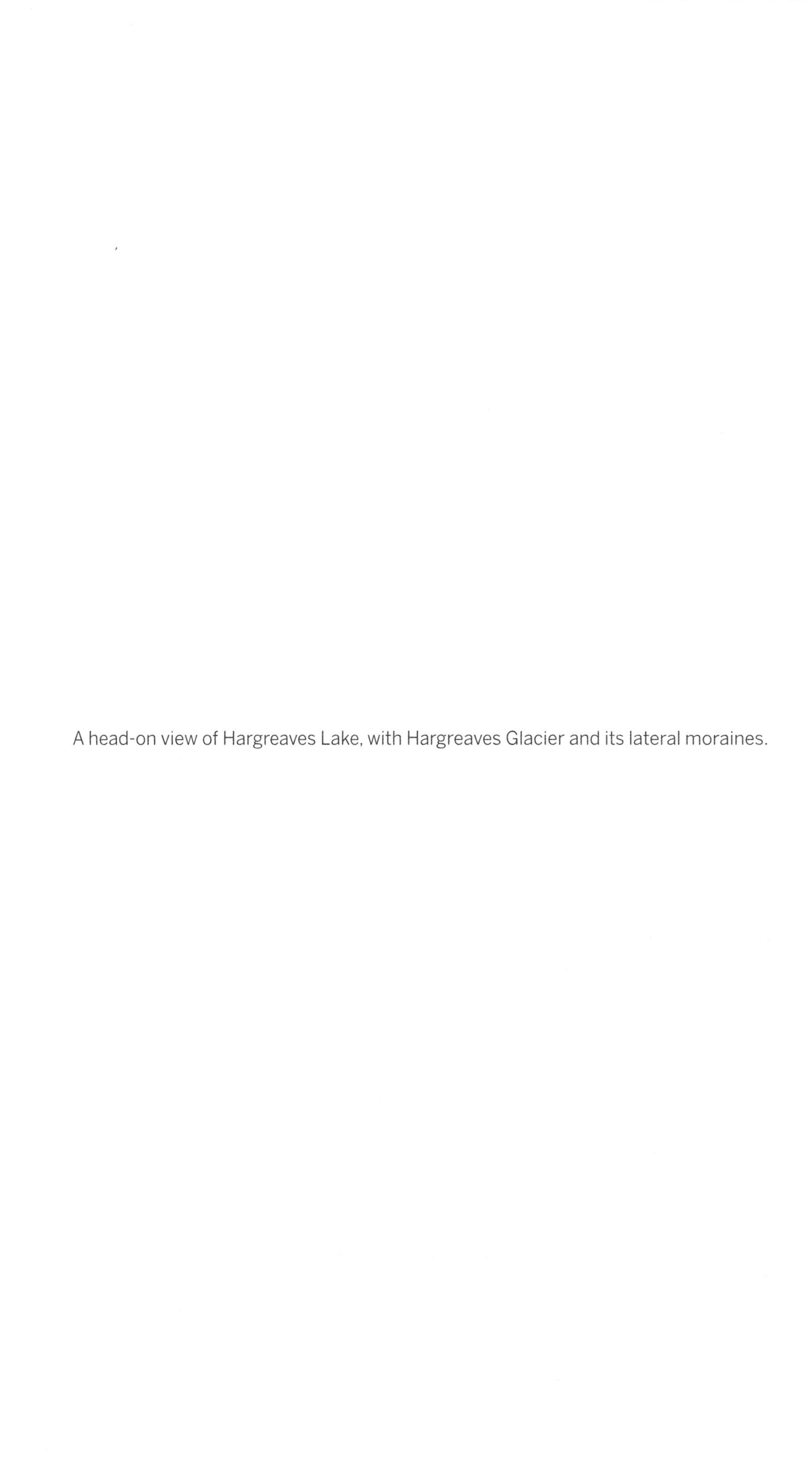

A head-on view of Hargreaves Lake, with Hargreaves Glacier and its lateral moraines.

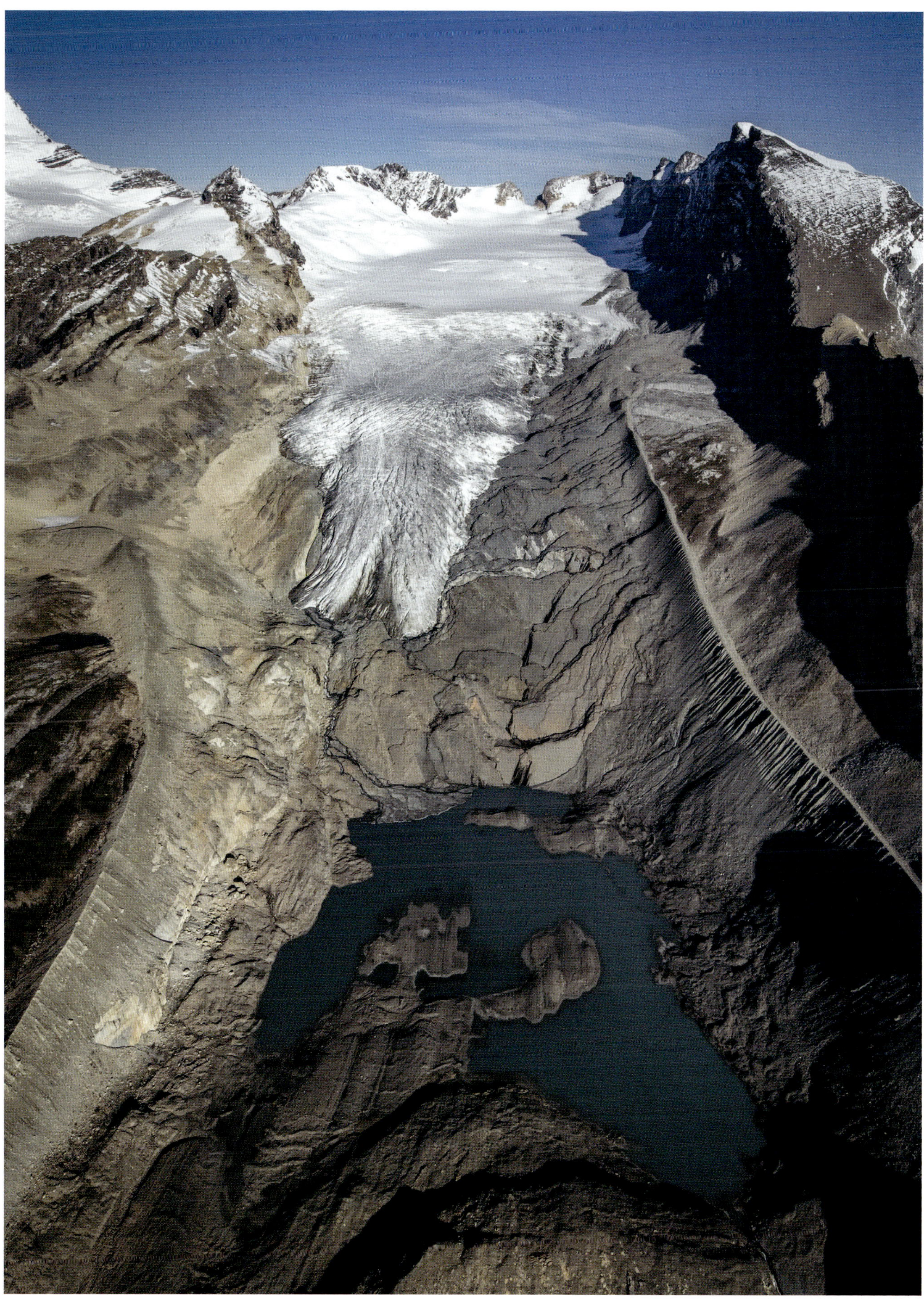

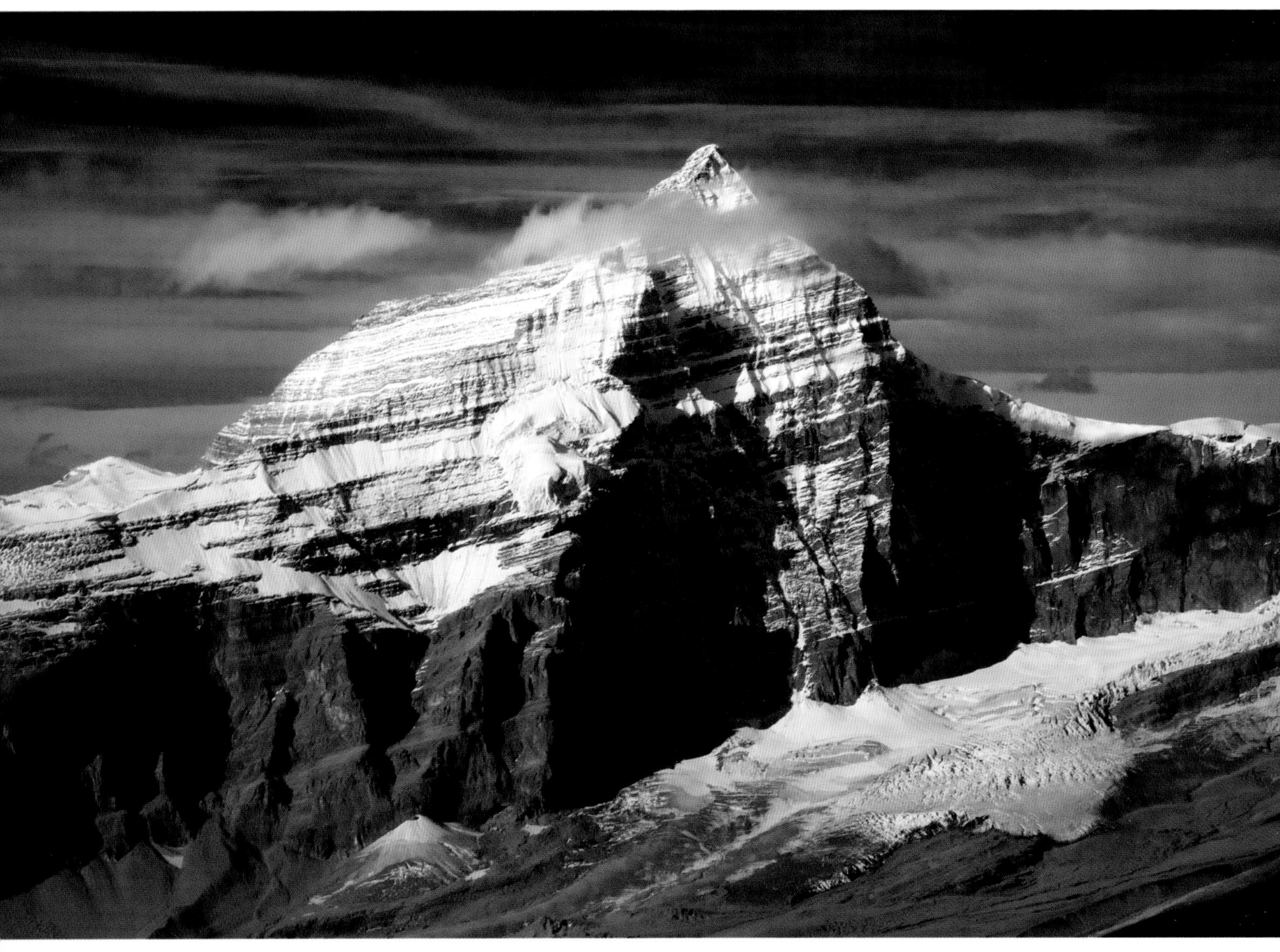

Above: The incredible east aspect of Whitehorn Mountain,
a neighbour to the west of Mount Robson.

Opposite: A heavily crevassed section of the Robson Glacier leads the eye towards the
highest point in the Canadian Rockies. Mount Waffl is on the right, while The Helmet
blends in with Mount Robson itself in the middle. The Kain Face is visible at the top right.

Overleaf: The rarely seen, absolutely stunning western sides of Whitehorn and Robson.
In between the horn-shaped peaks is Robson's trademark lenticular cloud.

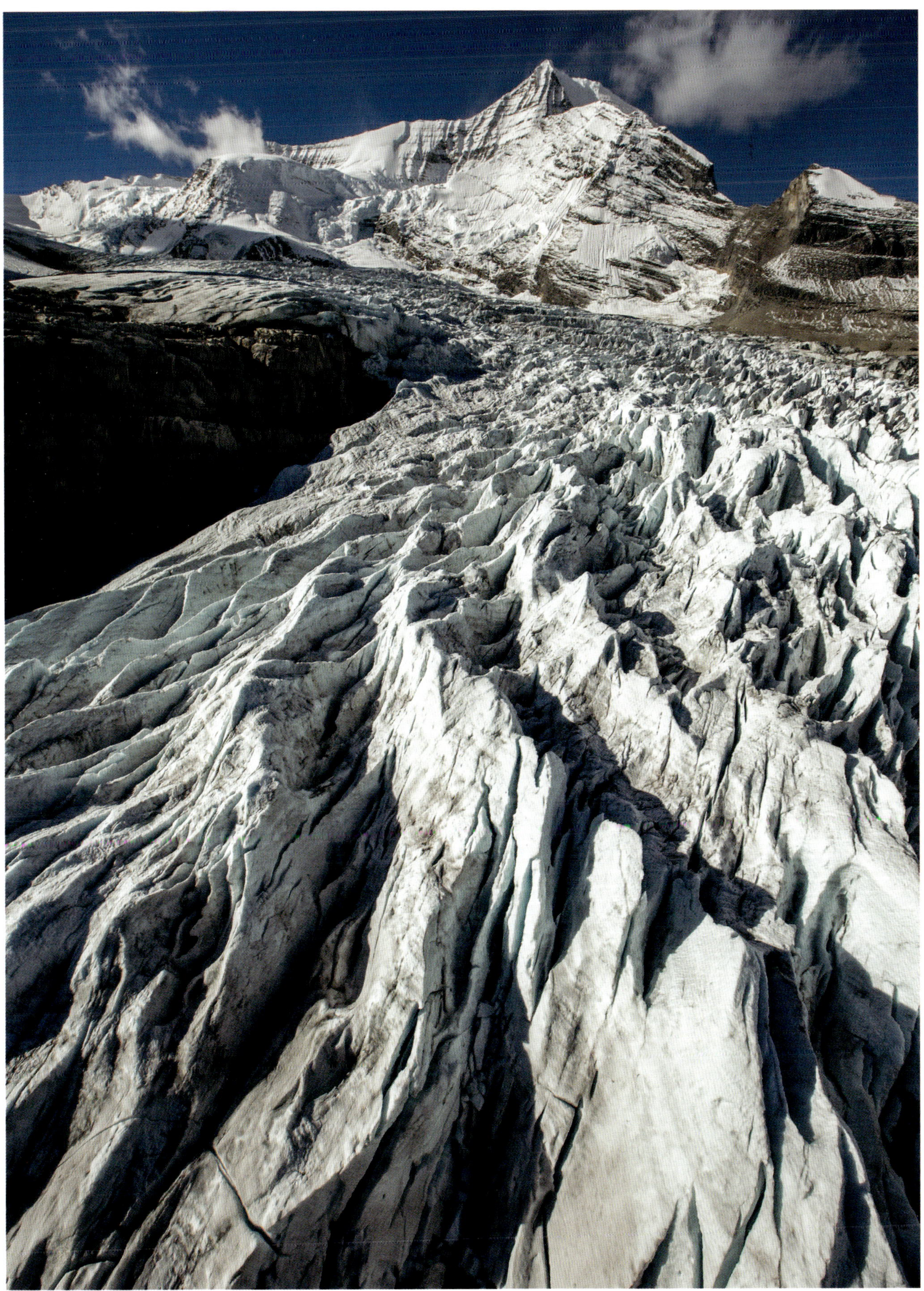

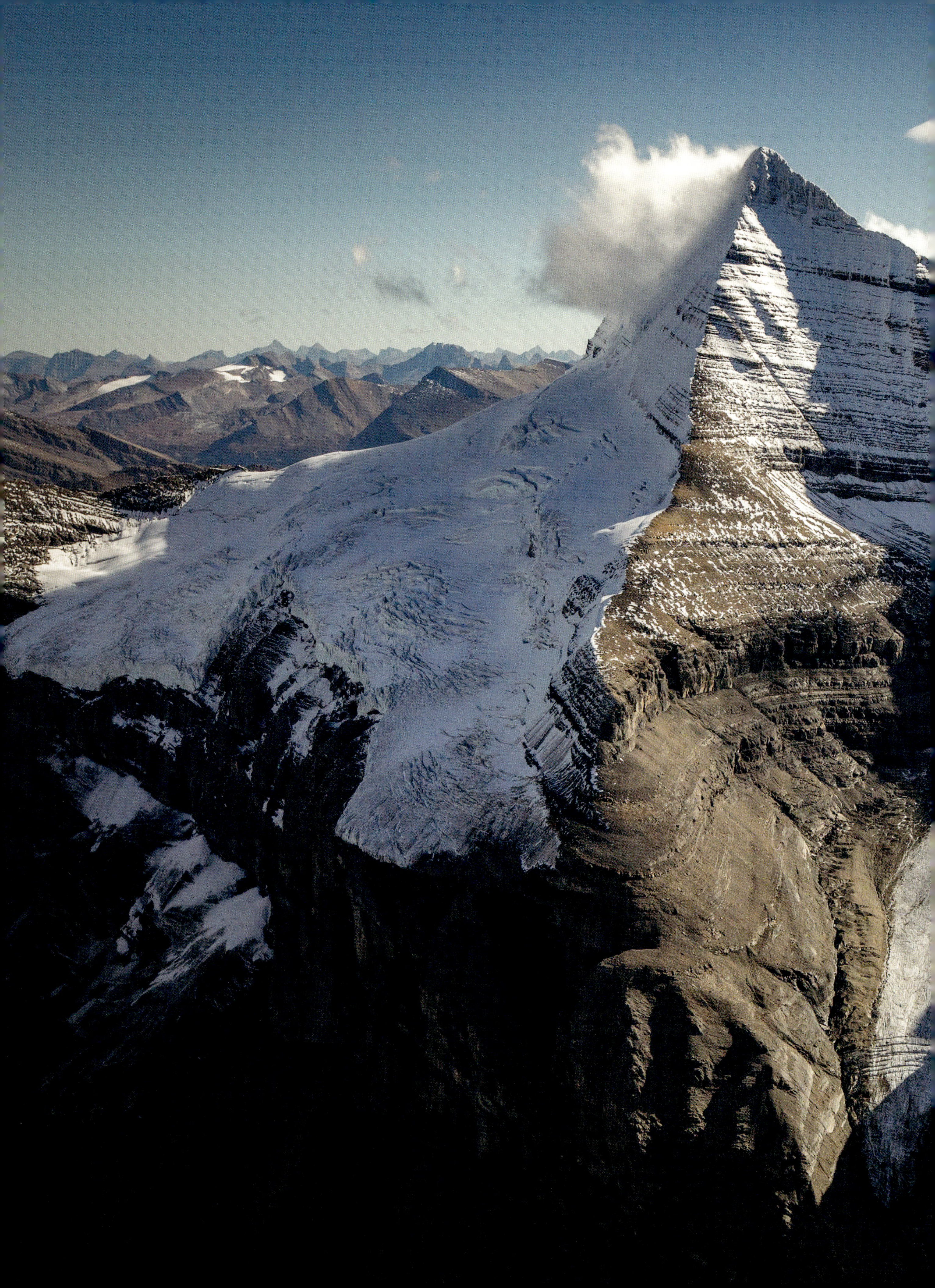

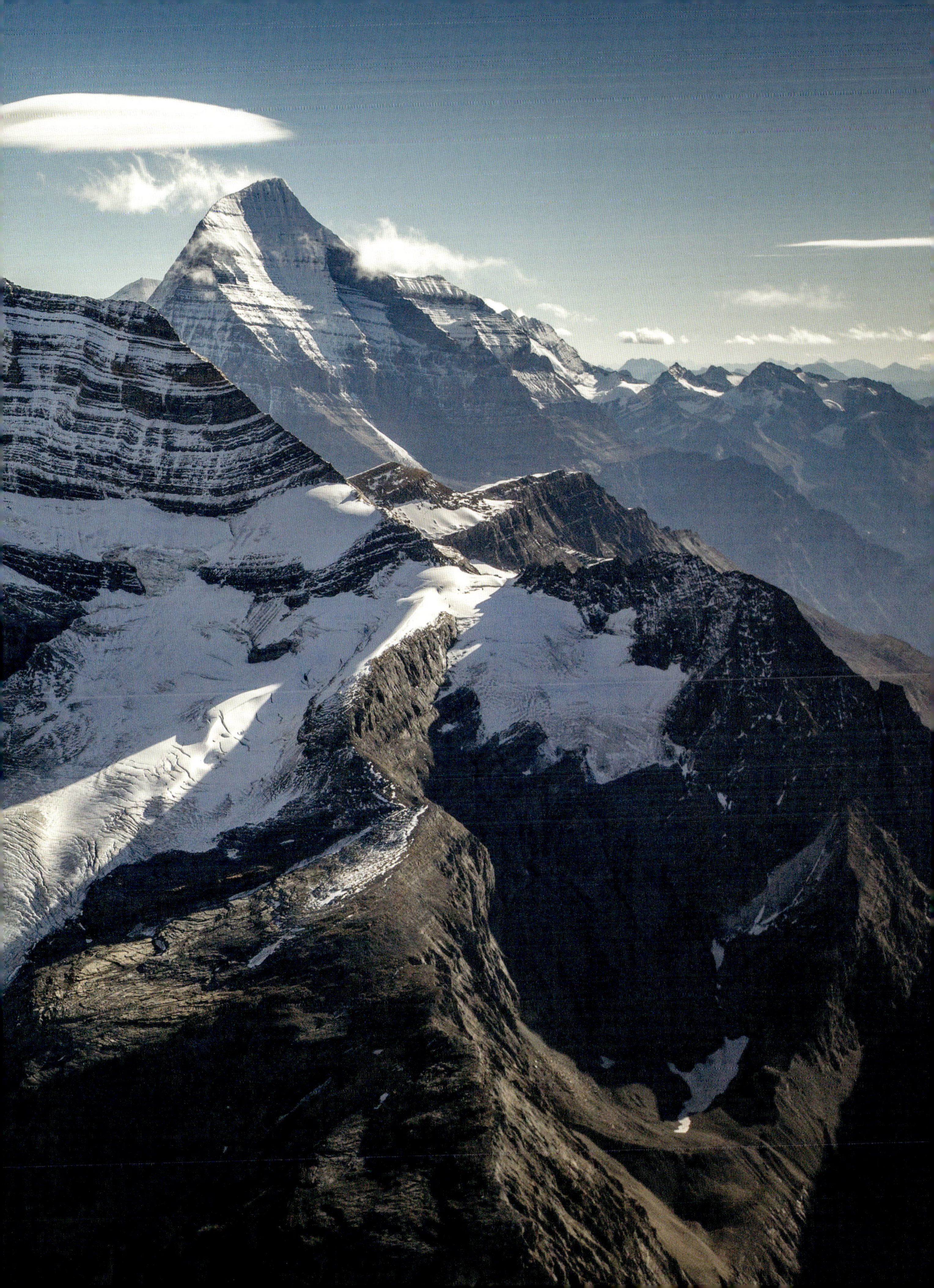

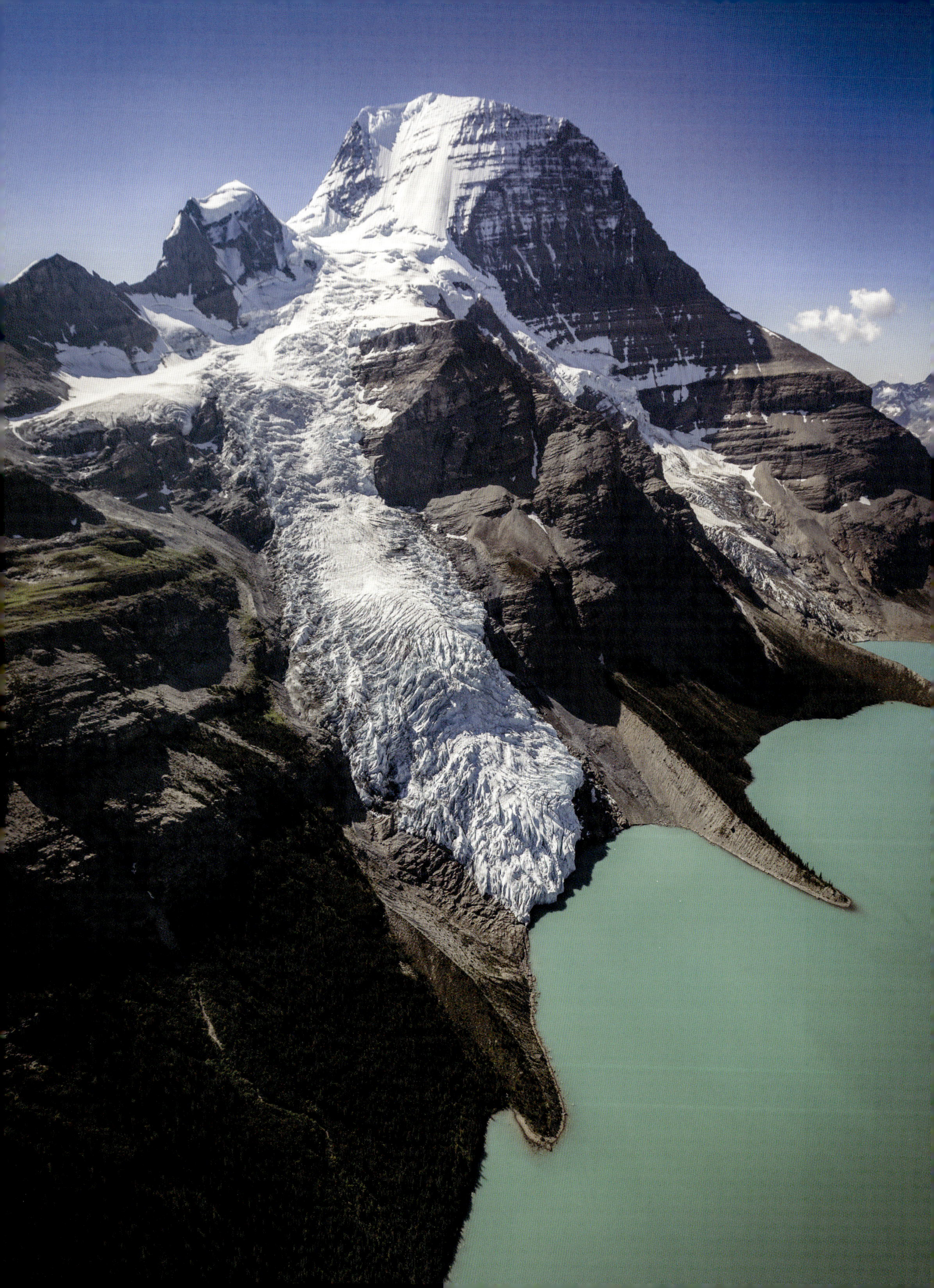

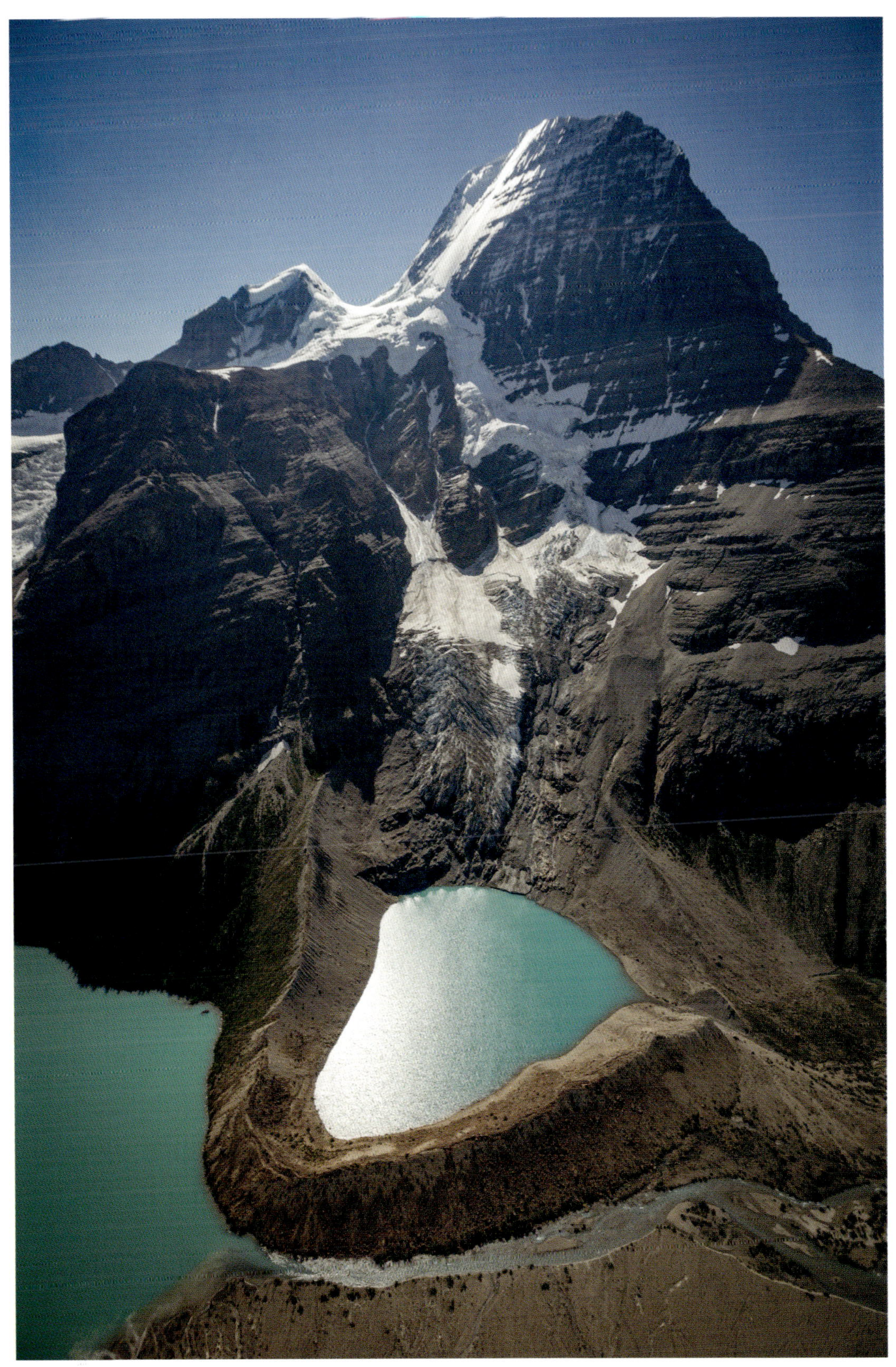

Opposite: Berg (l) and Mist (r) glaciers empty into Berg Lake from the heights of Mount Robson.

Above: Tall moraines keep Mist Lake from emptying into neighbouring Berg Lake.
Above the lake, Mist Glacier tumbles down from the north face of Robson.

TECHNICAL NOTES

All of the images in this book were obtained legally, with the required permits and with complete respect of the local laws. The photographs were created over a six-year period spanning 2013 to 2019 and were shot with Canon bodies (5D Mark II, III and IV, and EOS R) and lenses (16–35 f/2.8, 17–40 f/4 and 70–200 f/2.8).

ABOUT THE AUTHOR

Paul Zizka is an award-winning mountain landscape and adventure photographer based in the Canadian Rockies. Specializing in photographing in difficult conditions and hard-to-reach places, Paul has a passion for shooting alpine sports and backcountry experiences, capturing the spirit of adventurers and finding unusual angles of common mountain subjects. His award-winning images have been featured in a variety of periodicals, including *Maclean's*, *National Geographic Adventure*, *Canadian Geographic* and *Alpinist*, as well as six other volumes of photography published by Rocky Mountain Books. Combining a love of travel and a desire to help others expand their own creativity, Paul runs photography workshops throughout Canada and around the world. He lives in Banff with his wife, Meghan, and two daughters. See more of his work online at zizka.ca.

For information on purchasing bulk quantities of this book, or to obtain media excerpts or invite the author to speak at an event, please visit rmbooks.com and select the "Contact" tab.

RMB | Rocky Mountain Books Ltd.
rmbooks.com
@rmbooks
facebook.com/rmbooks

Cataloguing data available from Library and Archives Canada
ISBN 9781771603973 (hardcover)
ISBN 9781771606929 (softcover)
ISBN 9781771603980 (electronic)

frontispiece: Mighty Mount Assiniboine towers above Lake Magog on a cloudless October morning.

Printed and bound in China

We would like to also take this opportunity to acknowledge the traditional territories upon which we live and work. In Calgary, Alberta, we acknowledge the Niitsítapi (Blackfoot) and the people of the Treaty 7 region in Southern Alberta, which includes the Siksika, the Piikuni, the Kainai, the Tsuut'ina, and the Stoney Nakoda First Nations, including Chiniki, Bearpaw, and Wesley First Nations. The City of Calgary is also home to Métis Nation of Alberta, Region III. In Victoria, British Columbia, we acknowledge the traditional territories of the Lkwungen (Esquimalt and Songhees), Malahat, Pacheedaht, Scia'new, T'Sou-ke, and W̱SÁNEĆ (Pauquachin, Tsartlip, Tsawout, Tseycum) peoples.

We acknowledge the financial support of the Government of Canada through the Canada Book Fund and the Canada Council for the Arts, and of the province of British Columbia through the British Columbia Arts Council and the Book Publishing Tax Credit.

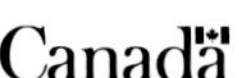
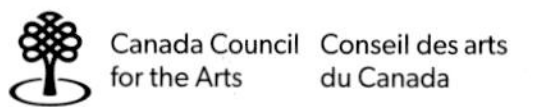
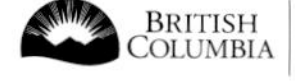
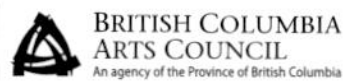